T0265760

THE
CRAZIES

THE CATTLEMAN,

THE WIND PROSPECTOR,

AND A WAR OUT WEST

AMY GAMERMAN

SIMON & SCHUSTER

NEW YORK   TORONTO   LONDON   SYDNEY   NEW DELHI

Simon & Schuster
1230 Avenue of the Americas
New York, NY 10020

First Simon & Schuster hardcover edition January 2025

SIMON & SCHUSTER and colophon are registered trademarks of Simon & Schuster, LLC

For information about special discounts for bulk purchases, please contact Simon & Schuster Special Sales at 1-866-506-1949 or business@simonandschuster.com.

The Simon & Schuster Speakers Bureau can bring authors to your live event. For more information or to book an event, contact the Simon & Schuster Speakers Bureau at 1-866-248-3049 or visit our website at www.simonspeakers.com.

Interior design by Carly Loman

Manufactured in the United States of America

10 9 8 7 6 5 4 3 2 1

Library of Congress Cataloging-in-Publication Data has been applied for.

ISBN 978-1-9821-5816-3
ISBN 978-1-9821-5819-4 (ebook)

For my father, Kenneth Gamerman
July 5, 1932–February 8, 2024
My mountain.

My favorite state has not yet been invented. It will be called Montana, and it will be perfect.

—ABRAHAM LINCOLN

Contents

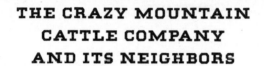

THE CRAZY MOUNTAIN CATTLE COMPANY AND ITS NEIGHBORS

Adapted from JA116, Demonstrative Map Exhibit, *Diana's Great Idea, LLC, et al. v. Crazy Mountain Wind, LLC, et al.*

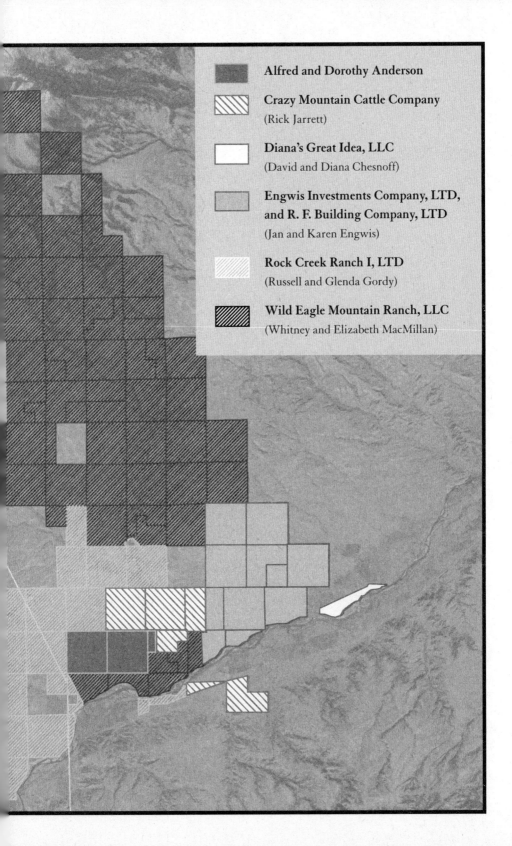

Alfred and Dorothy Anderson

Crazy Mountain Cattle Company
(Rick Jarrett)

Diana's Great Idea, LLC
(David and Diana Chesnoff)

**Engwis Investments Company, LTD,
and R. F. Building Company, LTD**
(Jan and Karen Engwis)

Rock Creek Ranch I, LTD
(Russell and Glenda Gordy)

Wild Eagle Mountain Ranch, LLC
(Whitney and Elizabeth MacMillan)

A NOTE ON SOURCES

The Crazies is a work of nonfiction. The thoughts and feelings attributed to the people in this book are drawn from their own words. In addition to interviews conducted over the course of nearly five years of reporting, I relied on transcripts and recordings of court hearings, public meetings, county commission hearings, Public Service Commission work sessions and hearings, and well over a thousand pages of court filings. Other sources include letters and email exchanges released through Freedom of Information Act requests, interviews with media outlets, and social media posts.

THE
CRAZIES

PREFACE

This story began on the ruins of an old hot-springs resort in the mountains of Montana.

Or maybe it began forty-nine million years ago, when the earth's crust turned itself inside out, its restless plates shifting and sliding, a volcanic arc spewing lava at the sky. The magma cooled and hardened into a forty-mile chunk of igneous rock. Eons passed. The world was hot, then it was cold. Slow-moving glaciers scooped out cirques and valleys, carving the rock into ridges. Millennia of ice and wind whittled those ridges into thirty-odd jagged peaks. Locals call them the Crazies.

The Crazies towered over wind-raked tundra where the first Americans chipped stones into spear points. They towered over shimmering grasslands where the Crow people hunted bison. Their frozen peaks shone through the summer haze as pioneers trundled along the Bozeman Trail in covered wagons, drawn west by dreams of gold. Now they look down on rangelands dotted with cattle and sheep.

It can seem like a mirage, this island of mountains rising from a sea of rolling hills. Your eye travels from the banks of the Yellowstone River to gray-green and gold-brown foothills as neatly humped as the model scenery on a child's train table, then sharply upward to the Crazies' splintery snow-frosted pinnacles, a chiaroscuro vision in pure white and midnight blue. People from the nearby town of Big Timber sometimes pull over on the frontage road that runs alongside the train tracks to take pictures of the Crazies at sunset or sunrise, or under a full moon. Those posts always get a lot of likes on the *Big Timber Buzz*, the community Facebook page.

The Crazies stand in magnificent isolation from the landscape they dominate, set apart by topography and by deed. The mountain range is as splendid as any national park, but for the most part it's private property. Crazy Peak, the loftiest of them all, is privately owned. So is Conical Peak, and Granite Peak and Kid Royal. The owners of those mountains are among the richest people in America.

The hot springs were part of a forty-four-thousand-acre mountain ranch owned by Russell Gordy, a Texas oil and gas billionaire. It was late spring in 2017 and I was writing a profile of Mr. Gordy and his $96 million collection of trophy ranches for the *Wall Street Journal*. Gordy owned so many ranches that he couldn't keep track of them all. There was a big ranch in East Texas, and a bigger one in South Texas. He had an eighty-thousand-acre spread in Wyoming, and a place in Colorado that he never visited—"It's a beautiful ranch, but I already got a bunch of gorgeous places." Later in our conversation, Gordy remembered that he owned a second ranch in Wyoming. He went goose hunting there sometimes.

Gordy's Montana ranch, some fifteen miles west of Big Timber, would be my first stop on a limited tour of his domain. He bought it in 2002 for over $40 million, a state record at the time. It was very windy that day; I had to borrow a hat to keep the hair out of my face. I'd learn that Big Timber is one of windiest places in the country. Wind, like water, flows faster downhill: the steeper the hill, the harder it blows. Big Timber is wedged between some very steep hills. Winds speed up as they're funneled through the Absaroka-Beartooth Range to the south. Chinooks from the west, honed by the sharp-toothed Crazies, double and redouble in force as they pour down the mountains' eastern slopes. It's a phenomenon called mountain gap wind, and Big Timber gets it from both ends. Crosswinds regularly hit gale-force speeds, nudging semitrucks sideways on Interstate 90 before shutting it down altogether. When the town makes the news, it's usually in the form of a high-wind advisory.

Gordy picked me up at my hotel in a muddy Land Rover. Tall, with a neatly trimmed gray beard, he wore shorts, a baseball hat, and a fly-fishing vest. He pointed out the sights as he drove. "You're on the ranch now. That's a buffalo jump rock—the Indians used to herd them off a cliff. That's the Yellowstone River—my boundary line." He turned onto a narrow, unpaved road that wound along a sandstone cliff. Prisoners from the state penitentiary in Deer Lodge had blasted the road in 1913; you could see scoring marks left by the sticks of dynamite they'd used on the cliff walls.

"I always tell folks that I live on Convict Grade Road in the Crazy Mountains," Gordy said with a grin, rocks spraying from the tires as we sped toward his $15 million lodge. A herd of startled pronghorns sprinted past. Gordy loves to hunt—elk, deer, grizzly bears. The antelope didn't get a rise out of him. "I could lean out my window and shoot one," he said. Gordy much preferred to hunt Hungarian partridges on his Montana ranch. The birds were delicious, he told me. "I like 'em fresh."

He pulled over at a creek wreathed in white steam. We got out of the Land Rover, the wind tearing at the pages of my notebook. Cows ranged across the rolling hills, a rumpled carpet shaken out at the mountains' feet under a heavy white sky. All that remained of the Mission-style hotel that once stood at the springs was a crumbling stone wall. A small blue above-ground pool with a ladder, the kind you see in suburban backyards, sat incongruously amid the sagebrush and cow pies.

"We were going to build a boutique hotel here," Gordy said, leaning hard on the first syllable in *boutique*. But then he found out that the owner of a small ranch south of his boundary line had leased his land for a wind farm. Gordy grimaced at the prospect of towering windmills next door. He had made the rancher an offer, tried to buy him out. But the man was set on doing that wind farm. "It's going to kill all the birds," Gordy said grimly.

In the years that followed, I thought about Gordy and the nameless rancher across his border—his neighbor. "We have no neighbors," Gordy had said during my visit, by way of describing the ranch's expansiveness, its absolute privacy. And yet, somehow, this one had made an impression. I wondered who that rancher was.

I didn't know that an epic story was unfolding in the Crazy Mountains, a story centuries in the making, with millionaires and billionaires, cattle barons and Crow warriors, prospectors and politicians, meat-packers and medicine men. It reached from the muck of Montana calving barns to the gleaming C-suites of Manhattan skyscrapers. It was a modern-day range war in a warming West—a fight for power in its most elemental form. It was a ghost story haunted by generations of dreamers and strivers, those drawn to the land and those who lost it, the dispossessed, the exiles. At its heart was an old cowboy in suspenders, and the all-American spectacle of neighbors suing each other.

Then I found out that my profile of Mr. Gordy had surfaced in the discovery for a lawsuit—the lawsuit to stop that cowboy from building Crazy Mountain Wind.

PROLOGUE

Montana's Sixth Judicial District Court sits on a quiet street in Livingston, some thirty miles west of Big Timber. The court, which has jurisdiction over cases in Sweet Grass and Park counties, occupies the footprint of the city's first courthouse, an imposing brick pile erected in 1896 as the last prairie schooners trundled through Yellowstone country. Livingston's fortress of justice was razed in the 1970s and replaced by a low-slung Ford-era box of pebbly gray concrete with smoked glass windows. Its best architectural feature is the free street parking. It's hard to imagine a less picturesque setting for the three-day showdown that was about to begin at high noon one gray winter day.

It had been brutally cold, the coldest February on record, with subzero temperatures in the double digits and gusting snow. But the first day of the hearing dawned clear, and it was a balmy eight degrees Fahrenheit as the plaintiffs and the defendants in the case of *Diana's Great Idea et al. v. Crazy Mountain Wind et al.* parked their battered pickup trucks, gleaming Escalades, and F-450 Super Duty Lariats on East Callender Street. They picked their way across the ice and frozen snowdrifts, stepped inside the county building's skylit lobby, and filed up the stairs to a courtroom painted the bright blue of a child's drawing of the sky.

Like guests at a wedding, they arranged themselves on opposite sides of the aisle; defendants to the right, plaintiffs to the left. Every time the heavy wooden doors to the courtroom swung open, people twisted in their seats to see who had arrived. Sometimes a newcomer would sit down, look around, realize they had picked the wrong side, and quickly scoot across the aisle.

Rick Jarrett removed his wool hat as he entered the courtroom, patting down his hair. His belly was round, his beard unruly. Rick had taken care with his appearance that morning. He wore a Western shirt with all its buttons, a leather vest, and clean, pressed jeans, secured with his good suspenders. There was a hitch to his step as he made his way to a royal blue bench a few rows from the front. Rick, sixty-eight, had been recently diagnosed with Parkinson's disease.

The cows were calving. Rick was out at all hours in the biting wind at this time of year, pulling calves and hustling the slick newborns into the warmth of the calving shed to dry off and suck before they froze to death. But lately, he had turned over more of this work to his daughter, Jami, and her companion, Harv. He was getting old too quickly, it seemed. He hoped the kids would be able to take over the ranch someday, buy him out so he could retire.

His land was worth millions, but Rick Jarrett was not a wealthy man. No IRA, no savings account. He drove a thirty-year-old Cadillac with a broken headlight, kicked out by one of his cows. Land rich, cash poor, that's how it was. The cows couldn't pay the bills anymore, which was why Rick had been fighting for fifteen years to get some wind development on his ground. A few years back, he mortgaged the ranch's two thousand acres for close to a million dollars. If Crazy Mountain Wind didn't get built, there might not be a goddamn ranch to pass on.

Four generations back, Rick's ancestor Cyrus B. Mendenhall might have rolled over the very ground where the courthouse now stood in his ox-drawn wagon on his way to the Montana goldfields. Like his great-great-grandfather, Rick Jarrett was an enterprising fellow with grit and ingenuity, determined to claim his share of Montana's rich resources. The wind that flowed over Rick's land was his treasure—a valuable crop ripe for harvest.

Wind turbines would scoop gold from the air, turning slashing westerlies into electricity that would power Big Timber and rain down money on Rick Jarrett and his kin. With his share of the profits from Crazy Mountain Wind, Rick could pay his debts, gift the ranch to his kids, and retire, secure in the knowledge that the place would be there for his grandchildren. The wind would provide for them all.

In the front row, Rick's neighbors Jan and Karen Engwis looked the other way as he settled on a seat across the aisle. Jan owned a 5,500-acre ranch on the Yellowstone where he ran a small herd of Black Angus cows and grew alfalfa. A former cop who made his fortune in the rock-blasting business, he saw it as his duty to preserve and protect his piece of Montana's sagebrush Eden from Rick Jarrett's obsessive wind development efforts. Jan grew up in Midland, Michigan, home of the Dow Chemical Company. Maybe people who grew up in Big Timber stopped noticing its natural beauty and open vistas. Maybe they'd been there too long.

The Engwises greeted David and Diana Chesnoff, who owned a two-hundred-acre ranch just east of theirs. The Chesnoffs had flown in from Las Vegas for the hearing. A criminal defense attorney, David was as much a celebrity in some circles as the pop stars, poker players, and mobsters he defended. Montana was his place to relax and enjoy the beauty, to get away from the work he did, because what he did was pretty stressful.

But not today. David was dressed for court in a tailored dark suit. The other wealthy litigants wore jeans, including Diana, who had paired her skinny denims with wedge-heeled Chanel snow boots. The Chesnoffs positioned themselves directly behind the table where the plaintiffs' team of lawyers would sit, the better to pass them notes, as David would do throughout the three-day hearing. Diana did not remove her oversized sunglasses.

Russell Gordy hunkered down on a pew at the back of the courtroom. He was sixty-eight, same age as Rick Jarrett, but he wore his years more lightly. February wasn't ordinarily a month you'd find Gordy in Montana. You might find him hunting quail at La Ceniza, his sprawling ranch in South Texas, or at one of his ski homes in Utah's Deer Valley. Or maybe you'd find him sea fishing for tarpon at the oceanfront retreat in the Bahamas that he bought as a surprise birthday gift for his wife, Glenda, who was more of a beach person. In any event, Gordy was due back in Houston on Friday, when he and Glenda would be honored at a black-tie gala. The Gordys had given $5 million to endow a new three-theater complex—The Gordy. There would be toasts and video tributes, and a three-course banquet served under trellises of tulip magnolias.

But first, there was this court deal to get through. Gordy had never met Rick Jarrett. But the prospect of Jarrett's giant windmills had loomed like a blight over Gordy's Montana ranch for well over a decade.

It was a beautiful piece of land, a small kingdom that stretched from the Yellowstone River to the Crazy Mountains. Gordy just loved the place.

Alfred Anderson entered the courtroom with his granddaughter and looked around for Rick, his business partner and codefendant. Alfred was eighty-seven and he didn't see so good, particularly at night, so his granddaughter would drive him home after the hearing. He'd gotten up at dawn to chop up the ice on the cows' frozen water tanks and throw square bales of hay to the buck sheep, and he still wore his square-toed work boots. Alfred found a seat near Rick and settled beneath the gaze of past Sixth District Court justices, whose black-and-white photographs lined the walls. Although Alfred had come to the courthouse to pay his taxes and serve his jury duty over the years, he had never been involved in a legal proceeding before. It didn't sit right. You should be able to do what you wanted to do with your land, Alfred thought. It was a free country.

Rick did not share his old friend's uneasiness. He was glad to finally take the fight to these neighbors of his. "The Oligarchs," his lawyer called them. They wanted to stop Rick from harvesting his million-dollar wind. They wanted to control what he did on his land. Well, Rick Jarrett knew his goddamn property rights. All right, he thought, eyes shining as he surveyed the courtroom. Let's start this son of a bitch.

1

RANCHING IT

February 20, 2019
Park County Courthouse
Livingston, Montana

RICHARD JARRETT, *having first been duly sworn, testified as follows*:
Q: Mr. Jarrett, did you decide to lease your ground to Crazy Mountain
    Wind?
MR. JARRETT: I did.
Q: Okay. And can you tell the Court why?
MR. JARRETT: It's tough to make a ranch, by itself, make ends meet.

Big Timber, Montana, population 1,650, is a railroad town. Like many small Western towns, it exists because someone put his thumb on a map and decided it would make a good spot for a train station. The Northern Pacific Railway Company laid track through the area in 1882, tracing the route of the Lewis and Clark Expedition along the Yellowstone. A year later, a railway surveyor platted a site at a bend in the Yellowstone for a town to go with those train tracks, and named it for the tall cottonwood trees that Captain William Clark had noted in his journal.

Big Timber's rail yard forms the top line of the town grid: twelve principal streets crisscrossed by nine numbered avenues. Turn-of-the-century buildings of rough-edged sandstone and weathered brick line its tiny business district; modest mid-century bungalows and carports dot its cross streets. The town's central axis is McLeod Street, a broad thoroughfare that dead-ends in the train tracks and a spectacular view of the Crazies.

When Big Timber was the wool capital of the world, a river of sheep flowed down McLeod Street every September, trotting back from summer grazing leaseholds in the mountains past the saloon of the redbrick Grand Hotel. The Grand still anchors McLeod Street, one of the few old buildings to survive the great fire that incinerated a third of the town in 1908. It sits opposite Cole Drug, Little Timber Quilts & Candy, and the Timber Bar, whose neon lumberjack lights up, red-faced, when the sun goes down. Many of the old storefronts are empty now. It's been more than a decade since anyone played pool at the Madhatter Saloon. Big Timber doesn't get as many visitors as the larger city of Livingston to its west, or the rodeo town of Red Lodge to its south. Mostly, it's a place you pass through on your way to Bozeman or Billings.

But it's a picturesque old town, with a weekly summer rodeo, huckleberry milkshakes, and some of the best fly-fishing in the state. Every summer, the Grand's fourteen rooms fill up and the Sorry sign switches on, in loopy neon cursive, at the Lazy J Motel. All through the night, guests hear the whistle of Burlington Northern Santa Fe (BNSF) freight trains hurtling past town. Each train stretches a mile or more, a conga line of hoppers, boxcars, tankers, and gondolas loaded with coal, crude oil, plastics, and fertilizers. The sound of the heavy cars juddering over the train tracks fills the quiet streets for a minute or more, when the wind doesn't drown it out.

The wind touches every aspect of life in Big Timber. It rattles plate-glass windows in their frames on McLeod Street, where tourists shop for T-shirts and tractor caps at Gusts department store and the old-timers gossip over coffee at Cole Drug. Golden eagles and red-tailed hawks use it to hunt, catching a gust as it bounces off a ridge and surfing it like a wave as they scope the prairie dog towns below. Townies joke about the wind, the way it will pluck the dollars from your hand and steal the lawn chairs from your yard. The uninitiated have been locked out of their vehicles when the wind slammed shut car doors left carelessly open.

But for cattle and sheep ranchers, the wind is an affliction. It sucks every drop of moisture from the soil, tosses thousand-pound bales of hay across pastures like tumbleweed, whips up brushfires into blazes that can consume thousands of acres in a night. Most people in Big Timber learn to live with the wind. Rick Jarrett sought his fortune in it.

Rick was a rancher. He never had the imagination to be anything else, he said. His people had ranched in Big Timber since 1882—cattle first, then sheep, then cattle and some sheep. Any Montanan who makes his living off livestock will tell you that what he really does is raise grass.

Rick raised fields of alfalfa and orchard grass and timothy hay and forage winter wheat, to be cut and baled for the long winters. When spring came in April or May, he'd turn the calves and the mother cows out on fresh green grass. Everything came in cycles on a ranch, just as it had for Rick's grandparents and his great-grandparents.

Being a rancher meant knowing how to do things. How to brand a calf, dock a lamb, break a colt. Mending a barbed-wire fence, cleaning out a clogged irrigation ditch so the water could flow clear and cold to your hay fields, knowing when to cut the hay and how many days to let it cure in the sun before you baled it—those were essential skills, along with a basic grasp of cattle futures, soil science, and veterinary medicine. You preg-checked your cows by sticking your arm up the rectum and giving a squeeze. If a calf got stuck in a heifer's birth canal, you'd loop a chain over its fetlock and slowly tug it free. Then you'd get some suture thread from the floor of your truck and stitch up the torn mother cow.

Not every calf lived, not every heifer survived. You saw a lot of death on the ranch. So you adapted. You'd skin the dead calf, then tie its pelt to the orphan, fooling the bereaved bovine into suckling it like it was her own.

It took a lifetime to acquire such knowledge. Rick could kill a rattlesnake with a rock or a rein, drive a fence post, cook beef goulash. If it busted, he fixed it. Rick always had a bit of wire or baling twine on hand if a gate didn't hook right or his suspenders snapped under the strain. When his tractor sputtered or the muffler fell off his 1987 Cadillac Brougham, he'd scavenge a spare part from one of the many junked vehicles that dotted his land. To be a rancher was to be a master of the work-around—to make do with what you had and get on with it. This was called ranching it. The corollary to ranching it was that your ranch looked like shit, because you never threw anything away. Rick's ranch was an open-air museum of historic farm machinery in various stages of decay, with the serrated white and blue peaks of the Crazy Mountains for a backdrop. He called it the Crazy Mountain Cattle Company.

Rick's connection to the place was earthy, sweat-stained, prideful. He took pride in the grass crops he grew on the land, pride in the cattle and sheep it sustained. The land gave him independence. He had the freedom to do what he wanted with it, to manage it how he saw fit, and that was more valuable to him than whatever he earned from it. Not everyone could find happiness in this life, one of punishing physical labor without much money or time off. But ranching suited Rick Jarrett. It wasn't a hard life if you'd never done anything else.

One July afternoon, Rick took me on a tour of his hayfields in his side-by-side—an open-sided, two-seat Yamaha Rhino built for rough terrain, like a Hummer crossed with a golf cart. Ten minutes earlier, over coffee at his kitchen table, Rick had seemed listless, his hazel-green eyes dull. I was asking him questions about the past and there were gaps in his memory. "I'm not exactly able to recall stuff," he said.

Now, at the wheel of his side-by-side, jolting across his domain at twenty miles per hour, Rick straightened and brightened like a cut plant dropped in a glass of water. We passed low fields of alfalfa sprouting tendrils of clustered purple flowers, and timothy hay whose nubby plumes nodded back and forth with the wind. The cows and their calves had moved to a summer grazing lease up on the Boulder River. Rick seemed infused with vitality by the sight of all the green things shooting up from his earth, their juicy vegetal fragrances mingling with the smell of warm dirt and sage crushed under the wheels of the Rhino.

"Holy shit, this is good!" he said as we drove through a pasture of orchard grass and smooth brome, so tall and lush that it completely concealed a startled deer, which leaped sideways and bounded away, vanishing again in the ocean of grass. "This'll be cut for hay, this is way too good to graze. Goddamn, holy shit. It's beautiful," he exulted. "Isn't it something? Isn't it goddamn something?"

Rick was born in 1950 on land that his great-grandfather Ralph Jarrett, the son of homesteaders, bought in 1908. The ranch sits in the foothills of the Crazy Mountains on Duck Creek, which winds through its sandstone bluffs under a canopy of silvery-leaved cottonwoods and golden willows, fringed with chokecherry bushes heavy with purple-red berries that generations of Jarrett women boiled into syrups and jams. Duck Creek is both the spine of the ranch and its main artery, gushing with fresh snowmelt from the Crazies every spring. The Jarretts rely on the mountain snowpack for water to irrigate their hayfields and water their livestock. Their rights to that water date back to Big Timber's earliest days.

In Montana, owning land doesn't confer ownership of the water that flows through it, the rivers, creeks, and streams. Ranchers must own a deeded right to draw that water, and the amount they can draw is measured to the inch. Those with the oldest recorded water rights have priority—"first in time is first in right," or so the doctrine goes. The Jarretts' deeded water rights are older than many of the higher-elevation mountain ranches above theirs—the trophy ranches with the best views—because their land was homesteaded first, in the 1880s. The growing season is longer in the valleys, the land more productive, which once made it more valuable. They were practical in the old days, Rick said. Today, people valued the scenery more.

Rick grew up in a farmhouse with a Northern Pacific boxcar pushed up against one side of it that had been repurposed as living space for his grandparents. He was the youngest of four boys. A fifth brother, Donald, died in his crib in 1941 at the age of six months. An old photograph shows the four surviving Jarrett brothers in a row, tallest to smallest: Billy, Ron, Ray, and Rick, a grinning, tow-headed toddler. The boys are dressed in Western shirts with pearly snaps sewn by their mother, Betty, who has wetted down their hair and brushed it neatly to the side. Rick's father, Bob, whippet-thin, his face shadowed by a white hat with a high, narrow crown—a gentleman's hat, for special occasions—smiles down at his sons from the top of the line.

Bob Jarrett was a sheep man; he didn't give a shit about cattle. He ran two thousand mother ewes on a ranch that sprawled across both sides of the Yellowstone River, some eight thousand acres in all. Rick's mother, Betty, was a Halverson, the granddaughter of the Norwegian sheep rancher who built the Grand Hotel. She was small enough to sit on a child's chair, with a short temper to match. They fought a lot, Rick's dad and mom. Ranch life could be hard on a woman.

From the time he was five years old, Rick went everywhere with Bob, one small hand tucked in his father's hip pocket. He tagged along when Bob irrigated the fields and tossed square bales to the sheep and drove the 1950 Studebaker truck high up Mendenhall Creek with provisions for the sheepherder, an old Norwegian who spent winters there in a humpbacked aluminum wagon with a sleeping bunk and a potbellied stove. The sheepherder would make them coffee on the stove, boiling the water with the grounds, maybe cut up some salt mutton. Rick sipped his coffee from a tin cup and felt like one of the men.

In the late winter, they sheared the sheep and Rick helped tromp the wool, stomping the gritty balls of fleece down into sacks with his feet. The Jarretts brought the year's clip to the wool house, a brick warehouse at the railroad depot near the stockyards, where the sacks were weighed and numbered and piled up to the rafters. The younger, spryer ranch hands clambered up the towering bales of wool to scrawl their names—and the occasional bit of smutty graffiti—on the warehouse's brick walls with the fat, ink-filled tubes they used to label the sacks. The names reached all the way to the wooden rafters, which had been salvaged from an older wool house that burned down in one of the fires that swept through Big Timber on a regular basis in the old days. All it took was a few sparks from a passing locomotive and a gust of wind to fan them into a blaze. The Northern Pacific Railway rebuilt the wool house in the 1880s, then built it again. Then built it twice more.

The town was busier, livelier, when Rick was a boy. Big Timber had a movie theater and a bowling alley, five churches, and five bars. Bob Jarrett would head for one of those bars, his little boy's hand tucked in his hip pocket, when he wanted to hire a sheepherder for the summer. Bars were a good place to find sheepherders, many of whom were drunks in the off-season. Bob rarely drank at home, but once he'd walked inside a bar and gotten himself settled, he could drink for a day and a night. He drank to get drunk; that's just the way it was. "I was too little, sometimes," Rick said, remembering. But somebody had to get the tough son of a bitch home.

From first grade through eighth grade, Rick and his brothers attended a one-room schoolhouse on Duck Creek with robin's-egg blue wainscoting and a Braumuller upright piano shipped by rail from New York City. The schoolhouse sat on the lower end of the Jarretts' ranch near the county road, which had once been a stagecoach road, and a Pony Express route before that. Rick rode his horse to school, stabling him in an ancient barn, a relic of the saloon that once stood at the stagecoach stop. The Jarrett boys nailed a basketball hoop under its eaves. Over the years, the barn slowly crumpled to the ground, its weathered gray boards folding and splaying like a pack of splintery playing cards, till only the rusted basketball hoop remained upright.

On summer days, Rick rode over to the Plunge at Hunter's Hot Springs—a giant concrete-bottomed pool fed by natural hot and cold springs a few miles east of the ranch. The springs were once owned by Rick's Great-Great-Grandfather Mendenhall, part of a spa resort. The hotel burned to the ground in 1932 but the Plunge survived. A local couple put a steel Quonset hut over it and charged thirty-five cents a swim, with bathing suits for rent.

At Sweet Grass High School, Rick joined the Future Farmers of America and played linebacker on the football team, the Sweet Grass Sheepherders. By senior year, he was going steady with Susan Davis, who had smooth, dark hair that flipped up at the ends and an assured, wide-set gaze framed by a pair of thick-rimmed glasses. Susan was smart—she and Rick were in the National Honor Society together—and she was bound for the University of Montana after graduation. At the senior prom, Rick and Susan danced to music by a local band called the Tijuana Trash. The theme was "A Taste of Honey."

The Jarrett–Davis wedding was announced in the *Big Timber Pioneer* that July. The ceremony was held without delay, as soon as the eighteen-year-old groom had returned from driving the sheep to the Jarretts' summer leasehold in the alpine meadows of the Absaroka National Forest, Hellroaring division. The bride, who kept her glasses on beneath her silk illusion veil, wore an empire-waisted gown; she was pregnant with the couple's first child, conceived the night of the Taste of Honey prom. Susan always believed that Rick got her pregnant on purpose, to keep her from leaving him. She'd never go to college.

Rick and Susan's son, Jay, was born the winter of Rick's freshman year at Montana State University in Bozeman. Susan cared for the baby while her young husband took classes on the care of sheep and swine, wool science, and soil fertility. He was in the second semester of his junior year when Betty called. It was late winter, just before the ewes started dropping their lambs, a grueling season. The pregnant ewes had to be fed, watered, and watched around the clock in the battering winds gusting off the Crazies. Betty told Rick that his father couldn't manage another lambing season on his own and needed his help.

Susan had different memories of that time. Rick's older brother Ron had moved back to the ranch with his wife by then, she recalled, and Rick was afraid that he'd be cut out. Rick wanted that ranch—he always had. He was just a few semesters away from completing his college degree, but after his mother's call, Rick dropped his classes and went home. He paid $5,000 for a trailer house, twelve feet wide, and towed it next to the farmhouse with a tractor. He never left the ranch again, never looked back or considered what might have been. Rick and Susan's second child, a daughter they named Jami, was born that September. Rick was twenty-one. "I was a happy boy," he said.

Rick worked on the ranch alongside his father for the next four years. On September 15, 1975, Bob went into Big Timber. Mid-September was when the Jarretts sold their lambs, so Bob had money in his pockets. Most likely, he'd been drinking for hours by the time he got in his 1967 Ford and pulled onto the highway. A little past 9:00 p.m., his truck veered into the opposite lane and collided with a double-trailer truck hauling diesel fuel. The semi plowed Bob's truck 150 feet down the highway before tipping over, fuel spilling from its ruptured tank. Bob was killed instantly. He was buried in Mountain View Cemetery a few days later, beneath a headstone carved with the jagged outline of the Crazies and a pair of soft-eyed ewes.

It's a common misconception that ranches like Rick Jarrett's are inherited, passed down from one generation to the next like family silver. They're not. Before an agricultural property changes hands, the market value of the land, livestock, ranch buildings, and equipment are assessed so the family can arrive on a fair price. If the parents are alive, the adult children usually have to buy them out. Ranchers don't have 401(k)s. Most spend their lives plowing every bit of money they have back into their agricultural operation. Their assets are the land and the livestock. If the kids want to take over, they have to pay their parents enough to retire on. Then it's up to them to figure out how to divide the land among siblings, or come up with the cash to buy each other out.

Rick was twenty-five years old when he buried his father. Youngest sons rarely got the chance to take over the family ranch, but Rick's older brothers had all left for more lucrative professions by then, like teaching high school and working for John Deere. Rick was the one who stayed. The brothers agreed that Rick would manage the ranch. But to claim title to the place, he'd have to buy out everyone in his family, starting with Bob's mother, Edna Jarrett, who hadn't been compensated for her ownership interest in the ranch at the time of his death. Paying off Grandma, that was Rick's first headache. Then he had to take care of his mother, Betty.

The four Jarrett brothers formed a partnership and drafted a promissory note, agreeing to pay Betty a principal sum of $209,500 over the course of twenty years, with interest—an amount far below the fair market value of the ranch, which was assessed at $568,000 at the time. Betty, who gifted the difference in the ranch's value to her sons, moved to town and went to work behind the lunch counter at Cole Drug.

For a time, Rick's brothers shared in the ranch's profits. Then they started breaking off pieces of land. Bill took an alpine parcel of land high on the Boulder River that generations of Jarretts had used as a stopping place for the sheep on their way to their summer grazing lease in the Absaroka Forest. At the time of Bob's death, the Jarretts still owned nine hundred acres of land on the southern side of the Yellowstone, on Mendenhall Creek. That land was sold, which went a ways toward paying off Ray and Ron, though not completely.

By 1985, the ranch was down to about two thousand acres, a fraction of its original size. That's the way it went with family ranches: they shrank with each generation. Rick ran several hundred head of Black Angus cows and kept a small herd of sheep. People weren't eating as much lamb or wearing as much wool as they once did, and beef had a better profit margin. But Rick wasn't earning enough on his cattle to make his payments to his mother, settle accounts with his brothers, and clear a profit, not even when beef prices were high.

The beef industry is dominated by a handful of multinational meat-packing giants, companies like Cargill, Tyson, and JBS, which set prices and control distribution. Beef prices are affected by everything from the weather and disease to geopolitics and export policies. Small ranches like the Crazy Mountain Cattle Company have no control over any of that stuff. Rick got one payday a year—the day he sold his calves.

Then they became part of Big Ag. The meat-packers shipped them off
to sprawling feedlots across the Midwest to bulk up on corn and other
grains, to give the beef the marbling consumers expected. Then they
were slaughtered, processed, packaged, and sold.

The buyers and packers were the pricemakers; cattlemen like Rick
were the price takers. Options for increasing his profit margin were limited. You couldn't starve money out of a cow by cutting its feed. You
couldn't increase the number of livestock you grazed without overtax-
ing the land. You could only grow so much grass, and in a dry year, you
might not be able to grow enough to feed your herd. Then you'd have to
buy feed or sell off your cows at a loss. Ranching was a starve-to-death
industry, Rick reflected. The only people who were successful at it were
those who came into it with a big enough cushion of cash not to care how
much they lost.

Rick and Susan were good at being poor; they didn't know any different. Susan drove a school bus and worked part time as a school clerk
to bring in more money. She raised a small herd of goats and sold the
offspring to kids for 4-H projects. Then she found a job in town, working for a financial planner. Once a month, the young ranch wives would
get together to drink coffee and share their troubles. "We used to talk
about what a myth the family ranch was—that it was this wonderful
family thing," Susan recalled. Family ranches were riven by jealousy and
conflict; that was the truth. The Jarrett ranch was no different from any
other. "Everybody fought everybody," she said.

Susan described Rick as a controlling husband who could be abusive,
slapping her or shoving her against a wall when he got mad. He was
unfaithful—Susan was sure of it. "He'd take a cow to Billings at eight
o'clock in the morning and not come home till six or seven at night," she
said. Selling a cow didn't take that long. There was a strip joint off the
highway to Billings called Shotgun Willies. Word got back to Susan that
everyone at Shotgun Willies knew Rick by name.

Susan divorced Rick in 1992. Jami and Jay were both married by
then—ranch kids marry young. Once the kids were gone, it was time
for Susan to fly, was how Rick saw it. So, she flew. "She got tired of me,"
he said. "She never really did feel a part of the ranch like she should."

Susan got half the money they had in savings and investments. She didn't ask for more than that, out of fear that the ranch would have to be sold to pay her divorce settlement. Despite everything she'd come to believe about the hollow myth of the family ranch, Susan wanted it to be there for Jay and Jami.

But Rick was struggling to hang on to the place even before the divorce. He confided his money troubles to a friend—Tim Owen, the financial advisor Susan had worked for. Owen would come out to the ranch and they'd shoot gophers together. Owen told Rick that if he wanted to keep ranching, he'd better find a partner. As it happened, he had someone in mind: his client Penelope Bell Hatten. Hatten, who originally hailed from Wayzata, Minnesota, was independently wealthy. Her great-grandfather James Ford Bell founded General Mills. Penny spent half the year in Bozeman, where she owned a stable and sat on the boards of various museums and schools. Apparently, she was interested in investing in a family cattle ranch.

For a wealthy person, owning an agricultural property can have certain financial advantages. A struggling cattle ranch makes a great tax write-off. But that was not what motivated Penny Hatten to buy a 50 percent stake in the Crazy Mountain Cattle Company, which she did shortly after she met Rick and decided she liked him. "It was never about making money; it was just about preserving some of the history of Montana," Hatten told me. "It was about maintaining the integrity of a true ranch."

Penny's husband and son went hunting on the ranch sometimes, but that was pretty much it. She left the decisions about the Crazy Mountain Cattle Company up to Rick, which suited him just fine. She didn't take any profits from the cattle operation, but she didn't pour money into it, either. Her investment was a one-time influx of cash that enabled Rick to pay debts to his various family members and go on doing what he'd always done. But even though everything still looked the same, the ranch was transformed. On paper, Rick now owned just half of the place.

In between irrigating hayfields and tagging calves and worming sheep, he began exploring other ways to make money—to diversify. In 1995, he got married again, to a woman named Linda who worked at Big Timber's assisted living facility. After Linda quit her job and moved into the farmhouse, Rick thought she could manage a new business venture he'd come up with: a game bird preserve for sportsmen. Rick raised the pheasants—"peasants," he called them—in a pen. When a sportsman booked a day of bird hunting with his dogs, Rick would go into the pen with a butterfly net, catch a pheasant, and tuck its head under its wing, rocking it back and forth until it went to sleep. He'd repeat this process several times, planting the drowsy pheasants under tufts of sagebrush around the coulees and hills of his ranch. This proved time-consuming and not very profitable, and fizzled out after a few years, along with his second marriage. Linda never took to the peasants.

In the late fall of 2001, Rick was working in his machine shop by the barn when a shiny truck wended its way down the dirt road along Duck Creek. It was too clean to belong to a rancher. A man got out, shook Rick's hand, and told him that he was a ranch broker. He worked with out-of-state clients who wanted to buy ranches. Had Rick ever thought of selling? He had a wealthy buyer who'd be interested in the place, willing to pay a lot of money.

Rick wasn't surprised. Rich people—famous rich people, even—were nothing new in Big Timber. The place was like a Hollywood fantasy of the West. Gene Autry, Hollywood's singing cowboy, bought a ranch just north of Big Timber in the 1940s and raised quarter horses there. In 1991, the Sundance Kid himself, Robert Redford, showed up in Big Timber to shoot *A River Runs through It*. Norman Maclean's fly-fishing novella was set in Missoula, but Big Timber was a lot more photogenic.

Sleepy as the town was, you might spot Michael Keaton eating a hamburger at the Grand, or bump into Tom Brokaw signing his latest book at Cinnabar Creek, a giftshop on McLeod Street. Both men owned big ranches nearby, along with a lot of people you hadn't heard of—big players from the worlds of finance, like David Leuschen, a private equity billionaire who bought an old dude ranch in the Crazies and turned it into a private playground for his family and friends.

Most of the year, these ranches were unoccupied, unless you counted the ranch managers, caretakers, cow bosses, and hired hands that maintained them. Then the summer would come, and with it, a stream of

Learjets and Gulfstreams screeching low over the Crazy Mountain Cattle Company on their flight path into Big Timber's tiny airport or Livingston's slightly larger one.

Now it seemed that a millionaire had a hankering for Rick Jarrett's land. Rick listened, stony-faced, as the ranch broker made his pitch. It wasn't a long conversation. Rick was dedicated to keeping the ranch in one piece for his kids, so fuck no, he wasn't interested in selling. He watched the man drive away in his shiny truck, and thought no more of it.

He had a new girlfriend by then, a dynamite lady named Karen. Unlike Linda and Susan, Karen was passionate about the ranching lifestyle. After she was laid off from her job as a hospital administrator, she traveled to Spain for an international conference on women and rural economic development. That's where she learned about European farm holidays, and how people would pay good money to stay on farms and help pick olives or crush grapes. Once Karen got back to Big Timber, she and Rick sat down at the kitchen table and began planning a new business, hosting working-ranch vacations for paying guests. Tourists who wanted to get up close and personal with a genuine cow-calf outfit could do it right there, at the Crazy Mountain Cattle Company.

Rick and Karen converted an old engine room into a bunkhouse, cleaning out the hives that bees had built in its walls and hanging curtains on the windows. Their first official guests were Penny and her son Max, who visited during lambing. Max helped brand the newborn lambs with sheep paint and funneled ewe's milk down the throats of the ones that were too weak to suck. "Lambing Camp," Rick called it. Max got sheep paint on his new coat, but Penny didn't seem to mind. After that, Rick and Karen put the word out to the state's tourism board and invited travel writers to stay. *Sunset* magazine ran a glowing feature on the joys of reconnecting with one's inner cowboy at the Crazy Mountain Cattle Company. Paying guests soon followed.

Rick took to the role of ranch host with gusto. He read in a travel magazine that you had to give your guests a truly memorable experience, something unique that they'd tell all their friends about, which is how he came up with the Tour. He'd drive new arrivals around the ranch in an old Suburban, pointing out the sights. At the climax of the Tour, he'd pause at the lip of a flat-topped hill overlooking the Yellowstone River, giving his passengers a moment to appreciate the view. Then he'd put the truck in gear and careen straight down the side. Sometimes, he'd pretend that his brakes had failed. A delighted teenage visitor compared the Tour to Disney World's Tower of Terror.

Otherwise, the roster of recreational activities at the Crazy Mountain Cattle Company was pretty much whatever work needed doing. Bunkhouse guests trotted along on horseback while Rick moved cows from one pasture to another, pulled on hip-high waders to help flood-irrigate his fields, and squirted worming medicine into the mouths of his sheep. Sometimes, they got to watch him castrate a horse. Rick enjoyed his visitors, by and large. But it was a lot of work, saddling up horses and packing lunches and making sure there was half-and-half in his refrigerator for their morning coffee. Guests from Japan complained about dead flies in the bunkhouse.

One day in 2004, Rick was in his truck when a feature on wind farms came on the radio. There was a market for wind, the radio host said, and Montana had some of the best wind in the country. Montana's winds blew hard and steady all winter long, providing a reliable form of renewable energy that could heat homes without the harmful carbon emissions that were heating up the planet. Rick snorted. He didn't believe in climate change. Heat and drought came in cycles same as they always had; that was nothing new. Montana had always been a dry goddamn place. Scientists predicted all kinds of things. You had to let the ball bounce a couple of times before you saw where it was going to go.

But when Rick heard how much money these wind farms were earning for landowners who leased their ground for the turbines, he turned up the volume. Millions of dollars, for wind. Rick didn't know what to believe about greenhouse gases, but he knew all about wind. The wind was a steady force that was always working against you. It dried up the soil something terrible. It took a cold day and made it even colder, turned a summer lightning strike into a brushfire that could destroy a season's grass crop in a few hours. The sandstone hills of his ranch were honeycombed with holes carved by its relentlessness. The wind was as much a part of Rick's legacy as the land itself. People were buying wind? Well, goddammit, he had wind to sell.

2

THE TREASURE STATE

February 20, 2019
Park County Courthouse
Livingston, Montana

RUSSELL GORDY, *having first been duly sworn, testified as follows*:

Q: And you and your wife, you said you purchased a property called Hunter Hot Springs.

MR. GORDY: That's correct.

Q: Can you tell the Court a little bit about that?

MR. GORDY: Hunter Hot Springs was a resort from 1870 to 1932. It went through various hands. It was originally done by Dr. Hunter. It had several different hotels on it. The last hotel was a three-hundred-room hotel called the Dakota Hotel. It had the hot springs, a big spa. They had their own brewery, they had their own dairy. They had what they called a golf course. Yeah, it was quite a thing.

The first tourist to record his impressions of the Crazy Mountains was Captain William Clark, who passed through Rick Jarrett's neighborhood, guided by Sacagawea, on July 17, 1806. The Corps of Discovery had split into two groups on its return from the Pacific Ocean. Meriwether Lewis headed up the Marias River, while Clark followed the Yellowstone River eastward. Sacagawea, an eighteen-year-old Shoshone woman, knew the Rochejhone from the seasonal buffalo hunts of her childhood, before she was kidnapped by enemy Hidatsa and then sold in a card game to Clark's interpreter, Toussaint Charbonneau, a gonorrheal French-Canadian fur trader.

Clark was infused with newfound respect for his teenage pilot, the "Squar wife to Shabono," who had brought his party safely across a mountain pass while wrangling her teething toddler. Now Sacagawea was leading Clark on an old buffalo road along the river, through grassy plains of wild rye, buffalo grass, and fragrant sweetgrass, with "a Strong sent like that of the Vinella after Dinner," Clark noted. He took in the sandstone cliffs, the cottonwoods growing in the creek bottoms, "a large gangue of about 200 Elk and nearly as many Antilope also two white or Grey Bear." Sacagawea pointed out a bark-covered fort used by Crow war parties, who dominated this part of the territory that Thomas Jefferson had recently acquired in the Louisiana Purchase. Jefferson's deal with France had doubled the size of the new nation. Lewis and Clark's mission was to explore the land and catalog its resources, to learn how they might be fully exploited.

It had rained hard the night before. Clark, who spent it huddled miserably under a buffalo skin, was still damp, and thus perhaps less enthralled by the future site of Big Timber than he might have been as his party rode their sore-footed horses across a ridge and through a low bottom, coming upon "a large Creek which heads in a high Snow toped Mountain to the N.W."

The creek was Big Timber Creek; the "snow toped Mountain," Crazy Peak. A mural painted on the cinder-block exterior of the Big T, the town supermarket, imagines the scene. Clark, in fringed buckskin and a Jackson Five–style applejack cap, clutches a rifle in one hand as he rides alongside Sacagawea, who wears her trademark long braids and a papoose. The sweetgrass tickles the horses' knees, so we cannot see the "Mockersons made of green Buffalow Skin" that Clark has strapped to their suffering hooves. Swathed in a luxuriant blanket of snow, the Crazies tower above the travelers, a vision in pure white and blue. Perhaps that is how they struck Clark. In his diary, he described the Crazies as a singular entity, "a high rugid Mtn. on which is snow."

Sacagawea's route along the Yellowstone—geographical coordinates, course distances, and landmarks scrupulously recorded by Clark in his journal—would provide a road map for white trappers and fortune hunters, then railroad surveyors and settlers.

Fifty-eight years and one day after Clark's ride-by, another traveler trudged past the Crazies on that old buffalo road—this time headed west, to the Montana goldfields. It was July 18, 1864. Andrew Jackson Hunter, Confederate Army surgeon and newly released prisoner of war, was on his way to the boomtown of Virginia City with his young wife,

Susan, and their children. All the family's possessions were heaped in an ox-drawn wagon under a canvas canopy: the family bible, a shotgun, a small sheet-iron stove. The day was clear; the peaks of the snowy mountains shimmered in the distance. They weren't the Crazies yet. White people hadn't been around long enough to name them.

The Montana Territory was in its infancy, created by an act of Congress and signed into law by Abraham Lincoln less than two months before. When the Hunters set off from Missouri, Montana was still part of the Idaho Territory. Large numbers of Southern secessionists— "seceshes" or "seshes," Northerners called them—had been flooding into the territory since 1863, when prospectors struck gold in Alder Gulch, scooping up millions of dollars in glinting placer deposits from its sandy streambeds with their wooden dishes. Lincoln wanted to claim the territory and its treasure before the Confederacy did. The Civil War was raging and the Union needed the gold.

Dr. Hunter's war had ended the summer before, after the Battle of Gettysburg, when he was swept up with the remnants of J. E. B. Stuart's cavalry and imprisoned at Fortress Monroe. Lincoln's Proclamation of Amnesty and Reconstruction granted freedom to Confederate prisoners of war in exchange for an oath to uphold the Constitution, the Union, and the abolition of slavery. Hunter swore the oath and returned home to Missouri, where a general store and pharmacy he owned was promptly burned to the ground by Union sympathizers.

"So we found ourselves in a short time almost destitute; then we decided to go West," Hunter's wife, Susan, wrote in an unpublished memoir in 1912. Andrew Jackson Hunter would gamble his children's lives on Montana and the "bright hopes of winning fortune in gold mines." The Hunters and three small children, each named for a hero of the Confederacy, fell in with John Bozeman's wagon train somewhere in Wyoming's Tongue River Valley. A prospector turned guide, Bozeman was charging five dollars per wagon to lead emigrants through Indian territory to Montana's fields of gold.

▼

The history of the land we call Montana stretches back to the beginning of human habitation in the Americas. The history of Montana the Treasure State sits lightly atop it. It's a short story driven by a simple plot line: the rush to grab up the land's wealth of natural resources before the next guy got there. The first chapters are all about various forms of extraction—animal, vegetable, mineral—serial tales of precious commodities and the boom-and-bust cycles they spawned. Consider Montana's state motto, emblazoned on its seal: *Oro y Plata*. Gold and Silver.

They came in waves. The fur trappers who all but wiped out the beaver population feeding the craze for beaver hats. The prospectors who blasted the hillsides for flakes of gold dust, burying valleys and streams in slurry. The buffalo hunters who slaughtered millions of bison for their hides, leaving behind mountains of skulls to be ground for fertilizer. The cattlemen who packed the grasslands with cows until the grass was gone. The copper kings who split open the earth with their glory holes and poisoned the air and the water with their smelters.

"Montana's growth, in one sense, has been a series of traumas," K. Ross Toole wrote in his indispensable history, *Montana: An Uncommon Land*. "There is little or nothing moderate about the story of Montana. It has ricocheted violently down the corridor of possibilities. What is good in reasonable measure is often bad in full measure, and Montana has been a place of full measure."

But a second theme emerges, a counterpoint to the materialist imperative that drove the invention of the Treasure State, and that is the deep emotional pull of the land itself. From the very beginning of the Crazies' many histories, recorded and unrecorded, the landscape's surpassing majesty has exerted a raw power that played on people's higher sensibilities, inspiring them with awe and terror, a sense of the divine. It wasn't long before the newcomers realized that there was value in that, too.

Now, as he forded the Yellowstone, driving his oxen against the current, Dr. Hunter was about to stumble down a new corridor of possibilities. The prospect was splendid: an open valley with miles of waving grass, guarded at the north by the Crazies' jagged palisade. A bright stream tumbled down from the mountains—Duck Creek, though it wasn't called that yet. Once the wagons had rattled their way atop the bluffs on the river's northern banks, Hunter's train struck camp. Susan gathered buffalo chips and clumps of sagebrush to fuel her stove, and the doctor shouldered his gun and went off in search of dinner. Pronghorns sprang up out of the high grass, bounding upland. Trudging after them, Hunter saw smoke wafting from a dip in the hills. He followed the smoke to its source—a hot springs, where a village of Crow Indians was encamped.

Hunter was in the heart of Crow Country, a 38,531,174-acre expanse granted to the Apsáalooke nation by the 1851 Fort Laramie treaty. The Crow, or Apsáalooke, were allies. They provided logistical support to the Union in its ongoing conflict with the Sioux and Cheyenne—their longtime enemies—and gave safe passage to white travelers. The Crow had visited the hot springs for centuries. They brought their old and sick to bathe and drink the waters, and treated sore-backed horses there. That summer, there had been many white visitors at the hot springs. The steaming thermal brooks and pools would become a landmark on the Bozeman Trail. People on a wagon train that passed through the month before Hunter's had the bright idea of washing their odiferous clothes in the boiling water they saw bubbling up from the ground.

But Hunter was the first white man to look at the springs and see money. He was a man of science, after all, aware of the latest medical trends. Back East, water cures were all the rage with well-to-do people. Hydropathy regimes—plunges in cold baths and hot baths of mineral-rich water—were embraced as the cure for everything from rheumatism and gout to insanity. It was one of America's first wellness fads. The spa towns that sprouted up around these natural hot springs were the nineteenth-century forerunners of Canyon Ranch and Miraval, catering to a wealthy, health-obsessed clientele. Before the war, Dr. Hunter had spent time in Hot Springs, Arkansas, a dusty backwater that burgeoned into a prosperous resort town in the space of a few decades.

As he beheld the steaming springs and sniffed their sulfurous tang—keeping a safe remove from the locals—Hunter resolved that if any white man should become possessed of these healing fountains, he himself should be that man. "He knew their value," Susan wrote. "But we could not stop there on account of savage Indians."

Hunter spent the next seven years in a fruitless quest for pay dirt, dragging his family from one mining camp to the next—Virginia City, Last Chance Gulch, Diamond City, Confederate Gulch—and staking one bad claim after another. Having strained out every particle of gold from the streams, prospectors were building flumes and using giant rawhide water hoses to power-wash the hillsides, tearing away trees and grass and topsoil and then feeding the runoff through sluice boxes—a process called hydraulicking. Hunter never found so much as a flake.

In 1871, the doctor threw in his dish, abandoned his worthless claims, and returned to the Crazies to claim squatter's rights to the place he was already thinking of as Nature's Sanatorium. The springs were no longer Crow territory by then. All Apsáalooke ancestral lands north of the Yellowstone—including the hot springs and the Crazy Mountains—had been stripped from the tribe by a new treaty.

In the winter of 1867, some twenty Apsáalooke chiefs left their hunting grounds on the Yellowstone at the government's request and traveled to Fort Laramie, an army outpost in the Dakota Territory, though doing so involved crossing enemy territory controlled by the Sioux.

"When I return, I expect to lose half of my horses on the way," Chief Bear Tooth said with bitter humor before launching into a litany of the abuses committed by the tribe's white allies. Crow Country had become overrun with silver and gold prospectors, trappers, and wolfers. These trespassers committed random acts of violence against Crow people. They devastated the elk, deer, and bison herds. "They do not kill them to eat them; they leave them to rot where they fall," Bear Tooth said. "All the old chiefs of former days, our ancestors, our grandfathers, our grandmothers, often said to us: 'Be friends with the white faces, for they are powerful!' We, their children, have obeyed, and see what has happened."

But a few months later, in April 1868, the Crow chiefs reluctantly signed a new treaty with the white faces. They agreed to surrender seventy million acres of territory in exchange for annuity payments, goods, and foodstuffs. The treaty, which affirmed tribal control over prime hunting grounds on both sides of the Yellowstone, marked the establishment of the first Crow reservation.

"The country across the river, where you go to hunt buffalo, the treaty says, you can go to while the buffalo are there; but when the game is gone away from there that is all to be the white man's land," a US envoy named Felix Brunot would clarify, five years after the treaty signing. Crow Country without buffalo—the idea was once inconceivable. But the bison were vanishing from the shrinking territory that remained to the Apsáalooke.

Bolts of calico, tin kettles, socks, and sacks of sugar and coffee were distributed at Fort Parker, a cottonwood log stockade that served as the headquarters for the newly established reservation, called Crow Agency. The fort was about ten miles east of the hot springs. Crow bands spent the winter encamped at the springs, as they had for centuries, visiting Fort Parker to collect annuity goods and to sell tanned bison hides to white traders—a source of income that had become essential to their survival, even as it contributed to the decimation of the herds that once sustained them.

Dr. Hunter dammed a hot-water creek that gushed from the earth at 148 degrees Fahrenheit at its juncture with a cold stream, creating a large pool of warm water suitable for a medicinal bath. On their first visit to the springs in July 1871, Susan and the children spent a day pouring buckets of boiling water into snake holes and killing the serpents as they slithered out. Hunter hired a contractor to build bathhouses from the sawn lumber he'd paid to have hauled out to the springs at great expense, and planted a few acres of potatoes, crop production being a requirement for claiming the land. The first guests at his natural sanatorium arrived in the fall of 1873, a wagonload of sick men transported to the springs by Dr. Hunter himself, who had been the lowest bidder for a contract to care for the county's indigent sick.

Whatever their feelings about the white interlopers who had claimed the hot springs as their private property, the Apsáalooke looked out for the Hunters and seemed to view the family's safety as a tribal responsibility. The Hunters were tending their potatoes one spring day when the Mountain Crow chief Iron Bull, a longtime scout for the US Army, appeared. He insisted that Dr. Hunter load his wife and children in their wagon and travel with him some distance, to be his guests at a sun dance—for good luck, he said. In fact, hostile Piegan Blackfeet were in the valley, and Iron Bull wanted to remove the white family from harm's way.

From then on, the Hunters planned their visits by the Apsáalooke calendar, staying away in the summer, when the Crow followed the bison herds across the plains, and returning in the late fall, when they set up winter camp at the hot springs and prepared their bison hides. "If anything happened to us they would be blamed. So they were a sort of protection for us," wrote Susan, who had no fondness for her protectors. "We were insulted on every turn we made by the Bucks," she harrumphed. "I or the children dare not go out without the men being with us, for they had no idea of virtue."

But nothing was more savage than the environment itself. Death could take many forms in the Crazies: a murderous blizzard on a spring day; the treacherous currents of the Yellowstone, in which Thomas Stonewall Jackson Hunter drowned at the age of eleven; the gust of wind that flipped the hay wagon Susan was riding in with her daughters, killing four-year-old Emma Sidney Johnston and crippling her older sister. And yet, the grandeur of the Crazy Mountains—"so grand, you cannot describe it"—never palled. "Many has been the days that I just drank in beauty of the scene before me," Susan wrote.

Wealthy tourists began finding their way to the Crazies, lured by many of the same things that would draw trophy ranch buyers at the turn of the twenty-first century: the dramatic landscape, the big game, the promise of adventure. "To the north and east the blue cloudy heights of 'Crazy Woman' Range swam and trembled in the haze," the Anglo-Irish aristocrat Windham Wyndham-Quin, the fourth Earl of Dunraven, wrote in *The Great Divide: Travels in the Upper Yellowstone in the Summer of 1874*, in which he recounts killing great numbers of bison and elk with a guide named Texas Jack.

The earl's visit to Crow Agency was the high point of his trip. He spent several days at Fort Parker ogling the Apsáalooke "bucks," who much impressed him with their "paint and finery," "long locks," and "brawny chests." Seating himself upon an empty candle box, Wyndham-Quin told his hosts "that a few blankets might be forthcoming if they gave us some good dancing." His interpreter was Tom Shane, a fur trader who had thrown in his lot with the Crow. Shane took the earl on a tour of the chief's lodges, brokering introductions while ribbing the men on their women troubles and flirting with the females in fluent Apsáalooke.

Dr. Hunter's health resort was an outpost of Victorian civility in the western wilds. An illustration in Michael Leeson's 1885 *History of Montana* shows a clutch of tidy bathhouses and a hotel with high, curtained windows. Women in bustled gowns and men in top hats stroll under the portico. Dr. Hunter, who had the long, white beard of an Old Testament patriarch, presided over his establishment in a silk stovepipe hat, an omnipresent wad of tobacco stowed in his cheek. His Crow protectors were long gone by then. The Apsáalooke had been forced onto a new reservation, one hundred miles to the east, driven there by a pair of congressional acts designed to open the entire Yellowstone Valley to white settlement. The laws took effect in 1882. Within months, Rick Jarrett's ancestors arrived in Montana to lay claim to their piece of the Crazies.

In photographs, Cyrus Barton Mendenhall, Rick's great-great-grandfather, exudes raffish charm. A handsome man with a weather-beaten face, unruly salt-and-pepper hair and a beard to match, he gazes forthrightly at the camera with a humorous expression. A hawk perches on the back of his thickly callused hand. Like Hunter, Mendenhall had been drawn back to the Crazy Mountains after first encountering them as a traveler on the Bozeman Trail. An Iowa farmer, Mendenhall followed the trail to the Montana goldfields in the summer of 1866 with a convoy of ox-drawn wagons loaded with stock goods, to sell to the prospectors at exorbitant prices.

The Bozeman Trail had become a flashpoint in Indian Country. Although Crow chiefs had tolerated the passage of prairie schooners through their territory to preserve their alliance with the US military, Red Cloud, chief of the Oglala Lakota Sioux, saw the trail as an existential threat. "This land has buffalo on it and we have children and that is what we feed them on. We don't like to have all these roads through our country," he protested to government officials. Shooting buffalo was a popular pastime for the pioneers, who would kill a hundred or so in a day to celebrate Independence Day, or to while away the tedium of the journey. The Bozeman Trail was littered with rotting bison corpses. Sometimes, the pioneers cut out the tongues, considered a delicacy.

Red Cloud declared war on the trail in 1866. Allied Sioux, Arapaho, and Cheyenne fighters attacked wagon trains and government outposts.

Mendenhall's train, which traveled with a military escort, came under attack several times, including a skirmish at the Tongue River in which one white traveler was killed. But the Iowa farmer and his merchandise made it to Virginia City intact. He stayed about a month, just long enough to sell all his wares, followed by his oxen and wagons. Then he boarded a flat-bottomed boat with $40,000 in gold dust packed in the hold and sailed home to Iowa City, a wealthy man. The Bozeman Trail was shut down for good that December after a war party lured a detachment of eighty-one US troops into an ambush outside Fort Phil Kearny in northeastern Wyoming, killing them all.

Mendenhall eventually left Iowa for Colorado, where he prospered in the cattle business. But his passage through the Montana Territory had made a deep impression on him. There was one place that stood out in his memory: a fine piece of country on the Yellowstone River where a sea of sweet-smelling grass waved beneath an island of snow-topped mountains. Mendenhall dreamed of filling that ocean of grass with cows. Now that the Indians were out of the way, it was time to seize the opportunity.

Mendenhall set off from Colorado in a caravan of twenty-two wagons with his second wife, his seven children, and a crew of cowboys to marshal his herds of 4,800 cattle and 700 horses. They arrived on the southern banks of the Yellowstone in August 1882. Mendenhall's cowboys built him a five-bedroom log house on a creek—Mendenhall Creek—with a magnificent view of the Crazies. He named the new settlement Springdale, for the hot springs across the river.

The Mendenhalls soon had neighbors: Spencer and Annie Jarrett, a young couple from Minnesota. Once the former Crow territory south of the Yellowstone was declared open for settlement, the Jarretts boarded the Northern Pacific Railway with their six-year-old son Ralph—Rick's great-grandfather—and rode it to the newly completed train station in Billings. There, they bought a narrow track wagon and traveled one hundred miles westward toward the Crazy Mountains. An old roan cow, trundling behind the wagon on a rope, served as a brake as it jolted downhill. The Jarretts staked their claim to a homestead three miles from Mendenhall's log manse. The 1877 Desert Land Act enabled them to claim 640 acres for just twenty-five cents an acre, so long as they irrigated some portion of it. The Jarretts built a sod-roofed cabin on a creek—Jarrett Creek—and planted an apple orchard. Clumps of mud fell from the roof into Annie's butter churn.

While all this building and planting was taking place, Chinese work crews were laying railroad track along the southern banks of the Yellowstone, from the newly platted town of Big Timber to the Springdale settlement. The arrival of the Northern Pacific put Dr. Hunter's sanatorium within reach of anyone who could purchase a train ticket. Sufferers of paralysis, dropsy, eczema, and diseases peculiar to the female sex came all the way from St. Paul. The water cure was not always successful. More than a few of Dr. Hunter's patients died at his health resort, their burial places long forgotten. One guest suffering from mental derangement wandered off and was never seen again.

While Dr. Hunter ministered to his patients, C. B. Mendenhall set about becoming a Montana cattle king. Just as the upper Yellowstone Valley had been cleared of Indians to make way for white people, the plains had been cleared of bison to make way for their cows. The buffalo were gone, hunted to the point of extinction, the culmination of an eradication campaign that began during Red Cloud's War.

General William Tecumseh Sherman—the government's chief strategist in its long offensive against Northern Plains tribes—saw the elimination of the buffalo as essential to the subjugation and assimilation of Indigenous people. He sponsored buffalo-hunting contests for wealthy New Yorkers and Russia's Grand Duke Alexei Alexandrovich, providing military escorts of hundreds of troops and awarding trophies, such as a silver drinking set embossed with buffalo heads. Buffalo Bill Cody, who guided many of these hunting parties, recalled elaborate dinners served by uniformed waiters, wagons loaded with fine carpets and crystal, portable ice houses of chilled wine. More than six hundred bison were killed in one contest. The hide hunters took care of the rest, slaughtering millions and sending the hides east by rail. By 1884, there were no hides left to ship.

The plains were now open for business—the beef business. Miles upon miles of open, bison-free rangeland—former Indian territory now owned by the United States—was offered to stockmen for pasturage, free of charge. It was the great grass giveaway. Cattlemen could fill the plains with livestock without buying a single acre. The Northern Pacific Railway put this grazier's paradise within easy reach. Stock cars of cattle arrived from the Midwest at Montana's new railway stations. All a man had to do was buy a couple thousand cows and a goodly number of bulls, put his brand on them, turn them out on Montana's incomparable bunchgrass for a season or two, then ship the fatted offspring back to the stockyards of Chicago and St. Paul.

Everyone wanted in: British aristocrats, Scottish lords, and a young Republican state congressman named Theodore Roosevelt, who invested in a large cattle operation that ranged across Montana and North Dakota. General James Brisbin's *The Beef Bonanza: Or How to Get Rich on the Plains* topped the 1881 best-seller list. Brisbin raved about Montana, whose "grazing cannot be excelled in any country in the world." There were over a million cows in Montana by the end of 1884. A new phrase was minted to describe the territory's lowing masses: black gold.

"The growth of the business has been one of the marvels of this marvelous age . . . Hundreds of men who embarked in the business a few years ago, with exceedingly limited means, are now ranked as 'cattle kings,'" Joseph Nimmo Jr., the chief of the Treasury Department's Bureau of Statistics, wrote in an 1885 report to Congress, calling for a large-scale expansion of cattle ranching across the northern plains. Washington's chief statistician proposed shrinking Indian reservations to free more land for grazing. The buffalo were gone, after all, "and the nomadic life encouraged by the possession of enormous reservations is not favorable to the formation of habits of industry." Nimmo noted that plans were already in progress to reduce the Crow reservation by half. "The portion to be released from Indian control is nearly all excellent bunch-grass range," he wrote, with palpable satisfaction.

Rick Jarrett's great-great-grandfather was swept up in the craze for black gold. In April 1884, the *Bozeman Weekly Chronicle* noted that C. B. Mendenhall—"one of our large cattle dealers"—would take delivery of 2,500 young cows from Minnesota at the Northern Pacific's depot in Fallon that Thursday, then return for another 1,600 cows on Saturday. By 1885, some 20,000 head of beef cattle bearing Mendenhall's brand—a triangular hatchet—ranged across hundreds of miles of prairie, from Wilsall in the southwestern foothills of the Crazies to Forsyth in eastern Montana. Mendenhall became one of the highest taxpayers in Park County, the owner of fine horses. His bay Billy took second money in Big Timber's Independence Day races.

While Mendenhall prospered, Dr. Hunter struggled. The healing fountains hadn't turned out to be the liquid gold mine he had envisioned all those years ago on the Bozeman Trail. When paying guests were in short supply, the doctor advertised the springs as a sheep dip; the mineral-rich waters provided an excellent preventive against blowfly and itch mites, for just two cents a head. To no avail: Dr. Hunter's name appeared on a list of delinquent taxpayers. In 1885, he listed his natural sanatorium for sale.

Dr. Hunter's medicinal baths had been eclipsed by the booming tourist attraction to its north: Yellowstone National Park—America's first—a wonderland of geysers, hot springs, and bubbling mud pots. The Northern Pacific platted a town some thirty miles west of Big Timber to serve as the hub for a new rail line to the northern entrance of the park, and named it after the railway's director, Crawford Livingston. The Northern Pacific's investors saw Yellowstone as another bonanza, a wellspring of profit. You could only sell one train ticket to a homesteader, but sightseers and pleasure-seekers would fill your trains every season.

The Northern Pacific launched a national marketing campaign inspired by Lewis Carroll's *Alice in Wonderland*. "Alice's Adventures in the New Wonderland," which described Yellowstone's many marvels, was distributed across Northern Pacific rail lines. Wealthy people traveled to Livingston in private Pullman cars with lavish staterooms, parlors, dining rooms, and observation decks—precursors of the private jets that would one day crowd Big Timber's little airport.

When Hunter listed his resort for sale, Mendenhall saw a unique business opportunity. With his considerable means, he could transform the sleepy sanatorium into a spa resort with all the improvements of the modern age. In 1886, Mendenhall bought Hunter's Hot Springs for $26,000. He formed a consortium called the Montana Hot Springs Company with two business partners a few months later and issued $150,000 in capital stock—$4.9 million in today's dollars—for the creation of a grand hotel at the springs. Then he bought out his partners and assumed control of the entire enterprise.

"C. B. Mendenhall, the proprietor and sole owner of the hotel, bath rooms and ladies' plunge, now under course of construction, is sparing no labor or money to place this resort foremost among the celebrated watering places of the United States and he is the possessor of all the natural advantages bestowed upon us by the Omnipotent Being," the *Livingston Post* declared. The new pools and bathhouses would be as fine as any to be found at Baden-Baden, the hot water delivered directly from the springs by newfangled covered pipes.

Mendenhall hired a civil engineer to plat a large township on a 160-acre site near the hot springs and named it after himself. The town of Mendenhall, Montana—reached by a new iron suspension bridge across the Yellowstone, which Mendenhall would build—would have wide avenues lined with shade trees, artificial canals, and row upon row of 50-by-150-foot homesites. Mendenhall submitted the plat survey to the Park County clerk and recorder and had it notarized. "The proprietor of Hunter's Hot Springs has tacked his own name to the famous springs, for what reason, except to gratify a possibly laudable family pride, no one can discover," the *Daily Yellowstone Journal* noted with displeasure. "Mendenhall is probably quite as pretty a name as Hunter, but in this case it cannot be considered as appropriate, unless to assert the fact that the springs are capable of 'menden' all' the ills that flesh is heir to."

On February 24, 1886, the *Bozeman Weekly Chronicle* reported that the $150,000 in capital stock issued by Mendenhall's Montana Hot Springs Company had been fully subscribed. Appearing alongside this notice was a letter to the editor from a reader concerned about overgrazing. "It takes a great many acres of thin grass to maintain the adult steer in affluence for twelve months, and the great pastures at the base of the mountains are pretty well tested," it read. "These great conventions of cattlemen, where free grass and easily acquired fortunes are naturally advertised, will tend to overstock the ranges at last, and founder the goose that lays the golden egg."

The Sagebrush Cassandra was right. Grass was disappearing from the upper Yellowstone Valley, eaten up by burgeoning herds of cows, horses, and sheep. But Mendenhall, who was busily overhauling Hunter's Hot Springs—repapering and repainting, laying new carpets, purchasing upholstered furniture for the parlor—had no time to worry about bunchgrass. He set eight carpenters and fifteen laborers to work that spring constructing a three-story frame hotel that he called the Da-Ko-Ta.

It was hot and dry that summer, a bad year for grass. There was less nutrient-rich forage on the range for the cattle to fatten on as they headed into the most brutal winter that new Montanans like Mendenhall had ever experienced. Ice storms swept through in November, with howling winds, followed by heavy snows that blanketed the range. The blizzards came in January. In February, temperatures dropped to forty degrees below zero.

Cows couldn't weather a Montana winter like bison—particularly not pilgrim cows, out-of-state bovines who hadn't had a few seasons to grow thick hides or acclimate to the severities of the climate. Those who did not freeze to death starved, unable to paw through the thick snow and ice to rustle out whatever grass was buried deep below beneath the drifts. Cattle died by the hundreds of thousands, huddled in ravines or along streambeds where they had tried to eat the bark off the cotton-woods and willows. They died where they stood, frozen stiff as boards or buried up to their ears in snow.

Across Montana, townspeople watched emaciated cows stagger inside city limits in search of food, then die on the streets. "Full many a heifer now bellowing loud will be found ere long in a snow-white shroud," the *Daily Yellowstone Journal* lamented. In February, the *River Press* re-ported that cattle were dying "by the wholesale," declaring, "There is no salvation for the stock interests except in a speedy and genuine chinook." But the chinooks—warm, snow-eating winds from the Pacific—didn't come.

During the winter that became known as the Great Die-Off, Men-denhall was living with his family at Hunter's Hot Springs. As the snowdrifts rose outside his windows and temperatures plummeted, Mendenhall paced the hotel's newly carpeted halls in a state of agonized distraction. Rick Jarrett's great-grandmother Inez would recall the morning her Pa came downstairs to the dining room in his nightshirt, so tormented by worry that he had forgotten to put on his pants.

When the chinooks finally arrived in March, they melted the snow-drifts and laid bare the corpses. Mendenhall took measure of his losses: six-

teen thousand head of cattle and countless horses dead, at a cost of $80,000.
His days as a cattle king were over. Five generations later, his great-great-
grandson could describe C. B. Mendenhall's terrible winter as though he
had been there himself. "It took the heart out of him," Rick said.

Mendenhall's big plans—the iron suspension bridge, the artificial canals and rows of shade trees, the bustling spa town bearing his name—
were all shelved. Hunter's Hot Springs would never be Baden-Baden
under his ownership. But it was still a grand place for a bath. John
"Liver-Eating" Johnson, the mountain scout reputed to have eaten the
innards of dozens of Crow Indians, was a regular; soaking in the hot
springs eased his rheumatism. Walter Goodall, former secretary to Khe-
dive Tawfiq, ruler of Egypt and Sudan, was dazzled by the scenery. "My
eyes are dilated as must have been Aladdin's when they first encountered
the palace which had arisen in a single night under the hands of his genii
slaves," Goodall declared of the view that greeted him from his hotel
window upon being awoken by Mrs. Mendenhall's canary.

Then standards began to slip. "Hunter's Hot Springs is a delightful
place to visit, or would be if things were kept up in better shape and some
attention paid to guests. A little elbow grease and soap expended on the
bathing apartments would also be vastly appreciated," the *Big Timber
Pioneer* chided in 1894. Mendenhall fell behind on his taxes. A few years
later, he sold the hot springs resort to a Butte millionaire, James Murray.

Montana became a state in November 1889. Big Timber flourished as
sheep ranching became the region's prime industry. Sheep were cheaper
than cattle, and hardier. They filled their bellies on the scrubby forage and
weathered the harsh winters snug in woolly coats that could be sheared
off in the spring and sold. In 1895, the town became the seat of the new
county of Sweet Grass, across whose rolling hills and coulees millions of
sheep now grazed. Five million pounds of raw wool were shipped out
of Big Timber on Northern Pacific freight trains that year. By 1907, the
frontier town would be known as the wool capital of the world.

Big Timber acquired all the accoutrements of civilization: a church, a
school, a printing press, a hardware store, a barbershop—with a female
barber, no less—as well as hotels, saloons, billiard halls, and a bowling

alley. It was a lively, polyglot place. Dozens of Chinese men from the rail-road crews stayed on, and some started restaurants and laundries. A sheep-herder fresh off the mountains could pay a dime to have his fetid union suit bleached white in Sam Lee's copper tubs with cobalt bluing balls. Lu Lung's O.K. Restaurant served chicken dinners at all hours; turtle soup and a good cigar were included with the price of a meal at Henry's Big Restaurant. Susie Sargent, a Black woman credited with bringing night-life to Big Timber, presided over the town's burgeoning red-light district. An 1893 Sanborn Fire Insurance map shows "female boarding houses" on both sides of Anderson Street, a stone's throw from the local calaboose—a little wooden jail. An opium den did business behind a washhouse.

"Rich and poor, high and low, clean and unclean were component parts of a common herd and all ate together . . . It made no difference whose elbow your elbow was rubbing," the *Big Timber Pioneer* remi-nisced in 1938. Susie Sargent dined with the justice of the peace and the founder of the town's first bank.

It didn't last. Sargent's female boarding house on Anderson Street was seized by the sheriff over missed mortgage payments and sold at the court-house door. Chinese residents—some of whom had been in Big Timber from its earliest days—were harassed under racist exclusionary laws. In April 1903, the *Pioneer* reported that a "special immigration inspector . . . looking up contraband chinks" had rounded up twenty-eight people "but found all of them entitled to remain here." Some men shot up a restaurant, as a prank. By 1930, Big Timber had only three Chinese residents.

Mendenhall retired to his old ranch on the Yellowstone to raise sheep. No longer trusting the grasses of the open range to provide for his herds, he grew alfalfa, irrigating his fields with water drawn from the Yellow-stone. When the Treasure State's first histories were written, Menden-hall would be hailed as one of its most stalwart pioneers. "While he has suffered losses that would have forever put out a less determined and active man, he has but surmounted them to show that it is not the luck but the man that makes the winning in this world of pushing business and whirling adventure," *An Illustrated History of the Yellowstone Valley*, published in 1907, declared.

Under Murray's ownership, Hunter's Hot Springs at last became the four-star resort that Mendenhall had envisioned in the heyday of his cat-

tle baronetcy. Murray built the Dakota Hotel, an imposing edifice with
a concrete Mission-style facade and every modern convenience: steam
heat, electric lights, and "intercommunicating telephones." Old postcards show the immense Natatorium, water shimmering under a high
arched roof, and a glass-walled solarium filled with palm trees. Gibson
girls in shirtwaists and full skirts wield rackets on the tennis courts made
of poured sand and molasses. A pair of gentlemen in bowler hats sip
water from a long-handled dipper under a kiosk. There was a nine-hole
golf course and a cricket pitch. In the spa, masseuses administered blanket sweats, needle baths, and salt glows.

A few decades later, it was gone. A new highway that would have
linked Hunter's Hot Springs to Yellowstone National Park was routed
along the opposite side of the Yellowstone River, bypassing the resort.
Prohibition shut down Hunter's Bar, a popular watering hole, known
for its selection of bonded liquors. Hunter's Hot Springs became a place
of dubious repute, a honky-tonk. A local entrepreneur opened a still
in an old lemon-soda bottling plant, or so the rumor goes. On a windy
night in November 1932, an electrical fire that started in Mendenhall's
old frame hotel burned the entire resort to the ground in a few hours.

Various commercial enterprises were launched amid the ruins in the
decades that followed. A local couple ran the Plunge as a public swim-
ming pool and opened a lunchroom. A Japanese natural foods company
drained the Plunge and grew organic vegetables in greenhouses heated
by the springs, until high winds blew the greenhouses away. The hot
springs were acquired by a rich man who made his fortune from a chain
of truck stops. He buried the Plunge and bulldozed or burned whatever
ruins remained.

Only the town of Mendenhall stayed the same, untouched by fire
or wind or the degradation of time. Plat No. 172, the survey that C. B.
Mendenhall commissioned back in 1886, was preserved in the amber of
the Park County Clerk's records system, where it became a permanent
appendage to the deed to Hunter's Hot Springs. To claim title to the
springs was to inherit the faded blueprint of another man's dreams. And
so the town of Mendenhall passed from one owner to the next for more
than a century, with its unbuilt streets, avenues, and bridges, its canals
and shade trees, and row upon row of rectangular lots, all for sale.

IF YOU GIVE ANYBODY LUCK,
SHIT WILL DO FOR BRAINS

February 20, 2019
Park County Courthouse
Livingston, Montana

RUSSELL GORDY, *Direct Examination*:
Q: So, you put together how many properties?
MR. GORDY: I think it was seven, overall.
Q: Okay. And why did you do that?
MR. GORDY: Well, it was a pristine area, and much more valuable
to me if I could own from the river to the mountains. That's what I
was looking for, and I was lucky enough to do that.

The new owner of Hunter's Hot Springs liked to tell people that he
was born dirt-poor, that he never thought he'd fly in an airplane, much
less own one. Now he owned two—a Gulfstream IV and a Beechcraft
B300 King Air, and a few helicopters besides. When the news of his
$40 million–plus, forty-four-thousand-acre Montana land grab broke in
the spring of 2002, Russell Gordy was in Alaska, hunting grizzly bears.
He declared himself shocked to learn that he had just set a record for the
most expensive ranch acquisition in Montana history. "I just thought it
was a beautiful property," he told the *Bozeman Daily Chronicle*. "They
don't make land like that anymore."

Gordy was a collector. He collected land the way other rich men collect art. Every time he sold an oil or gas property, he'd buy a quality piece
of land out West, transforming a share of the liquid profits into solid
earth. He *liked* land. Maybe there were better investments, but land was
real. You could see it. You could bow-hunt elk on it. You could watch
your bird dog flush a covey of Hungarian pheasants and take your shot

as they wheeled up from the grass in a noisy whirl. You could fly-fish for trout on your own private stretch of river. You could ride quarter horses through its coulees with your grandkids, maybe try your hand at roping some calves.

By the time I made Gordy's acquaintance, he had acquired some 200,000 acres of blue-chip ranchland across the American West. His collection has grown since then, great swaths of mountain and forest, river and stream. His name regularly appears on *Land Report* magazine's annual listing of the one hundred largest landowners in the country.

Gordy's collection, like his fortune, was built on fossil fuels—the catchall term for hydrocarbons formed in the earth's crust over many millions of years from the fossils of decomposed plankton, plants, and microorganisms. Transmuted into oil, gas, and coal, those ancient fossils became the bedrock of the modern age. There would never have been a steam locomotive or a steel mill without them. Hydrocarbons burn; that's what creates power. Exposed to heat and oxygen, their molecules of tightly bound carbon and hydrogen burst, releasing energy—energy that fuels cars and furnaces and electric grids. Fossil fuels also release carbon dioxide, methane, and other greenhouse gases that trap heat in the atmosphere, melting ice caps, shrinking glaciers, warming oceans, causing extreme droughts and hurricanes and all the other signposts of climate change.

And like that old joke about the Catskills resort, not only is the food bad, but the portions are small—limited, let's say. Fossil fuels can take different forms, depending on the type of organic matter, the degree of heat, the amount of pressure. They can be found deep below the ocean floor, trapped in subterranean reservoirs and caves, locked inside rocks and sand. But the supply is finite. Oil wells run dry, coal mines tap out, shale plays are exhausted. Hydrocarbons are not an all-you-can-eat buffet. So, since the dawn of the Industrial Age, there's been a constant pressure to find new sources of these fuels to keep the lights on.

Gordy was very good at finding and harvesting hydrocarbons in their more elusive forms, and this made him a wealthy man. But he'd be the first to say he was lucky. And perhaps his greatest stroke of luck was to come of age in Houston, Texas, the energy capital of the world.

Russell was born in 1950 in Savannah, Georgia, the only child of

Russell Wayne Gordy and Marion Agnes Shepherd, who preferred to be called Agnes for reasons no one could fathom. The Gordys moved to Houston when Russell, their only child, was three years old. Russell Wayne became a policeman. Agnes cared for her son during the day and earned money cleaning office buildings at night. Russell grew up in a cramped single-story home in Chatwood Place, a subdivision of mass-produced homes built to house the city's swelling population of blue-collar workers. The Gordy home on Woodlyn Road occupied a narrow lot, one-sixteenth of an acre in size. There was a patch of grass in the front and a patch out back. Russell attended M. B. Smiley High School, where everyone was poor, so no one minded. He grew to mind when his basketball team played schools in upscale Houston neighborhoods like Memorial and River Oaks. Russell gawked at the glass backboards in the gyms and the lockers full of fresh new footballs.

Decades later, when he had become a very rich man, Gordy would make a point of flying over his old Houston neighborhood every few months in the helicopter his wife, Glenda, had given him for a birthday present. (When her husband couldn't find the time to attend his flight lessons, Glenda bought him the helicopter company so that the flight instructors could work around his schedule.) Chatwood Place and its rows of small two-bedroom homes were still there—shabbier now, with sagging carports, sickly live oaks, and a collapsed backyard shed here and there. M. B. Smiley was gone—the school's main building burned to the ground in an arson attack in 1980.

After Officer Gordy caught his son stealing hubcaps for pocket money, he packed him off to his grandparents' farm in Vernon Parish, Louisiana, for the summer, to work his ass off hoeing and weeding and thereby keep from turning into a juvenile delinquent. Russell was ten or eleven at the time.

On the boot-shaped map of Louisiana, Vernon Parish is located right about where the Achilles' heel would be, on the Texas border. Gordys had lived in the parish since the Reconstruction Era, when Vernon was known for its virgin forests of longleaf pine, a tall, stately tree with fine, feathery leaves. When Gordy's great-grandfather Henry Clay Gordy was a young man, he could ride his horse all the way to Texas across a hundred-mile swath of airy, sun-dappled forest carpeted with golden pine straw.

Lumber merchants descended on Vernon in the early twentieth century. Russell's grandfather George Gordy went to work for the White-Grandin Lumber Company in the sawmill town of Slagle. He spent the 1920s tending the firebox of a company steam train that shuttled back and forth between the sawmill and the railway depot in Leesville, pulling flatcars of lumber. By 1930, the longleaf pine forests were gone. Vernon Parish had been cut over, cleared so completely that it was said that you could stand on a stump and see all the way to Lake Charles.

White-Grandin shut down its sawmill and abandoned its Leesville, Slagle, and Eastern Railroad line. George Gordy found work as a day laborer. He ran a prison work crew from the county jail. Eventually, he saved enough to buy a forty-acre farm near the old sawmill town of Alco—named for the Alexandria Lumber Company and deserted by the same. Abandoned tramways cut through the scrub of the lost forests like ghostly roads, their tracks and ties salvaged for scrap.

"If you give anybody luck, shit will do for brains," George Gordy told his grandson. "Without luck, it doesn't matter how smart you are." Russell resolved to become lucky.

His grandparents put him to work in the fields, tending watermelons and cantaloupes and butter beans and purple hull peas. When it got too hot, they'd knock off for a bit and play dominoes. Russell's grandfather took him on his first quail hunts in woods of scrubby slash pine that had been planted by the millions in a New Deal–era reforestation program. Russell spent hours mooning over the hunting guns in his Grandmother Ocie's Sears & Roebuck catalog—the Wish Book. Russell told Ocie that one day he'd buy them all. In the meantime, he made do with a BB gun, honing his marksmanship by shooting wasps on lazy summer afternoons.

Russell got his first job in the oil business the summer he turned fifteen, as a roustabout at a little oil field about a mile from his house. Despite the raffish job title, being a roustabout was drudge work mostly, cleaning up after the guys who knew what they were doing—the roughnecks. After a few summers on oil rigs, he became a roughneck himself. He put himself through college roughnecking on offshore oil platforms. Russell learned how to throw the chain—a technique for connecting the sections of pipe down an oil well. You took a steel link chain and wrapped it around the new section of pipe, then unwrapped it fast to twirl it into place. Some roughnecks lost fingers throwing the chain, but Russell held on to all ten. With his first paycheck, he bought himself his first gun, a 12-gauge Remington. He was halfway through college when his father died, killed by a heart attack at the family home on Woodlyn Road.

After earning a degree in business administration, Russell took a job with the Transco gas pipeline company. Right off the bat, he figured out that working for a big company and doing the same thing every day wasn't for him. At the time, a wildcat oilman named Joe Walter was making a name for himself in Houston with his knack for finding crude oil and natural gas in places that bigger outfits missed. His company, Houston Oil & Minerals, extracted five hundred billion cubic feet of fossil fuels from a layer of hydrocarbon-rich sand deposits right in Houston's Galveston Bay that nobody else in the industry thought existed. Walter was scrappy, intuitive, unafraid of risk. Russell Gordy didn't want to be a company man. He wanted to be an entrepreneur like Joe Walter.

After reading up on gas and oil deals at the Houston Public Library, Gordy cold-called Walter and asked for a meeting. The wildcatter took him to James Coney Island, a Houston hot dog joint, then made the twenty-four-year-old pay for lunch. ("Dadgum, I forgot my wallet," Walter declared upon being presented with the eight-dollar check.) A few weeks later, Gordy was hired on as Houston Oil & Minerals' thirteenth employee.

Gordy learned the oil business from Joe Walter, and much more. He learned to recognize opportunities that others overlooked, which is another way of saying he learned how to be lucky. Luck was seeing that opportunity and not being afraid to act on it. You had to be prepared to get lucky. So, Russell Gordy prepared.

In 1981, Walter sold Houston Oil & Minerals. Gordy founded an oil and gas company called Northwind Exploration with some of his colleagues, a bunch of guys all in their twenties with too much testosterone. Russell's wife, Glenda, kept the books. Russell and Glenda had been high school sweethearts, though he'd fallen for her long before then, in their elementary school Christmas play. Glenda St. Andrie, a tiny third-grader with starry blue eyes, was an angel. Russell was smitten.

Gordy and his partners found some nice oil and gas fields off the Gulf

Coasts of Louisiana and Texas. It was a boom time for oil, but they resisted the temptation to expand the business by taking on debt. They sold Northwind Exploration just before the oil industry crash in 1985. It was a stroke of dumb luck, and Gordy made the most of it. "I kind of had money when other people didn't," he said. During the bust, he scooped up oil fields at bargain prices.

Russell and Glenda bought their first piece of land in 1982: 113 acres in the piney woods of East Texas, with a lake and a tin-roofed barn with a woodstove. The Gordys would own much grander and more expansive properties, but there was nothing to rival the thrill of those first years on the East Texas ranch with their two young sons, Garrett and Shaun. The boys spent hours riding their three-wheelers through the trees and throwing pinecones at each other. Russell took them fishing on the lake and bird hunting in the piney woods, just as his grandfather had done when he was a boy.

The family stayed in the barn, sleeping on mattresses they laid on the floor. One night, Glenda woke up and locked eyes with a wood rat that was sitting at the foot of her bed. She refused to return until her husband built her a cabin, with a bathtub. Russell built Glenda her cabin and bought more land around the lake. Then he bought some more. The East Texas ranch grew to 7,800 acres.

In the mid-1980s, a friend of Gordy's brought him a deal on coalbed methane gas. He'd never heard of it. Conventional natural gas is free-flowing. It collects in underground reservoirs—often mixed with crude oil—and can be piped to the surface through wells. Coalbed methane gas was unconventional. It wasn't free-flowing; the methane was locked within the matrix of the coal seam. But if you drilled into the seam and pumped out all the groundwater on top of it and around it—if you dewatered that well—you could free the gas. The drop in water pressure triggered a chemical reaction that unlocked the methane, transforming it into a free-flowing gas that could be pumped to the surface, compressed, and fed into pipelines.

The federal government wanted to encourage coalbed methane exploration. The Iran–Iraq War had disrupted oil production, causing energy shortages and fears of an economic recession. In 1980, amid rising concern about American dependence on foreign oil, Congress approved tax credits for the production of fuels from "nonconventional" sources like coal beds and shale. Domestic natural gas production tripled. Critics called it drilling for credits.

The surge in domestic energy exploration came at a cost. Coalbed methane extraction used up a lot of water—a precious commodity in the arid West, where a lot of America's coalbed methane was to be found. A single gas well could pump out between seventeen thousand and twenty-two thousand gallons of ground water in a day; a field of gas wells could lower aquifers, sap streams, and drain residential wells. Then there was the problem of the water itself—the wastewater. Water flushed from coal seams was salty—up to five times saltier than seawater—and often contained heavy metals, which could damage soil and contaminate streams and rivers. But there were no federal regulations for the disposal or purification of coalbed methane wastewater. Coalbed methane drilling was the Wild West of energy exploration.

Gordy was a pioneer on fossil fuels' new frontier. In 1989, he formed SG Interests with his friend Lester Smith, acquiring coalbed methane wells in the San Juan Basin of New Mexico and Colorado. At first, this new venture seemed like a great way to get in the poorhouse quick, tax incentives notwithstanding. Gordy's coalbed methane wells pumped out two thousand barrels of water a day—eighty-four thousand gallons— but only produced a measly fifty thousand cubic feet of gas. It cost two dollars a barrel to dispose of that water, which was twice what Gordy was earning on the gas. But he figured it out. Gordy struck a deal with a big energy company that had an established water disposal system in the San Juan Basin; he'd sell them some of his conventional oil and gas holdings if they'd take his wastewater, at ten cents a barrel. Gordy kept pumping those coalbed methane wells until the water production dropped and the gas began to flow. After a year, his wells were producing just fifty barrels of water a day—and five million cubic feet of natural gas.

"As soon as we knew it was going to work, we bought everything in the area," Gordy said. "We probably drilled five hundred to a thousand wells."

Gordy had been looking for a classic Western spread in the Rockies for years. He found it in 1993: a fifty-thousand-acre ranch just south of Casper, Wyoming, that had once belonged to Bryant Butler Brooks,

Wyoming's seventh governor. Gordy paid $5 million for the place and named it Falls Ranch, for the waterfalls that cascaded over several of its box canyons. Falls Ranch became the home base of Gordy's new sideline, the Lone Star Cattle Company.

"You don't really make a living doing cattle, but it preserves the land," Gordy said. And it was fun. The Gordy family went on cattle drives into the mountains with their cowboys. They hadn't been horse people to start, but going on a three-day cattle drive, that sure turned them into horse people.

Glenda remodeled a small home on the ranch—nothing wrong with it, but modest, with a low iron fence and a cattle guard to keep the cows off the front lawn. She picked out a large stained-glass window of a cowboy on a white horse for the family room. Russell arranged some antique pistols on a low table, like coffee-table books. There was an old-fashioned jukebox. Now and then, Russell would pick out a song and sweep Glenda up for a jitterbug.

Coalbed methane accounted for more than half the natural gas produced in the US in the 1990s. Natural gas was touted as a pathway to energy independence and a cleaner-burning alternative to coal—a "bridge fuel" that would enable America to transition to carbon-free forms of energy. It's true that natural gas emits half the carbon dioxide of burning coal. But gas is primarily composed of methane, and methane in its raw form is a fearsome greenhouse pollutant. Leaked methane is more than twenty-five times more potent than carbon dioxide when it comes to trapping heat in the atmosphere.

The natural gas industry leaks a lot of methane. Methane leaks when gas is extracted, it leaks when it's compressed, it leaks from aging pipelines. By one estimate, anywhere from 2 to 6 percent of all the methane produced in the US escapes into the atmosphere every year in its most toxic form. (Natural gas production isn't the only source of methane emissions, of course; industrialized agriculture pumps billions of pounds of methane into the atmosphere, from fertilizer factories, pesticides—which are derived from fossil fuels—and feedlots packed with cattle, which belch out the greenhouse gas.)

When prices for natural gas reached new heights in 2001, Gordy sold some of his coalbed methane assets to Conoco for a nice chunk of money. Then he bought himself another high-quality piece of land: La Ceniza, a sprawling hunting ranch in South Texas, with doves and quail and deer ranging through the mesquite. La Ceniza's owner had a gambling problem. After renting the ranch for a time, Gordy began buying up chunks of it in 1998. By 2002, he owned all 19,200 acres—a steal at $18 million.

At first, Russell and Glenda thought they'd remodel a house at La Ceniza. Then Russell thought again: *nah*. Glenda taught herself how to use computer-aided design software and designed a fifteen-thousand-square-foot Spanish-style hacienda. Every time she showed Russell the plans, he told her to make it bigger.

Gordy killed some really good deer at La Ceniza. When he shot a thirty-three-point buck, a message board called Totally Texas lit up. The Uvalde buck had been a local celebrity. "The deer was hard to hunt only see him a few times a year," a user with the handle Fish On posted in February 2005, adding, "FYI Mr. Gordy lives in Houston area so if any one knows him or meets him might suck up and say sir. Ha ha. He has a lot of real nice bucks on ranch . . . just a regular guy when I met him. Talks like a plain working man."

Wild pigs also roamed the ranch, but they were a nuisance, an invasive species that competed with the deer and other wildlife for food. Now and again, they attacked Gordy's cattle. Then he'd have one of his pilots take him up in his helicopter, strap himself in, and lean out the open cockpit to lay waste to the pigs with an AR-15 semiautomatic rifle. Sometimes Glenda joined in. Lithe as a teenager well into her sixties, with baby-blond hair she wore long and straight with seventies-style bangs, Glenda handled the AR-15 with ease.

The early 2000s were an excellent time to be in the fossil fuel business. From his Texas twang to his extensive network of friendships in the oil and gas world, newly elected president George W. Bush was an oil patch lover's dream. Dick Cheney, even better. In between stints as George H. W. Bush's secretary of defense and George W. Bush's running mate, Vice President Cheney was chairman and CEO of Halliburton, a sprawling multinational corporation that provides a host of services to the oil and gas industries, including its own patented hydraulic fracking technologies and products.

On his ninth day in office, Bush created the National Energy Policy Development Group and tapped Cheney to lead it. The task force held some forty secret meetings with as many as four hundred representatives from the oil, mining, and gas industries. Four months later, Cheney's group released its proposals for a new energy policy. Chief among its recommendations: open up more public land for drilling—including environmentally sensitive areas like the Arctic National Wildlife Refuge (ANWR)—expedite drilling permits, and lift cumbersome restrictions limiting oil and gas exploration. In a sop to environmentalists, the report recommended earmarking $1.2 billion in oil and gas bid bonuses from the "environmentally responsible leasing" of ANWR for research into renewable energy sources.

Conservation and environmental groups, which had been shut out of Cheney's task force and its secret meetings, focused their outrage on the report's proposal for drilling in the Arctic. The call for expanded gas and oil exploration in the Rocky Mountains got a lot less attention.

The federal government owns a lot of land in the Rockies, amassed during the push for westward expansion by the forcible displacement of Native tribes, who were pushed onto reservations (or massacred) to make way for white settlers. In the Midwest, most of this government-appropriated land eventually passed into private ownership in the form of homesteads and land grants to farmers. But the rugged, high-altitude terrain of Western mountain states didn't attract as many homesteaders, creating a giant land surplus. Most of that federal land is now overseen by the Bureau of Land Management (BLM), which issues permits and leases for logging, grazing, mining, and energy exploration, but is also charged with protecting and conserving the most wild and scenic areas.

Cheney's task force had set its sights on the vast reserves of natural gas and oil that lay beneath the surface of BLM lands in the Rockies—Colorado in particular, where the federal government owns more than a third of all the land in the state. "Much of these potential resources have been placed off-limits or are subject to significant restrictions," the report's authors groused.

No longer. Under President Bush, the BLM began auctioning off drilling leases to federal land across the Rockies, including some very wild and scenic wilderness. It was like a new gold rush, or the great grass giveaway of the 1880s. Energy companies submitted their wish lists for parcels of public land; the BLM put those parcels on the block and sold the drilling rights to the highest bidder. This massive sell-off took place with scant public notice, and without the review processes mandated by the National Environmental Policy Act, which requires federal agencies to assess the environmental impact of any proposed use of federal land before issuing permits. The BLM had been directed by the president and the vice president to fast-track energy exploration, and it did.

For a study in contrasts, consider the fate of the 2002 farm bill, which earmarked $115 million for a new US Department of Agriculture (USDA) program to promote wind energy development on America's farmlands and rangelands. The goal was twofold: harness the heartland's untapped wind power while giving rural communities and farmers a needed economic boost. But in 2004, the Government Accountability Office declared the USDA's renewable-energy program a bust. Agriculture Department officials didn't implement key provisions, like providing government loans and loan guarantees to ranchers and farmers who wanted to put up wind turbines in their cow pastures and soybean fields. Small grants were available, but the application process was so complicated that few applied. In two years, the USDA had managed to award just $600,000 in grants from that $115 million kitty. Rural America's wind, the GAO report concluded, "remains largely untapped." By 2004, wind power accounted for less than one-tenth of one percent of the nation's electricity.

Around the time that Rick Jarrett got the idea of building his wind farm, Gordy was taking advantage of the BLM's garage sale of federal land, buying up oil and gas exploration leases at bargain prices in Colorado's Thompson Divide. Once home to the Ute people, the Thompson Divide was pristine wilderness with virgin forests, sparkling trout streams, elk herds—just the kind of quality land that Gordy might have added to his ranch collection under different circumstances. But the Thompson Divide sat atop reserves of coalbed methane and hydrocarbon-rich shale—another unconventional source of natural gas.

Gordy's SG Interests started out drilling wells for coalbed methane in the Thompson Divide. He thought he'd found the promised land when the very first well he drilled produced copious coalbed methane gas and very little water. But the second well made a whole lot of water, necessitating the drilling of a second well for a wastewater disposal zone. To Gordy's surprise, gas began issuing from the disposal well—far more gas than his coalbed methane wells were producing. Gordy had drilled into the Mancos Shale formation, which lies deep below the Thompson Divide. In the process of trying to get rid of wastewater, he had discovered something super special—a prodigious reserve of unconventional natural gas, locked in the shale.

A new technology called hydraulic fracturing was about to revolutionize the energy industry, and Gordy was about to get lucky again. Shale, like other hydrocarbons, is formed from fossils, but also contains minerals like clay and quartz, which make it harder than coal. Shale is fine-grained and impermeable. To get the gas out of shale, you've got to shatter it with a liquid battering ram called slickwater: a turbocharged mix of water, chemicals, and tiny particles of sand or high-strength ceramic beads. The chemicals thin out the water and speed its flow, smashing the rock. The tiny particles—called proppants—wedge themselves in the fractured rock to let the gas escape.

After his discovery, Gordy stopped pumping water for coalbed methane and started fracking for shale gas in the Thompson Divide. The environmentalists kicked up a fuss over the slickwater. It takes a lot of slickwater to frack shale—millions of gallons down every wellbore. Common ingredients include such toxic chemicals as methanol, ethylene glycol, and propargyl alcohol. But no one really knew for sure what mix of chemicals were in any fracker's brand of slickwater. It was considered proprietary business information under the law, like the recipe for Diet Coke. Only industry insiders like the folks at Halliburton knew for sure. Vice President Cheney's old company was one of the world's largest producers of fracking fluid.

The slickwater used in fracking and its flowback could seep into aquifers and other underground sources of drinking water, a source of untold environmental damage and risks to human health. But fracking fluid wasn't subject to the regulations of the Safe Drinking Water Act, which had been in effect since the 1970s. The Energy Policy Act of 2005, which baked many of the Cheney task force's recommendations into law, exempted hydraulic fracturing from drinking water regulations. This exemption became known as the Halliburton Loophole.

In 2011, Robbie Guinn, SG Interests' top landman, would declare that he was "reasonably certain" that SG Interests hadn't poured diesel fuel down its Colorado shale wells. This was not reassuring to the people who lived in the counties where SG Interests had its wells. At a Pitkin County Commission meeting to discuss new drilling permits, a man showed up dressed like an undertaker, with a bouquet of lilies. Every time one of SG Interests' guys tried to talk about the new shale well they wanted to drill, the undertaker laid down on the floor and held up a lily. "He'd say, 'Oooh, you're destroying Mother Earth,'" Gordy recalled. "It was like a clown show."

Gordy's SG Interests amassed forty thousand acres of BLM land in the Thompson Divide's Ragged Mountain area, prime fracking real estate atop the Mancos Shale. But he had some competition: the Gunnison Energy Corporation (GEC) also wanted a piece of that Mancos Shale. Gunnison's owner was William Koch, brother to Charles and David Koch. William—"Wild Bill" to his friends—was entranced with the Old West. He built an old-timey frontier town with five saloons, a church, a bank, a jail, and a pink and teal brothel—a guesthouse, he insisted—on a 6,400-acre ranch he owned in the shadow of the Ragged Mountains in Gunnison County, Colorado.

Now Wild Bill and Russell Gordy were headed for a showdown in the Thompson Divide. The rivals managed to coexist for a time. Gordy's SG Interests focused its drilling activity on the eastern side of the Ragged Mountain, where it controlled forty thousand acres of BLM land, while Koch's GEC bought up leases to fifty-two thousand acres in the south. But when SGI and GEC's interests in the region began to collide and overlap, they struck a deal. Why drive up the price of leases by bidding against each other, when they could work together and get the land for cheap?

Two days before a BLM auction in February 2005, attorneys for the two companies executed a memorandum of understanding signed by SGI's Guinn and a Gunnison vice president named Anthony Gale.

Under the terms of the memorandum, Gordy's SG Interests would bid on the leases at the auction while Gunnison Energy sat on its paddle. The memorandum set a maximum bid price of $300 per acre. If SG Interests was successful and won the leases for that price or lower, it would transfer a 50 percent interest to Gunnison, and the two companies would split the cost.

The plan worked perfectly. At the BLM auction that February, and at subsequent auctions through 2006, SG Interests placed the winning bids on leases to nearly twenty-five thousand acres in the Ragged Mountain area, scooping them up for as little as two dollars per acre. The deal was brash, creative, and quite possibly illegal. To anyone familiar with antitrust law, it looked a lot like collusive bidding, a violation of federal laws barring companies from conspiring to restrict or monopolize trade.

In 2009, Gale, who had left Gunnison Energy to start his own company, blew the whistle on his former employer and SG Interests, informing the Justice Department that the two companies had colluded in a bid-rigging scheme to acquire federal oil and gas leases. As proof, Gale produced the memorandum of understanding that he had signed with SG Interests VP Robbie Guinn.

The federal government had taken a hard line against those who abused the BLM auction process. Just the year before, a University of Utah undergraduate named Tim DeChristopher placed $1.8 million in fake bids at a BLM gas lease auction in Salt Lake City, Utah, in an effort to put the land beyond the reach of the fossil fuel industry. DeChristopher managed to win fourteen drilling leases to public lands in southern Utah before being removed from the auction by federal agents.

DeChristopher's actions, and the media coverage of his arrest, threw a spotlight on the BLM's negligence, its lax approach to the stewardship of public land, and its eagerness to cater to oil and gas companies. In 2009, the Obama administration's interior secretary, Ken Salazar, concluded that the BLM had failed to perform an adequate environmental impact review on the land it had auctioned off that day. Salazar canceled the winning bids on seventy-seven leases—including eleven of the fourteen leases DeChristopher had won with his phony bids. Despite that, a few months later the feds charged the Utah undergrad with two federal felony counts. Tried and convicted, he was sentenced to two years in prison and a $10,000 fine.

The Department of Justice launched a two-year investigation into Gale's whistleblower complaint. In 2012, it brought a civil antitrust suit against SG Interests and Gunnison Energy, but declined to bring criminal charges against the companies' executives. Litigation was time-consuming and expensive, with an uncertain outcome. So, rather than taking the case against the two companies to trial, the DOJ proposed settling the matter with a pair of $275,000 fines. The fines weren't punitive damages: they were a calculation of what Gordy and Koch's companies would have paid for the leases had they competed against each other at those auctions and bought them fair and square.

The federal judge in the case received dozens of letters from outraged citizens, asking why a college student was sitting in prison for an act of civil disobedience while two powerful corporations that had conspired to cheat the government were allowed to walk away without so much as a slap on the Rolex. The commissioners of Pitkin County, where Gordy's SG Interests owned leases to thirty-two thousand acres of public land in the Thompson Divide, were also dismayed. SG Interests had purchased twelve of its sixteen leases in the Divide's Lake Ridge area for just two dollars an acre—paying six dollars an acre for the remaining four. Those leases hadn't been the subject of the Justice Department's investigation, but the Pitkin commissioners wondered if they were a product of the same kind of illicit bidding arrangement.

In the end, the judge approved a settlement that increased the fines on both companies to $500,000 apiece—with no admission of wrongdoing. Both Gordy and Koch were allowed to keep the public land leases they had won through their companies' improper conduct, and to continue buying up more. The final judgment was issued on April 22, 2013—Earth Day. Tim DeChristopher had been released from a federal penitentiary just a few days before, having served twenty-one months of his two-year sentence.

Gordy's Wyoming ranch on the North Platte swelled. He kept adding to it: a 6,500-acre tract here, a 640-acre inholding with a spectacular waterfall over there. One by one, he bought out the old-timers clinging to a section of land that their great-granddaddies proved up in the homesteading days. Gordy bought land all the way up to the highway, land he didn't even really want, just to keep it from being turned into tract homes, like the subdivision he'd grown up in. Falls Ranch swelled to nearly eighty thousand acres. To see it all in a day, you needed a helicopter.

But just because you own a big piece of land doesn't mean that you'll get to enjoy it in peace. By 2001, Gordy had learned that the hard way. Although it sprawled across 140 miles, Falls Ranch was pocked and banded with tracts of public land—state trust land, BLM land. This caused no end of headaches. Gordy had a complicated relationship with what he called the public. And the public was forever finding its way onto Falls Ranch.

That it was private property didn't seem to matter to the campers who pitched their tents on his side of Muddy Mountain or the hikers who found their way to the forty-foot waterfall spilling over one of his box canyons. (There were five waterfalls on the Wyoming ranch, but in Gordy's estimation, the other four were more like Slip 'N Slides.)

One September evening, Russell and Glenda were coming home from a night at the movies in Casper when Gordy spotted the distant lights of a car going up the mountain road—*his* road—on Muddy Mountain. Having recently lost 1,500 acres to a brushfire, Gordy was not kindly disposed toward campers. He headed up the road after the car and eventually came upon a young couple. The tale, as Gordy told it, involved a campfire and a pair of flustered teenagers under a blanket. "I says, 'Can I help you, son?' and he says, 'I'm just here with my mother, barbecuing,' and then she pulls her head out from under the blanket and says, 'I ain't your mother!'"

He was less amused by the hunters. In the first years of owning the Wyoming place, Gordy allowed some hunting. He held drawings and gave away between ten and twenty elk permits a year, and thirty antelope permits. But the public abused the privilege. He'd go out and find fifty people hunting his elk, not twenty. They tore up his land and left their trash behind. There had been two fires on Muddy Mountain; Gordy blamed the hunters. He stopped giving away permits.

But even after Gordy locked the figurative gates to his ranch, the public found its way in. On opening day of elk season one year, a dozen hunters showed up. One of them told Gordy that a guy at the post office had said it was okay. The poachers who shot at his elk from the open windows of their four-wheelers were the source of particular outrage. Gordy bow-hunted his elk—a lot more challenging than shooting at them. The people who ran around in ATVs on his land trying to shoot something—that wasn't even hunting. Those people didn't respect his elk, and they didn't respect his land. Their four-wheelers tore up all the sagebrush. No, Gordy didn't have much use for the public.

For some time now, he'd had his people on the lookout for a place in Montana, a big place where every acre belonged to him, and to him alone. No neighbors. "I like people," he told me once. "I just don't want to be around them." Lucky for Russell Gordy, an old cowboy in the Crazy Mountains was getting ready to hang up his spurs.

John Moreland cut his teeth on saddle leather. He was born in 1915 near the Crow reservation in eastern Montana. He rounded up wild horses when he was small, trailed a herd of cows and horses to Wyoming at the age of nine, rode saddle bronc in rodeos as a teen. Hankering to see something of the world, Moreland went east to perform in Wild West shows, riding and trick roping for crowds at Madison Square Garden and Atlantic City. When he got tired of boardinghouse spaghetti, he came home to Montana, where he found honest work as a cowhand and courted his wife, Elta. "Cut 'er out of a bunch of heifers and ran her up a draw! Put my brand on 'er!" he'd say.

Moreland owned a fifteen-thousand-acre ranch in the Crazy Mountains where he ran cows, broke colts, and rode horses no one else wanted anything to do with. But at the age of eighty-six, Moreland was ready to take up more age-appropriate hobbies, like raising quarter horses. In the fall of 2001, he put the ranch up for sale.

A Livingston ranch broker named David Viers took notice. He'd heard about the Texas oilman who was looking for a big piece of country in Montana. As it happened, Viers was trying to sell another ranch nearby, a 12,250-acre property that had been in the Bonhomme family since 1913. Pete Bonhomme, the end of the line, fed his herd for the last time in 2000. Viers got the listing for the ranch after the executors of Bonhomme's estate failed to sell it at auction.

The Bonhomme ranch had been on the market for more than a year, and the executors were antsy. They started talking about selling the land to an oil and gas company. That kind of talk was very bad for business, from Viers's perspective. Just that year, a Colorado energy outfit bought the mineral rights to a ranch in the Jackson Creek area, to drill for coal-bed methane. Viers had a deal in the works to sell another ranch near Jackson Creek, and the very mention of possible coalbed methane development in the area killed it; his buyers walked.

"What we have in this country is a view with some dirt under it," Viers told a reporter for the *Bozeman Daily Chronicle*. He urged the executors to stay the course.

When the Moreland Sheep Mountain Ranch went up for sale, Viers saw an opportunity that might appeal to the Texas oilman. The Bonhomme ranch and the Moreland place added up to a nice piece of property. Gordy came to Montana, and Viers took him up in a helicopter so he could get a good look. It was beautiful mountain country. But as they flew over the two ranches, Gordy saw there was another property smack in the middle: a five-thousand-acre cattle ranch. Gordy wasn't interested in buying land that was divided up like that.

The ranch in the middle belonged to Dave Gibson. It had been in his family since the homesteading days. He spent his days farming, fencing, and raising cattle on that land. In the winter, when the work thing was done, Gibson liked to go snowmobiling in the mountains with his three children and their friends. The Crazy Mountains were his cathedral. Gibson had been born on that land and planned to die on it.

Gordy decided he'd buy it.

"They said the owner would never sell. It was a homestead," Gordy recalled. "But it was tough times for cattle."

The tourism industry was reeling in the wake of the September 11 terrorist attacks. People weren't traveling, which meant they weren't going to restaurants, which meant they weren't paying for burgers and steaks. A cattleman could hold on to his calves, let them fatten up in a Nebraska feedlot for a few extra months, and wait for the world to steady itself. But that would mean paying more for feed. By the time the calves finally came to slaughter, they'd yield bigger carcasses—increased supply, in other words, that would keep beef prices low. "Given the global events of the past six months," an article in *Beef* magazine warned in April 2002, "marketing your 2001/2002 calves has to be the ultimate marketing challenge."

Hard luck for some, an opportunity for others. Gordy asked for Gibson's phone number, called him up, and made an offer—no brokers or lawyers involved. When Gibson told Gordy he didn't want to leave the ranch, the Texan offered him a job. "I said, 'You just stay here and manage it all.'" Gibson told his friend Jim Hogemark, the ranch manager for the nearby Wild Eagle Mountain Ranch, that he didn't want to sell. "His parents were buried on that land. But he said, 'Jim, I just couldn't refuse. It was too much money,'" Hogemark said.

Gibson accepted Gordy's offer and told him about other ranchers who might be persuaded to sell. Viers did some digging, and found a few more. It was a mix of longtime ranching families and some moneyed newcomers, like the fashion photographer Bruce Weber, who owned 1,440 acres on the west fork of Duck Creek with his wife and agent, Nan Bush. Jonathan Foote, an architect, owned Hunter's Hot Springs. The old spa hotel was gone, but it was good grazing land, with three irrigation pivots for growing hay. Viers told the architect to name his price. "It was a deal you simply couldn't refuse," Foote said.

So there it was: seven ranches, forty-four thousand acres in all. "To me, it made it more valuable from day one," Gordy said. North to south, Gordy's new ranch stretched seventeen miles, with its figurative toes splashing in the Yellowstone River and its head in the Crazy Mountains, pillowed by clouds. On a surveyor's map, Gordy's Montana domain looked like a game of Tetris: an ungainly assortment of rectangles and squares stretched haphazardly across a grid. But contained within those squares and rectangles was an uninterrupted expanse of gorgeous scenery abounding in elk, deer, and pronghorns, with enough bears and mountain lions and wolverines prowling around to keep things interesting.

Best of all, there was no public land mixed in, apart from one section that was completely engulfed by Gordy-owned acres, and thus inaccessible to the public. Any day-tripper who wanted to visit would need a helicopter.

Gordy vowed to be a good steward of the land. He would never subdivide or develop his domain. He would not drill for gas or oil. "I won't mess it up," he told the *Bozeman Daily Chronicle*. "I think people will find I'm a good neighbor."

When the reporter asked if he planned to make money on cows, Gordy just laughed.

4

Awaxaawippíia

February 20, 2019
Park County Courthouse
Livingston, Montana

DEAN APOSTOL, Scenic Resource Assessor, *Direct examination*:
There's a lot of agreement within our culture about what we think
is scenic and what we don't, and there's a body of research and
methodology behind that work. So, when somebody says, "Well,
I think, you know, the Crazy Mountain area is scenic," they're not
just saying that as a—they may be saying that as an opinion, but it's
an opinion that aligns very strongly with what we know about what
people feel is scenic.

In the beginning, there were the mountains, and the wind flowed over
them. Sediment cores drawn from the muddy depths of an ancient lake
west of the Crazies are banded with thick layers of silt, blown there some
fifteen thousand years ago by masses of cold air whipping off the receding glaciers. There's pollen embedded in that ancient mud as well, borne
on great gusts from the grasses and sages and the flowering broadleaf
plants called forbs that flourished on the steppes and tundra that was
Sweet Grass County.

The first people arrived at the end of the last Ice Age. We know that
they traveled and hunted and gathered food in and around the Crazies for
thousands of years. The mountains are networked with aboriginal trail systems, some marked with ancient stone cairns that have sunk into the earth
like wisdom teeth. It was a fertile place, with abundant fresh water and
game. Streams flowed downslope from the mountains in every direction,
drawing herds of mastodons and woolly mammoths and ancient bison to
its valleys. Even then, the Crazies were a fantastic piece of real estate.

For the first people, the best places were ones where you could hide from the creatures that would kill you while scoping out the creatures you could kill. A mix of high and low places, wide-open places and enclosed hidden ones, an interplay of sunlight and shadow. *Prospect and refuge* is the phrase a geographer came up with back in the 1970s to sum up the essence of great scenery. Our most primitive instincts draw us toward landscapes that offer both safety and opportunity. Tens of thousands of years ago, the hills and river valleys sheltered by these mountains telegraphed a message: *Here, you will survive.* By 2019, that message had become a slogan on a T-shirt at Gusts department store: *Last Best Place.*

The mountains officially became Crazy in 1876, when a War Department cartographer labeled the island range west of Big Timber as the "Crazy Woman Mtns." There are various stories about how the Crazies got their name, the most popular of which involves a pioneer woman who went raving mad after her family was massacred by Indians, disappearing into the mountains and haunting them with her cries. This almost certainly did not happen. Although there were some gruesome attacks on wagon trains on the Bozeman Trail, none seem to have occurred in the Crazies. Diaries kept by emigrants from that period don't refer to the Crazies at all.

There are more prosaic explanations. The drainage from the mountains, which runs in every direction, is crazed. The toxic, purple-blossomed locoweed that grows in the foothills drives cows and horses crazy, causing weakness, extreme nervousness, and eyes dull and staring. The fierce winds that whipsaw the mountains and the dangerous unpredictability of the weather up there—truly insane. Some point to the irregular, or crazed, landforms of the mountains themselves.

But the word that the Crow, or Apsáalooke, people know the mountains by offers a better portal to their otherworldly mystique: *Awaxaawippíia. Awaxaawé* is the Apsáalooke word for mountain. The meaning of *Ippíia* is more elusive. It's an archaic term that means dangerous or ominous. You can find it in the Crow word for nightmare: *baashíalippiia.* Otherwise, *ippíia* no longer exists in the Apsáalooke language.

Awaxaawippíia—a high, jagged place with a bad reputation or omen. It's usually translated as the Ominous Mountains. Some call them the Bad Dream Mountains.

Big Timber's current residents don't know much about the people who lived there before white people arrived; some believe that the lands their families have ranched for generations were vacant before they got there. "We don't have ancient history, like Spain and France," Rick Jarrett told me once. "This is country that nobody lived in."

But Rick's land was prized long before Montana became the Treasure State. The Crazy Mountain Cattle Company lay in the heart of Crow Country.

"The Crow Country is in exactly the right place. Everything good is to be found there," the River Crow chief Eelápuash famously declared in Washington Irving's *The Adventures of Captain Bonneville*, published in 1837.* "It has snowy mountains and sunny plains; all kinds of climates and good things for every season. When the summer heats scorch the prairies, you can draw up under the mountains, where the air is sweet and cool, the grass fresh, and the bright streams come tumbling out of the snowbanks."

In 1873, Felix Brunot, an envoy from the Commission of Indian Affairs, went to Crow Agency at Fort Parker to persuade Apsáalooke leaders to cede more territory. It had been only five years since the chiefs Bear Tooth and Blackfoot signed the last treaty at Fort Laramie, establishing Crow Agency. They had already surrendered their claim to lands north of the Yellowstone River—the Crazies, Hunter's Hot Springs, and the land that would one day belong to Rick Jarrett. Blackfoot was bitter about the 1868 treaty. He accused government envoys of lying to their interpreter, a fur trader named Tom Shane who had thrown in his lot with the Crow and lived among them for years. "Shane was there the first time and what he interpreted to us are not the words that are in the treaty," Blackfoot told Brunot. "We told them we wanted a big country. They said we should have it, and that is not in the treaty."

Now the Great Father Ulysses S. Grant wanted more country, for white miners and cattlemen, and to build an iron road for the Northern

---

* Though Irving spelled the chief's name as Arapooish, Eelápuash is now preferred.

Pacific Railway. "The Great Father has heard that the country southwest of here is not of much use to the Crows, and that the whites are
going into it," Brunot told the head men. "Where is the best country you
know of for Indians to live on?" There was a long silence, then discussion among the chiefs.

"Why did you ask that question?" Blackfoot finally replied. "We
have land we like very much." The best country was Crow Country.

The arrival of the Apsáalooke people in the Crazies marked the climax
of a centuries-long odyssey. The Apsáalooke, or Crow—the name means
"Children of the Large-Beaked Bird"—are the descendants of people
who once lived in the upper Great Lakes region. According to Crow
oral histories, the ancestral tribe began its long trek west after a terrible
drought parched their land and the game disappeared. During a stop-
over in North Dakota, two brothers, Red Scout and No Vitals, fasted in
search of divine guidance. Red Scout received an ear of corn in his vision,
and the instruction to stay put. His band would become the agrarian
Hidatsa tribe. No Vitals dreamed that he and his followers must travel
onward, to a place with high mountains.

The Apsáalooke historian Joseph Medicine Crow, who drew on
stories passed down by sixteen generations of oral historians to create a
timeline and a map for the Crow exodus, dates its start to around 1500.
No Vitals' splinter group settled for a time with the Mandan people in
the Dakotas, where they lived in earthen lodges, made clay pots, and
grew corn and pumpkins. A ferocious argument between two women
over the choicest parts of a buffalo killed by their husbands divided the
community. No Vitals' tribe set off again, this time on a wide-ranging
quest that took them first to western Canada, then south to the Great
Salt Lake, then east all the way to present-day Oklahoma, and finally
west and north again, to Montana and Wyoming.

Medicine Crow theorizes that a journey that began for one reason
continued for another, as the Crow and other bow-and-arrow Plains Indians came under threat from Eastern tribes who had been displaced by
European settlers and were themselves being pushed west, armed with

rifles acquired in trade. Their travels were all on foot; the Apsáalooke had yet to acquire horses.

By the dawn of the eighteenth century, the Apsáalooke were well established in southern Montana and northern Wyoming. In 1743, the Verendrye brothers, a pair of French-Canadian traders, came upon a Crow settlement at the confluence of Montana's Bighorn and Little Bighorn Rivers. It was the tribe's first recorded encounter with Europeans. The Apsáalooke had undergone a complete revolution by then, having abandoned their pedestrian pumpkin-patch ways for a dynamic and much more exciting lifestyle centered on horses, warfare, and the hunting of bison. Struck by their statuesque good looks, the Verendryes called them the *Beaux Hommes*—the handsome men.

Crow Country was vast. Bison followed the smell of grass and water carried on the wind, and the Crow followed the bison, walking into the winds that blew across the greater Yellowstone ecosystem. As they moved between summer grazing lands in the alpine meadows of the mountains and their wintering places in the grassy river valleys and bottomlands, the bison traveled about a thousand miles a year. The Apsáalooke map traced those seasonal migratory corridors across Montana, Wyoming, and the Dakotas. In what would become Montana, the nomadic tribe's territory stretched from the Powder River and the Pryor Mountains in the east to the headwaters of the Yellowstone in the south, then west across the Absaroka-Beartooth range and north to the Musselshell River and the Crazy Mountains.

Everyone wanted Crow Country. "We stole the hunting grounds of the Crows because they were the best," a Cheyenne chief told an army colonel during Red Cloud's War. "We fight the Crows because they will not take half." As Crow bands followed the bison across the landscape— clans of men, women, and children traveling with horses, dogs, and loaded travois—they were under constant threat from the Assiniboine, Piegan Blackfeet, and Sioux. "There was almost continual war with those who coveted our country," Plenty Coups, the last of the Crow warrior chiefs, would tell his biographer, Frank Linderman. "No other section could compare with the Crow country."

The Apsáalooke were always primed for combat, ever ready to

seize an opportunity to steal the enemy's horses—warlike, but above all agile and adaptive. A man's social and political standing was defined by his prowess on the battlefield, by how skillfully he could disarm the enemy or capture his horse. The hallmark of a great warrior was to strike an enemy with a coup stick rather than lifting a gun or bow to kill him. This infliction of the ultimate humiliation was called "counting coup."

(Men were not the only warriors. Crow women fought and counted coup, as did people of a third gender the Crow call *batée*, or two-spirit. The medicine woman Pretty Shield described the heroics of "a woman and a *half*-woman" in the Battle of the Rosebud in 1876, in which the Crow fought alongside US troops against the Lakota Sioux and Cheyenne. Osh-Tisch—Finds Them and Kills Them—"who was not a man, and yet not a woman," jumped off their horse to defend a wounded Crow warrior, firing shot after shot at the advancing Lakota Sioux as fast as they could load their gun. The Other Magpie, "a wild one who had no man of her own," charged at a Lakota armed only with her coup stick, striking him just as Osh-Tisch shot him off his horse. The Other Magpie returned to camp, waving the Lakota's scalp in the air, then cut it into little pieces to give to the men to dance with. "The men did not tell you this, but *I* have," Pretty Shield told Linderman.)

The Apsáalooke maintained ties with their Mandan and Hidatsa cousins, traveling to their palisaded villages on the Missouri River to trade with them and with the white fur traders who were coming west in growing numbers. A new generation of French-Canadian traders called them the *Gens de Corbeaux*—People of the Crow. The mistranslation stuck.

Father Pierre-Jean De Smet, a Jesuit priest who traveled across the western territories and the Canadian Rockies in the early nineteenth century, evangelizing to the people he encountered, spent a few days riding with a Crow band that he ran into along the Yellowstone in 1840— "the best-formed savages I have met on my travels," he declared. Father Pierre-Jean was shocked to see that many of the women were covered in dried blood. The band had just passed a battlefield where some forty kinsman had been killed by Sioux two years before. The wives, mothers, sisters, and daughters of the fallen warriors had torn their faces and cut their arms and legs to honor them.

De Smet began proselytizing his blood-smeared companions forthwith. He had his work cut out for him. "The Crows are considered the most indefatigable marauders of the plains; they cross and recross the mountains in every direction, carrying to one side what they have stolen on the other," De Smet wrote. After telling his hosts about God's laws and the torments of damnation awaiting those who killed and stole, a chief exclaimed, "I think there are only two in all the Crow nation who will not go to that hell you speak of."

At the time of the Lewis and Clark Expedition in 1806, there were an estimated 3,500 Apsáalooke, spread out across Montana and northern Wyoming in different bands. There were River Crow, Kicked in the Bellies Crow, and Beaver Dries Its Fur Crow. The Apsáalooke who lived in the shadow of the Crazies were known as the Mountain Crow.

There are tipi rings all over the Crazies—circles of stones used to anchor the tipi skins and keep them tight to the ground—marking the seasonal villages of the Apsáalooke. The Indian Rings subdivision in Big Timber was named for scores of tipi rings that lay undisturbed for centuries, until the tract homes started going up in the late 1970s. ("Easy access, one mile to town. Beautiful view of Beartooth & Crazy Mountains," read the ad in the Big Timber Pioneer.) But even where the stones have disappeared, the names the Apsáalooke knew these places by endure.

Timothy McCleary, a scholar of Crow tribal culture and language, has led an ongoing project called the Apsáalooke Place Names Database since 1996 at Little Big Horn College at Crow Agency, as the reservation near Hardin is known. (Many enrolled tribal members refer to themselves as both Apsáalooke and Crow.) Because the Crow named places for the events that took place there, the database provides a vivid history—a story map of the past.

An area near Hunter's Hot Springs, about ten miles south of Big Timber, identified only by a highway mile marker, is Xoóxaashe Alatshíihile Awooshissee—"Where the Corn Was Planted but Did Not Mature." It was here that the Crow tried without success to resume the agrarian way of life they had led with the Mandans. The culture shift to hunting is recorded in the names for bison kill sites, like Long Ridge Where the Buffalo Were Driven Over. Sheep Mountain, a jagged, flat-topped butte, was called Hide Scraper—Iáxuhpish—for its resemblance to the tools used to process bison hides.

The Yellowstone River and the rangelands where Rick Jarrett grazed his cows were the winter hunting grounds of the Mountain Crow. The cottonwoods, birch, and golden aspens along Duck Creek provided sturdy lodgepoles for tipis and sweet cottonwood bark for Crow horses to eat when grass was scarce. Even in the coldest months, there was abundant game. Vast elk herds congregated at Iichíilikaashaashe Koón Bahaatawée, the Hot Springs on the Elk River. War parties also gathered at the hot springs, to soak and steam hardwood branches until they became pliable enough to make into snowshoes, the better to sneak up on the enemy unaware.

Battles were fought on this landscape. A boarded-up waterslide park on I-90 east of Big Timber marks the place where the warrior chief Pretty Eagle returned from a war party. White people and their diseases left their scars. Where There Are Many Human Skulls, a site near Billings, is a mass grave for the victims of one of the smallpox epidemics that decimated the Apsáalooke tribe and many others, reducing their numbers to fewer than two thousand by 1870, by Medicine Crow's estimate. The place name is the only memorial that remains.

The spread of white diseases was compounded by the soul sickness of the reservation era. That left its mark, too. Fort Parker, the headquarters of Crow Agency, was located near the Yellowstone on Mission Creek. The Apsáalooke called the spot Where They Laid Down Yellow Blankets, for the cheap and often useless government-issued goods that were distributed there. "We are tired," Iron Bull told Brunot at the 1873 summit. "When you gave us flour did we ask for it? Did we ever ask for sugar or beef? What made you give it to us? We never asked you to give us pants or stockings." Iron Bull was tall, like many Crow men, with a Kirk Douglas dimple in his chin and an air of quiet command—the kind of man you did not say no to when he told you to get in your wagon and accompany him to a sun dance. Now he was suffering from erysipelas, a bacterial skin infection that had spread among the Apsáalooke, sickening many.

Though they'd never asked for it, the Apsáalooke had become dependent on the food rations distributed at Crow Agency. The bison were disappearing from Crow Country, along with the elk and antelope and deer. Government agents began giving away meat at a location west of Big Timber. The Apsáalooke called this place Where They First Ate Beef—the bitter taste of colonization encapsulated.

But the most fearsome place on the Apsáalooke story map would forever be Awaxaawippíia, the Ominous Mountains. The island mountain range is the spiritual locus of Crow Country, with Crazy Peak at its epicenter: a notched black pinnacle, piercing the sky. The Crazies were a place to experience life-changing visions, a literal dreamscape. If you were an ambitious young person, eager to prove yourself to the elders, you climbed high into the mountains, built a fasting bed from rocks, and lay there for days, praying to be visited by a presence from the spirit world. Dreams were power. Fasting in the Crazies as a teen in the early 1800s, Eelápuash—also called Sore Belly—saw a fearsome thunderbird who imparted the art of war to him while shooting out lightning bolts. That vision—paired with his prowess as a horse thief—propelled Sore Belly's rise to chiefdom.

The Crazies are still held sacred by Apsáalooke people. The mountains are a repository of stories. Some are rarely spoken of. The Apsáalooke Place Name Database contains a tantalizing fragment of information provided by Barney Old Coyote Jr., a revered elder. In the Second World War, Old Coyote was a gunner on B-17 Flying Fortresses and a windtalker—part of an elite group of Crow combatants who used Apsáalooke code words to relay crucial information about enemy positions during bombing sorties. He flew seventy-two combat missions, earning seventeen medals for his service—the most decorated Native American to serve in the Second World War. Old Coyote, who died in 2012, was posthumously awarded the Congressional Gold Medal in 2015.

Old Coyote spent some of the last days of his life driving around Montana with McCleary, pointing out places that were important to the Apsáalooke people and telling stories about the things that happened there. Old Coyote told McCleary that the Crazies were where the Outcasts went—people who had been scalped but survived. Scalping was the ultimate insult. If you had been dishonored in this way—whether in battle or in an enemy raid—you could no longer live among your own people. It was too embarrassing, Old Coyote explained, and offensive to others. "When a person is scalped the skin on their forehead droops over their face, so yeah, it's kind of gruesome," McCleary said.

The Outcasts occupied an existential gray zone. They became another kind of being: alive, yet not alive. Barney Old Coyote's daughter, Rachel Sue Old Coyote, told me a story about her nephew, who once hiked into the Crazies with some friends to a mountain hot spring they knew about. They sat in a hot pool, laughing and drinking. A rock hit her nephew from behind. He looked around, but didn't see anyone.

"And everybody else started saying, 'Hey, somebody just hit me with a rock.' And a couple of the guys, emboldened by alcohol, got out and were scouting around, and then a couple of larger rocks started landing in the pool," Old Coyote told me. The young people left in a hurry. They were not welcome there, she said. "I attribute it to the lack of respect that was being shown."

Rachel Sue Old Coyote described the Crazies as a massive battery, a storehouse of energy and collective memory. You could also say they are a magnet. The mountains have drawn human beings almost from the moment they emerged from the ice sheets that covered Montana in the Last Glacial Maximum. The Apsáalooke had always known this; the rest of the world would begin to discover it one spring day in 1968, when a construction worker named Ben Hargis tore into a sandstone cliff near the town of Wilsall with his front-end loader.

The cliff was on a piece of land directly west of the Crazies' Wilsall Peak, which was owned by Melvyn Anzick, a large-animal veterinarian. Mel and Helen Anzick brought their children there on weekends to picnic and fish on Flathead Creek, which wound around the cliff. Anzick had given Hargis permission to collect talus, or loose rock, for a construction project at the local high school.

Hargis had scooped about ninety yards of sandstone talus out of the side of the outcropping when a large, shiny rock slipped out from the front-end loader's claws. It was a fluted stone tool of some kind, with a fine, tapering point. Hargis collected a bucket of talus to dump in a pothole, and another shiny stone—a large biface of hard, fine-grained quartz, called chert—fell out. It was oblong and the size of a hubcap. Both stones were coated with powdery red stuff.

That evening, Hargis returned with his wife, Faye, and their friends Calvin and Mary Sarver. They went to the spot where the stone objects had tumbled out of the outcropping and started to dig. They soon found more artifacts—many more, about a hundred in all. Each time they pulled out a stone, another one clinked down on top of it. The tools were as neatly stacked as a row of candy bars in a vending machine. The treasure hunters dug and dug until they came upon something that stopped them short: the delicate skull of a child, covered in the same thick, red dust that coated the tools.

Hargis and his friends had unearthed the oldest grave in the Americas. The skeletal remains of the person who would become known as the Clovis, or Anzick, child have since been radiocarbon dated to between 12,707 and 12,556 years. The child, who was between the age of one and two, had been buried beneath an extraordinary trove of objects. There were large projectile points—some a half foot long, the tips and edges still sharp. There were blades and hand axes and large, irregular, flaked stones the size of potlids, and delicately cross-hatched, beveled rods of bone or antler. The stones were glossy, richly colored—moss agate, chalcedony, porcellanite. Some came from ancient quarry sites hundreds of miles from the burial grounds. All the artifacts were coated in red ocher—a ferrous iron-oxide mineral that Paleo-Indian people often carried with them on their travels.

The stone tools were the product of untold hours of work. They had been created by a complex process that involved slowly heating the stone to a high temperature, which made it easier to flake into sharp-edged instruments for hunting, butchering, and scraping hides. Heat produced chemical alterations in the stone, giving it luster and translucency. Different types of stone require different temperatures; the people who made the objects understood that. Each projectile point had a shallow groove so that it could be fitted to a spear—the product of a distinctive flaking technique called fluting that is the hallmark of the late-Pleistocene Clovis culture.

Although one of the bone rods had been deliberately—perhaps

ritualistically—broken, none of the stone tools showed any signs of wear. They had been created to be buried. The array included flaking tools and preforms—partially worked points that had yet to be knapped and turned into tools—and large stone pieces called cores, from which more tools could be made. The child had been buried with everything one would need in the afterlife. Because the lithic artifacts represented every phase of the toolmaking process, some scholars have compared the burial assemblage to a teaching kit—an instruction manual with an ancient culture's most vital information, written in stone.

Hargis and Calvin Sarver eventually revealed their discovery to Mel Anzick, who suggested that they divvy up the find. He numbered the stone and bone artifacts with a pencil and they drew lots: Anzick got half, Hargis and Sarver each got a quarter. He sent the skeletal remains, which Hargis had been carrying around in the glove compartment of his dump truck, to the University of Montana.

The Anzicks' daughter, Sarah, was about two years old at the time of the discovery—the same age as the buried child. As a little girl, she caught her first fish in Flathead Creek, just below the ancient child's resting place. For many years, the Anzicks kept their share of the stone and bone artifacts in their home, in glass-topped boxes lined with cotton. From time to time, Sarah would take out the stone tools from the box and run her fingers over the swirled patterns and the flaked edges. They were heavy, the colors ranging from bright yellow to purple, brown and blue. A few still had traces of red ocher on them. Holding one made her heart drop. It was an indescribable sensation, the pull of deep time. Part of a child's skeleton was found with the tools, she'd been told. She wondered where the rest of the child was.

Because the human remains and stone tools had been discovered on private property, they were not subject to the Native American Grave Protection and Repatriation Act, which applied only to artifacts recovered on federal or tribal land. The skeletal remains were kept at the University of Montana until 1999, when they were returned to the Anzick family in a bankers box.

By then, Sarah Anzick had become a molecular biologist with the National Institutes of Health, a member of the team working on the human genome project. In 2001, the project's international consortium published the first draft of the human genome sequence. Inspired, Sarah decided to try to crack the genetic code of the Clovis child—her spectral twin. Working on her own time, she tried to extract DNA from one of the child's rib bones, but was unsuccessful. In 2010, she contacted Eske Willerslev, an evolutionary geneticist at the University of Cophenhagen who was doing pioneering work with ancient DNA. Willerslev had sequenced the entire genome of a Paleo-Eskimo man from a four-thousand-year-old clump of human hair dug out from the Greenland permafrost. Willerslev asked how soon Anzick could get herself on a plane to Copenhagen with the bones.

Working with a tiny fragment of DNA retrieved from the dense bone of the child's inner ear, Willerslev and his team would spend the next four years identifying and organizing over three billion jigsaw pieces of ancient code. By the time they were finished, they had created a genetic snapshot of the oldest skeleton in the Americas, who they now knew had been a little boy.

The toddler's genome told an extraordinary story—an origin story. About one-third of his DNA linked him to a boy who lived twenty-four thousand years ago in Siberia, whose skeleton was unearthed near the village of Mal'ta. The other two-thirds of his genes flowed from ancient East Asia—specifically, from a forty-thousand-year-old man who left his bone fragments in the Tianyuan cave near Beijing.

When it came to pairing the child with people living today, the researchers found no relationship to modern Chinese or Siberians—or to any population west of the Bering Strait. But there was no question whom this child belonged to. The Clovis child—the most ancient American ever discovered—was related to 80 percent of all indigenous North and South American groups from whom DNA exists for comparison. He was a direct forebear of people in forty-four tribes in Central and South America, and a close relative of seven northern Native American tribal groups from Canada and the Arctic. He is very likely an ancestor of Native Americans in the United States as well, though limited genetic data exists to establish this. (After decades of ethical abuses by the American scientific and medical establishment, many tribes have rebuffed attempts at genetic research, and some have banned it altogether.)

Willerslev's theory goes like this: two groups of Upper Paleolithic people—ancient Siberians and ancient East Asians—encountered one another in Beringia, a vast region that once extended from Siberia's Kamchatka Peninsula to the Yukon, joined by a land bridge across the Bering Sea. They banded together to form a new nomadic tribe. Willerslev believes it was a small group—perhaps as few as a hundred people. These people were among the first human beings to reach Montana as it emerged from the ice sheets some thirteen to fourteen thousand years ago. Their descendants peopled the Americas. The proof was right there, in the child's genome.

The discovery drove a Clovis spear point through the Solutrean hypothesis, which held that the first Americans were actually European seafarers who crossed the Atlantic Ocean—a hypothesis popular with white nationalists that still held currency in some circles. The Clovis child affirmed what Native Americans said all along: *We've always been here.*

Willerslev describes the boy as the Adam of the Americas. "If you should ever use a word like 'Adam' in a scientific context, then it is the Anzick child," he said. "I mean, this child, and the group he belonged to, have delivered a legacy across all the Americas. It's an evolutionary success story."

Nothing is known about the boy, how he lived or how he died. The only thing that can be said with any certainty is that out of all the places the child's people could have chosen for his final resting place, they chose this one.

The ancient ones knew it well. The sandstone cliff was a landmark visible for miles, the nexus of several trail systems. It occupied the highest spot in a fertile river basin sheltered by mountains on all sides. It rose up from the valley floor like the prow of a ship, sailing toward the Crazies. The boy's people dug out a small chamber in the side of the cliff and placed him there with all the tools he would ever need—the finest tools in creation. His resting place faced directly east. It would be lit by the first rays of the sun as it climbed above the Crazies every day, for all days. The views, needless to say, were spectacular. It was a very good place—the best place in the world.

If the child was America's Adam, then this was Eden.

5

COYOTE WIND

February 20, 2019
Park County Courthouse
Livingston, Montana

RICHARD JARRETT, *Direct examination*:

Q: Can you tell the Court how you went about trying to find a wind
project?

MR. JARRETT: Well, I called a few people that had worked with
wind a little bit that I knew in the Livingston area . . . I contacted
them, and they put me in touch with a Mr. Marty Wilde.

Q: Okay. And then how did you get to the point where you were
negotiating a lease agreement?

MR. JARRETT: He drove out one day and we took a grand tour . . .
We took a grand tour, and he says, I think we can make something
happen here.

It was the first day of summer vacation, June 2004. Jaffe Wilde, high school
sophomore, stared out the passenger window of his father's truck as it
bumped over a gravel road west of Big Timber. A flatbed trailer hitched
to the back of the truck rattled behind them. The trailer was loaded with
sixteen-foot-long sections of steel tubing and cables, the disassembled
pieces of a two-hundred-foot-tall meteorological tower that Jaffe's father,
Marty, would put up on a cattle ranch that day. Marty drove with one
hand on the wheel, windows down, shaggy hair blown back by the wind.
No seat belt; a metal clip was jammed into his seat belt buckle so the alarm
wouldn't ding. Marty Wilde didn't let his truck tell him what to do.

Jaffe spent a lot of his free time driving around Montana with Marty,
helping him set up met towers at windy places all over the state. It was
part of the indentured servitude he had entered into when he was twelve

and decided to live with his dad in the old schoolhouse on the Blackfeet Reservation. Growing up, it was never "Hey, you're a little kid, let's go throw a football around in the yard." That dude Marty Wilde, he was hard-core. They'd been on the road nearly six hours that day.

Marty turned off the county road at a signpost marked "Crazy Mountain Cattle Company," the letters peaked like mountaintops. The truck, the trailer, and its load of cargo rattled over a metal cattle guard onto a dirt road. Black Angus cows lifted their heads to watch them pass, jaws working sideways. The road traced the path of Duck Creek, winding past an old wooden grain silo, sagging cow sheds, and a machine shop. Marty steered off the dirt road and drove over the sagebrush toward a high bluff jutting up from the rolling hills like an anvil. Marty had picked it as an ideal site for the met tower. Following a crude cow path, he floored the accelerator and drove the pickup truck up the side of that steep-ass hill, rocks spraying and three thousand pounds of steel jangling on the trailer behind them.

Marty Wilde was a wind prospector. He didn't pan for gold in a stream; he sought it in the air. The meteorological tower, banded with sensors, wind vanes, and anemometers, was his dish. Montana had some of the best wind in the Lower 48. No one knew that better than Marty Wilde. He worked alone, a wildcatter with a gift for persuading ranchers to let him put up his jury-rigged met towers and secondhand anemometers on land where the good wind flowed.

Marty was as cagey and territorial about his wind as any old-time gold digger guarding his patch of pay dirt. He'd had one of his sites stolen right out from under him by a rival developer and might have stolen one or two spots himself. Wind was becoming a big business. Investors in renewable-energy projects could write off millions of dollars in taxes in direct proportion to the number of megawatt-hours of carbon-free energy those projects generated. Large multinational companies were trickling into Montana, eager to get in on the action. Marty was an outlier in that world, doing business out of the back of his truck, not some glass tower with a leaf logo over the reception desk. The met tower he was putting up that day on the Crazy Mountain Cattle Company was one of a dozen or so that he had set up at sites across Montana, each one a wet index finger held up to the breeze.

There were no overnight fortunes in wind; it had to be tracked and studied for years before you knew it was worth anything. Once the met tower was up, Marty would spend the next year or two analyzing the data from its various instruments. Then he would create a three-dimensional wind map that charted its flow in minute detail—over the course of a day, through different seasons—capturing its fluctuations in speed, direction, intensity. He calculated for wind shear—variations in wind speed over different distances from the ground—to determine the ideal height for a turbine on the site.

If the data checked out, he'd move on to the next stage, which involved getting site permits, doing environmental assessments, hashing out interconnection agreements with utility companies. He'd have to figure out a way of transmitting the power the wind turbines would generate; you couldn't sell the electricity if you didn't have a way to feed it back into the main grid. But nail down all those elements, and a prospector like Marty would have a multimillion-dollar business proposition, a project that he could flip and sell to a big player in corporate wind. If he didn't go broke first.

The wind in the Crazies was famous; everyone in the business knew about it. ASOS—the Automated Surface Observing System—a joint program run by the National Weather Service, the Federal Aviation Administration, and the Department of Defense, has more than nine hundred weather stations across the country that provide a nonstop flow of information, every minute of every hour of every day, on a full spectrum of weather conditions, including wind speed and direction. There was an ASOS station twenty miles west of Rick's ranch that had collected data for decades, and that data showed that the wind off the Crazy Mountains was wind you could take to the bank.

Marty had been nosing around the Crazies for years, sniffing out opportunities to capitalize on that million-dollar wind. Back in 1999, he drove high up Duck Creek Road into the mountains until he ran out of road and it was all sagebrush. Wild Eagle Mountain Ranch, the place was called. Marty didn't get any interest whatsoever from those folks. The owners didn't welcome visitors—the ranch was private and they wanted to keep it that way. Marty learned that there were quite a few wealthy landowners around the Crazies like that. The folks at Wild

Eagle had a different opinion about wind development than, say, a guy who was trying to scratch out a living on two thousand acres. Rick Jarrett, a hardscrabble Montanan looking for a way to make his land work for him, was Marty's kind of rancher.

The other thing that Marty liked about Rick was that his ranch had its own power substation. Technically speaking, the substation belonged to the Park Electric Cooperative, the local utility. Rick had sold Park Electric a patch of land on lower Duck Creek in 1999 to build the substation when the co-op was looking for a way to transmit power to the Sibanye-Stillwater mine. The mine, Sweet Grass County's biggest taxpayer, extracted palladium and platinum from the bowels of the earth below Big Timber and sold it to the auto industry, which used the rare-earth metals to build catalytic converters. But with some technical upgrades, the substation could deliver the power generated by Rick's wind to the main grid.

The Crazy Mountain Cattle Company ticked off three essential boxes for Marty: a willing landowner, a means of energy transmission, and a brilliant wind resource.

Marty drove around the top of the bluff while Jaffe, who had climbed onto the flatbed, dropped the tower pipe sections over the side in the approximate order that they would be assembled. Another truck pulled up: Marty's friend and sometime business partner Dave Healow had come to help raise the met tower.

Dave, a fifty-four-year-old wind hippie in wire-rimmed glasses, was an anesthesiologist who had put up some of the first turbines in Montana, near Livingston. Wind was his passion. When Marty was struggling for cash, Dave provided the financing to keep his projects afloat. Their bro code for these projects was "Save the Planet I" and "Save the Planet II." Dave was a true believer, but for Marty, it was tongue-in-cheek. Wind development for Marty Wilde was all about making money.

Dave helped Marty and Jaffe lay out the tower pipe sections and unspool the cables. They threaded lightning wire through the outer tubes. Lightning struck met towers all the time; the wire would keep it from shorting out Marty's sensor equipment or sending the tower up in flames. Then they began coupling the sections, bolting them together like Lego pieces. Booms outfitted with anemometers and wind vanes would be attached to the tower at twenty-meter intervals to measure wind speed and direction; sensors at the top and bottom would capture air pressure and temperature. Information from those instruments would be recorded by a data logger mounted at the base of the tower, once it was raised atop the bluff like the mainmast of a ship.

Putting things together, taking things apart, that was what Marty did. He loved machines—fast cars, old trucks, vintage motorcycles. Marty did his own engine-mount repairs, replaced radiators. Sometimes he'd let Jaffe hand him a tool. Maybe he'd say, "This is a carburetor—the float goes up and down as fuel comes in." But it wasn't really a father-son thing. Marty didn't have the patience to teach him. Or maybe it was that Jaffe didn't have the patience to learn, being more interested in skiing, playing video games, and smoking weed with his friends, so, like, whatever, Dad. They both loved music; they had that in common. Marty was an expert pianist, a quality player. He could play anything by ear on his Korg keyboard—Tom Waits, the Eagles. Always some throwback to when he was a teenager and Elton John was the biggest fucking thing in the world. Marty had his own original material and he played that, too: songs about one-eyed men and midnight rodeos and last-chance hotels.

Marty was in recovery from his first career, as a child prodigy of substance abuse. He got his start smoking weed in the back of the school bus, became a drunken bastard while enrolled in the University of Pittsburgh's engineering program, then developed a taste for cocaine after he dropped out and went to work in an auto body shop. That dude Marty Wilde, he did it all. His life thoroughly derailed by drugs and alcohol by the age of twenty-seven, he lay down on the grass by a highway overpass one day and thought about jumping. A prayer came to him: *Hey motherfucker, if you're there, I'll do this AA thing.* That was the day he got sober. The Prayer of St. Marty, one of his girlfriends called it.

Admitting his own powerlessness and acknowledging a power greater than himself was transformative. Marty rolled hard on the spiritual aspect of his sobriety, really wore it on his sleeve. He met Jaffe's mom at an Alcoholics Anonymous meeting in Columbus after he resumed his studies at Ohio State, where he'd go on to earn a master's degree in engineering. They dated for a while, broke up. Then she found out she was pregnant with Jaffe's big sister, Chloe, and they decided to get married instead.

Jaffe was born seventeen months after Chloe, in 1988. Marty named his son for Japhy Ryder, the hitchhiking, mountain-climbing Zen Buddhist hero of Jack Kerouac's *The Dharma Bums*. He was still a baby when his parents split for good. Marty would show up on Wednesdays and Saturdays—his visitation days, per the custody agreement—and take the kids for a drive. Some of Jaffe's earliest memories of his dad were of riding around in his truck, listening to Tom Waits howl about a murder in the red barn and dirt in the ground and going out west where the wind blows tall.

Then, one day in 1992, Marty got in his Toyota Tundra and headed west, just like that song. He pulled onto Highway 70 and started driving. No real plan. He drove and kept on driving. He drove for the sensation of driving, drove as though a dream was pulling him toward the Rockies. He didn't stop until he reached the Blackfeet Indian Reservation in northwestern Montana, on the Canadian border.

Marty had once visited the reservation on a horse-packing trip and was awestruck by the raw beauty of the land, a million-and-a-half-acre expanse east of Glacier National Park. He befriended his guide on that trip, a Blackfeet man named Nelse St. Goddard. St. Goddard told Marty he could stay in an old schoolhouse on his ranch, on Little Badger Creek. The building was abandoned, full of old bottles and trash. People went there to party. Marty roughed it for a while, then bought a camper to live in while he renovated the schoolhouse, replacing the plumbing and the electrical wiring and the broken windows.

Marty got a job teaching math at Blackfeet Community College in Browning. He bought a horse and a couple of cows, let his hair grow down to his shoulders, and lost a lot of weight, turning gaunt and angular like some wild white man of the plains. Leo Sure Chief, a Blackfeet elder with cataracts in his smoky eyes, brought Marty into the sweat lodge one day and gave him an Indian name, singing as he dipped a sweetgrass whip in a bucket of water and splashed it on the glowing red rocks. Leo Sure Chief flicked water from the sweetgrass whip on Marty and named him Siyeh—an auspicious name, the name of a nineteenth-century Blackfeet chief who climbed mountains. In English, it's Mad Wolf.

The wind blew tall on the Blackfeet Reservation. Marty had an Indian name, but like a tourist, he never remembered to hold on to his car door when he opened it. The second or third time a gust of wind almost tore the door off, it got Marty's attention. He started looking at ways to harness its force.

The Energy Policy Act of 1992 provided funding for tribal nations to pursue energy self-sufficiency, including grants to "private sector persons"—white outsiders like Marty. Although most of the tribal governments that applied for these grants used them for feasibility studies, Marty resolved to erect the first wind turbine on Native land.

He won a Department of Energy grant to raise a ninety-foot meteorological tower on a hill at Blackfeet Community College. Then he persuaded a California wind energy company to donate a one-hundred-kilowatt Vestas wind turbine. Tribal members were hired to do construction, and students at the community college got part-time jobs as environmental observers. (Over the course of a year, they found one dead bat.) Glacier Electric Cooperative, the local utility, agreed to buy the power the turbine produced, offsetting it against the college's electricity use. In the first year, the power generated by the turbine paid most of Blackfeet Community College's electricity bill.

The turbine occupied a prominent spot in Browning on one of the main routes into Glacier National Park. Tourists got a good look at it as they passed through Blackfeet land, which was the point. Marty wanted the Blackfeet wind turbine—the first ever erected on tribal land, he boasted—to serve as a vivid demonstration of how tribes could take the initiative with renewable-energy projects. Wind offered a way that Indigenous people could claim power for themselves in the most literal sense of the word. "Historically hustlers have promised the world to these tribes, only to let them down time and time again," Marty told *Windpower Monthly* in 1996. Wind would give the Blackfeet the power to determine their own destiny.

Jaffe and Chloe spent summers on the Blackfeet Reservation with Marty. Wild horses ranged over miles of open land, and Little Badger Creek tumbled just past the schoolhouse door. Jaffe chased the wild horses and tried to ride them, and roamed the creek with a fishing pole and Marty's dog, Dr. Wu, for company. Just before the start of sixth

grade, he told his dad he wanted to stay with him and go to school on
the reservation. Marty said no, then changed his mind when Jaffe didn't
act like a momma's boy and whine about it. A little kid needs to be with
his dad.

Marty built another wind project, securing Energy Department
funding to install four small turbines to power Browning's wastewater
treatment plant. It was a good project, but modest. Marty pushed for
the creation of a tribal corporation, 100 percent owned by the Blackfeet Nation, that would spearhead renewable-energy projects and other
business ventures on their land. It was called Siyeh. Marty got a seat on
Siyeh's board of directors and took the lead on developing the Blackfeet
Wind Park, a thirty-five-megawatt commercial wind farm.

It never got off the ground.

"We spent thousands of hours and over two years to learn that to build
a 35-megawatt wind farm would cost $65 million and that the Blackfeet
Tribe did not have 65 cents to invest in this business venture. The wind
farm would have been owned by some big money person or business,
and the Blackfeet Tribe would have owned a minuscule portion of the
business venture," Virgil "Puggy" Edwards, Siyeh's chairman, wrote in
2009 in the *Glacier Reporter*, Browning's local newspaper.

Marty's relationship with Siyeh's board and the Blackfeet tribal council soured. In 2000, Marty quit as project manager of the wind project at
the Browning wastewater treatment plant, packed up his belongings in
a borrowed horse trailer, and left the life he had built on the reservation.
In his absence, the wind turbines shut down for good. Ten years later,
Marty was still hounding Browning officials for payment for his services. Lockley Bremner, who was Browning's mayor in 2010, recalled,
"He was bill-collecting me, that was pretty much our interaction: getting
his check." He added, "Marty was always fun to visit with, always."

Hard luck and hard feelings would be a recurring theme in Marty's
business dealings over the years. There were unpaid bills on used equipment he bought, unpaid legal fees. When you shake hands with Marty
Wilde, count your fingers, a wind industry veteran said.

After leaving the reservation, Marty supported himself by putting up
wind turbines for other developers and doing consulting work for utility companies and state and federal agencies. He bought a house in the

Flathead Valley so that the kids could go to a good high school, in Columbia Falls. Chloe had joined the household by then. Marty laid down some rules. "Here's how it's going to be," he said. "We're going to do this commando-style." That meant the kids had to pull their weight around the house and stay out of his way when he was working. If Marty could hear Jaffe and Chloe watching *Friends* or giggling when he needed to concentrate, he'd become enraged. He'd kick them out, lock the door, and tell them to go play in the woods.

That door stayed locked for eight hours at a time. Chloe and Jaffe invented a game. They pretended they were abandoned children who had to find ways to survive in the wild. It didn't bother Jaffe so much—he always was an outside dog—but one time, Chloe did something that made Marty mad and he pushed her outside without her shoes on, then turned off the lights in the house. It was winter. Chloe stood out there, barefoot in the snow, banging on windows until Marty's girlfriend let her in.

Marty seemed disappointed by the childishness of his children—how short their attention spans were, how selfish they could be. Chores were assigned, and his standards were exacting. If Marty wasn't pleased with the job Jaffe did sweeping the floor, he'd take Chloe night skiing and leave Jaffe at home. Looking back on it as an adult, Jaffe thought you just had to respect the principles of a guy like that. Marty wasn't trying to make his son feel good about himself; he was trying to teach him how to sweep the floor properly. A real tough-love dude.

The principles behind other aspects of Marty's parenting were harder to decipher. Jaffe and Chloe both got an allowance of ten dollars a week. Marty made them play Texas Hold'em for it. Every Sunday, he'd hand out the bills, shuffle the cards, and say, "Here's your allowance, let's gamble." Sometimes, he'd let the kids win a few hands. Then he'd just shark them, cleaning them out and pocketing the allowance money he had handed out not an hour before. It was hard finding steady work in wind. Marty, a single parent with a mortgage, was deep in credit card debt by then.

Y

On the bluff at the Crazy Mountain Cattle ranch, the wind had started to pick up. A golden eagle soared high on a thermal current, dipped its wings, and dove. The tower's base plate was bolted, its fifteen anchors sunk deep in the earth, the cables secured. Using a hydraulic winch and a pulley attached to a gin pole, Marty started to raise the tower, then stopped. The tower was listing to one side, the guy wires uneven. The wind was blowing harder now.

Marty and Dave began arguing over what to do next. Dave was a gearhead whose nickname was "Dr. Science." Where Marty was stolid, gravel-voiced, Dave was effusive and shiny-faced, like some kid genius inside an adult male body, doing complicated math in his head. The men had met in AA: two big heads with egos to match. Now they were yelling at each other. Jaffe didn't understand the technical details of their disagreement, but it looked like his dad and Dr. Science were about get into a fistfight. It was always a rodeo, raising a met tower.

Another pickup truck was powering its way up the hillside, a couple of border collies panting in the passenger seat. The rancher, an irascible cowpoke with a bristly mustache, got out to see what was going on, observing that whatever it was, it looked like they were having a hell of a time getting it done. Marty explained the trouble in his usual no-bullshit manner. He knew how to get with these old-time Montana dudes. He won their confidence by being real with them. Spend five minutes with Marty Wilde and you'd know who he was, the good and the bad.

Rick grinned, showing the gap between his teeth. He knew enough about Marty to know he was running this business on a dream and a shoestring, but that was all right. Marty could be a hard-to-like guy, a little arrogant and stuff. He had his way. But Marty did speak Rick's language, and Rick liked him. Birds of a feather. Somebody who was not a big curser himself might feel different.

It was a busy week on the ranch. *Sunset* magazine was doing a feature on working-ranch vacations at the Crazy Mountain Cattle Company, and the writer was due the next day. Rick would take him on the Tour, put him on a horse, lend him a pair of hip-high waders, and take him irrigating. There'd be breakfasts of elk sausage and apple strudel French toast, and a rattlesnake rearing up from a clump of sagebrush, which Rick would stone to death as his stunned guest looked on. After the photographer left, a Taiwanese TV crew was coming for a week of riding and cattle roundups, which they'd film for an episode of a show called *King of Adventure*.

Collecting royalties from a wind farm on his land would be a much easier way to make ends meet, Rick reflected. But first they had to get the son-of-a-bitch tower up. Healow, who'd had enough, got in his truck and ripped out of there. Rick set his squashed short-brim Stetson more firmly on his head and went to work alongside Marty and Jaffe. By the end of the day, the met tower stood tall, cables taut, wind vanes and anemometers set to capture prevailing winds. Coyote Wind, LLC, was launched.

Across the barbed-wire fence on the eastern boundary of Rick Jarrett's ranch, an old windmill of weather-scoured steel sat on a hill, its wind vane sticking out like a fishtail. The ranch belonged to his new neighbors, Jan and Karen Engwis. Rick Jarrett's windmills wouldn't be the first in the Crazies.

The basic mechanics of a windmill are simple: The wind blows on a set of blades, or sails, connected to a hub—the rotor—which is attached to a drive shaft. As the blades turn, the drive shaft spins, transmitting the energy to a geared mechanism that goes up and down, like a water pump, or revolves, like a millstone. The kinetic energy of the wind is transformed into mechanical energy.

Ancient Persians invented the *asbad*, a vertical-axis windmill that looks like a revolving door made of panels of wood and straw, to grind grain. (In the blustery Iranian village of Nashtifan—"Storm's Sting"— asbads have been in continuous use for a thousand years.) Upright post and tower windmills began appearing in the eighth and ninth centuries across the Middle East and Asia, then throughout Europe. By the fifteenth century, windmills with scoop wheels were being used to drain wetlands for farming in the Netherlands.

But in America, windmills were heroic. Windmills were how the West was won.

The nation's first great wind power moment kicked off during the nineteenth-century push for westward expansion. Access to water was the difference between proving up a homestead claim and starving out on it. Windmill-powered well pumps enabled homesteaders to collect and store water. The rotating blades powered a geared mechanism that drove a pump rod up and down inside a pipe fed down a well. The upstroke of the pump rod sucked the water up from the well and spat it into a water tank, where it could be used for drinking and bathing, watering livestock, and irrigating crops.

By the 1880s, wind pumps were being produced by the thousands in factories across the Midwest as they struggled to keep pace with the waves of migrants trundling across the Great Plains. The windmills were made of wood first, then steel and iron. These were self-regulating windmills with tail vanes that turned to capture the wind as it shifted, a major technological advance on the old-country ones, which had sails that had to be adjusted by hand whenever the wind changed direction.

Innovation succeeded innovation. Windmills were built with centrifugal governors that regulated speed by changing the angle of the blades—preventing them from self-destructing when the wind blew too hard. Back-geared windmills got more revolutions out of every stroke, with curved metal blades to scoop up more wind. Each new windmill promised smoother pumping action, greater power.

The Great Display of Windmills caused a sensation at the 1893 World's Fair. Scores of windmills of all types and sizes were arrayed by a lake near the fair's Agriculture Building, "blazing in all colors and whirling away together" like so many giant pinwheels, according to George R. Davis's *Picturesque World's Fair: An Elaborate Collection of Colored Views*.

The spectacle drew "an army of admirers," Davis wrote, adding, "It is safe to say that, because of this remarkable display noted by so many hundreds of thousands, and because of the practical utility of the machines so thoroughly demonstrated, windmills will become more and more a feature of the American landscape." Sounding a note of caution, the *Chicago Times* warned that the sight of so many spinning wheels could cause dizziness, particularly to the inebriated.

Advertisements for the Eclipse windmill, the Woodmanse, the Aermotor, the Climax—made of malleable iron with "the strongest and lightest wheel in the trade"—filled the pages of newspapers across Montana. Salesmen packed sample models on locomotives and headed west to demonstrate the wonders of the wind pump to farmers and ranch-ers. Tall windmills lined the railroad tracks—one every twenty miles—pumping water into fifty-thousand-gallon tanks to keep the steam engines from running dry.

Innovation in windmill design meant that farmers in arid or semi-arid territories could irrigate a tract of land and harvest crops from it. The *Big Timber Pioneer* tracked the wind-engine trend in its Irrigation Matter column. There were reports of windmill pumps that could raise a hundred barrels of water per hour, or four hundred, or even thirty-seven thousand gallons—in a single hour.

Those stories would have been of tremendous interest to a home-steader like Spencer Jarrett, Rick's great-great-grandfather, who made final proof of his desert land claim in July 1892 before a Livingston judge. Witnesses from Big Timber and Springdale attested to Jarrett's complete reclamation of the land through irrigation. He planted and harvested an acre-sized patch of yellow dent corn that summer, pro-ducing fifty bushels—an accomplishment of sufficient magnitude to be reported in the newspaper. "This indicates that Montana soil and cli-mate will produce anything that can be grown in the western states," the *Livingston Enterprise* declared of Jarrett's bumper crop.

Windmills sprouted across Montana to irrigate vegetable patches, water livestock, saw wood. A lumberyard owner rigged a windmill to an elevated water tank with a hose, to keep it full and ready in case of fire. John Quinn put a windmill atop his livery in Big Timber to water his horses; a windmill went up at the new high school to pump water for the students. "There is no cheaper power than the windmill, and in the wind there is no monopoly, it blowing alike on the rich and poor," a *Pioneer* correspondent wrote in July 1895— though he looked forward to the day "when electricity is more fully developed."

The Big Timber Electric and Power Company set up shop in a con-crete building near the fairgrounds the following year. The town's first electricity was produced by steam turbine—a system that involved a three-hundred-foot flume, a waterwheel, a coal-fired boiler, and a sec-ondhand dynamo acquired from a mining company that went bust in the silver crash of 1893. "The deeds of darkness committed in the past (under cover of Æolus) will no longer prevail," the *Pioneer* exulted as the power plant neared completion in May 1896. Big Timber was plunged back into darkness in January, when the newly constructed flume was demolished by a gale, then again the following November, when the ditch that was dug to replace it froze over. In the summer of 1902, a prolonged power outage was caused by a visiting circus elephant that wandered off from the fairgrounds for a cooling wallow in the Big Timber Electric Light Ditch.

And so began the slow finale of America's great windmill era. For decades, electricity was a privilege reserved for townsfolk. In 1899, electrical wires were strung across McLeod Street and hung with dangling bulbs; Big Timber's streetlights lit up that September and were declared first-class. But ranchers a few miles outside town were using kerosene to light their homes well into the next century. The Jarretts didn't get electricity until 1947; Rick's parents relied on thirty-two-volt generators—housed in the engine room—to power the ranch.

Nonprofit electrical cooperatives were created under the Rural Electrification Act. Power poles went up along dirt roads and across alfalfa fields and were strung with electrical wire from giant spools off the backs of pickup trucks. It took a while, but once a ranch was wired up to that energized line, the windmill became a relic. Ranchers could now use electrically powered pumps to get their water.

It wasn't until the energy crises of the 1970s that people started to think about wind power again. War and revolution in the Middle East disrupted oil exports throughout the decade, resulting in skyrocketing fuel prices and gas rationing. Aermotor—one of the last three windmill manufacturers still in business—was suddenly inundated with orders. President Richard Nixon put NASA to work developing experimental prototypes for utility-scale wind turbines.

In 1978, Congress enacted the Public Utility Regulatory Policies Act—PURPA for short—to expand and diversify America's energy industry, in large part through the development of renewable resources like hydropower, wind, and solar. Until then, big power companies had pretty much had the electricity market all to themselves. PURPA required those big utilities to buy electricity from independent wind, solar, and hydro companies. The law created a new class of generating facilities: qualifying facilities, or QFs for short. QFs were small power production plants gen-

erating a maximum of eighty megawatts. Under the new law, a certified
QF had the right to sell its electricity to utilities for a fair market price,
which PURPA described somewhat opaquely as "avoided cost"—the
price the utilities would have paid to generate that power themselves.

The federal government wanted to foster QFs. An Energy Tax Act
passed the same year that PURPA went into effect rewarded alternative
energy investors and developers of wind projects with tax credits, grants,
and loans. California, which offered an additional 25 percent state tax
credit for investment in renewable-energy projects, became home to
some of the world's first large-scale wind farms.

Unlike old-fashioned windmills, which turned wind into mechanical
energy to pump water or grind grain, wind turbines use that aerodynamic
force to create electrical energy. Picture a pinwheel of fiberglass and steel.
A rotor with propeller-like blades sits atop a tower. The rotor—the wheel
of the pinwheel—is connected to an oblong nacelle, which houses a gearbox and a generator. A yaw system keeps the nacelle upwind; a pitch system adjusts the blades, angling them in and out of the wind to control the
rotor speed. A software-powered controller in the nacelle coordinates and
oversees all these moving parts while monitoring atmospheric conditions,
shutting down the rotor when wind speeds are too high.

When the wind blows, spinning the pinwheel, a main shaft from
the rotor spins, too, activating the drivetrain in the nacelle. The gearbox
transmits the rotational torque from the main shaft to a second, high-
speed shaft, which spins the generator at ninety times the revolutions
per minute of the revolving blades. That spinning generator produces
electricity, which flows through underground collection cables to the
substation, then travels over transmission lines—with some adjustments
along the way to the current and voltage, to make it compatible with the
main grid.

Turbines have a lot of bells and whistles: ultrasonic wind sensors with
built-in heaters, aerodynamic brakes, lightning detectors. But the most
technologically advanced wind turbine isn't all that different from an
Aermotor: the wind blows, the blades turn, and kinetic energy is transformed into power. A NASA report on windmill technology concluded
that a medieval gristmiller would feel right at home on a California
wind farm.

Now Rick was going to get a windmill of his own—a slew of them. The wind would blow and the blades would turn, performing a magical alchemy that would erase his debts and narrow the gap that separated him from his neighbors. The wind that blew alike on the rich and the poor had the power to make Rick Jarrett a wealthy man.

In June 2008, the summer after his freshman year in college, Jaffe returned to the Crazy Mountain Wind Company as a paid employee of Coyote Energy, LLC. Jaffe's college career hadn't gotten off to a brilliant start. He smoked a lot of weed, failed three classes, and had to drop out for a year because Marty refused to cosign any more student loans. Instead, he offered Jaffe a job on his install team. Marty gave him a Saab turbo convertible to drive, so that was chill. Then he sent him to Rick Jarrett's ranch with a trailer of more met tower equipment. It was nearly four years to the day that Jaffe helped his dad and that irascible cowpoke raise the met tower. These were exciting times at the Crazy Mountain Cattle Company. A big renewable-energy company wanted to build Coyote Wind.

After the met tower went up in 2004, Marty came by Rick's ranch every month or so to check the average wind speeds recorded on its data card and make sure none of the sensors had frozen over. Month after month, the data confirmed his hunch: Rick's wind was top-tier. It flowed over his ranch at an average speed of eighteen miles an hour—the Goldilocks zone for power generation. If the winds are too high—anything much over fifty miles per hour—the turbines shut down. If they dip much below eight or nine miles per hour, the rotors stall.

What's more, Rick's wind blew without fail all winter long. That was critical, because the electricity generated by wind turbines couldn't be banked and stored—that technology didn't exist yet. Year after year, the data showed that Rick's wind was at its peak when Montanans needed it most, to heat their homes through the bitter winter months.

In 2005, Marty offered Rick a one-year wind lease agreement for $1,000. Rick's payment would go up by an additional $1,000 each year the lease was extended. It wasn't a lot, but the lease fee was just a placeholder. The real money would come when Marty flipped the project to

Big Wind and it got built. Once those turbines went up on his ranch and started spinning, Rick would earn annual royalties on the electricity they generated. Most lease agreements in his part of the country promised landowners approximately 3 percent of the annual gross revenues, or a minimum annual payment based on the number of turbines and their nameplate capacity—how many megawatts they could produce. A standard clause awarded them whichever was greater—the 3 percent or the guaranteed minimum.

Say Rick locked down an annual rate of $2,000 per megawatt from the turbines installed on his land. If he got one Vestas wind turbine with a nameplate capacity of 1.8 megawatts, he'd earn at least $3,600 a year. If twenty such Vestas wind turbines went up on his ranch, he'd earn at least $72,000—on top of one-time installation fees, annual land rental payments, and other incidentals. The pay rate per turbine would scale up over the life of the project, based on the consumer price index or an agreed-upon factor for inflation. And the payments would go on for decades. That was the best part. Utilities and ratepayers like stability when it comes to electricity supply and utility bills, which translates into long-term power purchase agreements with electricity providers—contracts of twenty or twenty-five years. Over the life of this theoretical project, Rick could collect over $1.8 million.

More turbines meant a bigger profit margin. Marty was determined to develop Coyote Wind as an eighty-megawatt QF—the maximum size of a wind farm entitled to preferential treatment under PURPA. A project that size would generate enough to power for twenty-six thousand Montana homes. But to put up all the turbines he'd need for eighty megawatts, Marty would have to expand Coyote Wind's footprint beyond Rick Jarrett's property line. He got in Rick's truck, and the two paid a visit on Jarrett's neighbor to the south, an old Norwegian named Alfred Anderson. Marty asked the man if he'd like to have a couple of income-generating wind turbines on his land. Anderson laughed and shook his head. He didn't seem all that interested.

There was another option: a section of state trust land adjacent to the Crazy Mountain Cattle Company that Rick had leased for years: Section 36. Rick grazed his cows on it. Marty wanted it for Coyote Wind.

Every township in Montana has sections of trust land—640-acre parcels set aside by the state constitution for the benefit of Montana's schools. Any revenue generated by the lease or sale of trust land is funneled into the state's public education system. Rick Jarrett paid a grazing fee for his section; other school sections, as they are called, were leased for oil and mineral rights or coalbed methane. There had been wildcat oil wells dug on school sections of land not far from Jarrett's ranch.

Wind development in Montana had lagged behind states like California, which offered generous tax incentives to developers. California liked wind. Montana, which has thousands of oil and gas wells and the largest recoverable coal reserves of any state in the nation, preferred fossil fuels.

But there had been a change in the state's weather. Governor Brian Schweitzer—a farmer in a bolo tie who'd never held office before his election in 2004—was a centrist Democrat with strong views on renewable energy and energy independence. He believed Montana could lead the way in developing biofuels from soybeans and synthetic diesel fuel from gasified coal—and by harnessing the power of its extraordinary wind. Soon after taking office, Schweitzer signed a law requiring the state's utilities to buy at least 10 percent of their electricity from wind farms by 2010. "Let those sheiks and dictators and rats and crooks from all over the world boil in their own oil," he declared.

Officials in the state's Department of Natural Resources and Conservation (DNRC), which oversees its trust lands, were already onboard. Wind development dovetailed with traditional agricultural uses on state land: you could even lease the same trust section twice, and let cows graze under the turbines. Montana's first large commercial wind farm, the Judith Gap Wind Energy Project, in Wheatland County, was built on a mix of private and state land. Fifteen of its ninety turbines were sited on trust land, generating $50,000 a year for Montana's schools—on top of millions of dollars in tax revenue for the county.

In 2004, the same year that Marty, Rick, and Jaffe raised the met tower on Rick Jarrett's ranch, DNRC officials hired an independent consultant to identify trust sections with the best potential for wind energy development. Their consultant flagged Section 36 in Sweet Grass County—the very section that Rick had leased for years to graze his cattle—as the second-best trust land for wind development in the state, right after Judith Gap.

The DNRC's paid consultant was one Martin Wilde, the same Martin Wilde who had applied to put up a met tower on Section 36. By the time the DNRC study on potential wind development came out—a study that drew on his findings as a consultant—Marty had already planted his flag on Section 36 as a private developer.

Internal emails by DNRC staffers, released during the discovery process in the first of several lawsuits filed by Rick Jarrett's neighbors, reveal that Marty was a pain in the ass—cagey, distracted, an epic procrastinator. Impatient to lock down the wind lease to Section 36 before any of his rivals could get their hands on it, Marty sent nudgy emails embellished with his corporate logo, a baying coyote. But once he had secured the lease, he blew deadline after deadline, delaying months, even years, when it came to filing mandatory applications, completing environmental assessments, and paying fees—especially paying fees.

Jeff Bollman, acting manager of the DNRC's Southern Land Office, was Marty's point person on Section 36. Bollman, an easygoing person who ran ultramarathons in his free time, had a high tolerance for pain. Marty tested its limits.

"The timeline for this project is totally out of our control," Bollman emailed his colleagues in a January 2007 update on Coyote Wind. Bollman didn't want to be a dink about timelines, but he was still waiting for Marty to turn in a land use application he'd sent him two years ago. Marty, perennially pressed for cash, had been dragging his feet on paying the $960 fee.

Coyote Wind wasn't his only project—far from it. The wind prospector had planted met towers all over the state, like a lobsterman dropping traps along the coastline. Marty was overextended, which made him disorganized. His proposals were riddled with careless errors; his net revenue spreadsheets were overly optimistic. The man was shameless. When a DNRC supervisor asked for an update, Marty responded with an email link to one of his new business ventures: "Want to invest for partial ownership?"

In January 2008, Bollman sent Marty a sternly worded email about the land use license, along with a request for $1,920 in back fees. Marty promptly forwarded the bill to Alternity Wind Power in New Jersey, which had just bought an interest in Coyote Wind. A Spanish company called Enerfin was negotiating to buy Alternity's majority share. Suddenly, everyone wanted in on Coyote Wind.

After years of data tracking, wind mapping, haggling, and wrangling, Marty had created a multimillion-dollar blueprint for a wind farm. The site plan called for forty-four 1.8-megawatt turbines, which would be spread across Rick's Crazy Mountain Cattle Company, Section 36, and Alfred Anderson's ranch. The old sheep rancher had finally agreed to allow some turbines on his ground.

Twenty-four Vestas V90 1.8-megawatt turbines would be sited on the Jarrett ranch. They couldn't go up soon enough, from Rick's perspective. He was struggling to keep the bunkhouse thing going, now that he and Karen had split up. The working-ranch vacation business had really been her baby. Montana Bunkhouses, she called it, and it had caught on—so much so that Karen had recruited more ranch hosts, including Susan Metcalf, Sweet Grass County's school superintendent. (In 2009, Anthony Bourdain booked a stay at the Metcalf ranch on Deer Creek and shot an episode of his series *No Reservations* there. Metcalf liked Bourdain, but didn't enjoy being filmed as she whipped up a dish of Rocky Mountain oysters for him. "The cameraman asked me, 'Can you do that again—only more professionally?'" Metcalf wrote on Facebook. "I'm sorry, but has he ever tried to cut a slit in a slippery calf testicle and squeeze out the oyster?")

Karen took the business with her when she moved out, leaving Rick and his bunkhouse behind. But a Montana rancher with crinkly green eyes, a booming laugh, and an easy way with horses will not be lonely for long. Several of Rick's bunkhouse guests were smitten. Stacey from Hollywood, a would-be filmmaker, swore she'd never forget their time irrigating together. A romance novelist vowed to base the hero of her upcoming Western-themed bodice-ripper on Rick. *Good luck with your womenfolk, ha ha*, a bemused visitor wrote in the bunkhouse guest book.

Rick's daughter, Jami, stepped in to help. While Dad made memories with the guests, Jami did most of the grunt work, packing sack lunches, saddling horses, and cleaning the bunkhouse. Jami was thirty-six, a single mom with two kids. She had Rick's green eyes and the same forthright, no-bullshit manner. One bunkhouse visitor said that meeting Jami was like meeting a young, female version of Rick—an open book of knowledge, with a heartfelt love for the land.

Jami had worked on the ranch since she was eight and her brother, Jay, was ten and Rick paid them a penny for every gopher they killed. Jay and Jami cruised the fields in a little Subaru, one at the wheel, the other hanging out the passenger window with a .22, firing at gophers. As the kids got older, their responsibilities grew. When Jami was in the fifth grade, her mom went to work for a financial planner in town and left her with a bunch of recipe cards. From that point on, it became Jami's job to cook the meals for the family and the hired men, and to do all the ranch laundry.

In high school, she was that girl—the one who was an officer in lots of clubs and played lots of sports, the one who took the hardest classes and got straight A's. Over dinner at the ranch, a family friend, a college professor from the University of Rhode Island who spent his summers in Big Timber, told Jami she should apply to Brown. "The guy who was with him said, 'Oh, she could never get in—it's incredibly selective.' So of course, I applied," she said.

Jami had never been on a plane until the day she set off for New England by herself at the age of seventeen. At Brown, she majored in international relations and played rugby and struggled to adapt to East Coast humidity. Summers were spent working on the ranch and hanging out with J. V. Moody, whom she'd met the summer before college. JV, who was five years older than Jami, had enlisted in the army after graduating from Sweet Grass High School. He was back home after a three-year stint as a military policeman in Germany, earning a bachelor's degree in criminal justice at Montana State University with the goal of working for the state highway patrol.

Back at Brown, Jami pined for JV, so much so that she decided to take a leave of absence her senior year to find out if they were meant to be together. The following June, Jami put on an ivory satin dress with a princess train and married JV in Big Timber's Lutheran church. The wedding announcement in the *Pioneer* said the bride would finish her degree at MSU in Bozeman. Once, Jami had thought she'd leave Big Timber behind for a high-powered career on the East Coast. After a few years at Brown, she had decided that wasn't her thing. But there it was: she'd left it all for a man.

JV went to work for the Montana Highway Patrol. Their daughter, Jordan, was born in 1996; a son, Jess, was born two years later. Interesting job opportunities were scarce in Big Timber, and when the county attorney offered Jami a job as his assistant, she took it. JV was promoted to regional commander and worked long hours. He was gone many nights, and the marriage floundered. Jami suspected that JV was cheating on her. They separated in 2005.

Jami and the kids spent almost all their free time on the ranch with her dad. By 2008, she was taking days off her real job to help run the bunkhouse vacations. Jami was determined to keep the ranch going so that it would be there for her children. So, it was good news when the Spaniards showed up.

Enerfin, a Madrid-based renewable-energy developer with a portfolio of projects in Europe and Brazil, had succeeded in securing a majority interest in Coyote Wind. This delighted Governor Schweitzer, who had traveled to Spain to meet with Enerfin executives to lobby for wind development in his state. Rick liked the Spaniards; they were good people. Now that they were involved, Marty didn't come around so much, but that was all right. The Spaniards were ready to pay Rick handsomely for his wind once the project got built—$108,000 in royalties and installation fees for the first year alone.

But there were red flags fluttering over Coyote Wind, issues that gave DNRC officials like Jeff Bollman concern. The project would be partly on state trust land, so the state had to comply with the requirements of the Montana Environmental Protection Act, which involved a thorough review of its potential impact on the environment, the economy, and local residents. The state also had an obligation to keep the public informed. And there were signs early on that some members of the public were not at all happy about Coyote Wind.

In January 2008, Bollman got a phone call from a lawyer who represented a landowner whose ranch abutted Section 36—one Jan Engwis.

Jan and Karen Engwis had moved to Big Timber from the suburbs of Denver in 2001, buying the first piece of a ranch on the Yellowstone that would grow to about 5,500 acres by 2004. Along with three and a half miles of river frontage, the ranch had a cameo role in American history: Captain Clark's expedition passed through the Engwis ranch in the summer of 1806. Rick knew it better as the old Myrstol place.

Jan, who had a Wilford Brimley mustache and a florid complexion, embraced the ranching lifestyle. He bought himself a tractor and a couple dozen cows. Karen, an amateur photographer, took hundreds of pictures of the pronghorns and deer. Their idyll was disrupted one morning in November 2008, when Jan looked out his bedroom window and saw men in hard hats drilling holes on the northwest corner of his land. That particular strip of land, on the border of Rick Jarrett's ranch, had been traded in an informal land swap between Rick's grandfather Tom Jarrett and Elmer Myrstol back in 1950. The Myrstol place had changed hands several times, but the Jarretts still held the title to the land. Engwis had always assumed it was his.

Engwis stared in disbelief as contractors traipsed across his land with their surveying equipment and drills. Two metal fence posts, their tips spray-painted orange, had been driven into the dirt—*his* dirt, by the terms of a historic agreement. Wooden slats marked *Center Turbine 10* and *Center Turb 11* leaned against the posts. An infuriated Engwis confronted the workers, who told him Mr. Jarrett was taking his land back, and he could have his back, too. Engwis demanded a copy of the site map and called his lawyer.

Rick shrugged when he heard about the fence post incident. Maybe the contractors had crossed a corner of the man's land. It didn't concern him. That was the Spaniards' problem now.

Jarrett's wind farm had been fixed in Jan Engwis's sights for months. His lawyer peppered Jeff Bollman's in-box with regular emails, demanding updates on the project. Some of the Big Wind guys had become concerned about the possibility of a lawsuit. "We received word that there is a Gordy party that also has a lawyer that is against turbines for the State land," an Alternity executive emailed Bollman. "Are you aware of them?"

"That name does not ring a bell," replied Bollman, who had other worries. As part of his due diligence, Marty had hired Dr. Al Harmata, a wildlife biologist and eagle specialist at the Montana Raptor Conservation Center, to assess the potential impact of the Coyote Wind project on wildlife. Harmata documented over a hundred different bird species in and around Rick's ranch. There were meadowlarks and horned larks, ravens and vesper sparrows. There were peregrine falcons and northern goshawks—raptors that Montana's Fish and Wildlife Service classed as species of concern because of their declining populations and threatened habitat.

But mostly, there were eagles—bald eagles, golden eagles, lots and lots of eagles. Golden eagles were the most frequently observed avian species on the state parcel, throughout all four seasons of the year. Section 36 had a prairie dog town, and eagles loved prairie dogs.

It's a crime to kill eagles—or to hunt, possess, or sell them—under a federal law passed in 1940 to protect America's national symbol. An even older law—enacted in 1918, when snowy egrets were almost eradicated in pursuit of their plumes—protects all migratory birds. There are exceptions to these laws. Incidental takes—bird deaths caused by otherwise lawful activities—are not a criminal offense. Energy development kills millions of birds, with rare legal consequences. Coal ash fly—the waste product of the coal burned at power plants—leaches heavy metals into the soil, streams, and groundwater, poisoning birds and all manner of wildlife. The oil industry kills birds by exposing them to toxic, uncovered waste pits. Then there are headline-grabbing disasters like oil spills. The Deepwater Horizon spill killed between 800,000 and one million waterfowl.

But the fossil fuels industry isn't the only culprit. Anyone who has ever flipped on a light switch or charged a mobile phone has killed birds, and maybe even an eagle or two. Eagles are routinely electrocuted when their wings brush high-tension power lines, which kill up to sixty-four million birds a year; collisions with communication towers account for another seven million avian fatalities.

Bollman knew that wind turbines had been deadly for birds—eagles in particular. One of America's first commercial wind farms was Altamont Pass, a sprawling development of six thousand turbines, sited within a major raptor migration corridor in Northern California's Diablo mountain range. Altamont Pass was infamous. The turbines killed thousands of birds each year. They were especially deadly for raptors, which nested in the latticed towers and collided with the blades, or were electrocuted by turbine cables as they hunted California ground squirrels. Prior to 2005, up to 117 golden eagles, 300 red-tailed hawks, and 380 burrowing owls were killed in a single year at Altamont, along with dozens of kestrels, falcons, vultures, and owls.

Altamont was the ugly face of industrial wind—a vivid example of the environmental cost of green energy. It had a chilling effect on wind development. Turbine design evolved in response. Blades were mounted on tubular towers instead of latticework structures where birds could nest. Gearboxes, generators, and other parts were now encased in smooth, perch-resistant nacelles. Electrical cables and conduits were buried underground, so birds wouldn't be electrocuted by them. Wind developers began to pay more attention to where turbines were sited, moving them away from nesting areas and prime hunting grounds.

Wind turbines also grew taller. Taller, more powerful turbines mean fewer turbines overall, which was better for birds. The blades of these larger turbines turned more slowly. Eagles avoided them more easily, it seemed. But their elongated blades swept a greater area, creating more turbulence in their wake. That was potentially worse for small birds and for bats, which were vulnerable to barotrauma—internal damage caused by sudden changes in air pressure. Wind farm operators began hiring seasonal avian monitors, shutting down some turbines during peak migratory periods. Many of these measures were implemented at Altamont. By 2013, fatality rates for golden eagles and red-tailed hawks had dropped by 70 percent and 61 percent, respectively, and total bird deaths had been cut in half.

After the Judith Gap wind farm became operational in 2006, a monitoring program was implemented during the fall and spring migratory periods. Based on the number of carcasses found in targeted searches, researchers estimated that 1,206 bats and 406 birds would be killed by Judith Gap's ninety wind turbines every year. Eagles weren't among the casualties. Mostly, the monitors found dead grebes.

A dead grebe was one thing. A dead eagle—well, people got upset about dead eagles. Although there were no laws outlawing wind development in places where eagles fly, the state was bound to ensure that any projects on trust land minimized any risk to the fullest possible extent. A more expansive scoping report was compiled at Bollman's urging by Garcia and Associates, an environmental permitting company.

Raptor counts were conducted over the course of a year's spring and fall migratory periods. A fixed-wing Piper PA-18 Super Cub, modified for slow flight, conducted aerial surveys to locate every bald eagle, golden eagle, and hawk nest within a four-mile radius of the project site. Each nest, active and inactive, was documented and mapped; the number of chicks in each nest was counted.

The environmental specialists didn't just look at eagles. Every aspect of the state trust parcel was examined to assess the potential effect of the eight wind turbines—from the ground up. The dirt on Section 36 was surveyed and broken into sixteen different soil maps, calculated to the acre. Wildlife biologists conducted acoustic monitoring for various bat species and documented the movements of grizzly bears, Canada lynx, and wolverines within a ten-mile radius of the wind farm site. A gray wolf pack was active in the West Boulder River area; biologists analyzed their movements to assess how likely they were to visit Section 36. Not very, they concluded.

A state archaeologist was dispatched to see if the trust land contained any cultural resources. During a thorough inspection of all 640 acres, he found two low stone cairns of indeterminate age, a small rock wall, and two isolated stone artifacts—a biface thinning flake of lavender-colored chert and a flake of butterscotch-colored chert. One could say that the state and its agents had literally left no stone unturned in their assessment of Section 36.

To a casual observer, the land might have seemed untouched, pristine. But Section 36 had been leased for development long before Coyote Wind. Devon Energy, an oil and gas company, held a lease to the mineral reserves below its surface and could drill for oil or coalbed methane there if it liked—though if it ever did, it would have to steer clear of a petroleum pipeline that traversed the trust land's entire southern half. Montana is home to four oil refineries, which process crude oil from Canada and Wyoming. Gasoline, jet fuel, and diesel fuel had flowed below the surface of Section 36 through this pipeline—the Yellowstone Pipeline, named for the river it crosses on its way to Idaho and Washington— since it was built in the 1950s.

The Yellowstone Pipeline also passed through Russell Gordy's Rock Creek Ranch, where it could be spotted near Duck Creek Road, arcing up from the dirt like a shiny white porpoise, then diving back below. The hoop of exposed pipeline was set behind a high fence topped with razor wire, a pimple of industrial unsightliness on Gordy's domain. It was a block valve station owned by Phillips 66, the oil company that controlled the pipeline. Should the pipeline spring a leak—the pipes were old, the seams worn, it happened—workers could block or shut down the valve there. The oil company had held title to that patch of land since 1960, and no one complained about it, an agent for Phillips 66 told me. "People say, 'That's such an eyesore,'" she said. "Someone who is used to it says, 'I don't even see it.'"

In August 2009, the DNRC issued a draft environmental impact statement on Coyote Wind. It was nearly two hundred pages long, not counting the seven appendixes. A photo simulation on the cover showed what the project would look like from the interstate highway, near the Springdale exit. Several rows of skinny white turbines rose on the northern banks of the Yellowstone River, their blades facing east toward Springdale—a tiny community on the fringe of the railroad tracks, with a smattering of homes and a white clapboard schoolhouse. The train tracks appeared in the foreground of the picture, the Crazy Mountains far off in the distance. Juxtaposed against the mountains' looming bulk, the turbines seemed as slight as toothpicks, though each would be four hundred feet tall at the height of its rotation, with a three-hundred-foot wingspan.

The DNRC report examined the wind farm's impact through two lenses: Proposed Action and No Action. Proposed Action looked at what would happen if the eight wind turbines went up on the parcel of state land, while No Action examined what would happen if the state parcel was not developed, while the Coyote Wind project went up next door on Rick Jarrett's ranch. In the DNRC's analysis, Coyote Wind was a reality. It was going to be built, with the state's involvement or without it.

Special attention had been paid to Springdale's raptors. The eight turbines on Section 36 were set fifty meters back from bluffs, hills, and ridges to reduce the risk to eagles and hawks, which catch the updrafts created at the edges of ridged land formations to fly and to hunt. No turbines were sited within two miles of any known eagle's nest, or near the prairie dog town, the golden eagles' favorite canteen. Once the wind farm was up and running, Montana's Fish, Wildlife, and Parks would monitor the site and track avian fatalities.

Public hearings were held on the afternoon and evening of September 2, 2009, at Big Timber's Carnegie Library. Bollman was there, along with senior ecologists from Garcia and Associates and representatives from Enerfin. Rick took a seat and looked around to see if any of his neighbors had shown. His boundary dispute with Jan Engwis raged on. In March, Engwis filed a lawsuit against the Crazy Mountain Cattle Company and Coyote Wind over that strip of land Rick's grandfather had traded with Elmer Myrstol. The lawsuit was a public notice that anyone with plans to survey or develop that land would do well to cease and desist. In fact, Enerfin had already decided to relocate the two turbines off the disputed strip of land. The lawsuit was moot, at least so far as Coyote Wind was concerned.

As the hearing got underway, a woman named Cindy Selensky raised her hand. Cindy and her two sisters had grown up on Wild Eagle Mountain Ranch, north of the Jarrett ranch. Their parents, Jim and Roxie Hogemark, managed the ranch for the owners, Whitney and Betty MacMillan. The MacMillans lived in Minnesota, where the Cargill agribusiness empire—the family business—was based.

Selensky had known Whitney and Betty her whole life. They might have been among the richest people in America, but they were like a third set of grandparents to the Hogemark girls, bringing them souvenirs from their travels and helping pay their college tuition. When the girls came by the house, Betty would pour them a bowl of cereal and sit down on the floor with them while they ate. The MacMillans were private people. Cindy's father, Jim Hogemark, had probably been the one who turned Marty Wilde away when he dropped by the ranch some years back.

Selensky had a lot of questions about Coyote Wind. Mostly, she was upset at the idea of seeing a lot of windmills in front of the Crazies. "I guess from an emotional and personal perspective, it's really difficult for me," she said.

Jose Antonijuan, a representative for the Elecnor Group, Enerfin's parent company, assured Selensky that the turbines would be difficult to see from the road—a dubious assertion. The DNRC's environmental impact statement included several simulations, including one in which eight turbines were plainly visible from North River Road, near the Duck Creek schoolhouse. The greatest visual impact would be experienced by motorists on Interstate 90, which ran roughly parallel to the project site. But the turbines would not block views of the Crazy Mountains. In the simulations, the towers were a visual footnote, a white scribble in the margins of the low foothills.

"I mean, there is certain things that you will notice. You will see antennas, transmission antennas . . . The thing is that the wind flows, and this is a way to generate electricity without having to import more oil from the Arabs, without burning coal," Antonijuan told Selensky, adding, unconvincingly, "And I think you will be amazed to see that it's not disturbing."

Selensky wasn't having it. "If I was to go any place in time, I'd be back here in Montana in the early 1900s, where there isn't, you know, anything out there," she said.

Darlene Fahrenbruch raised her hand. Her family had ranched in Sweet Grass County a long time, since the days of kerosene lamps and hand-dug well pumps. She remembered when the electricity came through, and it was horrible. The rural co-op wanted to put up poles on her father's ranch, but he was totally against it. He didn't want to see those electrical wires strung through his land. He didn't want telephone poles going up in his alfalfa fields, either. And he prevailed. The utilities did not dig electrical poles or string wires across her dad's land. The family ranch was left off the grid, without electricity or a telephone.

"Cindy, I really understand where you're coming from. I really do," Darlene said. But she remembered what it was like being without electricity. It was like primitive times. "We were bypassed when Dad made his decision," she said, ". . . and we adjusted to the little telephone poles, you know."

Not that Darlene didn't have her own doubts about the windmills. She had lived in California for a time, and she hated the sight of those huge things—everyone did. But she got used to it. She adjusted. That's what humans did—they adjusted, because they needed to, to survive. Whether she was for the wind farm or against it, she just didn't know at that moment. "But I do know that I survived those telephone poles," Darlene said, and sat down.

Two days later, on the final day of the public comment period, Jan Engwis, Russell Gordy, and Whitney MacMillan submitted lengthy letters through their various attorneys, objecting to the DNRC's proposed land lease to Coyote Wind. The Engwis letter was thirty-one pages long and included a recap of the fence post incident. Enerfin had already resited the two turbines. Nonetheless, Engwis attached a photograph of the spray-painted fence posts to his lengthy list of objections.

In his email to Bollman, Gordy pointed out that his Rock Creek Ranch was home to the historic Hunter's Hot Springs, three miles southwest of Section 36. "It has been my intent since acquiring the property to restore it to its former glory," Gordy wrote. "I believe it will be rather easy to prove that a wind farm will diminish the value of my property so as not to allow the development of Hunter Hot Springs and therefore decrease the economic benefits to the State of Montana."

Jarrett's wealthy neighbors were not the only ones to object to Coyote Wind. Ray Mulé, a wildlife program manager for the state's Department of Fish, Wildlife, and Parks, had serious concerns about the project's impact on eagles and other species, particularly bats. Springdale just wasn't a good site for a wind farm, in Mulé's opinion. The head of Montana's Audubon Society wrote to express similar fears, as did the director of the Lewis and Clark Trail Heritage Foundation.

In November, the DNRC issued its final Environmental Impact Statement, which included pages of point-by-point responses to all 177 comments and complaints it had received—ninety-two of them from Jan Engwis. ("Still wading through Engwis," Pam Spinelli, a senior wildlife ecologist with Garcia and Associates, wrote Bollman in late September.) The substance of the final report was fundamentally the same as the ini-

tial draft, but it now had an appendix of fifty-five pages of corrections
and clarifications. The most significant correction was to upgrade the
project's potential risk to wildlife from moderate to high. The report's
authors qualified this by saying the risk was at the low end of high, and
that "a high rank does not preclude development."

As for Gordy's objection that the wind farm would diminish the
value of his hot springs and rob the state of its economic benefits, the
report's authors responded that such concerns were outside the scope of
Montana's Environmental Protection Act. But the consultants had done
additional photo simulations, to show what the view would be from a
hill above Hunter's Hot Springs. A line of white turbines stretched halfway across the panorama, blades spinning, in full view of the springs.

In January, Montana's land board approved the lease of Section 36 to
Coyote Wind, LLC. Governor Schweitzer, who presided over the land
board meeting, was delighted. Long ago, Spanish explorers had come to
Montana searching for gold, he declared exuberantly, if erroneously. He
welcomed the Spaniards back to Montana to reap new treasure from its
winds.

A few months later, Wild Eagle Mountain Ranch, Rock Creek Ranch,
and Jan Engwis's two holding companies, Engwis Investment Company
and R. F. Building Company, filed a lawsuit against the Department of
Natural Resources and Conservation, which they accused of acting arbi-
trarily in approving Coyote Wind's lease to Section 36.

Rick shook his head when he heard the news. Marty had put up his
met towers and mapped the wind for years. He had looked at every piece
of available land to figure out the best spot for each turbine. But Marty
hadn't seen this one coming.

DNRC lawyers read through the filing, an everything-but-the-
kitchen-sink complaint from a strike team of attorneys that faulted the
state for its inadequate analysis of the potential impact on property values, wetlands, bat and bird mortality, roads and water use, Federal Aviation Authority lighting requirements, and the true value of potential
oil and gas development on the state parcel. Now that the spaghetti had
been thrown against the wall, they'd see what stuck.

In October 2011, Judge John McKeon issued a summary judgment against the DNRC and Coyote Wind. In his decision, the judge agreed with Rick Jarrett's neighbors on several key points. The DNRC's No Action alternative, which considered the presence of a wind farm on private land as a given, was invalid. It ignored a crucial fact: there were, as yet, no windmills on the Crazy Mountain Cattle Company. Maybe there never would be.

The judge took issue with other aspects of the DNRC's final environmental impact statement. He seemed particularly irked by the DNRC's position that oil and gas drilling on the state parcel was unlikely. If Devon Energy, which owned the gas and oil lease to the property, got a drilling permit and struck oil, the state would collect a one-time payment of $105,320. Judge McKeon thought the department had lied by omission by not mentioning that.

But as far as golden eagles, bats, and other wildlife went, the judge found that the DNRC had given rational consideration to all the plaintiffs' primary concerns.

None of McKeon's findings exposed fatal flaws with the plan to lease Section 36 for wind development, at least not in the minds of Bollman and other DNRC staffers who had been working on Coyote Wind since 2005. The business about the oil and gas lease, in particular, seemed like bullshit from a fossil fuel–friendly judge.*

The DNRC was ready to appeal. But Enerfin was wavering. The Spaniards were having trouble nailing down a complicated multiparty agreement to transmit Coyote Wind's electricity from Montana to the Pacific Northwest. This would involve an agreement with NorthWestern Energy, Montana's biggest utility, to deliver Coyote Wind's electricity over its transmission lines to the Bonneville Power Administration, which would in turn transmit it across its system to customers in Washington and Oregon.

---

* In 2016, Judge McKeon would make national headlines when he sentenced a man who had repeatedly raped his twelve-year-old daughter to sixty days in jail—minus the seventeen days he had already served. The prosecutor in the case had recommended a sentence of at least twenty-five years. The judge, who defended the sentence as "quite rigorous," cited testimonials from the man's friends and his church as justification. He retired the following month with full benefits, despite widespread calls for his impeachment.

There are only so many power lines and substations and transformers in Montana, and transmission capacity on that system is limited. The Spaniards had run into a roadblock that would derail other American renewable-energy projects: an exhausted and outmoded electric infra-structure, desperately in need of technological upgrades and expansion. Enerfin's transmission headaches, combined with the trouble over the state lease and Rick Jarrett's litigious neighbors, were too much. In 2012, the Spaniards walked. Under the conditions of Enerfin's conditional sale agreement with Coyote Wind's original developer, the ownership and management of the project reverted to one Martin Wilde.

Wind development was a long game. Marty took stock. Next time, there'd be no state land—no poking around for arrowheads, no acoustic monitoring for bats, and no requests for comments from the neighbors. If you wanted to get a wind farm done in Montana, then you had to do it on private land. Coyote Wind was finished. It was time to develop Crazy Mountain Wind.

6

ALFRED AND WHITNEY AND A $10,000 BULL

February 20, 2019
Park County Courthouse
Livingston, Montana

ALFRED ANDERSON, *having first been duly sworn, testified as*
   follows:
Q: How old are you?
MR. ANDERSON: Pardon?
Q: How old are you?
MR. ANDERSON: Eighty-seven.
Q: Okay. And are you still working, actively, every day?
MR. ANDERSON: Yes. Yah, feeding livestock, chopping ice, and
   watching livestock.

SPRINGDALE, MONTANA

Alfred Anderson wasn't for it, not at first. Rick brought the wind-business man over to his ranch one afternoon, was how he first heard of it. Alfred, a tall, lean man with bright blue eyes and perennial stubble on his chin, listened to Marty Wilde talk. Marty was wanting to put one meteorological tower up there, on Alfred's ground. Alfred didn't think much of that idea. Marty asked if Alfred owned that land to the west. When Alfred said that he did, Marty said, well, you could make a lot of money off that land with a few turbines. Alfred laughed and shook his head.

So, Alfred let it go. But the wind thing, it kept a-going. More met towers went up on Rick's ranch, then on the school section, north of Anderson ground. As Coyote Wind took shape, Alfred thought about it some more. The next time Rick and Marty paid him a visit, Alfred said that some windmills might be all right. On December 27, 2006, he signed a one-year lease agreement with Marty, giving him the wind rights to four hundred acres for $1,000 down.

Alfred's ranch was just two sections of ground, but it straddled the county line, so he had a foot in both Sweet Grass and Park. His father, Alfred Anderson Sr., bought the place in 1950. Alfred Sr. came over from Norway as an infant. The family settled in Wisconsin, but at the age of fourteen, he set off on his own on the Northern Pacific. For reasons no one knows or can remember, he got off in Big Timber. The year was 1905.

Alfred Sr. drove a stagecoach for the mail service for a time, then found work as a hired hand. He married Cora Talle, a schoolteacher who taught at a log schoolhouse at Sioux Crossing, a remote spot in the Crazies at the juncture of some old Indian trails. Young Alfred was born in 1931; his sister, Alice, was born two years later. The family lived on different ranches over the years, as Alfred Sr. followed work as a laborer, then began leasing land of his own.

There were no tractors on the ranches Alfred grew up on. Draft horses pulled the feed wagons and drove the disc harrows and pushed the haying rakes, which were like giant toothed combs, parting a sea of grass. Alfred learned how to gather the cut hay with the buck rake when he was little. He'd harness an old workhorse and climb up on the box, his face inches from its rump. You wanted gentle horses when you were bucking in a load, nothing too pippy. If they bolted, you'd have a wreck. He'd coax the old mare along the windrows, the cut hay tumbling forward in a great pile. Once Alfred had bucked in a load of hay, the men pitched it onto a towering stack with an overshot—a catapult, powered by a horse. They was pretty proud of their haystacks, all right, Alfred said.

What wasn't done by horse was done by hand, every task a memory his muscles carried. Bundling the cut sheaves of wheat and oats and stacking them in shocks to dry, pitching those bundles into a wagon with a tined bundling fork, then hefting them into the threshing machine to separate the grain from the chaff. Because there was so much manual labor in those days, ranchers traded work, helping each other out with branding and shearing and threshing—thrashing, Alfred called it. There was only one threshing machine in the county, and it made a circuit from ranch to ranch. When it reached your ranch, all your neighbors would pitch in to help get your thrashing done. That was quite a get-together. The women always cooked a big meal, and there'd be neighbors around from quite a ways.

The Andersons worked and saved for decades to buy their own piece of ground. Cora taught at one-room schoolhouses across Sweet Grass County, from Glasston to Duck Creek, where the Jarrett boys were her pupils for a time. In the summer, she worked as a maid at the Lazy K Bar, a dude ranch high up in the Crazies that was popular with wealthy people from the East. Cora cleaned their log cabins, made their beds, and served their meals in the dining room.

Alfred graduated from Sweet Grass High School in 1950. The graduates listed their aspirations and dreams alongside their senior portraits in the *Timberline* yearbook: go to college, become a secretary, teach high school math, play professional basketball. Alfred's was just one word: *rancher*. That fall, his father bought the T. O. Murray place in Springdale, and Alfred began his chosen profession. He found out that much of ranching was about trial and error. You do something, and if it ain't right, you do it over.

The Andersons couldn't afford livestock in the beginning. They farmed the land and sold the hay and grain and saved up to buy cows. A year or so after they got their first cows, Alfred started in with sheep: Targhees, a dual-purpose breed good for meat and wool, and some Rambouillets, whose wool was almost as fine as merino. If you crossed a Rambouillet ram with a Targhee ewe, you'd get meaty lambs and sturdy ewes with dense, soft fleece.

Around the time that Alfred was puzzling out the complexities of crossbreeding, he went to a card party at the Laubachs' place in Springdale, where he met Dorothy O'Leary. Dorothy's father was a hired man for a wealthy Californian who owned a ranch nearby. Dorothy, a vivacious girl who had recently graduated high school, was working at an ice cream parlor in Livingston and exploring an interest in photography. When Dorothy's sister told her there sure was a good-looking guy at the ranch down the road, she decided that maybe she'd go to that card party at the Laubachs' after all. Alfred made his mind up to marry her that night.

The newlyweds built a small frame house behind the senior Andersons' farmhouse. Then Alfred decided it would be better to live closer to the barns and corrals, where the work was. The neighbors helped him load the house on log skids, and then they towed it three miles down the county road with an International Harvester TD-9 crawler and a pair of John Deere tractors. Alfred and Dorothy never left that house, not even after they had bought the ranch from his folks. They added onto it over the years, cobbling on rooms as their children, Kevin and Karen, grew.

Now they were old. Kevin moved back onto the ranch to help with the calving and lambing and seeding and irrigating, living in a camper he parked out front. But Alfred never stopped working. He rose before dawn on the coldest winter mornings to feed and water his herd, breaking up the ice on the tanks with a pitchfork, or if it was frozen real thick, an ax. The wind would get in your face and sting it pretty bad. It was hard to stand up when it was gusting. When it blows hard, you gotta lean into it. Alfred had learned that over the years.

He stood straight and tall well into his eighties, though he couldn't hear too good or see too good anymore. Macular degeneration made his eyesight kind of blurry. Couldn't read fine print or nothing without a magnifying glass.

But your eyes could fool you even if your vision was sharp. Although the landscape around Alfred's ranch looked much the way it always had—open grazing land, tawny range grass, gray-green sagebrush, irrigated fields—so much had changed. The families he had known for more than half a century, the ones who gathered for card parties and helped each other out at thrashing time and shearing time and brought food when you had a death, were mostly gone, having sold their land or moved on to their own plots at Mountain View Cemetery. His neighbors were millionaires and billionaires now. Alfred wouldn't know the Texan if he saw him.

He knew Jan Engwis. They were in the same ditch association, the Hunter Hot Springs Canal Company, which provided the water to irrigate his fields. Alfred had been to Engwis's home for a ditch meeting or two. Sometime after Engwis bought the ranch, Alfred noticed an old steel windmill setting out on a hill that never used to be there in the Myr-stols' day. Yard art, they called it, he supposed.

Whitney MacMillan was in the same ditch association, but he didn't attend the meetings, sending one of Wild Eagle's ranch managers in his place. Alfred had never met MacMillan, though he knew the ranch well. The schoolhouse at Sioux Crossing where his mother once taught was on MacMillan ground, though only the old stone foundations remained. Now and again, Alfred passed MacMillan on the county road. The snowy-headed Minnesotan always gave a courtly wave.

Alfred and Whitney were contemporaries. Born in 1929, MacMillan was the great-grandson of W. W. Cargill, a Union supply corps captain who founded the grain business that would become Cargill Incorporated, the largest privately owned company in the United States at one time. Cargill produces, distributes, transports, and sells every kind of commodity, from cocoa beans, crude oil, and cotton to chicken feed and the liquid eggs that McDonald's turns into breakfast biscuits and McGriddles. At the time of the hearing on Crazy Mountain Wind, MacMillan ranked as the 128th-richest American on the Forbes 400, with a net worth of $5.1 billion.

Whitney was the last member of the Cargill-MacMillan family to head Cargill Incorporated. He began working for the family company after his graduation from Yale in 1951, starting off as a trainee merchant in the vegetable oil division, then onward and upward to grain, eventually ascending to the summit of the seed, salt, and cargo carrier divisions. He became president of the company in 1975, then chairman of the board and CEO, positions he held until his retirement in 1995. Under MacMillan's leadership, Cargill became a global juggernaut whose agricultural, industrial, and financial products and services have become inextricably enmeshed in the planetary food web.

In the mid-1970s, MacMillan oversaw Cargill's expansion into the beef packaging and processing business. Within a few years, a large percentage of the world's beef was coming from Cargill. Cargill cattle—raised by ranchers like Alfred Anderson and Rick Jarrett, then sold at auction—filled feedlots built with Cargill steel products. The cows fattened on Cargill-produced animal feed that had been grown with Cargill fertilizers and stored in Cargill grain elevators. They were then slaughtered and processed in Cargill meat packaging facilities, vacuum-packaged in portions with the precise proportion of fat that Cargill data analytics found customers were most likely to buy, and transported in Cargill container ships to China, Taiwan, and Hong Kong. Whatever ingredients in this meat pie Cargill didn't produce, it secured through its network of subsidiaries and affiliates.

During his time at the helm of Cargill, MacMillan expanded the company's theater of operations from thirty-one countries to fifty-three and quadrupled the number of employees. Cargill was everywhere, but remained a private family business, its corporate headquarters housed not in a Minneapolis skyscraper, but a sixty-three-room ersatz French château near Lake Minnetonka. The Cargill Castle, some called it. MacMillan resisted pressure to take the company public, preferring to run the company the way the family saw fit—privately, free from interfering shareholders. Cargill's corporate ethos mirrored his personal value system: a mash-up of the Protestant work ethic, Scottish thrift, and Minnesota nice, served with a dram of ancestor worship.

"W. W. Cargill was a Midwesterner, and he was a Christian—specifically, a Presbyterian," Whitney MacMillan wrote in *Common-Sense Business*, a manifesto on corporate leadership that he coauthored with Theodore Roosevelt Malloch in 2017. "His company has taken on the character of its founder. In typical Midwestern fashion, WW wasn't interested in the fastest or the flashiest. He exercised prudence in his business, and his common-sense, practical wisdom has built the vast powerhouse that his family carries on today." MacMillan called this blend of prudence, patience, principles, and practicality—"the four P's"—the Cargill Way.

Common-Sense Business is a primer on the Cargill Way, studded with more biblical proverbs than a church sermon. It contains a seven-page, trademarked "Ethics Audit" for CEOs—"Does the company violate the Golden Rule?" "Does the company take ethics cases seriously?"—and an "Oath of Virtuous, Common-Sense Capitalism" to safeguard the interests of shareholders *and* "to create virtuous economic, social and environmental prosperity worldwide."

The emphasis on virtue was a hallmark of MacMillan's leadership style. In 1975, as the company's newly appointed president, MacMillan wrote an internal memo to Cargill employees responding to a recent spate of bribing scandals involving grain companies and government inspectors at export elevators. "Cargill does not want any profit from any practice which is immoral or unethical," he wrote.

Common-Sense Business is silent on Cargill's role in the destruction of rain forests across the world, including in South America and Indonesia, where much of the grain, soybeans, palm oil, and other commodity crops it sells are grown. In 2006, Cargill and a few other Big Ag companies signed a voluntary moratorium on purchasing Brazilian soybeans harvested from newly deforested land in the Amazon. But even as press releases heralding this act of corporate virtue went out, Cargill was gobbling up soybeans grown on freshly razed rain forest land in Paraguay. From a historic standpoint, Cargill does not seem to have regarded damaging the environment—other people's environments, anyway—as immoral or unethical. At least, not enough to refrain from profiting off it.

Nor does MacMillan make any reference to forced child labor on cacao farms in Côte d'Ivoire, which supply Cargill with tens of thousands of cocoa beans every year for its cocoa products. A group of former child laborers from Mali sued Cargill for aiding and abetting in their enslavement by subsidizing those farms, in a case that reached the Supreme Court in 2021. The court sided with Cargill and its codefendant, Nestlé. The corporations couldn't be held accountable for overseas human rights abuses on the basis of "general corporate activity" like "providing training, fertilizer, tools, and cash to overseas farms," Justice Clarence Thomas wrote in his majority opinion. (Cargill maintained throughout that it had done nothing wrong and was committed to combating child labor.)

MacMillan himself gave almost no interviews, and managed to say nothing on the few occasions he did. ("Food has become such an interesting issue in the nation and the world," he observed in a rare sit-down with the *New York Times* in 1986.) By many accounts, he conducted his personal life the Cargill Way, with prudence, patience, practicality, principle—and one more *P*: absolute privacy. In his 1998 family history, *MacMillan: The American Grain Family*, W. Duncan MacMillan wrote that his cousin Whitney "has maintained an extremely private and understated lifestyle. Conservative and taciturn by nature, he prefers modest cars which he drives himself and has never indulged in the excesses of power or luxury."

One can't imagine Whitney was happy about his cousin's book, which is stuffed with gossipy anecdotes about prep school high jinks, cocktail parties—"mother loved her martinis"—and quickie divorces. "I didn't ask," Duncan said, when questioned about Whitney's reaction to its publication.

MacMillan and his cousins grew up in Orono, a wealthy enclave on the shores of Lake Minnetonka. A bosky Twin Cities suburb, Orono was thickly settled with Pillsburys, Daytons, and Bells, who built estates there and played tennis on one another's courts. Whitney's grandfather John Hugh MacMillan built a turreted castle called Longridge, which he filled with crystal chandeliers and Louis XV furnishings manufactured in St. Paul.

The younger MacMillans arranged themselves around the family patriarch. Whitney's father, Cargill MacMillan, and mother, Pauline Whitney MacMillan, built a colonial-style house on MacMillan Lake, an artificial lake that his grandfather created at considerable expense. The family called it Rudolph's Pond, for the hired man who pumped water around the clock for over a month to fill it.

Whitney and his siblings, Cargill Jr. and Pauline, grew up next door to their cousins W. Duncan, John Hugh III, and Marnie, who occupied a sprawling manse named Craigbank, for the ancestral family home in Scotland. Whitney and W. Duncan were playmates, born just one year apart. The cousins sailed catboats on MacMillan Lake, played tennis on Craigbank's tennis courts, and jumped off the roof of their grandfather's goose house, where MacMillan Lake's swans were kept. Duncan and his best friend, David Winton Bell—whose family founded General Mills—liked to play Jacques Cousteau. They put on heavy diving suits and walked around on the bottom of the lake, breathing through rubber tubes attached to an air tank in a rowboat. (Bell, a US Marine who died in a plane crash in Japan in 1955, was the father of Rick Jarrett's silent partner, Penny Hatten.)

Later on, there were sailing lessons at the Minnetonka Yacht Club, debutante balls at the Woodhill Country Club, and winter getaways to Jamaica, where Uncle John bought a one-thousand-acre plantation called Green Castle. ("At its peak as a sugar plantation it boasted four hundred Black slaves," W. Duncan declared.) Around the time that Alfred Anderson graduated high school, the MacMillan boys joined their fathers on a two-week cruise to British Columbia aboard the *Carmac*, the 115-foot family yacht, to inspect Cargill's Canadian lumber operations and to spearfish for salmon. There would be seven *Carmac*s over the years, each grander than the last.

But a shadow hung over these scenes of privilege—the small, toddler-sized shadow cast by Charles Lindbergh Jr., the twenty-month-old son of the aviators Charles Lindbergh and Anne Morrow Lindbergh. The baby was stolen from his crib in 1932 by kidnappers who left a ransom note on his nursery windowsill, demanding $50,000. The child's body was discovered a few months later in a shallow grave less than five miles from the Lindbergh home, his skull crushed.

The kidnapping of the Lindbergh baby riveted the American public. It also spawned a rash of kidnappings of wealthy Americans, many of whom were now looking anxiously over one shoulder. In the Twin Cities, a prominent brewer was abducted and held for ransom. After the ransom was paid and the brewer was released, the gang kidnapped a St. Paul banker.

The Lindbergh baby, who was about the same age as Whitney and W. Duncan, haunted the cousins' childhood. "The possibility that my brother and sister and I might be kidnapped when we were children curtailed our activities. We didn't go to camp, and we were under constant surveillance, if not by our parents, then by the household staff. For a time we couldn't go anywhere, but we had our cousins," W. Duncan wrote. They spent their earliest years sequestered from outside world—a childhood that was clannish in the extreme.

The MacMillan boys loved playing cowboy. An undated photograph shows Whitney with cousins and his brother, Cargill Jr., in cowboy hats and bandannas, brandishing toy pistols from the back of a wagon that has been converted into a makeshift stagecoach, with the words *Wells Fargo* dabbed on the side in white paint. The freedom, adventure, and boundless horizons that the West represented must have had a powerful appeal for the cloistered princelings of Orono.

"Owning a ranch has been a childhood dream of mine," MacMillan told the *Big Timber Pioneer* in a rare interview in 1987. He was in his late fifties then, and in his second decade at the helm of the Cargill empire. Although MacMillan avoided the press at home in Wayzata, Minnesota, he made an exception for the *Pioneer*, which had reached out to him before a talk he was set to deliver at the Grand Hotel on trends in the beef industry. The event would be open to the public, with a roast beef dinner provided by Cargill's boxed beef subsidiary, Excel.

The local reporter had caught MacMillan in a chatty mood. When he and his wife, Elizabeth, found the means to acquire a ranch, MacMillan explained, they began looking at properties across the West.

"While skiing in Vail and Aspen, we looked at ranches in Colorado; we also looked around Wyoming," he said.

But there was nothing to compare to Roger Whidden's ranch in Montana's Crazy Mountains. The Whidden place covered all the bases. It had a solid cattle operation. The climate was good. And it was private. The ranch was so remote, its terrain so mountainous and rugged, that Big Timber's Explorer Post 521 once conducted search-and-rescue drills there. Back when Rick Jarrett was in high school, he and his fellow search-and-rescue trainees ranged across the Whidden place with walkie-talkies in search of a dummy named Charlie, which had been air-dropped from a small plane. Kid Royal Mountain—named for a notorious horse rustler who hid out up there—was included in the bill of sale, along with a few peaks so desolate they didn't have names.

MacMillan bought the twenty-thousand-acre ranch in 1979, three years after being named Cargill CEO, and named it Wild Eagle Mountain, which shared a monogram with Whitney and Elizabeth MacMillan.

How can a man—even one as wealthy as Whitney MacMillan—own a mountain? It seems somehow not kosher—like keeping a bald eagle for a pet. Owning a bald eagle is, in fact, against the law. But private citizens do own mountains across the Rocky Mountain West. The scion of a Texas oil family owns Culebra Peak in Colorado. Most of Wyoming's Elk Mountain is the property of a pharmaceutical magnate from North Carolina.

In the Crazies, the key to the conundrum lies in the checkerboard. The mountain range is locked within a grid-like pattern of private and public ownership that predates the state of Montana itself. Squares of private land alternate with squares of Forest Service land—each section 640 acres in size—forming a fifty-thousand-acre patchwork quilt the size of the range, a literal crazy quilt.

The checkerboard was created in 1864 by Congress when it established a charter for the nation's first transcontinental railroad, the Northern Pacific Railway Company. The Northern Pacific would run from Lake Superior to Puget Sound, traversing the breadth of the newly created Montana Territory. The nation was at war with itself, its very future in question. Nonetheless, Lincoln, a former railroad company lawyer, saw the creation of this line as a national priority. Montana's ample resources would boost the nation's economy. At the height of the gold rush, its gulches produced more than $2 million worth of gold a month, generating more tax revenues for the federal government than any other territory and several states. Mining companies needed the railroad to bring in heavy equipment, like stamp mills; the stockmen who followed closely on the heels of the prospectors would need it to transport livestock to and from the range.

The federal government couldn't underwrite the construction of this infrastructure project, so it provided the newly chartered railway company with collateral to attract investors in the form of territory: a land grant of more than thirteen million acres across the West. In Montana, the Northern Pacific would be granted forty square miles of land for every mile of track that it laid, a corridor of alternating 640-acre sections that would extend twenty miles on either side of the rails. The railway would get every odd-numbered section, while the government held on to the even-numbered sections.

Only a small fraction of this land would be used for track and rail yards. The Northern Pacific could, and would, do whatever it wanted with the rest: mine it for coal or iron, or sell millions of acres of forest to lumber companies, to be clear-cut for timber. In 1870, the Northern Pacific's financier, Jay Cooke, launched a mass marketing campaign with newspaper ads and paid editorials to sell bonds backed by the grant lands and the promise of the West—"a vast wilderness waiting like a rich heiress to be appropriated and enjoyed," in the words of the sales prospectus. By 1871, Cooke's campaign had raised nearly $30 million.

The Northern Pacific was granted fifty thousand acres in the Crazy Mountains, land the federal government had taken from the Crow tribe in the 1868 treaty and by subsequent acts of Congress. In June 1883—a year after the tracks were laid through Big Timber—a topographer employed by the Northern Pacific surveyed the Crazies. He climbed to the top of Crazy Peak and built a stone cairn at its summit, which he used to triangulate its height. The topographer was followed later that summer by a geologist, who marveled at the Crazies' rough peaks and beautiful waterfalls, its glaciers and many colorful varieties of igneous rock. "Scenically I have never seen in such small compass, so great variety," he declared.

After several financial collapses—the first of which sank Jay Cooke's bank, triggering the Panic of 1873 and a full-blown depression—the railway company sold off its holdings in the Crazies. The Northern Pacific executed a bill of sale for the land on Duck Creek in 1891 to William Wright, a gold prospector and one-time scout for the railway. Wright disappeared—presumed drowned in the Yellowstone—and the ranch was acquired by Lewis C. Romans, a stockman who succumbed to influenza in 1902. Rick's great-grandparents—Ralph Jarrett and Inez Mendenhall—bought the place in 1908 in an auction arranged by Inez's father, C. B. Mendenhall, who had been named administrator of Romans's estate. Attached to the land were water rights that entitled the Jarretts to draw 168 miner's inches of water from Duck Creek— equivalent to 11.22 gallons per minute. These rights, the most senior of which date to 1884, were older than the state of Montana.

The even-numbered sections of public domain land in the Crazies became national forest in 1907—a patchwork forest, interwoven with sections of private land. Nonetheless, the General Land Office—the precursor to the Bureau of Land Management—surveyed the Crazies in their entirety. In 1916, a deputy surveyor named Ranney Lyman was dispatched to Township 3 North, Range 12 East, which contained within its borders Crazy Peak and Fairview Peak. Lyman's report described forbidding crags and cliffs, lakes like deep-set gems, and above all, the "surpassing grandeur" of the views. The mountains were a national treasure, Lyman wrote. "With very small outlay the scenic grandeur of the Crazy Mountains could be made easily accessible to tourist travel . . . so to spread abroad their incalculable inspirational value to the people of Montana, and to the United States."

It never happened. The Crazies' inspirational value remained locked within the checkerboard. There are sixty-six miles of trails that wind around the trunks of the mountains and high up into the interior, many centuries old. But there are few ways that most people can reach them. There is a public access road to the west of the mountains, and another to the east, in Big Timber, which leads to a campground and a public trailhead. To call it a road is generous. Big Timber Canyon Road is a five-mile stretch of coccyx-bruising, molar-rattling ruts and loose rock, narrow and unpaved.

In 1988, Congress passed the Montana Wilderness Bill, safeguarding 1.4 million acres of the state's public land from development. There was turmoil within the Forest Service over whether public land in the Crazies should be included in the bill. The mountains' untouched, "primeval character" met the essential criteria for true wilderness: "a visitor would find little evidence of man's influence," Forest Service analysts wrote in their report to Congress.

But those same analysts argued against designating the Crazies as protected wilderness, for one reason: the checkerboard. "Because there are over thirty owners of private inholdings, acquisition of all private lands within the boundaries could pose difficulties. It is likely that some of the private landowners would be unwilling to sell," they concluded. Not that it mattered in the end. The Montana Wilderness Bill was vetoed by Ronald Reagan a few months before he left office.

Access to the Crazies shrank with each decade, despite historic right-of-way agreements known as easements—dirt roads, trailheads, and trails on private land. Landowners stopped honoring those agreements in the early 1940s. Locked gates appeared at the entrance to disputed trails. No Trespassing signs replaced old Forest Service signs on trailheads on private land. The people who owned land that sandwiched sections of national forest effectively controlled that, too. A contentious game of chess unfolded on the Crazies' vast checkerboard, pitting private landowners against Forest Service rangers, hunters, Apsáalooke who wanted to fast and pray on Crazy Peak—anyone who wanted to experience the Crazies' surpassing grandeur but couldn't, because of the squares of private land blocking their way.

When the Whidden ranch became Wild Eagle Mountain, any access that hunters and hikers might once have had to the public inholdings within its borders ended. Privacy was paramount to the MacMillans.

Whitney and Betty, who had two children and four grandchildren, built a home on the east fork of Duck Creek and filled it with books. The MacMillans always spent the Fourth of July at the ranch and liked to be there at branding time. It was just like the movies. Riders on horseback lassoed the calves, and then teams of cowhands wrestled them to the ground and dragged them to the fire. Each calf was branded above the left rib with Wild Eagle's brand—*WM*, with a slash. The MacMillans didn't ride or rope or drag or brand the calves themselves, but they enjoyed the spectacle. MacMillan expanded the cattle operation to 750 pairs of mother cows and calves. In 1985, he bought a ranch on the Yellowstone, eleven miles from Wild Eagle, to grow the hundreds of acres of hay needed to feed them.

Whitney and Betty were down-to-earth people: they didn't employ household staff at Wild Eagle. Roxie Hogemark, the ranch manager's wife, stocked the refrigerator before their visits, but the MacMillans washed their own dishes. The MacMillan grandchildren learned how to drive on a 1979 Ford F-250 with manual transmission. Whitney taught them how to fly-fish on the east fork of Duck Creek and on Henry Creek, where an eight-foot waterfall cascaded down from the mountains. In 2013, he built a hunting lodge above Sioux Crossing so they could spend days hunting elk in the Crazies.

Whitney no longer hunted much himself, but he loved to fish. Well into his eighties, he would drop to his hands and knees to crawl through the brush to his favorite fishing holes. He liked to walk down to the stream that ran by the house and fly-fish for trout to cook for his breakfast, cracking a Pabst Blue Ribbon when Betty wasn't looking. MacMillan particularly loved casting for Yellowstone cutthroat trout, a handsome fish with speckled golden-brown skin and a rosy blush along its gills.

Brown trout also swam his streams, but Whitney was less attached to them. Brown trout were a non-native species, European interlopers that had been introduced to the Yellowstone watershed along with rainbow trout, brook trout, and bass in the late nineteenth century by national park guardians to draw sports fishermen to Yellowstone.

Although he didn't have much patience for greenies, as he called environmentalists, MacMillan really did care about the Yellowstone cutthroat trout. He made an effort to improve their aquatic habitat on his ranch. He hired a pond consultant to restore a stream on the upper reaches of Duck Creek. The consultant built plywood overhangs over degraded streambanks, then sodded and seeded them with smooth brome, to attract the insects trout liked to eat. This was not a success: the plywood overhangs tended to collapse into the stream, and smooth brome, a non-native plant, lacked the deep root structure necessary to stabilize the banks.

Over the years, MacMillan noticed that the Yellowstone cutthroat trout population was dwindling, and this troubled him. The cutthroat trout had once been abundant in his streams and he had caught plenty of them for breakfast. By the 2000s, MacMillan was reeling in more and more brown trout. He wondered if the interlopers were edging out his beloved cutthroats.

In July 2007, he met Carol Endicott, a biologist with Montana's Department of Fish, Wildlife, and Parks. Endicott was working with ranchers to restore degraded streams through a landowner-incentive program that included matching some of the costs of restoring or fencing the streams with state grant money. The man who built MacMillan's artificial pond knew Endicott and brokered the introduction.

MacMillan was cagey. He wanted to know why he should work with the government. Endicott, who didn't believe in getting state money for rich people who could reach into their own pockets to clean up their streams, told him he didn't have to. Nevertheless, he proceeded to spend the day showing her around Wild Eagle's creeks and streams.

"My ranch manager says the greenies are telling us to fence all the cows off the streams. This is a cow operation, not a fish operation," MacMillan told Endicott, pulling the truck over by Duck Creek. They got out and walked past some grazing Black Angus. Cows had trampled the creek and eaten away all the grass. The banks were badly eroded and muddy, the water cloudy with sediment. MacMillan took a long look, then turned to Endicott. "We have to fence this," he said.

It had been twenty years since MacMillan had visited this particular part of his ranch, he said. Wild Eagle Mountain was a very large ranch, after all, and MacMillan never got to spend as much time there as he would have liked. Endicott waded into the creek to take a temperature reading and was startled by how warm the water was: seventy-seven degrees Fahrenheit, dangerously high for a cold-water fish like Yellowstone cutthroat trout.

After the tour, the two went up to the house and MacMillan cracked open two beers. Endicott, who was in uniform and driving a state truck, passed on the PBR. But it was all good: any ice between MacMillan and the state greenie was broken. He told Endicott that he was open to implementing trout conservation measures and improving the streams on his ranch, so long as they didn't interfere with his cow operation—or his privacy.

Whitney MacMillan was a conservative in the literal sense: he wanted to keep the place the way he had found it, and he had found it with those Yellowstone cutthroat trout. The brown trout, an aggressive, bullying sort of fish, were the usurpers; MacMillan did not want to be the one to allow those barbarians through the gate. From that point on, the rule on Wild Eagle Mountain Ranch was that MacMillans might fish for Yellowstone cutthroat trout, but they could only eat the brown trout.

Endicott proposed dosing MacMillan's creeks with rotenone, a plant-derived piscicide once used for fishing by Indigenous people, to rid Wild Eagle's watershed of the invasive trout species. That would clear the slate. Then, after a few years, they could reintroduce the Yellowstone cutthroat trout. MacMillan didn't like the idea. Rotenone would kill all the fish, not just the brown trout. Any proposal that would prevent him from fishing his creeks with his grandchildren and great-grandchildren during his brief visits to Wild Eagle was a nonstarter.

One of Whitney's grandchildren suggested that he contact a college friend of his from Dartmouth named Adam Sepulveda, who was working toward a PhD in ecology at the University of Montana. Sepulveda's focus was aquatics. MacMillan gave the young ecologist a call. "He said, 'I've got some questions about the fish,'" Sepulveda recalled. "'Would you mind coming out to take a look?'"

Sepulveda came out for a look, and a decade-long research project was born. While he was finishing his PhD, he began sampling the lower and upper streams to determine whether the brown trout were altering the food web in a way that was killing off the native Yellowstone cutthroat trout. He continued his research after he went to work for Montana's Fish, Wildlife, and Parks Department, then began publishing his findings with his colleague Robert Al-Chokhachy as an aquatic ecologist with the US Geological Survey's Northern Rocky Mountain Science Center in Bozeman. Every July and October, Sepulveda visited Wild Eagle to sample fish from both groups, comparing their growth and survival rates and pumping their stomachs to see what they'd been eating—a nonlethal procedure called gastric lavage.

Betty put out a platter of Ritz crackers and dip after Sepulveda's gastric lavage sessions and told the young man to call her Buddy, her family nickname. During the MacMillans' annual visits in July, Sepulveda and his family were invited to dinner parties and family gatherings. One afternoon, Sepulveda's three-year-old son became fascinated by a papier-mâché sculpture of a golden eagle in the MacMillans' home. As the child groped the eagle, MacMillan mentioned that it had been a gift from a Chinese leader, then tut-tutted as the boy's parents lunged to stop him. "I can't remember if it was Whitney or Betty, but it was just like, 'That's fine! Have at it, we don't care about that thing,'" Sepulveda recalled.

When the windmill controversy began heating up, MacMillan's thoughts turned to the Yellowstone cutthroat trout. "He asked every which way to find some way that the wind farms are going to affect the trout," Sepulveda said. "And it was like, 'Sorry.'" As a government scientist—a federal employee—there were certain limitations on the kinds of questions he was authorized to answer. But no. Wind turbines, however unsightly, would not harm the finned inhabitants of Wild Eagle Mountain Ranch.

By then, Sepulveda's work on Wild Eagle had expanded to a wider-ranging examination of environmental factors affecting the MacMillans' chunk of the greater Yellowstone watershed, including studying its creeks for signs of climate change–induced drought.

For millennia, snowpack in the Crazies had functioned as a water tower for the rangeland below, storing up water over long winters in its frozen form, then gradually releasing it as snowmelt when the seasons changed. Duck Creek swelled every spring with gushes of deep, cold water flowing down the south slope of Fairview Peak. The snowpack continued to provide fresh water through the summer, gradually melting as the temperatures rose.

But in Montana's warming climate, more winter and early spring precipitation took the form of rain, not snow. Rain melted the snowpack, which caused flooding in the spring and drained the mountain water tower. By summer, the rivers had become sluggish, with low streamflow and higher water temperatures—stressful conditions for native cold-water fish species. In the summer of 2016, the spread of a deadly parasite that thrives in warmer, slower waters would kill off more than ten thousand mountain whitefish in the upper Yellowstone River, engulfing its banks with the reek of rotting fish.

MacMillan touched lightly on the topic of energy and the environment in *Common-Sense Business*. "Energy consumption, especially of a polluting type, is, of course, part of our problem," he wrote. "More sustainable solutions are therefore sought on every front . . . Wind and solar power are gradually gaining greater acceptance."

But when it came to Wild Eagle Mountain Ranch and its environs, wind energy was quite simply unacceptable. "Wild Eagle has a direct and substantial interest in the environmental effects that will result from the Project," MacMillan's attorney huffed in a 2009 letter to the Department of Natural Resources and Conservation, opposing the land lease to Coyote Wind. Furthermore, Wild Eagle noted, the DNRC had already leased that parcel of land—to Devon Energy Production Company, for oil and gas exploration. "Presumably, by entering into the oil and gas lease, the DNRC expects that the lessee will develop the property for its oil and gas potential."

As it happened, Whitney MacMillan had just signed his own oil and gas lease with Devon Energy Production Company. Fracking fever had swept Sweet Grass County. Energy companies were suddenly very interested in the shale formations that lay thousands of feet below the county's surface, shale that no one had ever thought was worth much until hydraulic fracturing came along. Landmen swamped the county clerk's office, looking up deeds to oil and gas rights. Sherry Bjorndal, the county clerk and recorder, set up extra chairs for them in the hall. At a state land lease auction in September 2008, mineral leases that had been valued at just $1.50 an acre only a few years before sold for as much as $251.

The money the fracking outfits were offering "made you stand up and pay attention," a rancher named Matt Cremer told a reporter that December, after the first exploratory hole for a shale gas well in Sweet Grass County was drilled on his land in Melville, a small community north of Big Timber in the eastern Crazies. Some of Cremer's neighbors worried that the fracking would contaminate their groundwater, but there was nothing they could do about it—it was private land, after all, and fracking was minimally regulated by the state.

Whitney MacMillan's lease with Devon Energy gave it oil and gas rights to twenty thousand acres of his ranch, in exchange for undisclosed royalties. It seems baffling that MacMillan would even consider allowing a drilling rig on his land, given the impact on his open vistas, wildlife habitat, and so on, to say nothing of his beloved Yellowstone cutthroat trout. The reason may have something to do with the complex nature of deeded mineral rights. When MacMillan bought Roger Whidden's ranch back in the late 1970s, he didn't secure full title to the riches that might lie beneath its surface. The land's mineral rights were split among multiple past owners and their descendants. The MacMillans owned just 25 percent.

In 2008, Whidden's adult children executed an oil and gas lease with Devon Energy in exchange for one-sixth of any royalties that might be produced from it. The descendants of another past landowner entered a similar lease arrangement. If the other mineral rights holders chose to lease the land to Devon, there wasn't much MacMillan could do about it.

So, a few months after those oil and gas leases were inked, MacMillan signed one of his own. MacMillan did not want frackers on Wild Eagle Mountain Ranch, according to his ranch manager, Jim Hogemark. But it was just common sense: if the well drillers were going to come, the MacMillans might as well get their share of the money. "They're going to be on your property doing their mineral stuff anyway; you might as well go along with it. You're not going to stop them," Hogemark explained.

And yet. Surely a man with MacMillan's boundless resources could have found a way to eliminate the threat of shale gas exploration on his land. Or perhaps he knew how unlikely it was that there'd ever be any actual drilling. At the height of Big Timber's shale speculation, a petroleum engineer on the state's Board of Oil and Gas voiced his skepticism that any of those speculative leases would pan out. Eighty holes had been drilled in Sweet Grass County since 1915; every one of them was dry as dust.

Absent the risk of actual drilling, an oil and gas lease was a very nice source of mailbox money. And Whitney MacMillan wasn't one to leave money on the table. He collected over $25,000 in USDA crop subsidies for the hay and barley he raised for his cattle between 1996 and 1999 on Wild Eagle Mountain Ranch. He also applied for, and received, nearly $290,000 in conservation subsidies for another ranch he owned: the fifty-thousand-acre PN Ranch in north-central Montana, where he was restoring an 1866 fort and a ghost town called Judith Landing.

Whitney MacMillan was not a romantic. Practicality—a cornerstone of the Cargill Way's four P's—was a fundamental driver of his business decisions, and Wild Eagle Mountain was a business above all. It was a working cattle ranch, a distinction MacMillan insisted on, lest anyone confuse it for a trophy ranch like the one next door.

Russell Gordy's redoubt bordered Wild Eagle Mountain on the west, matching MacMillan section for section and then some. The MacMillans called it Texas. On Wild Eagle Mountain, they joked that they had the Texan to the west and the Italian—Lodovico Antinori, the scion of an Italian wine dynasty—to the east. Marchese Antinori owned the Morris Place Ranch, an old homestead on the eastern flank of the Crazies, where he built an elegantly rustic compound with logs reclaimed from an old sheep-shearing barn.

The MacMillans weren't entirely unaware of the Andersons. Sometime in 2010, one of Whitney's lawyers reached out to Alfred to ask if he'd be interested in selling his ranch. Alfred told the lawyer he didn't think so, and that was the end of it.

After the met tower went up on their ranch, Alfred and Dorothy began thinking about the many ways it could be improved with the money they'd get for their wind. You could always upgrade fences, it seemed like, and the Andersons had several miles of fence that needed fixing. The corrals were rundown, too. Alfred had heard about the corrals that a professor of animal sciences at Colorado State University had designed, with curved fences and chutes and diagonal sorting pens that didn't spook the cows. The professor down there, Temple Grandin, was altogether different than some people, but she was quite a livestock handler and her corrals worked out good for the cattle. Alfred decided he would like to buy some of Temple Grandin's blueprints and build those corrals.

The more you thought about the money, the more ways you could think to spend it. There had never been a machine shop on the ranch; Alfred could build one. He supposed he could get better livestock, too. Alfred bred his heifers to a $4,000 bull he bought from a breeder named John Michael in Livingston. He was a good bull for $4,000. But $10,000 would get you a bull with superior genetics, a high-growth sire. If Alfred could service his cows with a $10,000 bull, they'd throw calves with better slaughter value.

Wind energy was clean—no pollution, dust, or smog. Alfred thought it was all right. The sheep and cows could eat grass right under the turbines; wouldn't make any difference to them. And the tax revenue would be all right for the county—Alfred had that in the back of his mind the whole time. Big Timber didn't have near the business it once did. When Alfred graduated high school in 1950, Big Timber had two or three grocery stores, a creamery, four farm machinery dealers, six car lots. Now there was just one place to buy groceries—the Big T, which was about going out of business, it seemed. As for car lots, there wasn't even one, and no farm machinery shops, neither. There was a John Deere in Livingston; if you rode green, you could get a tractor part there. But if you had a Case or a Massey Ferguson and that broke down, well, then you might have to drive all the way to Billings or Belgrade.

Alfred and Dorothy wanted Kevin to own the ranch someday. When he wasn't working on the ranch, Kevin worked two jobs. He had his own business trucking livestock in his semi, and he drove a snowplow for the state Department of Transportation. When it was gusting at seventy-five miles per hour, Kevin went out and put barriers and closure signs on the interstate, to keep semitrucks from tipping over on that hill by Livingston, which happened sometimes in high winds. The Andersons also relied on two hired men from Peru, sheepherders who lived in separate campers on the ranch. They were hardworking and kind, and often cooked lunch for Dorothy and Alfred on the hot plate she had set up in the main room. Sometimes, they baked a cake in the oven, which was tucked away in a small room down the hall. The home had no kitchen to speak of.

The Andersons never thought of themselves as poor. However bad things got, they had the land. You could weld up busted machinery to keep it going. You could throw another plank or an old pole on the brokedown corral. You could even sell your cattle if it came to that. But you'd keep your ground. You could still farm it and sell the grain and the hay. Yah, you'd keep working, that would be it. You'd keep working till the day you died.

7

HIGH ON THE HORSE IN BIG TIMBER

February 20, 2019
Park County Courthouse
Livingston, Montana

JAN ENGWIS, *Cross-examination*:
Q: Mr. Engwis, isn't it true that in 2014 you sued Sweet Grass County
over Mr. Jarrett getting a letter of support for this wind project?
MR. ENGWIS: No.
Q: You didn't?
MR. ENGWIS: What we sued—
Q: Okay. What did you sue over?
MR. ENGWIS: Do you want me to answer or not?

DECEMBER 6, 2013
SWEET GRASS COUNTY ANNEX BUILDING
BIG TIMBER, MONTANA

Lindsey Erin Kroskob, staff reporter for the *Big Timber Pioneer*, arrived
early at the Sweet Grass County Annex for the eleven o'clock county
commission meeting about Rick Jarrett's wind farm. Although she was
sometimes the only member of the public who showed up at commission
meetings, it was important for the *Pioneer* to be there—Kroskob really
believed that. She was passionate about community journalism, which
was why she had left a job at a big daily newspaper in Wyoming for the
Pioneer, a small-town paper that published just once a week.

Big Timber residents relied on the *Pioneer* to tell them the score of
the Lady Herders' volleyball match against Park City, the game count
on opening weekend of deer season, and which Big Timber resident

had been charged with conspiracy to distribute methamphetamine. The *Pioneer* was full of news they could use. It published the weekly lunch menu at the Hospitality House Senior Center, and On the Record, a summary of every call that had come into the sheriff's office: a drunk driver on First Avenue, a door-to-door salesman being a nuisance, a cow loose on Old Boulder Road. Obituaries were a staple. When a Big Timber rancher fed her herd for the last time, you read about it in the *Pioneer*.

Given that it had been twelve below when she left the *Pioneer*'s office, Kroskob wasn't expecting to see a lot of people at the annex that morning. But there were a good half dozen milling around the meeting room in addition to the three commissioners. Bill Wallace, Susie Mosness, and Bob Faw sat in their swivel chairs at the head of the gray Formica-topped conference table. Each had their own walnut nameplate set out in front of them. A framed copy of the Declaration of Independence hung on the wall between the American and Montana state flags, whose spear-tipped poles brushed the acoustic tiles of the low ceiling. Wallace, Mosness, and Faw were all Republican. Sweet Grass County hadn't turned blue since Franklin Delano Roosevelt swept Montana in 1936.

Sweet Grass County, which occupies a total area of 1,862 square miles, had about 3,600 residents. The commissioners oversaw its annual budget, set and levied taxes, maintained roads and bridges. You could find them in the meeting room most mornings, sipping coffee and hashing over the cost of new grandstands at the fairgrounds or the state of the county roads, which needed more gravel and some mowing to keep them from drifting when the snow came. The county agent might stop by to share some gossip from the Sweet Grass County Stockgrowers and Wool Growers annual banquet and an update on when they'd be selling the wool pool. Susan Metcalf, the county school superintendent, sometimes brought in treats like Norwegian Christmas cookies or sour cream drops. Metcalf wrote a weekly cooking column for the *Pioneer*— Cooking on the Long Trot.

Anyone could stop by and visit with the commissioners—their door was always open. But when Rick had come by earlier in the week to talk about his wind farm and the permits he'd be needing, the commissioners told him they'd have to schedule a formal meeting and notice it forty-eight hours in advance. That's what today was: a discussion of the proposed Crazy Mountain Wind project.

Kroskob scoped the room. Wearing a wool hat with earflaps and smelling like cows, Rick Jarrett stood by the window, talking with Marty Wilde. Lindsey first met Marty when she started at the *Pioneer* and Coyote Wind was in the news. He always made her think of a used-car salesman—just in the way he was so gregarious and talkative. Talking to Marty, Kroskob always felt like she was being sold something. Jan Engwis sat on the opposite side of the conference table with Jim Hogemark, the ranch manager for Wild Eagle, the MacMillan place. Jim was two months into his winter beard. You could mark the seasons in Big Timber by a rancher's beard. Jim grew one every fall and shaved it off in the spring. Come summer, the patch of forehead covered by the brim of his tractor cap would be several shades paler than the rest of his face. There was a third man seated on that side of the table, but Kroskob didn't recognize him. He was tall and heavyset, with a swoop of gray hair that curled at the base of his neck, and smooth, uncallused hands.

Jami Jarrett Moody hurried in, carrying the cold on her coat. She had come straight from the courthouse on Front Street, and was dressed in her office clothes, earrings dangling. Jami said a quick hello to Page Dringman, the Sweet Grass County planner. Page, who projected an air of brisk efficiency, was married to Pat Dringman, the county attorney—Jami's boss. Kroskob found a seat next to Sherry Bjorndal, the clerk and recorder, and got out her notebook. The room was quiet; no small talk beyond some discussion about how it really was cold that morning.

"Okay, this is a meeting to talk about Crazy Mountain Wind," Mosness began. The commission's longest-serving member, Mosness had founded Little Timber Quilts & Candy in the old Solberg store on McLeod Street. She sold the store in 2007 before running for office, but the new owners had kept everything the same, from the bolts of colorful fabric on the shelves to the glass jars full of bridge mix and chocolate-covered jellies.

Mosness asked everyone to go around the table and introduce themselves. This was a formality. Susie Mosness knew who everyone was. Jim Hogemark was practically family: Susie's husband Gary's grandmother had married Jim's grandfather after his first wife passed away. Jan Engwis was next—another family connection. Jan's ranch once belonged to Gary's Aunt Edith and Uncle Elmer, who had a potato farm there. Susie and Gary knew Jan and Karen from the classic-car circuit. Both couples collected old cars and trucks, though Susie's collection couldn't hold a candle to Jan's. She had visited his workshop, which occupied the first level of his home. It was full of gorgeous vehicles—vintage trucks and rare Corvettes, including a 1965 fire-engine-red coupe with all its original parts that had cost close to $200,000.

Mosness hadn't been introduced to the tall man sitting next to Jan, but she knew who he was before he said, "David Chesnoff, resident." When you build a big house right on the Yellowstone, people are going to find out who you are. Chesnoff's sprawling timber-and-stone lodge was a prominent landmark on the river, visible from I-90. A few years back, the Las Vegas attorney and his wife had petitioned the commissioners for permission to name the private road they had built to their lodge. Sanctuary River Lane, they called it. The locals called it Cabela's on the Yellowstone, for its resemblance to the timber-and-stone-clad superstores of the outdoor-sporting goods chain.

"Thanks, everybody, for coming," Mosness said, once Sherry had recorded all the names in the minutes. "I think we'll just turn it over to Rick and Marty."

Rick hadn't expected to see so many people. When he had stopped by earlier in the week, he just wanted to give the commissioners an update on the wind farm. "It wasn't as big a deal, I don't think, today," he said, with a nervous laugh.

"Why don't you just go ahead and talk about what your project entails and how big it is," Mosness prompted.

Marty stepped in. "So, I'm happy to give you kind of an overview of the project," he said. The overview began with a short history of Marty's work in wind development. Almost everywhere there was a wind farm in Montana was a place where Marty Wilde once stood, according to Marty, so this took a few minutes.

"That fast-forwards us to the project on Rick's land," Marty said. "Coyote Wind, that was the original name of the project out there." Coyote Wind didn't get built. There had been pushback from some of the folks who lived around there. "There's different sorts of folks, you know, and Texas guys that own half a township tend to have a different opinion than a guy who's trying to make a living on two thousand acres," he said.

Marty didn't mention the successful lawsuit that the Texas guy, Jan Engwis, and Hogemark's boss Whitney MacMillan had brought against the Montana DNRC and Coyote Wind. The reason Coyote Wind failed, he told the commissioners now, was that the Spanish company that bought Coyote Wind couldn't secure a contract with NorthWestern Energy, Montana's primary electricity provider.

NorthWestern didn't like giving contracts to wind developers, Marty said. NorthWestern owned Colstrip: a sprawling coal-fired power plant in Colstrip, Montana, named for the coal that was first strip-mined there by the Northern Pacific Railway to fuel its steam locomotives. North-Western really liked coal, Marty said. Mostly, NorthWestern liked coal because the utility could make more money from the coal-fired power plants it owned than if it bought renewable power from someone like Marty Wilde. The capital that the utility had invested in Colstrip was factored into the rates it was allowed to charge consumers, which translated into a higher profit margin and increased revenues for its shareholders. "They don't like wind and they really don't like wind that they don't own," Marty said.

But now NorthWestern had no choice: it had to buy power from small wind and solar farms, thanks to the new Community Renewable Energy Program (CREP), which Montana's state legislature had enacted as part of the Renewable Power Production and Rural Economic Development Act. Under CREP, NorthWestern Energy was obligated to purchase approximately sixty-five megawatts of electricity every year from renewable-energy projects developed in Montana—small, homegrown projects, no larger than twenty-five megawatts.

So far, NorthWestern Energy hadn't come close to meeting that benchmark. Rick's wind farm could change that. Marty and Rick had retooled Coyote Wind as a twenty-five-megawatt CREP called Crazy Mountain Wind. Crazy Mountain Wind would be a much smaller wind farm than its predecessor, with just fourteen turbines, set entirely on private land. Marty applied to have Crazy Mountain Wind certified as a CREP the year the program went into effect, 2012. The project almost won the coveted certification, but failed because Marty couldn't show NorthWestern how he was going to finance construction on his own. A twenty-five-megawatt wind facility would cost about $58 million. Marty didn't have that kind of money: no independent wind developer did.

But just a year later, in 2013, scrappy wind prospectors like Marty Wilde got a lucky break: Congress resurrected the federal production tax credit for wind projects, to help lure investment from the private sector. Every megawatt-hour produced by a wind or solar farm would be worth a $23 tax credit to the equity investor—the big player that provided the capital to build it. Say a corporate investor provided the financing for an eighty-megawatt wind farm, and that wind farm produced 280,000 megawatt-hours of electricity per year. That investor would collect $6.44 million in tax credits per year—$64.4 million over a decade.

Very few corporate investors had pockets deep enough, or tax bills high enough, to take advantage of a tax credit that size. But investment wizards at banks like J. P. Morgan saw how the wind energy production tax credit could be used as a financial instrument. They calculated what the tax savings would be on the revenues from a wind farm once it was fully operational, then picked the wind project whose average megawatt-hours would translate into enough production tax credits to cover, or at least defray, their tax bill. They became equity investors—investors whose capital built the wind farm, entitling them to partial ownership.

As part of the deal, the equity investor got to pocket most of the profits from the wind farm for the first decade. After a decade, 95 percent of the revenues from the wind farm would begin flowing to the original owner, but the equity partner would continue to collect a piece of the profits every year for the life of the project.

If you wanted to write off millions of dollars of taxes while earning annual returns on your investment—all while draped in the green mantle of environmental stewardship—then you wanted to put a big chunk of money in a wind farm. It was all upside for the bank, so long as the wind farm actually got built. That was the catch: the wind farm had to produce the energy its developers promised, over two decades or more, or the equity investor would lose its stake. Wind farms were not junk bonds; no one made money off a failed project. If a wind farm didn't deliver the power promised in its contract with a utility like NorthWestern Energy, its equity owner would have to cover the shortfall out of its own pocket. Consequently, banks that wanted to take advantage of the production tax credit were very picky about which renewable projects they would invest in, putting their money on the safest bets.

Big financial institutions loved the federal production tax credit. So did corporate behemoths like Apple and Amazon and Facebook, which began figuring out ways to get in on wind energy investment. So did some of the most powerful Republicans in Washington, DC. The self-declared father of the wind energy production tax credit was none other than Chuck Grassley, the hard-right Republican senator from Iowa, who pushed through a package of nearly $15.5 billion in federal tax incentives for wind and other forms of "Iowa-grown" renewable energy like ethanol when he chaired the Senate Finance Committee.

Marty didn't mention any of that.

"So, that brings us to Crazy Mountain Wind," he said.

Just over a month ago, he said, NorthWestern Energy had put out a fresh request for CREPs—proposals for small Montana-grown renewable-energy projects. And this time around, Crazy Mountain Wind grabbed the brass ring. NorthWestern had chosen the project as its next CREP. The CREP designation would secure a guaranteed power purchase agreement, good for twenty-five years.

Marty was confident that with the power purchase agreement in hand—and the juicy incentive of the federal production tax credit—they'd have no trouble securing the capital investment from J. P. Morgan or Morgan Stanley or General Electric Capital to get Crazy Mountain Wind built. After all, Marty had ten years of solid wind data on Rick's ranch to show investors, not to mention exhaustive environmental studies—all that work on birds and bats he'd done for the state on Coyote Wind.

"Do you have a contract with NorthWestern Energy?" Faw asked. Elected in November 2012, Faw was the most junior member of the Sweet Grass County Commission. He had just returned from a training session for new commissioners in Helena.

"Yeah. I mean, Monday, we're signing a power purchase agreement.

That's what we refer to my contract as. They agree to purchase power at a given rate for twenty-five years," Marty said.

There was one small technicality: according to the wording of his contract with NorthWestern, Crazy Mountain Wind would have to be formally declared a CREP by the Montana Public Service Commission (the PSC), a quasi-judicial body of five elected officials that regulated the state's utilities, for the power purchase agreement to go into effect. Marty didn't mention that.

He asked what kind of permits he'd need to start moving dirt on Rick's ranch so that Crazy Mountain Wind could qualify for the tax credit before the year ended. Marty was pleasantly surprised by Mosness's answer: none. If construction affected county roads, he'd have to apply for an encroachment permit. But beyond that, there were no required applications, no special permits. Rick could do pretty much whatever he wanted on his land. Beyond Big Timber city limits, the county had no zoning regulations. The county commissioners had no authority over private property. They couldn't stop Rick Jarrett from putting up a windmill, any more than they could have stopped Matt Cremer from drilling a shale gas well on his land in 2009. Not that anyone had tried.

Bob Faw wanted to know why Marty was hurrying so fast to get his foot in the door. "This might affect a lot of people," he said in a slow drawl.

Before getting into county government, Faw had owned the Chevrolet-Oldsmobile dealership on McLeod Street, across the street from Little Timber Quilts & Candy. Faw ran that dealership for more than twenty years. Then General Motors started sending guys with briefcases. They told Faw that if he wanted to keep selling Tahoes and Suburbans, he'd have to sell little cars, too. Nobody wanted little cars in Big Timber. But GM thought it knew better than Bob Faw. He'd bet you that half the time those GM guys had nothing but their lunch in their briefcases.

Faw sold the dealership in 2007 and turned his attention to the political system. He and his wife, Judy, moved to Helena for the legislative session so they could sit in at sessions at the statehouse and see for themselves what was wrong with government. Folks told him that if he really wanted to make a difference, he should start at the ground level, and the county commission was the closest thing to it. When a commissioner seat opened up in 2012, Faw threw his hat in the ring, facing off against two Republican opponents. There were no Democratic candidates.

Faw didn't like zoning, but he didn't like the sound of Rick Jarrett's wind farm, either. At commissioner school the other week, they were talking about the big wind farm up north in Shelby—Glacier Wind Farm, it was called. He had seen pictures of that thing, windmills with generators the size of railroad flatcars. "I'd actually like to see it go to a vote so that the people would have some input on how this is supposed to look in this community," Faw said.

Jan Engwis couldn't contain himself any longer. "Can I shortcut this a little bit?" he said, his voice tight with emotion, cheeks reddening above his bristly mustache. "I have a question, and then I'd like to speak a little bit."

Engwis's border war with Rick Jarrett had been settled earlier that year. After a court-ordered mediation, Engwis paid Rick $35,000 and an amended deed was executed, giving him full title over that disputed strip of land. But he was still seething over the surveyors, the drilling, the core holes on his land. Jarrett had certainly acted maliciously—Engwis was convinced of it.

In his own telling, Jan Engwis was a humble son of the Midwest, a self-made man smitten by the beauty of Montana's Crazy Mountains. People like Rick Jarrett, maybe they didn't notice it anymore. "But to a flatland boy who came out here and is still awestruck by it, it's absolutely irreplaceable," he'd tell the judge in 2019.

Engwis was born in 1946 in the central Michigan town of Midland, the home of Dow Chemical and a major manufacturing plant. Agent Orange and napalm were produced for the Vietnam War there. After graduating Midland High School (its yearbook was the *Chemic*) in 1964, Engwis attended a nearby community college, then went on to earn a bachelor's degree in police administration and public safety from Michigan State University. Jan worked as a Michigan police officer for seven years.

By 1975, he had become president of the Police Officers Association in the university town of Ann Arbor. POA President Engwis had strong views on crime, law enforcement, and a controversial topic of the day: hollow-point, or dumdum, bullets. Ann Arbor cops were allowed to buy hollow-point bullets with their ammunition allowances. Civil rights groups protested: the bullets expand on impact, tearing bodies apart from within. Under pressure, Ann Arbor's police department agreed to stop using the bullets, but Engwis wasn't happy about it. "Factual information surrounding the effect of this type of handgun bullet on the human body remains inconclusive at this time," he said in a statement. "Certainly conjecture and emotionalism have taken the place of necessary scientific documentation."

Engwis moved to Golden, Colorado. He worked for four years as a training specialist at the Colorado Law Enforcement Training Academy, then took a job as an administrative officer in the district attorney's office. In the 1980s, Engwis changed careers, joining a contracting company that specialized in explosives and rocks—exploding rocks for major projects like widening interstate highways and stabilizing rock walls by cabling and bolting them.

Jan and Karen Engwis never responded to my letters or phone messages, or the note I handed to Karen's son on a fruitless visit to their ranch. So, I can't explain how he made the leap from law enforcement court administrator to blasting company mogul.

But Engwis would tell a version of his rocks-to-riches success story to the court in 2019. A small construction company called Yenter was in search of an administrator. "It was a mom-and-pop operation. They promised me some shareholding, share involvement, if I came to work for them, basically at subsistence. I did that and worked at the company for fifteen additional years," Engwis said.

He began buying out the Yenter family, acquiring shares in the company through a multiyear purchase plan. Under his leadership, business boomed. By 1995, Engwis was the company's majority owner and Yenter was running through a million pounds of explosives a year on its blasting runs, with projects across the country.

"Jan didn't blast, he was just a good businessman. When I first started working for Yenter, they were making $500,000 gross. Jan doubled it to $1,000,000," Bill Roberts told me. Roberts, who joined Yenter in 1989 when he was in his early twenties, worked his way up from laborer to blaster to project foreman. He described himself as Engwis's yes-man. "He'd tell me, 'I've got a meeting—I don't want you to say anything un-

less I ask you a question, and if I ask you a question, the answer is yes,'"
Roberts said.

Engwis gave his employees bonuses when year-end profits were high,
a practice Roberts believed was motivated by a desire to avoid paying
taxes ("He hated paying taxes to the government back then"), but bristled when they asked for time off. Engwis never took vacations himself.
"What's to see?" he'd say. When Roberts asked to take four days for his
honeymoon, Engwis was incensed. "I really had to battle him for it,"
Roberts recalled. "He didn't even come to my wedding, he was so pissed."

In the 1990s, Engwis offered Roberts and a handful of other senior Yenter employees the opportunity to buy the company from him
through an employee stock ownership plan—an ESOP. Roberts and
his colleagues would acquire shares of the company over a period of six
years, assuming full responsibility for all bonding and loans, and paying
Engwis up front for his equity stake in Yenter.

"That's how Jan ended up in Montana with about $12 million of our
money," said Roberts, who became a copresident of the company after
Engwis's departure. "It was a really good deal for Jan—that's why he
pushed for it. We took out company loans, but we were all personally
responsible for those loans. Our wives had to sign, too." But the deal was
fair, he said. Roberts and his fellow employee-stockowners paid off the
loans and made good money until the construction industry collapsed
during the 2008 recession. He eventually left the blasting business to become an undertaker. By then, Jan Engwis had embarked on a new chapter, as a gentleman rancher in Big Timber. He soon became a familiar
presence in the Sweet Grass County annex building.

Engwis had a question for Mosness about Rick Jarrett and his wind
farm. "Do these folks still have the unequivocal endorsement of you,
Mrs. Chairman, and you, Mr. Wallace, that was expressed to them in
writing last year?"

"Yes, we have that letter right here," Mosness said, looking through
her papers.

About a year before, Rick had stopped by the annex to ask the commissioners for a letter of support for a new wind project on his land.
Coyote Wind had died and been reborn as Crazy Mountain Wind by

then, and Marty told Rick that a letter of support from the county could help attract financers.

None of the commissioners saw anything particularly controversial about Rick's request. The Sweet Grass County Commission was pro-business. Anything that would help grow the local economy was seen as a good thing. Mosness wrote the letter of support, and all the commissioners signed it. They didn't issue a formal notice first, announcing their intentions to draft such a letter; they just did it. Now Engwis was waving a copy at Susie.

"Let me read this last paragraph of your letter, if you don't mind," he said. "'This letter expresses our support for the project. We look forward to a good working relationship with Crazy Mountain Wind on responsible energy development in the county and wish you success in the future.' Well, that's wonderful. Thank you for speaking for me in advance and in private. I do not condone this. I do not accept this. I will not tolerate this."

The more he spoke, the angrier Engwis became. It was absurd. It was abject idiocy. The wind farm would devalue his private property. Construction of the wind farm would affect his ability to get to and from his property. All on a whim, without a cloud in the sky, because Marty Wilde had come in and asked for it ten minutes ago. It was unimaginable. The commissioners had made a mockery of the process by writing that letter.

"This is a sham. Just like every other wind project," Engwis said, his voice rising. "The people who come here, that buy multimillion-dollar properties, people that spend big money here, the tourists that come here, don't come here for the windmills. They don't want to see Rick's windmills out there. And I don't, either."

Commissioner Wallace shifted uncomfortably on his swivel chair. He had been there that morning in 2012 when Rick stopped by. Here comes a rancher walking in, someone they've known forever, asking for a letter. It was just a simple one-page little thing, something they'd do for anyone, fully noticed in the minutes. They had signed a similar letter of support for the Sibanye-Stillwater mining company when it was building the new East Boulder mine. No one objected. The Stillwater mine accounted for 41 percent of Sweet Grass County's tax base. They mined platinum-group metals for one little piece of a car part there. If anybody figured out how to make catalytic converters with something other than palladium, Sweet Grass County was toast.

It kept Wallace up some nights, worrying what would happen when Sibanye-Stillwater went away. The mine's lease was up in 2044. He didn't like the idea of giant windmills near the Crazies any more than Jan Engwis did. Wallace owned a gamebird farm on Otter Creek. The trophy ranchers who didn't want to see Rick's windmills were the same folks who bought the pheasants he raised for bird hunting. But he believed in private property rights. That framed Declaration of Independence hanging up there, it said something about the right to property, Wallace thought.

Marty took it all in with a serene expression. He wasn't ruffled by Engwis's outburst. He attended a lot of county commission meetings. The tense atmosphere in the conference room was nothing new. Almost every county meeting on wind that he had attended over the years had featured brisk discussion. Sometimes there was actual yelling, he said now, with a chuckle. There wasn't a whole lot of in-between folks when it came to wind energy—you were for it or against it. "That's one of the advantages of working on private land," he said.

Page Dringman, the county planner, reminded everyone that Sweet Grass County did have a citizen-initiated zoning process. If the majority of landowners in one part of the county agreed that they didn't want any wind development, they could start the zoning process to ban windmills there. But you couldn't use it to zone your neighbor: everyone had to agree to the same restrictions on their land. Page noted that she had been mentioning this citizen-initiated zoning option on and off for about five years now, ever since local landowners began objecting to the first wind farm, Coyote Wind. No one had ever taken her up on it.

Only one community in Sweet Grass County had embraced zoning. Back in the 1970s, a group of ranchers in the unincorporated community of Melville banded together to create a zoning district to prevent ticky-tacky subdivisions in the eastern Crazies. Page knew all about it. Page was a Van Cleve on her mother's side, and the Van Cleves had been in that part of the Crazies longer than Montana had been a state. Page's great-great-grandfather Paul Ledyard Van Cleve Sr. came to Big Timber in 1885 and built a thirty-six-room lodge with a tennis court and a polo field at the foot of Porcupine Butte, where he entertained Chief Plenty Coups, Calamity Jane, and Liver-Eating Johnson. Page's great-grandfather Paul Ledyard Van Cleve Jr. founded a famous dude ranch called the Lazy K Bar high in the mountains. The Van Cleves had recently sold the Lazy K Bar to a private equity billionaire for $9 million, but Page's branch of the family, the Carroccias, still owned the Sweet Grass Ranch, another guest ranch in the Crazies.

Page's grandmother Barbara Van Cleve had opposed the creation of the zoning district on principle. She thought it was appalling the way the government harassed ranchers with regulations, controlling them to death. Zoning had always been a tough sell in Sweet Grass County. Ranchers were independent-minded people. They liked to make their own decisions about what they did on their land, and bristled at anything that took even a little bit of that independence away.

"Countywide zoning would be very, very difficult. In this county," Page said now.

Kent Morgan, a Spanish teacher and basketball coach at Sweet Grass High School, had slipped into the meeting room. Morgan, who lived on a fourteen-acre property on Cow Creek Road with his wife, Kathy, had moved to Big Timber from Colorado in 2003. Even after a decade, he still felt like an outsider there sometimes. If you weren't descended from a homesteading family or you didn't have a Norwegian last name, folks in Big Timber could make you feel that way. But there wasn't a time he drove home without looking at the Crazies and thanking the Lord for the beauty he and Kathy enjoyed there. One of the neighbors had told him about the wind farm meeting that morning, and Morgan thought he'd stop by during his free period.

"I don't begrudge any individual the right to make a living. I come from a long line of agriculture and ranching and whatnot, and so I don't begrudge Rick that at all," Morgan said. "My dad's in a rest home now because of what ranching and farming has done to his body."

But Morgan had talked to some local real estate people, and they all told him that if a wind park went up nearby, it would hurt the value of his home. "I just would kinda dig in my heels at the decrease of my property value, which my wife and I have worked long and hard to establish," he said.

Morgan's tone was respectful. But privately, he had to admit it, he'd always found Rick Jarrett kind of abrasive. Not to sugarcoat it, but Mr. Jarrett could be a real jerk. Once, he was driving on the Old Boulder Road and saw Rick stranded by the roadside, his vehicle having broken down. Morgan offered him a ride; Rick asked for a tow. Morgan helped him set up the tow lines, and then Rick got behind the wheel of his dead sedan while Morgan towed him to a garage. But he didn't take him to the right garage, or maybe he didn't pull up in the right spot—Morgan wasn't sure which—and Rick chewed him out for it, asking why the hell he had stopped there. That was Rick Jarrett for you. You just had to chuckle.

One by one, Jarrett's neighbors chimed in. Sherry Bjorndal noted each comment in the minutes:

"Jim Hogemark expressed that he knows we need energy but not in his backyard."

"Mr. Engwis told the commissioners that they are a sham."

"Mr. Chesnoff concurred with Mr. Engwis that this project would affect the roads and the value of his property as well as the view of the Crazy Mountains."

Chesnoff's ranch lay east of the Crazy Mountain Cattle Company. All the talk about landowner rights grated on him. What about the neighbors? Didn't they have the right to enjoy the beautiful scenery? "They don't write books called *The Last Great Place* for no reason," he said in a low rumble. Beauty was irreplaceable. Beauty was more valuable than money. "And also, I'll tell you this, I've been close to them, and the noise from these things, it's very, very real. And it's constant. And it's like being locked in a room and having rock music played—'Zoom!'—it's constant."

Chesnoff's exposure to rock music was mostly confined to his law office. He had defended many rock stars and music executives against criminal charges—drunk driving (Mötley Crüe's Vince Neil), drug possession (Bruno Mars), domestic battery (Scott Weiland of Stone Temple Pilots). He helped them get out of sticky situations, like blackmail threats (René Angélil, Céline Dion's husband). The walls of his law office were lined with signed glossy headshots of prominent people who had come to see him after their mug shots appeared in the tabloids.

"I'm just going to open another can of worms," Morgan said. "What can you tell me about the flicker effect?" He'd been all over the internet, looking this stuff up. Windmills had made people physically sick. Cows had quit giving milk and chickens had quit laying eggs, and they said that was due to the flicker effect. The propellers got in the way of the sun, or the moon—interrupting the moon rays, or the sun rays.

Marty said that question was above his pay grade.

Rick Jarrett had kept quiet and let Marty do the talking. But it was past noon by now, past time for lunch, and he was becoming impatient. He snorted at Morgan's moon ray question.

"You're not going to be living a mile away from it and have that happen," Rick said, in much the same tone he had taken when Morgan had towed him to the wrong garage.

"All righty, that concludes it," said Mosness.

"How does the commission intend to proceed from here?" Engwis asked her. "Are you going to reconsider your position in general on this wind energy?"

"It's on private property, Jan. There's no teeth in anything we have at the moment to do anything about it," Mosness replied tightly. She was still trying to get over her shock at being called a sham. Jan had always been friendly when she and Gary ran into him at car shows.

Kroskob went back to the *Pioneer*'s offices on 2nd Avenue to write her story. All in all, the spat over Rick's wind farm seemed minor compared to the hubbub over an ordinance proposed earlier that year to allow chicken coops within Big Timber city limits. People were really up in arms over that one. If you started allowing chickens in town, what would come next—potbellied pigs? The chicken-coop meeting had to be moved to the public library to accommodate all the people who showed up, including one man dressed in a chicken suit.

After he got back to his ranch, Rick went for a soak in his hot tub, as he did every night, sub–zero degree temperatures notwithstanding. The hot tub sat outside the farmhouse door in what would have been its front yard, had Rick observed such niceties, a bubbling vat of dirty water cut with industrial levels of chlorine that he kept at 104 degrees. It eased his aching back and the pain in his leg which had been crushed when a horse rolled on him some years back. That leg had never set right.

Rick did his thinking in the hot tub, surrounded by the nighttime sounds of the ranch: lowing cows, owls in the cottonwoods, the shriek of a red fox. Nearly ten years had passed since he helped Marty raise that first met tower on his land. In 2005, he had taken out a mortgage on the Crazy Mountain Cattle Company. Then he'd borrowed some more on top of that. He now owed Citizens Bank & Trust $500,000. Ranching was done with the common man, Rick thought. The land was worth so much more than anything that ran around on it.

Until those wind turbines went up and started turning his wind into cash, Rick had no idea how he'd square things with the bank and get the ranch on a secure footing. It was his land. It should have been simple. But there was nothing simple about this wind farm. Behind all of it was a lot of goddamn politics and confusion.

On Valentine's Day, two months after the meeting with the county commissioners, David Chesnoff, Jan Engwis, the MacMillans, and Russell Gordy filed a lawsuit against the Sweet Grass County Commissioners, accusing them of a pattern of suppressing public input and participation in the case of Crazy Mountain Wind, "an industrial wind energy development project" on Rick Jarrett's Crazy Mountain Cattle Company.

Susie Mosness was upset to see that the letter of support she had drafted for Rick Jarrett back in September 2012 was Exhibit 1 in the plaintiffs' complaint. The lawsuit described "the Mosness letter" as the product of a secret meeting held behind closed doors, in violation of Montana's right-to-know and open-meetings statutes. Although she had been warned during commissioner training sessions in Helena after she was first elected that all county commissioners get sued eventually—it was not an *if*, but a *when*—Mosness was shaken. She resolved to be extra careful from then on.

As it happened, the commissioners had two meetings about Crazy Mountain Wind scheduled the following week, including a public forum at the library to solicit feedback from the community on the issue of tax abatement. In Montana, wind farms were considered a new and expanding industry, and as such, were eligible for tax relief during the first years of operation. Counties weren't obligated to grant tax abatement, but the statute was viewed as an incentive to attract development.

Marty showed up at Big Timber's Carnegie Public Library that evening armed with maps and project schematics, ready to make his case to the citizens of Sweet Grass County. Rows of chairs had been set up in the basement. Marty, who wasn't particular about whether his T-shirts had holes in the armpits, had donned a striped button-down shirt and gotten a haircut for the occasion.

As the meeting got underway, Marty explained that this was a local project, by Montana folks, for the benefit of Montana folks. It would be entirely situated on Rick's ranch, and Rick's people had been in Big Timber since before the dirt was there. The turbines would be from General Electric, the people who made your toaster, a good, old American company. Outside financiers would fund the project, just the way you'd go to a bank to get a mortgage to buy a house, Marty explained. Tax abatement would attract those financiers and help their little project find its legs.

Kory Hofland from the state's Department of Revenue walked everyone through the math. Sweet Grass County would collect over $3 million from the wind farm over twenty years if it granted tax abatement; without tax abatement, it would get $4.1 million.

Rick Jarrett stood up to make his case to his neighbors. "I think this is a good deal for me. It's a good deal for my family, and I think it's a good deal for the community," he said. "I know that a lot of people don't want to look at wind power, and I appreciate that. There's nothing that's all good or all bad about anything. But if you look at this thing as a whole, I think it's a real positive deal for this community."

But some people at the library that night didn't see it that way. They questioned why you'd give a Wall Street bank a tax break so that they'd come in and build a project that wouldn't be profitable to begin with. There was confusion about taxes: some thought, erroneously, that their own taxes would go up if the wind farm was built. Some thought the tax break would go directly to the Jarretts.

Others vented their ire at the county commissioners. "It seems as though the commissioners gave support to this wind group before we ever had a public hearing," a woman said.

"I guess that would be part of the lawsuit you're talking about," said

Bill Wallace, who had assumed chairmanship of the commission that January. "I guess we better leave that alone, huh, Pat?" Pat agreed that they should. Susie Mosness, who was hunkered down in a corner of the room with her back to the wall, didn't say a word the entire evening.

Several people did speak up in favor of the wind farm that night, including a rancher named Arnold Breck Jr., whom everyone called Steve. Breck had leased his land for a small wind farm project called Kelly Hills that was under development by Gaelectric, an Irish wind energy company. There'd be between eight and twelve turbines set on 2,500 acres of private land, just north of the Engwis ranch. Unsurprisingly, Kelly Hills had drawn fire from some of the same people who were fighting Crazy Mountain Wind—including Jan Engwis and David Chesnoff.

Sweet Grass County needed money—for the schools and the roads, Breck said. What would happen when the Stillwater Mine faded out? The people at the library that night who were complaining about stuff, they milked that mine to death.

"I don't think you ought to kill a goose that laid a golden egg. I say take the $3 million and invite the company in instead of just run 'em on out the county," Breck said. "This town ain't that stable . . . So, maybe this county should look at some of this here stuff and not be so high on the horse."

But the following month, the commissioners voted to rescind the 2012 letter of support for Crazy Mountain Wind. Marty would have to request a new letter, the commissioners announced. Then they'd properly notice a discussion about it and schedule new hearings on tax abatement. They'd go the whole nine yards all over again, all because of the kerfuffle kicked up by the first letter.

But Jan Engwis, who was present for the vote, was dissatisfied. Rescinding the Mosness letter didn't solve the issue, as he saw it. It didn't address the tremendous damage that had been done, personally, to him, to his family, to his property, to his ability to freely and pleasurably enjoy his property. Kroskob quoted him at length in the next edition of the *Pioneer*: "'I do not take this lightly,' Engwis said. 'This doesn't solve the problem as far as I see it.'"

As far as Jan Engwis was concerned, the toothpaste was out of the tube.

8

DIANA'S GREAT IDEA

February 19, 2019
Park County Courthouse
Livingston, Montana

DAVID CHESNOFF, *having first been duly sworn, testified as follows*:
Q: What is your relationship with Montana?
MR. CHESNOFF: I think it's the most beautiful place in the United
   States. My wife and I made a decision a long time ago, to find
   a place in Montana that we could call our own . . . We looked
   everywhere, across the state, from top to bottom, and eventually,
   almost at the point of exasperation, the Realtor took us out to Big
   Timber to look at the site that we eventually chose. At the time,
   it was separated into five separate parcels. We got there, and we
   looked at one parcel, and then we looked at next parcel, and we
   went the whole length, and I asked my wife which one she wanted,
   and—hence the name Diana's Great Idea—she said all five.

MAY 13, 2005
LAS VEGAS, NEVADA

Even by Vegas standards, David Chesnoff's fiftieth birthday party at
Caesars Palace was quite a shindig. More than seven hundred guests
flew in from around the country and from overseas, a cross-section of
people from the worlds of litigation and law enforcement, entertainment
and sports, high-stakes poker and high-profile skulduggery. Las Vegas
mayor Oscar Goodman—Chessie's mentor and former law partner—
was one of the party's five hosts.

   In a nightclub called Pure, judges and Hells Angels rubbed elbows on a dance floor doused in hot pink lights. Cocktail waitresses in tea towel–sized black dresses circulated with canapes on a fourteen-thousand-square-foot terrace overlooking the Las Vegas Strip. Jugglers and dancers performed. Leonid the Magnificent, a six-foot-seven Russian burlesque performer famous for balancing swords between his teeth while clad in feathered wings, platform go-go boots, and a slick of baby oil, wrapped the birthday boy in a fervid embrace.

Other guests kept a low profile. There were people there that night who, if not for David Chesnoff, wouldn't have been there—or indeed, anywhere outside the gates of a federal penitentiary. Chesnoff got his start defending accused mobsters and drug dealers, gradually building a glittering client roster studded with professional athletes, pop stars, and poker whales. But he didn't turn away less savory individuals, like the son of a Bonanno crime family capo accused of breaking a tourist's neck at the strip club he managed. Or the Hells Angel charged in a gang riot at a Nevada casino that left three people dead. Chesnoff represented both men that year. He didn't judge people; that wasn't his job. His job was to present his clients in the best light he could, to leave the judging to others and let the chips fall where they may. Often, the chips fell in his clients' favor, which is why many of them had shown up at Pure to celebrate Chesnoff's half century with him.

"With as many prosecution enemies as Chesnoff has made over the years, I have to wonder who is going to taste his birthday cake," an item in the *Las Vegas Review-Journal* teased that morning. "It's just a rumor, but I heard the FBI is handling all the photography for the party."

If the FBI had been stationed outside Pure that night, they'd have gotten a picture of the rap mogul Suge Knight, whom Chesnoff defended against parole violation charges, being turned away at the door for wearing sneakers. A gossip columnist reported that Suge later returned to the party in proper footwear.

Years later, Chesnoff remembered the story differently. He had a word with Pure's management, and a sneakered Suge was quickly welcomed inside. But he decided that he liked the gossip columnist's version of the story better. It was pretty cool, actually. The Death Row Records founder definitely would have gone home to change shoes for him; he believed that. There was very little Chesnoff himself wouldn't do for his clients, and they knew it. Hadn't he once gotten Suge a table for fifteen at the Palm in Miami the night before the Super Bowl at a moment's notice? Then, when Suge canceled and asked Chesnoff to get him seven steaks and seven lobsters to go instead, he took care of that, too.

Not all his favorite clients could join him that night. Chesnoff's old friend Martha Stewart, whose legal team he had joined in 2004 in an unsuccessful appeal of her conviction on obstruction of justice and conspiracy charges, was stuck at home in Bedford, New York, with an electronic monitoring device on her ankle, serving out a five-month term of home confinement after five months in a minimum-security prison in West Virginia. Chesnoff flew out there to visit her, sent her books to read. Martha was a great American.

Chesnoff spent his birthday dancing with his wife, Diana. He drank and he ate. Mostly, he schmoozed, making his way from one knot of guests to the next. He tried to talk to everyone—the hotel and casino owners, the poker legends and sports bettors, the lawyers and private investigators he had worked with on cases across the country, from Texas, to California, to Massachusetts, to Montana. For Chesnoff, the party's sprawling guest list reflected the way he had tried to live his life: by engaging with all kinds of different people. It was a testament to the relationships he had forged since he showed up in Las Vegas in 1980, a twenty-five-year-old kid from Long Island with all his worldly possessions packed in a Fiat Brava.

For guests at the party and anyone who happened to be taking notes on the other side of the velvet rope, the night at Pure confirmed what everyone already knew: David Zeltner Chesnoff had summited the apex of his profession and become one of the most connected men in Las Vegas.

Just a few months after his birthday, Chesnoff would grasp the token of all that success: a two-hundred-acre Montana ranch with two miles of frontage on the Yellowstone River and a staggering view of the Crazy Mountains. Buying all five parcels might have been Diana's great idea, but the land and all its beauty was David's trophy.

It didn't take a lot of imagination to see how people who spent time around casinos could wind up in trouble. Chesnoff was the guy you called when a glassine bag of cocaine fell out of your Chanel purse during a traffic stop, or if a security guard spotted you throttling your girlfriend at the MGM Grand. If you were accused of murder, you called Chesnoff. No matter what time it was, he'd pick up the phone. And then he'd start figuring out what had to be done, who to call, and what motions to file first thing in the morning.

If you were going to be arrested, for example, he'd make arrangements with law enforcement so that you could surrender politely instead of being paraded in handcuffs in front of a bank of cameras. At your bail hearing, he'd make sure you had family members there, to humanize you in the eyes of the judge—to let the court see what Chesnoff himself saw in you. Or, if you were a whale with too many overdue multimillion-dollar markers at the casinos, he'd negotiate to have you installed in a palatial hotel suite with an electronic ankle monitor and your own butler while he sorted things out.

Then the real work began. Chesnoff hired investigators to uncover information about the witnesses who would testify against you. He picked through every detail in the police reports. He'd read every page of discovery to sniff out any instance of government overreach or law enforcement misconduct, anything that could be used to undermine the state's case. Chesnoff had a genius for catching prosecutors and police on the wrong foot.

"When I'm representing somebody, I do it as zealously as the law allows, and I don't apologize for that. My client is the most important thing to me. And sometimes, you know, a real good lawyer puts himself between him and who's ever going after him," Chesnoff said. Criminal law was really a form of constitutional law, he explained. "First of all, you make sure that that law enforcement follows the rules. I mean, that's what a real good criminal lawyer does—make sure that the Constitution is followed."

Case in point was the triumph Chesnoff had scored just a month before his milestone birthday, when a federal judge in Boston ruled that his client Vincent Ferrara, aka the Animal, a capo for New England's Patriarca crime family, had been deprived of his right to a fair trial.

In 1990, Ferrara had been indicted under the Racketeer Influenced and Corrupt Organizations Act and charged with a Whitman's Sampler of criminal offenses that included ordering the murder of a mafia foot soldier. The FBI had wiretapped an induction ceremony Ferrara attended, during which four aspiring mafiosi swore loyalty to the family at the risk of eternal hellfire while cupping burning holy cards in their hands. The feds produced testimony from a key source who swore that the Animal had ordered the hit.

Ferrara admitted to the murder as part of plea agreement to avoid life in jail. But it didn't sit well with him. In an interview room at the Terminal Island federal prison in California, where he was serving a twenty-two-year sentence, Ferrara told Chesnoff that the informant's testimony was false; he had been coerced into admitting to a homicide he didn't commit. Chesnoff believed him.

If you asked Chesnoff why he believed the Animal was framed, he might point out that he was a graduate of Boston College. He probably wouldn't mention that Ferrara had started calling himself the Animal to overwrite his original nickname, which was Pinhead.

Chesnoff discovered that the government's key witness, a detective, had recanted the most damning testimony against Ferrara before his trial in a memo—a memo the federal prosecutor withheld from his lawyers. Chesnoff appealed and got a new trial for Ferrara. He put the detective on the stand and questioned him till he came clean about the recanted testimony and the memo that would have exonerated his client. The guy didn't break down crying, but it was a little bit of a *Perry Mason* moment all the same. The judge called the withheld memo "the smokingest gun I've ever seen," proof of extraordinary misconduct by the government and a clear-cut violation of Ferrara's rights. The Animal was released from prison the following month. Score one for the Constitution, and for David Chesnoff.

It was one of Chesnoff's proudest moments, made sweeter by how arrogant the prosecutors had been to him years back, when he had first approached them about a deal to reduce Ferrara's jail time. Those lawyers literally laughed in his face. Now look who was laughing.

But Chesnoff didn't just do criminal stuff. His reputation as the city's top problem solver was cemented in 2004, when Britney Spears's people contacted him early one January morning in a panic. The pop princess had spent the night drinking and dancing with Jason Alexander, a childhood friend. Sometime around dawn, after watching *The Texas Chain-saw Massacre* in Spears's suite, they decided to get married. The limo driver walked Spears down the aisle of Vegas's Little White Wedding Chapel; the groom reported that the newlyweds consummated their union in the limo's back seat.

Chesnoff had the marriage annulled inside of fifty-five hours.

As it happened, a pregnant Spears was having a private party of her own at Caesars Palace the same night as Chesnoff's birthday party. Did she stop by to wish him many happy returns? Years later, he couldn't remember. There were a lot of boldface names at Pure that night. But it was a nice coinkydink, he said.

Chesnoff was a big man, as bulky as a nightclub bouncer, with a tattoo on his arm and floppy curly hair that he brushed back straight over the top of his head for a more senatorial air. For fun, he rode Harley-Davidson motorcycles—the only motorcycle, as far as he was concerned—and played poker. He had learned from the great poker players, legends like Doyle Brunson and Chip Reese, whom he met in his early days in Vegas. Poker players always had problems. Chessie helped them out with their legal issues on occasion, and that got him interested in the game. He'd sweat Brunson and Reese at the poker tables—watch them play from the rails—and eventually began playing himself.

He got pretty good at it; good enough to compete in the opening rounds of the World Series of Poker. The night before one big tournament, Reese and Brunson spent four hours teaching him how to play Omaha, a variation on Texas Hold'em, so he wouldn't embarrass himself. Chesnoff's clients became friends, and his friends often became clients. For someone in his line of work in Las Vegas, the lines blurred. One day, he might be representing Andre Agassi in a lawsuit against Rolex; the next, the two would be playing a round of golf, or his son, Max, might be getting a tennis lesson from Agassi's father at the tennis star's home.

The Agassi estate was a long way from the North Shore of Long Island, New York, where David Zeltner Chesnoff grew up, a Jewish kid descended from a line of prodigious extroverts—movers and shakers, entertainers, and occasional lawbreakers. Audacity was embedded in his DNA.

Chesnoff's maternal grandfather, Louis Efraim Leib Frederick Zeltner—aka Wireless Louie—was one of the great characters of early-twentieth-century New York City. A journalist and political operative, Zeltner got his start as a copy boy for the *New York Sun* in the 1890s. He caught a lot of stories hanging around Essex Market Court, a courthouse and jail on the Lower East Side. When he filed a story about the escaped parrot of a prison warden with such dispatch that a pair of lawyers were still chasing after the bird to collect the reward money, a *Sun* editor asked him how he did it. "By wireless!" Zeltner quipped.

The name stuck. "Louis, as everybody knows, is the great east side newsgatherer. Stories come and perch on him like homing pigeons. So great is his newsgetting ability that he is popularly supposed to use the Marconi system and private pipelines in his business," declared the *New York Times* in 1908.

Zeltner got into politics. After serving as a city alderman and campaigning unsuccessfully for Congress, he founded the New York League of Locality Mayors, handpicking his favorite local characters to preside over the city's various neighborhoods. The mayors of Grand Street, Avenue A, and the like gathered every year to elect a chief mayor at raucous banquets at the Hotel Astor. No one took the block mayors very seriously, except perhaps themselves, but they formed a network of local influencers with Zeltner at its center. Any politician who wanted to win votes in New York City made it his business to win over Wireless Louie.

Chesnoff's paternal grandfather Barney Chesnoff was a Russian immigrant who opened a saloon in Paterson, New Jersey, in the early 1900s. Unlike Wireless Louie, Barney preferred to keep a low profile, though his name appeared in the newspapers throughout Prohibition. In 1922, a pair of detectives confiscated two jugs and a bottle of wine that Barney had stashed in a safe; a judge fined him $100. The following year, enforcement raiders seized a quart of wet goods Barney had stashed behind the bar. A 1925 raid on the saloon uncovered a pair of fifty-gallon hogsheads of mash, with another batch bubbling away in a twenty-five-gallon boiler. In 1932, when Prohibition was in its twilight, federal agents relieved him of four barrels of ale. Nevertheless, Barney Chesnoff persisted. His saloon never closed.

Perhaps Chesnoff's saloon owed its survival to one of the organized crime networks that sprang up in New Jersey during Prohibition, or to officials willing to look the other way. "I'd venture to guess that he had, um, political and other assistance," David Chesnoff said. Grandpa Barney wasn't the warm and fuzzy type. In any event, he made enough money during the 1920s and 1930s to support his family, pay for his kids' violin lessons, and send his son, Lew, to law school.

David's father, Lew, never practiced law. He made a career as a musician, playing bass at the Copacabana nightclub and touring with the USO. In 1951, he made his screen debut playing a glow-in-the-dark bass fiddle with Frankie Carle's orchestra in *Footlight Varieties*, an RKO feature hosted by Jack Paar. But life on the road was tough for a married man with kids at home. By the time *Footlight Varieties* opened, Lew had mothballed his bass fiddle and bought a liquor store.

David was born in 1955, a late-in-life baby with two brothers, eighteen and fifteen years his senior. Lew, who made some bad investments, wasn't the best financial planner, so David put himself through Alfred University with a combination of loans and scholarships.

Young Chesnoff was brash and outspoken. When challenged, he could be combative; even then, Chesnoff knew that the best defense was an aggressive offense. As the chairman of Alfred's student assembly, he once rescheduled a meeting on short notice so that he could catch an 8:00 p.m. movie. Fellow students complained; he strenuously defended the constitutionality of his actions. When a reporter for the student newspaper, *Fiat Lux*, questioned him, a "plainly angered" Chesnoff told her to write whatever she wanted, so long as her article reported that the assembly had discussed a $2,000 loan that the paper's editor-in-chief had given herself from the *Fiat Lux* savings account. "He then added that the matter will be investigated more thoroughly."

During summer vacations, Chesnoff earned money by working as a dishwasher and a barback, by shucking oysters and valet-parking cars. A cousin got him a job working for Martha Stewart's catering business as a busboy. He graduated college in three years and entered Suffolk University Law School in Boston in 1976. Chesnoff always knew he wanted to be a lawyer: he liked the idea of fighting for the underdog.

In 1980, a law school mentor told Chesnoff that Dominic Gentile, a Chicago criminal defense attorney, had started a practice in Las Vegas and needed an associate. Chesnoff, who was then working for a staid corporate law firm in Houston, jumped at the chance. Criminal law offered a lot more opportunity to try cases in a courtroom, which was where he wanted to be. It also appealed to his antiauthoritarian inclinations. A criminal lawyer held law enforcement accountable, made sure that the government followed the rules.

Under the sequins and ostrich feathers, Las Vegas was still a rough-and-tumble Western town in those days. You could drive from one end to the other and run out of road in the Mojave Desert. People rode horses across scrubland now covered with shopping malls. Judges wore cowboy hats and pointy-toed boots.

Organized crime figures still ran the casinos. People like Frank "Lefty" Rosenthal, who operated a shadowy sports betting empire out of the Stardust for the Chicago Outfit, and Tony "The Ant" Spilotro, who skimmed the profits and whacked anyone who skimmed from the skim—the real-life models for the characters in Martin Scorsese's *Casino*.

When Chesnoff arrived, a whole new generation of lawbreakers was coming into its own. The 1980s saw the rise of the Cali drug cartel, and Colombian kingpins used Vegas as a major distribution hub. Gentile represented coke dealers who paid his retainer from aluminum cases packed with cash. Chesnoff was the rookie everyone called Chessie. He wasn't intimidated by his new clients. Growing up on Long Island, he'd had friends who were very intellectual, and other friends who weren't quite so cerebral—the ones he'd borrow motorcycles from when he was fifteen. It was just like anything else: if you treated people with respect, you didn't have problems.

He got to know the Binion family, who owned the Horseshoe casino. Benny Binion, the family patriarch, was a career criminal from Texas with a wide-ranging résumé: horse trader, bootlegger, gambling syndicate boss, convicted murderer. At Binion's Horseshoe, you could bet without limits at the craps tables, drinks were on the house, and there was $1 million in $10,000 bills encased in plastic inside a giant horseshoe in the casino lobby. The cheap steaks served at the Horseshoe came from the cattle Binion raised on his sprawling ranch in eastern Montana, near Jordan. Binion wore ten-gallon hats and Western shirts with gold coins for buttons. At lunchtime, you'd find him dining on squirrel stew in the

Horseshoe's restaurant, often in the company of his good friend Judge Harry Claiborne, the federal judge for the Nevada district, who usually ordered the ham hocks.

The Binions' friends were always getting into trouble. Chesnoff represented a few of them in court and had some success. Soon, he was having lunch at the Horseshoe with Benny and his sons and grandkids, and getting comped everywhere, from the Dome of the Sea to the Villa d'Este.

In 1983, Gentile and Chesnoff argued a case before Benny Binion's old friend Judge Claiborne involving Joseph Agosto, the Tropicana's former entertainment director and the Vegas point man for the Kansas City mob. Gentile and Chesnoff didn't represent Joseph Agosto; they represented his thirty-two-year-old son Charles, who had been ordered to testify in a grand jury investigation into his father's activities.

Spouses can't be compelled to testify against one another, but children can be compelled to testify against their parents. Chessie put on his thinking cap. Forcing a son to testify against his father—that made him think of the way the Nazis forced children to turn against their parents. He reached out to the famed Nazi hunter Simon Wiesenthal and asked him to provide a statement about the Third Reich. Then he went looking for expert witnesses who could speak on behalf of God and his commandments. A Roman Catholic priest who specialized in canonical law took the stand to explain that Charles's subpoena violated the commandment to honor thy father. The priest was followed by a rabbi, who educated the court about the Talmud.

Judge Claiborne was impressed. In his ruling, he wrote that the privilege that protects a spouse should also apply to parents and children. His precedent-setting decision made national headlines before being overturned on appeal. After the judge got into serious trouble himself a few years later for tax fraud, he hired a pair of lawyers to defend him in his impeachment trial in the US Senate. (Although Claiborne had already been convicted and was serving a two-year sentence, he didn't want to give up his federal judgeship—hence the impeachment trial.) Oscar Goodman, a Vegas lawyer famous for his mafia clientele, was the lead lawyer. The other was the brash young attorney who had used the Bible to cockblock federal prosecutors.

Judge Claiborne lost his case, but a powerful new partnership was born. Goodman embraced the moniker "mob lawyer." (He titled his autobiography *Being Oscar: From Mob Lawyer to Mayor of Las Vegas*.) Lefty Rosenthal and Tony "The Ant" Spilotro were Goodman's longtime clients; Robert De Niro and Joe Pesci came to him for pointers when they were preparing to play lightly fictionalized versions of the men in *Casino*. For the role of Oscar Goodman, Scorsese cast Oscar Goodman, who appeared in a courtroom scene, arguing for his client Ace Rothstein. Chesnoff, an extra, can be glimpsed sitting at the back of the courtroom.

Chesnoff and Goodman became partners in 1987. Goodman's flamboyant style and his vocal distrust of the government made a profound impression on his protégé. Goodman routinely invoked the Constitution in his unapologetic advocacy for scary men accused of unspeakable acts—"defending the right of the United States of the amendments of the whatever," in the words of Goodman client Charlie Moose Panarella, a Columbo family capo said to have forced one victim to eat his own testicles. And Goodman shared his clients' hatred for rats. He kept a plastic rat in his office as a kind of chew toy, smashing it against the floor to vent his rage at those who made deals with the feds to implicate his clients.

Chessie took it all in. "He was working with two of the brightest attorneys the city's ever seen," said Jack Sheehan, an author and longtime columnist for the *Las Vegas Review-Journal* who first met Chesnoff in the early 1980s. "Even then he was bombastic and kind of volatile at times, but extremely bright . . . He and I both agreed that we had landed in a really rich garden to ply our trade."

Chesnoff met Diana Willis in a restaurant. She was attractive, poised, and a deft hand at dispatching overconfident men who hit on her, having worked as a maître d' in Vegas restaurants. He asked her out and she told him to go back to high school football practice. David got Diana's number and kept calling her until she agreed to go on a date with him. They married in 1985.

The Chesnoffs bought a small ranch on a former alfalfa farm on the outskirts of Las Vegas, far from the Strip. They built a home with a barn and horse stalls. Diana, who had grown up in Michigan, loved animals—dogs, birds, horses. Chesnoff liked to say Diana was a horse whisperer before there was a word for it. Diana filled the stalls with

Friesian horses. David was happy to help her muck out the stables and feed the rescue dogs. A life-size statue of a mare and her foal presided over the pebbled drive.

Chesnoff's star rose. In 1995, he appeared on the *Charlie Rose* talk show with a panel of criminal defense lawyers for a segment on the Cali cartel. Chesnoff had represented a few reputed cartel members himself by then. Rose asked his panelists what they'd say if the head of the Cali cartel wanted to hire them. While the other attorneys hemmed and hawed, Chesnoff declared, "I would welcome it!"

It was a drug case that led Chesnoff to Montana. Daniel Jones, a professional gambler and casino owner, was arrested in Helena and charged with money laundering and involvement in a methamphetamine ring. Jones was a friend of the Binion family, which promptly dispatched Chesnoff to the Treasure State to defend him. It was 1991, and the war on drugs was at a fever pitch. The assistant US attorney prosecuting the case, James Seykora, called Jones a threat to society. Chesnoff secured his release on a $250,000 cash bond, paid by the Binions.

During the trial of Jones and three codefendants, Chesnoff made short work of the prosecution's star witness, a very impeachable fellow who buried his meth-making equipment before serving a stint in prison, then dug it up as soon as he was released. "Do you have any lab equipment buried now?" Chesnoff asked, after the star witness admitted to lying about his own misdeeds under cross-examination. To show the jury that his client had come by his money honestly—or honestly enough, anyway—Chesnoff called on none other than his poker buddy, Doyle Brunson. Brunson, a native Texan who wore his cowboy hat on the witness stand, testified to Jones's gambling skills. "How is it you know that Danny is a good gambler?" Chesnoff asked. "Because he never gambles against me," Bruson replied, poker-faced. It took a while, but Chesnoff eventually won the whole shooting match—full acquittal for Jones on all charges.

Montana was an interesting place, Chesnoff reflected. You might expect the people there would be conservative law-and-order types, but the state had always had an anti-government bent. If you were able to undermine the government's argument, you could win cases in Montana. Chesnoff spent months in the Treasure State on that case. During his free time, he'd go exploring. When he saw the Crazy Mountains for the first time, he was actually blown away. The mountains were wreathed in clouds. Sometimes they seemed close, sometimes they seemed far away. Chesnoff thought it was very mystical.

When Oscar Goodman was elected mayor of Las Vegas in 1999, Chesnoff lost a partner, but gained a friend at the summit of the city's government. He cultivated his connections to powerful people. "No matter who you're dealing with, you go right to the top. Everything happens at the top in Vegas," he told a journalist in 2014.

Access to the top was lubricated with money. Chesnoff made generous donations to the political campaigns of judges, the sheriff, the district attorney, the attorney general, the governor—Republicans and Democrats. Over the course of three election cycles starting in 2013, he gave $30,000 to Steven Wolfson, the Las Vegas district attorney. His law office partner, Richard Schonfeld, donated $20,000; Diana contributed an additional $15,000. The donations were completely legal, but invited questions about preferential treatment for Chesnoff's clients, whose drug possession, felony battery, and DUI cases came under the DA's jurisdiction.

David Ferrara, a former court reporter for the *Las Vegas Review-Journal*, was struck by Wolfson's deferential body language when he appeared alongside Chesnoff to announce a plea deal in one high-profile case, before a gaggle of reporters. "The DA kind of looked at Chesnoff, like, 'You go first,'" Ferrara recalled.

As Las Vegas became more corporate and its casinos were scrubbed clean of the last vestiges of organized crime, Chesnoff got involved in more white-collar stuff involving the big hotels and casinos. He understood how to work within the system. But even as he smoothed the way for his clients behind the scenes, Chesnoff cultivated a tough, street-smart persona.

A month after his birthday party, he made his screen debut in *Vegas, Baby*, a low-budget movie about a raunchy bachelor-party weekend that made *The Hangover*—released four years later—look like *Citizen Kane*. The movie was financed by Chesnoff's friends Tim Poster and Tom Breitling, who owned the Golden Nugget. Chesnoff appeared in a brief cameo as a badass biker in a motorcycle gang led by Chuck Liddell, the mixed-martial artist. Dressed in black leather and sunglasses, hair blown back, Chesnoff zooms the wrong way down a one-way street on a custom chopper, trailed by his law partner, Schonfeld.

The cameo was totally on-brand for Sin City's top litigator, who had defended various members of the Hells Angels over the years and had *81 Not Guilty* tattooed on his bicep ("81" is biker code for Hell's Angels). "I told the defendants, who happened to be members of the Hells Angels, that if we were successful, we would get tattoos," Chesnoff said. "We were successful. And a couple of shots of Jack Daniel's later, I had a tattoo."

Vegas, Baby went straight to video after its premiere at the Cine-Vegas Film Festival at the Palms, but Chesnoff continued to make occasional off-screen appearances as a Vegas heavy. A newspaper columnist described running into Chesnoff at a Montana airport after he wrote an item about a spat involving Diana at a charity event. "He let me know that I was playing with fire," the columnist said. "He could pass for a bodyguard—he is a stout, well-muscled guy—a serious guy." After that incident, the columnist made a point of running upcoming items about Chesnoff past him for his approval first.

By then, David and Diana were searching for a Montana ranch, somewhere he could really get away from the stress of the courtroom. They looked for years, but nothing was right. Then the real estate agent showed them those five parcels on the Yellowstone near Big Timber.

The Chesnoffs were immediately taken with the land, just smitten. David thought the Realtor had planted the eagles on the place before they got there. The river was absolutely beautiful, and the land was surrounded by mountains. Nobody had a better view of the Crazies than that place. As the broker showed them around, Diana elbowed David and whispered not to act excited. After they closed on the sale, David was proud to tell people that they bought all five parcels, because they preserved the land in its full form, which would have been subdivided otherwise.

Back in Vegas, the cases got bigger, and so did the names attached to them: David Copperfield, Paris Hilton, Charles Oakley, Cristiano Ronaldo. In 2009, Chesnoff represented the World Series of Poker champion Phil Ivey in his divorce. He won Ivey such a favorable settlement that the poker crowd began referring to Chesnoff as the Phil Ivey of attorneys. (Just as Chesnoff had once sweated the poker greats at the card tables, Ivey once turned up in the courtroom to watch Chesnoff handle a hearing in a publicized DUI manslaughter case.)

But the network of relationships with influential people at all levels of Vegas society that made Chesnoff a formidable advocate could also create conflicts of interest—or at least the appearance of such. The Iveys' divorce ended in bitter litigation. Ivey's ex-wife Luciaetta claimed that Chesnoff had "directed" her to hire an attorney named John Spilotro—the nephew of Tony "The Ant" Spilotro, Oscar Goodman's famous late client, who turned up dead in an Indiana cornfield in 1986. Luciaetta said that Spilotro sabotaged her financial interests by failing to trace $8 million her ex-husband had earned during their marriage. She sued Chesnoff, Spilotro, and Ivey for conspiring to defraud her. The Nevada Supreme Court ruled against her petition, and that was the end of it. (John Spilotro was never charged with any wrongdoing.)

Then there was the case of Michelle McKenna. McKenna was a cocktail waitress at Pure nightclub; she might have been one of the minimally clad women serving drinks at Chesnoff's fiftieth birthday party. In 2009, McKenna was allegedly assaulted at Pure by Patrick Jones, the son of Jan Jones Blackhurst, a top Caesars executive and a former Las Vegas mayor. Blackhurst had comped her son and his guests at Pure; McKenna, who was their server, claimed that Jones pulled her onto his lap, then throttled her when she rebuffed his advances. She blacked out, fell, and hit her head, suffering a concussion.

Chesnoff and Schonfeld agreed to represent McKenna in a personal injury lawsuit against Jones, Pure, and Caesars Entertainment. But, according to McKenna, the lawyers sat on her case for years. They didn't request key documents or interview any witnesses—or seek damages for lost wages and the ongoing care she needed as a result of her injuries. She eventually fired Chesnoff and Schonfeld, hired new counsel, and settled her case for a disappointing $225,000.

McKenna's lawsuit claimed multiple conflicts of interest that she maintained should have barred Chesnoff from representing her, including an undisclosed financial stake in Pure nightclub, and an ongoing representation of Pure's top executive, Steve Davidovici, in a tax evasion case. Days before the trial was to begin, Chesnoff and Schonfeld made a confidential settlement with McKenna.

Steven Aaronoff, a Los Angeles–based litigator, described a run-in with Chesnoff when he was representing Robert J. Cipriani, a professional gambler, FBI informant, and all-purpose Vegas gadfly who has been banned from casinos on occasion for changing blackjack bets and other antics. Cipriani, who goes by the moniker Robin Hood 702, filed a lawsuit against MGM Resorts International for a grab bag of complaints in connection with the 2017 mass shooting at the Route 91 Harvest Music Festival. The shooter fired from the Mandalay Bay Hotel and Casino—an MGM Resorts property. Cipriani claimed to have inside knowledge about security lapses there. According to Aaronoff, Chesnoff—for reasons that are unclear—tried to nip the lawsuit in the bud.

"He basically said, 'I'm friends with the governor, I'm friends with anyone who's anyone in Nevada, and we're going to go after you,'" said Aaronoff, who subsequently dropped Cipriani as a client.

Robin Hood 702 went ahead and filed the lawsuit himself. It was eventually dismissed. However dubious its merits, the description of that call to Aaronoff in Cipriani's florid DIY legal filing appears to capture some flavor of the Chesnoff modus operandi:

> On one occasion, Chesnoff told Plaintiff's former counsel, "I've been Man of the Year in Nevada. I've got the Governor, the Attorney General, the D.A. speaking about me. I've got the most prominent people in town. I have never done anything corrupt in my forty years as a lawyer." . . . To further his intimidation agenda, Chesnoff also stated to Plaintiff's former counsel: "I'm a street guy too, Steve. I graduated whatever, cum laude or whatever, but I've also been around."

Chesnoff had no comment.

David and Diana's Montana home, a sprawling, one-story gabled lodge of wood, stucco, and stone, was finished in 2011. The builder posted a picture of the portico, upheld by towering tree trunks, with one of his construction trucks parked nearby for scale: "CAT looks awfully small!" There were more trees inside the home: wide split-log rafters and great, thick trunks set like columns around the central living area, where a wall of windows overlooked the Yellowstone. A massive stone fireplace occupied the center of the room—the biggest stone fireplace outside Yellowstone National Park, Chesnoff bragged.

The ranch compound included a guesthouse, a boathouse, and a home for a ranch manager, who would oversee the place when they weren't around, which was about ten months out of the year. The Chesnoffs put in an artificial pond, so David could fly-fish for trout without walking down to the river. They built trails through the property for hiking and driving their four-wheelers. Sometimes, David rode the Harley he kept out there, or rafted the river under a full moon. Or he and Diana would just go outside and look at the stars. David had an app on his phone that told you all the constellations, and they would try to match it up with the night sky.

Now and then, he'd stop in at the American Legion for a beer. David didn't hang out with famous people when he was in Big Timber. Michael Keaton owned a ranch by McLeod. He was very pleasant to say hi to and stuff. Chesnoff was sure he could make a connection if he wanted to get to know Keaton—or Tom Brokaw, who also owned a place nearby. But why? Chesnoff already knew a lot of famous people. Without naming names, there were a lot of people he had helped with their issues—alcohol, drugs, psychological. After Mike Tyson was charged with driving under the influence in 2006, Chesnoff got him to go through rehab and get counseling, helped him turn his life around. Now he considered Tyson a good friend. They did the ice bucket challenge together, Tyson climbing up on a step stool to douse Chesnoff with cold water on the grass in front of his office.

It was a big responsibility, keeping someone out of jail. Once you told someone you were going to help them, you were all in. Chesnoff went at it full throttle. Montana was his refuge from all that. Karen Engwis gave David and Diana one of her photographs as a housewarming gift—a beautiful eagle picture. He kept it in Las Vegas, so he could remember what it was like on his ranch. It was where he went in his mind when he wanted to get away from the work he did, because what he did was pretty stressful. Diana's Great Idea was David's sanctuary.

So, Chesnoff wasn't happy to hear about Rick Jarrett's wind farm. There were millions of acres and lots of wind in Montana, plenty of space for windmills that wasn't in the heart of the most beautiful area of the state, within view of Sanctuary River Lane. Chesnoff talked to his neighbors. He went to the county commission to register his objections. And when that didn't work, Chesnoff did what anyone in his position would do. He got a lawyer.

9

BOXING IN PRISON

February 20, 2019
Park County Courthouse
Livingston, Montana

JAN ENGWIS, *Cross-examination*:

Q: You testified that you monitor the Public Service Commission's website and you watch it very carefully to determine whether or not anything is going on.

MR. ENGWIS: No, I didn't say very carefully. I periodically monitor it, meaning maybe once a month, whatever is available to me. For example, I am now—

Q: Okay. Can we stop. I'm asking questions, sir.

FEBRUARY 25, 2014
BOLLINGER ROOM
PUBLIC SERVICE COMMISSION
HELENA, MONTANA

The Public Service Commission is one of Montana's smallest government agencies. Picture a Monopoly board with its pastel squares for the Reading Railroad, the Electric Company, the Water Works. The PSC oversees those squares, and a host of other utilities: telephone and sewer companies, garbage trucks and taxis, petroleum pipelines and natural gas. The grab bag of companies that provide these services all have one thing in common: each is a for-profit corporation with a corner on the market and a lot of captive customers—otherwise known as ratepayers. The Public Service Commission oversees those utilities and the rates they charge, balancing ratepayers' interests against those of the utility providers. Just like the board game, the PSC is all about monopolies.

NorthWestern Energy is the biggest monopoly on the Montana PSC's game board. The utility is the modern incarnation of the Montana Power Company, which was itself an offshoot of John Ryan's Anaconda Copper Mining Company, the monopoly that controlled the state's copper mines. Ryan, the last of the Montana copper kings, consolidated a bunch of small electric companies into one big electric company in 1912 to secure cheap electricity for his mines and smelters.

Today, NorthWestern Energy sells electricity and natural gas to more than 764,000 customers across Montana, South Dakota, and Nebraska. NorthWestern owns dams that produce hydropower, coal-fired generating plants, and natural gas generators. It owns a few wind farms, too, which at the time of writing constituted less than 6 percent of its portfolio of in-house assets. Whatever energy NorthWestern doesn't produce itself, it contracts from independent wind, solar, and hydropower outfits.

But, as Marty Wilde told the Sweet Grass County Commissioners, NorthWestern really didn't like buying power from power plants it didn't own, and for a very simple reason: doing so ate into its profits. Understanding why requires a short history of the American marketplace for electricity.

As power companies proliferated in the early twentieth century, it became clear that a free-market approach to the buying and selling of electricity bred chaos. A city street might have three or four different sets of power poles strung with a rat's nest of wires—each owned and operated by a different electric company—while farmers out in the countryside were left off the grid entirely, because there was no financial incentive to put up miles of power line for a handful of customers. Worse, from the electricity industry's perspective, was that none of those companies could turn a real profit. It just wasn't worth it to build and maintain all the infrastructure required for a power grid unless you could capitalize on the economies of scale, free from competition.

So, big electric companies cut a deal with municipalities: give us an exclusive franchise to deliver power, and you can regulate us to make sure we do a good job and charge fair prices. That became the standard operating model for electricity providers across America. States gave single utility companies monopolies over regional power markets and established state agencies—public service commissions—to oversee the utilities and regulate the rates they charge. Utilities are a strange beast in America's free-market zoo. Although some utilities are publicly owned, they are the exception. The vast majority are for-profit corporations—owned by shareholders—that operate in the public interest, at the state's behest.

When public service commissions across the country set rates for kilowatt hours of electricity and dekatherms of natural gas, they rely on a century-old calculation to come up with what's known as the utility's revenue requirement. There is an actual mathematical formula for the revenue requirement, but I find it easier to think of it as a cake. The first layer is made up of the utility's operating expenses: everything from the cost of moving electricity over the grid to staff salaries, office supplies, the gas in line workers' trucks, and the expense-account lunches consumed by its executives. The second layer is the utility's tax bill. North-Western Energy pays the highest property taxes in the state—nearly five times more than the second-highest taxpayer on the list, the Burlington Northern Santa Fe Railway—because of the Brobdingnagian footprint of its grid infrastructure. Finally, regulators look at all the money that NorthWestern has invested in its infrastructure—power plants, substations, transmission lines—and the debt it has assumed to build those capital assets. Those capital costs—amortized over time, with calculations for depreciation—form the third layer of the rate cake.

Once the three layers are stacked, the PSC adds some frosting: a percentage return on the utility's equity—the capital it has invested in its power plants, generators and so on—of anywhere from 7 to 11 percent. Percentage returns are how the power company makes a profit. Suppose NorthWestern Energy spent $50 million on a new coal- or gas-fired power plant unit. With a PSC-approved return of 10 percent, the utility would reap $5 million on top of the actual cost of the unit. But should that unit break down and fail to deliver electricity—as Colstrip's Unit 4 did for seven months in 2013, at a cost of nearly $20 million—the price is passed straight to the ratepayers. The way this game works, the monopoly and its shareholders are insulated from financial risk with every throw of the dice.

Because all its costs are covered, NorthWestern has little motivation to operate more efficiently. To the contrary: it has every incentive to gold-plate its rate base—to spend on new substations, high-tension wires, and hydroelectric dams—because the more money it invests in infrastructure, the greater its profits. A disillusioned former Montana public service commissioner once observed that when a C-suite executive decorates his office, the utility earns a return on the new curtains.

But when NorthWestern bought wind power from an independent developer like Marty Wilde, it didn't get anything back. There was no frosting. The utility couldn't claim a percentage return on Marty's wind turbines, because it did not own them. Every contract that NorthWestern signed with an independent power producer, be it a small hydroelectric dam or a solar project or a wind farm, represented lost revenues for its shareholders.

And so, even though federal law—and Montana's own state legislature—required NorthWestern to buy energy from small, independent providers of renewable energy, the utility was very creative at finding ways not to. NorthWestern's cadre of high-paid lawyers—their salaries paid by Montana ratepayers—were frequent visitors to the PSC's Bollinger Room in Helena, a windowless box painted a watery shade of blue, where hearings about tariffs, rate adjustments, power purchase agreements, and other matters took place before a dais of five public service commissioners. The commissioners were charged with two tasks: making sure that ratepayers get adequate service at the least cost, and that utilities earn just enough profit to provide that service. "Just enough," a statement on the PSC's website declares. "No more, no less. It is this public interest protection that makes the PSC unique."

The definition of public interest is a narrow one. Electricity generation is responsible for nearly 45 percent of Montana's carbon emissions. In 2005, the state enacted a renewable portfolio standard that required utilities to source more electricity from non-carbon-generating sources like wind and solar. But carbon emissions and greenhouse gases were not spoken of in the Bollinger Room. In 2011, the same state legislature that had enacted the renewable portfolio standard, amended the Montana Environmental Policy Act to bar state agencies from considering "actual or potential impacts that are regional, national or global in nature" in their decision-making. That was widely interpreted to mean climate change.

Renewable-energy developers like Marty Wilde knew better than to mention the environmental benefits of their projects when they stepped inside the Bollinger Room, only how cost-effective they were. This is not unique to Montana; public service commissions in states around the country operate with the same myopic focus on ratepayers' pocketbooks. Tiny agencies with a handful of regulators hold tremendous sway over how people in those states will get their power, for decades to come. A *Harvard Law Review* study put it this way: "PSC decisions meaningfully affect our environment, but the environment does not meaningfully affect PSC decisions."

In most states, the job of utility regulator is filled by government appointees, supposedly qualified people tapped by the governor or the state legislature. Their work takes place largely behind the scenes. But not in Montana. The Treasure State is one of just eleven states that elects its public service commissioners. Despite the highly technical nature of their work, commissioners are not required to have any expertise in the industries they oversee, such as energy and telecommunications. They don't need a background in government administration or consumer affairs, or indeed, anything at all.

Although there's nothing red or blue about paying a utility bill, partisan politics have colored electoral contests for the Montana PSC. From 2012 and throughout the decade that followed, Republicans had a solid lock on the commission. Among the commissioners were a former chairman of the Yellowstone County Republicans and a former Republican state senator who owned an animal feed company. Roger Koopman, the commissioner for District 3—the region of south-central Montana encompassing Park and Sweet Grass Counties—was a former Republican state representative who had once worked for the NRA. The PSC has no say over firearms or abortion, but Commissioner Koopman ran on his endorsements by the NRA and the Montana Pro-Life Coalition. He handed out campaign flyers at gun shows, with live factory rounds glued to them: *Roger Koopman, The Firepower for Rate-Payers on the PSC.*

The commission's weekly work sessions, live streamed on the PSC's website, provided a handy soapbox for the commissioners, who were not shy about voicing their political opinions for the benefit of whatever audience chose to tune in as they plowed through an alphabet soup of regulatory issues: DCFs and LEOs, BPA credit exchanges, ARM waivers, ETC certifications, MCR transmission lines, FCC notices and EIA forecasts, etcetera.

Few letters of the alphabet were more likely to trigger speechifying from the commissioners than QF—for qualifying facilities, the small, independent wind, solar, and hydropower producers endowed with the right to sell their power to big power players like NorthWestern Energy under the Public Utility Regulatory Policies Act of 1978. PURPA required monopoly utilities to buy energy from QFs at a fair price, which it defined as the utility's "avoided cost"—the money it would have spent to generate that power from its own coal-fired plants and hydroelectric dams.

It was the PSC's job to make sure that avoided-cost rate, known as the QF-1 tariff, was fairly administered in contracts between the monopoly and QFs. But Montana's solidly Republican PSC tended to take a dim view of PURPA (Jimmy Carter–era big government) and QFs (handouts for wind developers). Why award a multi-decade power purchase agreement contract to a wind park when Montana had so much cheap coal? Wind was unreliable. It might stop blowing just when you needed it the most. Coal could be counted upon to burn.

When it came to approving power purchase agreements for wind farms, as it was legally bound to do, the PSC was pickier than Goldilocks: this one was too big, that one was too small, nothing was just right. Its yardstick was the PSC's own Montana Rule, enacted in the 1990s. Under the Montana Rule, wind farms that produced more than three megawatts of power had to compete in an open solicitation with all power generators—coal, gas, hydro, solar—to win a contract with NorthWestern, PURPA be damned.

It was a contest they were almost certain to lose. Wind was free, but the cost of capital for building a wind farm made it more expensive than coal. On the upside, the price of wind energy dropped with greater installed capacity—an industry term that refers the number of megawatts a project can generate. The bigger the wind farm, in other words, the cheaper the wind power. But developers who wanted to build those bigger, more ambitious projects ran into another set of bollards: a PSC rule that effectively allowed NorthWestern to cap the total amount of wind energy it would buy from qualifying facilities to fifty megawatts—all Montana wind QFs combined.

All those policies, preconditions, and restrictions were like so many chicanes blocking any wind developer's path to the state's energy market. For them, the game was more Mario Kart than Monopoly. NorthWestern Energy used the Montana Rule and the PSC's fifty-megawatt cutoff as a justification for ignoring QFs that wanted to sell them power, or as a wedge to force QF developers to accept lower prices and unprofitable short-term contracts, instead of the favorable long-term avoided-cost rate—the QF-1 tariff it was obligated to pay under PURPA.

But Marty Wilde knew his way around the Bollinger Room. His strategy, refined over two decades, was to tailor his projects to just squeak past those state regulations so that the PSC had no choice but to sign off on the deal. In 2008, Marty had seized on a temporary change in the Montana Rule that lifted the competitive solicitation requirement for wind projects from three megawatts to ten megawatts and won a power purchase agreement (PPA) for Fairfield Wind, a 9.6-megawatt wind farm now under construction in Teton County. After the Spaniards pulled out of Coyote Wind, Marty had an idea: he would split the project into two ten-megawatt wind farms, set one mile apart—Crazy Mountain Wind, LLC, and Crazy Mountain Wind II, LLC. But North-Western refused to give him a PPA for either one.

But now Marty had a new weapon in his arsenal: the Community Renewable Energy Program—CREP, an especially distasteful spoonful of letters for the free-market warriors on the commission to swallow. As part of the state's path toward decarbonization, CREP mandated North-Western Energy to buy sixty-five megawatts—about 15 percent of its annual power needs—from independent, Montana-owned wind, hydro, and solar energy producers. Marty had won a coveted twenty-five-year PPA with NorthWestern by repackaging Crazy Mountain Wind as a model CREP and, what's more, by promising to deliver that clean power for less than NorthWestern Energy's avoided cost. Crazy Mountain Wind would be a good deal for Montana's ratepayers.

But NorthWestern had inserted a few poison pills into the wording of

Crazy Mountain Wind's contract. One was that the wind farm had to be built and operational within eighteen months, an absurdly tight deadline, given the many steps that go into financing and building a wind farm. Even NorthWestern's own representatives admitted that getting a project from bid to completion took at least two years. The other condition was that Crazy Mountain Wind had to file for CREP certification with Montana's Public Service Commission, which oversees public utilities.

In January 2014—about a month after his meeting with the Sweet Grass county commissioners—Marty filed a petition asking the PSC to put a ring on it by declaring Crazy Mountain a CREP. There was one small, worrying wrinkle: according to language in the CREP statute—inserted at the public service commissioners' insistence—Montana residents had to own a majority stake in any CREP project. They wanted to give Montana corporations a piece of the lucrative market that was increasingly dominated by large multinational companies like Enerfin, the Spanish energy company that had tried to develop Coyote Wind.

The problem was that it was impossible find any Montana companies with the money to build a $58 million wind farm. There were maybe twenty corporate entities in the United States with tax bills high enough to reap the production tax credits for a wind farm of that size. None of them were Montana mom-and-pop outfits. It was a classic catch-22: By law, the owner of a CREP had to be a small local business, or group of small businesses, with less than $50 million in gross revenues and less than $100 million in assets. But a business that size wouldn't have $40 million or $50 million in tax liabilities, and therefore no use for an eight-figure tax credit—the prime driver for investment in wind development. It certainly wouldn't have the ready cash to build a $58 million wind farm. The well-intentioned state legislators didn't have a clue about how project financing works in the wind industry.

In his petition to the PSC, Marty said exactly what he had told the county commissioners: he planned to use the federal production tax credit as a carrot to lure out-of-state equity investors, financial industry giants like J. P. Morgan and GE Capital, to underwrite Crazy Mountain Wind. Under the terms of the production tax credit statute, those equity investors would have a controlling interest in Crazy Mountain Wind for the first ten years of the twenty-five-year life of the project. But after that, over the next fifteen years, the controlling interest would revert to its Montana owners—Marty's WINData and Dave Healow's Montana Marginal Energy. Rick Jarrett, who owned the land where the wind farm would be built, would receive leasing fees for the entire quarter-century life of the contract. No one could deny that Rick was a Montana resident, or that the Crazy Mountain Cattle Company was exactly the kind of struggling Montana business that the Renewable Power Production and Rural Economic Development Act had been created to support.

It's possible the PSC commissioners would have simply waved Marty's petition through, stamping it with the CREP seal of approval and moving on to the next item on their agenda, had no one objected. After all, NorthWestern had been directed by the state legislature and the governor to award PPAs to eligible renewable resources in Montana—the power company would be fined if it didn't—and Crazy Mountain Wind checked all the right boxes. What's more, under the terms of its agreement with NorthWestern, Crazy Mountain Wind would provide savings to ratepayers by providing electricity at a decent price.

If no one had challenged Marty's petition, perhaps that's what would have happened. But in early February—just a few days before they filed their lawsuit against the Sweet Grass County Commissioners—attorneys for Jan Engwis, Whitney MacMillan, David Chesnoff, and Russell Gordy submitted four separate sets of comments to the PSC, objecting to CREP status for Crazy Mountain Wind. Marty's plan to lure out-of-state investors was at the crux of their separate, but similar, complaints. If tax equity investors would hold the controlling interest in Crazy Mountain Wind on day one, how could it be considered Montana-owned? "The CREP statute was never designed nor intended to be a means of enriching out-of-state financiers who are interested in capitalizing on the entitlements conferred by the federal Production Tax Credit," the letter from Engwis's attorney declared. Crazy Mountain Wind should be kicked out of CREP.

On February 25, the PSC commissioners met in the Bollinger Room to review Marty's petition with one of the commission's lawyers, Jason Brown. The opponents to the wind farm were correct to point out that the present-tense wording of the CREP statute suggested that Montana residents had to be majority owners of the wind farm from the get-go, Brown said. But then again, the statute really didn't account for the complexities of an ownership agreement that was structured over twenty-five years. You could argue that, over the life of the project, local owners would hold a majority interest in the wind farm—their fifteen years to the tax equity owners' ten.

The public service commissioners had broad authority to implement the law as they saw fit. They could examine the proposed financing for Crazy Mountain Wind in a vacuum, the in-house lawyer said, or they could look at it in the context of the wind business, where equity tax investment ownership was standard practice.

Given the relative newness of CREPs, the commissioners didn't have much past precedent to guide them. Only two wind farms had been awarded power purchase agreements as CREPs, and both were much smaller projects, less than half the size of Crazy Mountain Wind and thus significantly easier to finance. One of those CREPs, the Gordon Butte wind farm, was a 9.6-megawatt project owned by the powerful Galt family. The Galts were the second-largest private landowners in Montana at the time, and prominent in Republican politics. The price tag for Gordon Butte Wind was $20 million—about one-third of what it would cost to build Crazy Mountain Wind.

Commission chairman Bill Gallagher invited Commissioner Koopman to kick off the discussion, since Crazy Mountain Wind was in his district. Koopman, who had a thatch of thick white hair and a fondness for baseball metaphors, appreciated the opportunity to be the leadoff batter. But first, there were a few things he had to get off his chest.

"I'll keep this observation to about thirty seconds," Koopman said. "But you know, we're dealing here with a situation where economic activity is being driven, not by rational economics, not by an even playing field, but by political goals that create an uneven playing field . . . decision-making based on governmental incentives and subsidies and tax credits and so forth. And I find that extremely unfortunate. Essentially, politicians are saying, 'We know more and we're better than freedom and free markets and free people.' And I'll leave it right there. I just simply had to get that out."

In the matter of Crazy Mountain Wind's petition, Commissioner Koopman was ready to put his personal feelings about wind farms aside and follow the law. But there were so many what-ifs. What if, in year eight or year nine, lightning struck all the turbines and the whole project just disappeared? Then local owners would never have had a controlling interest in the wind farm, he mused. The opponents to Crazy Mountain Wind made some strong points. They correctly pointed out that the commissioners were not at liberty to change the law.

Brown, the PSC attorney, observed that if Crazy Mountain Wind was not declared a CREP, it wouldn't be able to attract investors. Who would be willing to build a wind farm that couldn't meet the terms of its own PPA?

But a cloud of doubt had settled upon the Bollinger Room. Commissioner Bob Lake thought there were a lot of assumptions built into the wind farm's plan for financing, and assumptions drove him crazy. Commissioner Kirk Bushman didn't understand why the state legislature hadn't set up a process for monitoring ownership of these projects. Commissioner Gallagher wasn't convinced that Crazy Mountain Wind would last twenty-five years. In his experience, wind projects didn't last that long. And he didn't buy Marty's argument that he couldn't find the financing for a twenty-five-megawatt wind farm in the state of Montana. Maybe he just hadn't tried hard enough.

But when you came right down to it, the four commissioners agreed, the real problem with declaring that Crazy Mountain was a CREP was that the CREP law as written simply didn't allow it.

The year 2014 was the tail end of the Tea Party era, when hard-right politicians in Washington, DC, evoked the literal wording of the Constitution—and what they interpreted to be the intentions of its framers—to explain their positions on a variety of hot-button issues, like universal health care and the federal deficit. This legislative philosophy was referred to variously as originalism, constitutionalism, or constructionism. But the Constitution didn't come up for discussion very often in Montana PSC work sessions, so the commissioners had to content themselves with the CREP statute, which they now parsed as carefully as if it had been penned by a Founding Father.

"In order to find for this petition, it seems to me that we would have to insert in Subsection Four the phrase, 'over the life of the project.' And we would have to adjust the 'is'—you know, the present tense—to 'would be.' And then in Subsection Three, we would have to insert 'over the life of the project . . .' and so forth," Commissioner Gallagher said. "I really empathize with these developers and I wish I could find a circumstance where I could find in their favor, but I am a strict constructionist so I'm disinclined to do that."

"I would have to agree with the chairman that it is adding to the law. It is taking liberties beyond our authority," said Koopman, who considered himself more of an originalist, hewing faithfully to whatever it was that the original people who wrote the law intended. In the profile picture on his Facebook page, he appeared in the frock coat and tricorn hat of a Continental Army soldier circa 1776, waving an American flag with the original thirteen stars.

The PSC's lone dissenter was Travis Kavulla, the commissioner for District One—the northeastern quadrant of the state—who was participating by speakerphone from his home in Great Falls. Kavulla had become the youngest public regulator in Montana history when he was elected to the PSC in 2010 at the age of twenty-six. His CV was impressive: a graduate of Harvard and Cambridge University, he was a former journalist who ran for the PSC after returning to Montana from a freelancing stint in Kenya. Kavulla had always been an energy policy nerd. The young would-be commissioner had studied the subject in his free time while working toward his bachelor's degree in history, he told the *Harvard Crimson* in 2010.

Although Kavulla initially saw the PSC as a stepping-stone to a bigger career in politics, he had become fascinated by the complexities of energy regulation. Kavulla was a Republican. But soon after taking office, he carved out a role as the commission's resident contrarian. In 2011, when there were still a few Democrats on the commission, he sided with them to oust Gallagher from the chairmanship for helping cover up another commissioner's use of public money for an undeclared trip to Washington, DC. The following year, both Democratic commissioners lost their bids for reelection and Commissioner Gallagher was restored to the chairmanship.

Beyond the petty squabbles, a widening philosophical chasm divided Kavulla from his PSC colleagues. The young commissioner had become skeptical about NorthWestern Energy and the disproportionately powerful hand it held in its dealings with contractors and small, independent developers like Marty Wilde. Marty was one of the first renewable-energy developers Kavulla met after he was elected; the two men worked out at the same gym in Great Falls—Peak Health & Wellness. Kavulla always knew he was in for it when he saw Marty's car in the Peak's parking lot. Marty had no hesitation about strolling over in the buff for some animated shop talk when he spotted the PSC commissioner in the locker room. He'd talk so long, Kavulla would almost stop feeling awkward about the naked thing. Sometimes, Marty would buttonhole Kavulla on the status of one of the projects he had before the PSC, which was even more uncomfortable. Then the commissioner would have to sidle away and be like, "Marty, I can't really talk about that," while clutching a towel.

Kavulla had sympathy for Marty. A wildcat developer had to do so many different jobs. He had to understand the quality of a wind resource and persuade the landowners to sign leases. Then he had to secure interconnection rights to the electrical grid and negotiate power purchase agreements with the all-powerful NorthWestern Energy. Big developers like Enerfin had specialists, entire departments, to handle each of those tasks, but Marty did it all on his own. Although PURPA had been a legislative attempt to level the playing field, Kavulla realized that it fell far short, at least in the state of Montana. There were near-insurmountable structural inequities baked into a system in which a monopoly utility got all its costs covered by a captive set of customers. That monopoly was willing to spend a great deal of its customers' money on lawyers and expert witnesses to fight people like Marty, who had to pay all his costs out of his own pocket. The inherent unfairness of the system—a system designed to shut down the little guy—was frankly outrageous. So was the fact that it was entirely subsidized by ratepayers.

"I don't necessarily agree with the chairman that being a strict constructionist leads you to one conclusion or another," Kavulla said now, over the Bollinger Room's speakerphone. He suggested that his fellow commissioners were getting into the weeds by delving so deeply into Crazy Mountain Wind's financing structure, which looked a lot like a mortgage, albeit one that was front-loaded rather than spread out over the twenty-five-year lifespan of the wind farm.

"You know, this so-called strict-constructionist view is actually a very sort of liberal reading of the law in some ways, in the sense that it gives more power to a government agency to decide what instruments of financing are acceptable," Kavulla said, waggishly.

Marty's petition failed by a vote of four to one, with Kavulla dissenting. In their ruling, the commissioners declared that an eligible renewable resource couldn't qualify as a CREP unless "local owners had a controlling interest at the time of its interconnection and at any point thereafter."

The PSC commissioners' strict-constructionist interpretation of the CREP ownership rule as it applied to Crazy Mountain Wind would paralyze the development of homegrown renewable-energy projects in Montana. In the months and years that followed, the commissioners would evoke their own precedent-setting decision about Crazy Mountain Wind to put the kibosh on other would-be CREPs that depended upon outside financing to get built—which was pretty much all of them. Kelly Hills—the project that Rick Jarrett's neighbor Steve Breck had leased his land for—failed to win CREP status in 2014 and was never built. Greycliff Wind, a twenty-megawatt project east of Big Timber, died after being denied CREP status in 2015.

Years later, after he had left public service for a job in the private sector, I asked Kavulla if the PSC would have rejected Marty's petition for CREP status—and all the would-be CREPs that followed—if Rick Jarrett's neighbors hadn't filed their objections questioning the legitimacy of Crazy Mountain Wind's tax equity ownership plan.

"Oh, probably not," he said. He qualified his answer by explaining that the way the commission operated was largely reactive: the commissioners considered the arguments that were brought before them. They didn't do a deep dive into every statute for the fun of it, absent any formal challenges. "I don't think there would have been as much parsing had it not been" for the neighbors' objections, he said. They were well-made legal arguments. "Although honestly, when I see pleadings like that, I just assume that these are wealthy landowners who want to keep their view," Kavulla said.

Year after year, all through the 2010s, NorthWestern Energy failed to buy the mandated sixty-five megawatts of power from eligible local renewable resources. There were penalties on the books for this—in the board game of Montana energy policy, the rules were that if you didn't buy enough power from CREPs, you had to pay a $1.2 million annual fine. But each year, NorthWestern's attorneys appeared before the PSC and asked the commissioners to waive that penalty, claiming in the utility's defense that it was just too hard to find renewables that fit the CREP description. After all, look at what had happened when it signed a CREP agreement with Crazy Mountain Wind.

And the PSC obliged. The commissioners gave NorthWestern a decade's worth of passes. By 2018, there was widespread consensus that the CREP program was a failure, and that the most significant renewable resource in NorthWestern's portfolio was its Get Out of Jail Free card.

George Stigler, a Nobel Prize–winning economist, coined the phrase "regulatory capture" in 1971 to describe what happens to government agencies that are established to oversee powerful industries. Stigler, in a wide-ranging critique that examined everything from the petroleum and airline industries to the licensing of barbers and beauticians, argued that the more powerful the industry, the more completely it would "acquire" whatever body was set up to regulate it, shaping its rules and conditioning its functions for its own benefit. What's more, the industry would use its regulator to block any newcomer that challenged its dominance over the market. It would do this by influencing and molding regulatory policies in such a way as to restrict any potential rival who might peel away customers.

If you were Marty Wilde, regulatory capture looked a lot like the inside of the Bollinger Room. Former commissioner Kavulla, reflecting upon CREP's sorry history, put it more simply: "That's almost just an example of regulators who decide they just don't like a law, and decide they're not going to make it work."

The Montana regulators weren't unique in that. The *Harvard Law Review* analysis found examples of institutional bias in public service commissions across the country. In states with vague environmental mandates—and even in those with very clear, directly worded ones—"disinclined PSCs . . . will often narrowly interpret their governing statutes to avoid consideration of climate impacts."

Marty had now invested a decade in Crazy Mountain Wind, and well over $100,000 on site-development work and environmental studies and interconnection agreements and legal fees. And once again, he had come up empty-handed. By rejecting his CREP petition, the PSC had effectively killed Crazy Mountain Wind's power purchase agreement with NorthWestern Energy. And without that PPA, the wind farm had no chance of winning tax equity investors. The PPA was the lifeblood of any wind project. Without one, Crazy Mountain Wind didn't stand a chance.

But Marty was pressing ahead, because that was what Marty did. Trying to develop wind in Montana, he liked to say, was like learning how to box in prison. A difficult environment, period. Marty told Rick that there were alternative methods for obtaining contracts, other avenues to pursue. They could even try to sell Crazy Mountain Wind outright to NorthWestern, to be folded into its portfolio of in-house assets. "It was always 'I'll try to do A, B, C, or D—and if that doesn't work, there's E, F, G.' His wheels were spinning always, always," Marty's former girlfriend Annette Dea-Dart told me.

That winter, Marty started a blog he called *Warrior Medicine*. On the home page, he posted a sepia-tone photograph of his namesake, Siyeh—Mad Wolf, the Blackfeet holy man and leader known for acts of courage so rash that his own warriors thought twice about joining him on raids. The blog was where Marty explored his fascination with Blackfeet wisdom, Celtic lore, Greek myths, the *Book of the Samurai*—spirituality in all its forms. After the CREP debacle, he posted a link to a lecture by Robert Bly, the poet and men's movement founder, about the gift of grandiosity. Grandiosity, Bly said, was an implant from God. It could make you feel indomitable.

If you were a wildcat wind developer in Montana, you probably had the grandiosity implant.

As if to confirm this, a few weeks after his rejection at the PSC, the federal government handed Marty a victory. Marty and his friend Dave Healow had been part of a tiny group of Montana renewable developers that filed a complaint about the Public Service Commission's obstructionist policies with the Federal Energy Regulatory Commission (FERC), the independent government agency that regulates the interstate transmission of electricity, natural gas, and oil. That March, FERC ruled that Montana's Public Service Commission had violated federal law. The feds agreed with Marty and the other frustrated QF developers: the Montana Rule requiring a QF to win a competitive solicitation and the fifty-megawatt cap on wind created unreasonable obstacles to wind development. "A utility may refuse to negotiate with a QF at all," federal regulators observed. FERC declined to bring any enforcement action against the Montana PSC, but in the right hands, the federal ruling could become a bulldozer to clear a new path to Montana's energy market.

On April Fool's Day, Marty returned to the Sweet Grass County annex building with Rick Jarrett to formally request a new letter of support for Crazy Mountain Wind.

This was mostly an exercise in futility, given the fatal blow the PSC had dealt Marty's CREP petition. But a letter would show potential investors that Sweet Grass County still welcomed new industry. Marty Wilde coming down to Big Timber to ask the commissioners for that letter was how he showed the wankers in Big Timber they didn't have him beat.

"My understanding is that there's quite a few forces trying to obstruct the project, you know," Marty said, his voice lower and raspier than usual, after he introduced himself yet again to a roomful of people who already knew who he was, some of whom were staring at him with expressions of open dislike. "Things have changed since the last time we met with you, but we still have every intention of building the project, one way or another. And I am available for questions. I think Commissioner Faw asked that I be there to answer questions, so."

"I have several, as a matter of fact," Faw said. "So, how does this affect the project, Mr. Wilde, where the CREP program was turned down by the PSC?"

Marty seemed to have no idea what the commissioner was talking about. "I don't understand. What do you mean it was turned down by the PSC?"

"Well, it looks to me like if you go on the internet and take a look at it, that the community renewable-energy project was turned down by the PSC by four to one. You're not aware of that?" Faw said.

"I guess I don't understand your question. Maybe say it another way," Marty said.

This was what boxing in prison looked like. Marty blocked and parried every move Faw made to pin him down, to make him cry uncle and admit that his wind farm was officially DOA. "We do have other plans. The project will continue," he finally said.

Commissioner Bill Wallace asked if anyone else had comments they'd like to make.

Engwis pulled out a six-page list of questions typed up on his lawyer's letterhead.

"Commissioners, may I please ask some questions, and hopefully you'll be able to answer them on the record for me," he said. "Do you have a written set of policies or procedures for granting letters of support to private developments in the county?"

"Not that I'm aware of," said Susie Mosness, who had less patience than usual for Engwis's inquisitions. It had been a hard couple of weeks. Her mother had died in early March. The following week, Cindy Selensky had announced she was going to challenge Mosness for the commissioner seat in the upcoming November elections.

"The voters and I have a common belief that government has run amuck and our elected officials have stopped listening to the voters," Selensky told Lindsey Kroskob in an interview for the *Pioneer*. One of her top priorities, she said, was to put the wind energy issue to a public vote. Cindy was at the county commission meeting that afternoon, seated on the same side of the conference table as Jan Engwis.

Engwis worked his way down his list of numbered questions, sparring with the commissioners when they responded and needling them when they hemmed and hawed. Did the commissioners not have a formal process for issuing letters? Engwis thought there should be one. He didn't think government should run by whim or fancy. "Have you given any thought to the liabilities or obligations that you might incur as a county, and you might expose the county to, by issuing a letter of support in this case?" he asked.

"What number is that?" said Mosness.

"Number fifteen," said Engwis. His lawyer had emailed the list of questions to the commissioners just before the meeting, so they could follow along.

When Cindy Selensky told the commissioners that they should hold a public hearing to find out how people felt about the wind farm, Rick couldn't contain himself.

"Crazy Mountain Wind, it's all on private property," he said. "When Jan builds a building on his place, he doesn't have to go to a public hearing to find out if he can do it. If he wants to put a center pivot in, he doesn't have to go to the county commissioners to find out if he'll put a center pivot in," he said, referring to the large irrigation line that Engwis had installed to water his alfalfa fields. Rick's new girlfriend, Lois, hated Jan's center pivot. She said it pissed her off every time she drove down the county road, that stupid pivot blocking her view of the Yellowstone.

Engwis, indignant, observed that he had paid for his center pivot himself without asking the commissioners for a letter of support or tax abatement. Jami pointed out that Jan's pivot didn't benefit Sweet Grass County one iota, whereas their wind farm would bring in tax dollars for the county.

Jami tried to make it clear that she was attending these meetings as a private person, not a county employee. She made a point of writing, "Jami Jarrett Moody, taxpayer" or "Jami Jarrett Moody, citizen," on the sign-in sheets. But her comments rankled Engwis and his fellow wind farm opponents. After the meeting, a woman named Robyn Roberts fired off an email to Pat Dringman, the county attorney. "Is there a provision that allows for a county employee to engage in speech that might be questionable if he/she is 'off the clock'?" Roberts demanded. Jami was afraid she might lose her job. Dringman reviewed the matter with the general counsel of the Montana Association of Counties, who confirmed that Jami had a right to free speech, even if she was his assistant.

The motion to grant Crazy Mountain Wind a new letter of support passed, two to one.

"Forget it's a wind farm, I don't care what it is. It's still private property rights," Wallace said. Faw, who voted against, wanted to go on record as saying that he didn't think they'd had enough public meetings.

The 231-mile drive back to his log house in Augusta, on the Rocky Mountain Front, gave Marty time to mull over his options. Letter or no letter, in the wake of PSC's ruling, it would now be impossible to finance Crazy Mountain Wind under CREP. CREP had been designed to help homegrown qualifying facilities win power purchase agreements in Montana. However flawed, the law had been an acknowledgment of how difficult it was for QFs to find their feet in Montana's energy market. It compelled NorthWestern to do business with small renewable developers. The problem was, NorthWestern refused to do business with QFs. Marty knew this from bitter experience. The utility would cite the PSC's Montana Rule—the one that forced wind farms of three megawatts or bigger to go through the competitive bidding process—or the PSC's fifty-megawatt cap on the total amount of wind energy it could buy. "NorthWestern cannot bargain away the Commission's authority," Frank Bennett, a NorthWestern contract administrator, declared grandly in a 2013 email, swatting off one of Marty's attempts to sell his wind power.

Sometimes, the utility's administrators would offer him a lousy short-term rate for his wind power, well below the favorable QF-1 tariff. But mostly, they ignored him. "This guy keeps pestering me. I'm starting to have a better appreciation for Frank's life," one of NorthWestern's attorney wrote in an internal email to Bennett, the contract administrator. The lawyer asked to be taken off group emails with Marty. "I think at this stage everyone has the same feelings," Bennett replied, with a virtual sigh.

Marty had retooled Crazy Mountain Wind as a CREP so that he could jam his foot in the monopoly's door. Then the PSC slammed it shut again. The only souvenir he had for his trouble was the draft power purchase agreement that Crazy Mountain Wind had received from NorthWestern after it won the CREP beauty pageant.

Which got him thinking. As Marty drove north on US Route 87, AC/

DC blasting, a strategy began to take shape. The federal government had just called out the PSC for violating PURPA. FERC said the Montana Rule was illegal, and so was the PSC's fifty-megawatt cap. Crazy Mountain Wind would never be a CREP. But it was still a QF, with the right to sell its power under federal law—a right that the federal government had just reaffirmed, with a slap at the Montana PSC. And it so happened that Marty Wilde had a draft power purchase agreement from NorthWestern with Crazy Mountain Wind's name on it.

When he got home, Marty printed up the agreement, signed it, and sent it to NorthWestern with the demand that it be executed without delay. By giving Marty that draft power purchase agreement, North-Western had opened itself to a jiujitsu hip throw, Wilde-style. The PPA, Marty argued in an email to Bennett, the disdainful administrator, constituted a legally enforceable obligation—a LEO, in regulatory speak. Marty, by signing it, had committed Crazy Mountain Wind to NorthWestern; now the utility had to commit to Crazy Mountain Wind. Thanks to that timely FERC ruling, it would have trouble using the Montana Rule, or any of the other obstructionist policies it had long relied upon, as an excuse to say no. So—no bidding contest. No fifty-megawatt cap. And since the project wouldn't be a CREP, no fussing over Marty's plan for tax equity financing, either. Sign the tendered PPA immediately, Marty wrote Bennett. Time is of the essence. Otherwise, he'd pursue all legal options.

So pleased was Marty with this plan that he printed a second PPA form and wrote in the name of another twenty-five-megawatt wind farm he'd been developing in Teton County, called Greenfield Wind. He sent that off, too—a second LEO for the wankers at NorthWestern. He thanked them in advance for their attention and signed it, "Kind Regards, Martin Wilde."

NorthWestern would try to knock him down. But Marty knew how to box. Now he just had to find the right sparring partner.

10

THE ENGINE ROOM

February 19, 2019
Park County Courthouse
Livingston, Montana

DAVID CHESNOFF, *Cross-examination*:

Q: Good afternoon, Mr. Chesnoff.

MR. CHESNOFF: Hi, how are you?

Q: How are you doing?

MR. CHESNOFF: Fine, thank you.

Q: I'd like to put this map up, if I may.

THE COURT: You may.

Q: You told us not to get too close to each other, so I don't know what the safety zone is here. Can I come up here?

THE COURT: You certainly may.

MR. CHESNOFF: You seem nice enough.

JULY 28, 1996
LAKE LANIER OLYMPIC PARK
GAINESVILLE, GEORGIA

Monica Tranel Michini, six seat on the United States women's eight rowing team, watched the frogmen move through the greenish water of Lake Lanier. A clutch of pipe bombs had exploded at Atlanta's Centennial Olympic Park two nights before, spraying masonry nails into the crowds and killing one woman. Now, as the best female rowers in the world lined up at the start pontoon to race for Olympic gold, a tactical dive team was checking the hulls of their boats for concealed explosives.

It was day ten of the 1996 Summer Games, the day of the race that the world expected the American women to win. Monica and her teammates were the reigning world champions. "Women's crew route seems paved in gold," was the *New York Times* headline. Six feet tall and rippling with muscle, Monica was part of the boat's engine room—rowing lingo for the middle four seats of the eight, reserved for the strongest rowers.

The counter-explosives team gave the all-clear: the race could begin. Stripped down to her red-white-and-blue unisuit, an American flag and a pair of crossed oars over her heart, Monica adjusted her grip on the portside oar. She was thirty years old, an admitted member of the Pennsylvania bar. And an Olympian. In the space of four years, she had punched her way to the top of an elite sport she'd never heard of as a Montana ranch kid.

Monica grew up baling hay, feeding livestock, and fixing fence with her brothers and sisters on a ranch in Ashland, at the edge of the Northern Cheyenne Reservation. She was the sixth of ten children. Her father, Ned Tranel, had moved the family there to take a job as a school psychologist with the St. Labre Indian School, a boarding school founded by Ursuline nuns in 1884.

It was a ragged, isolated place, but the Tranels could afford land there—a beautiful piece of land, overlooking the Tongue River, with pastures for cows and horses. To Monica's mother, Virginia, the ranch seemed the ideal setting for a family-centered life. "For a while longer, we could shelter our family from the frenzied world while they learn lessons only the land can teach," she wrote in her 2003 memoir, *Ten Circles upon the Pond*.

The St. Labre school's dark history has yet to be fully uncovered. Many children are presumed to have died at the boarding school in the late nineteenth and early twentieth centuries, their burial places unknown.* Northern Cheyenne children who attended St. Labre in the 1950s had their braids cut off and their mouths washed out with soap for speaking Cheyenne. Reservation schools were reported dumping

---

* In 2022, the St. Labre Indian School Educational Association appointed a commission to investigate deaths and locate unmarked graves at the three schools it oversees on the Crow and Northern Cheyenne reservations.

grounds for priests known to have molested children. In the late 2010s, multiple allegations of sexual abuse by priests affiliated with the St. Labre school began surfacing. Their crimes had gone on for decades, from the 1950s well into the 1980s.

Ned and Virginia didn't know these things when they moved their family to Ashland in the early 1970s. They liked the idea of their kids going to mission schools with Northern Cheyenne and Crow kids, sharing cultures. The family attended Sunday mass at a stone church shaped like a tipi, with a giant cross jutting out from its stylized smoke hole. From first grade through third grade, Monica was the only white kid in her class. She was chased home, groped, had rocks thrown at her. Ned, who had trouble seeing past the beautiful scenery to the cycles of poverty, violence, and generational trauma that had shaped this community, urged his children to learn from the experience of being a minority.

The Tranel kids became their own tribe. While Virginia was occupied with whatever baby and toddlers she had at home, the older kids took charge of the younger ones. It was like being raised by wolves, Monica said, dangerous and wild and awesome. In the summer, one of Monica's big brothers would lead the kids out to the fields to bale and stack hay. Her job, at the age of eight, was to drive the tractor. When a summer storm swelled the irrigation ditch with rainwater, they'd peel off their clothes and jump in for a swim. In the winter, they built snowmen with the ranch's front-end loader. Tranel snowmen were over twenty feet high.

The Tranel kids shared everything—bedrooms, even beds. All that sharing was good training for rowing in an eight-woman boat—to be the sixth of ten children was to be a born team player. But Monica's place in the pecking order made her sensitive to the slightest degree of unfairness. Nothing bothered her more than someone getting more than their share. When Virginia opened a can of fruit cocktail, Monica was the one who carefully cut each maraschino cherry in half and made sure that each sibling got exactly the same portion.

She chafed at the way chores were divided between boys and girls. Monica didn't want to shell peas in the shade with her mother; she wanted to fix fence in the hot sun with her brothers, stripping off her shirt just like the boys did. Full of passionate convictions, she'd climb to the top of the grain bin and deliver speeches to the hills. When she grew up, Monica announced, she was going to play football for Notre Dame.

In 1976, Ned started a private practice in Billings and moved the family to a 2,400-acre wheat and cattle ranch in Broadview, a prairie town that consisted of little more than a grain elevator. Virginia's rosy vision of the ranching lifestyle had become clouded and cracked by then. Ned was an alcoholic. When he picked up the kids from high school in Billings, he'd grab a six-pack of beer on the way, then drink two or three while one of the older kids drove home. After dinner, he'd settle on his recliner with a twelve-ounce tumbler of whiskey. The family staged an intervention when Monica was an undergrad at Gonzaga, a Catholic university in Washington State.

She saw her first racing boat there freshman year. It was beached on a grassy quadrangle, dragged there by members of Gonzaga's newly formed crew team to whip up interest in the sport. Monica had busted her knee playing basketball. She was looking for a team to join, and Gonzaga's Jesuit Navy was eager for recruits. The first time she went out on the water, Monica was hooked. The catch of the oar at the start of each stroke, the fluid loop as you drove it through the water and feathered it back. The cool morning air and the feel of the water on your hands as the boat powered forward, cleaving the elements.

Before Monica's first race, the coach told her, "All this is about is pulling hard." Monica may not have gone to a prep school with a crew program, but she knew how to pull hard. A rival coach from a university with a bigger, better crew program said he'd never seen worse technique than from the Gonzaga rowers who had just beaten his boat and won the race.

After graduation, Monica went to Rutgers Law School. The Camden, New Jersey, campus was just a bike ride from Philadelphia's Schuylkill River and Boathouse Row. Even if you had rowed in a second-rate crew program on the other side of the country, you'd heard of Philadelphia's Boathouse Row. Monica rode her bike over the Benjamin Franklin Bridge and started knocking on boathouse doors.

When she got to the Vesper Boat Club, a neogothic pile at 10 Boathouse Row, J. B. Kelly III opened the door. Kelly was rowing royalty; his father and grandfather were Olympic champions; his aunt was Princess

Grace of Monaco. Monica had never heard of him. Kelly invited the tall Montanan inside Vesper, showed her around, and told her she was welcome to row with the club anytime.

Monica began spending all her free time on the Schuylkill with some of the strongest rowers in the country. At first, she was just killing fish with her oar. Someone at Vesper let her use a single, and she flipped it. After she flipped it again, people started calling her "Flipper." But she kept hanging around the boathouse, always with an eye out for a spot in a boat, any boat—sculling in a single or a double or a quad, rowing sweep in any four or eight with an open seat. She stopped killing fish.

As she refined her technique on the Schuylkill, Monica became aware that there was such a thing as class, and that she occupied a different one than many of the people in the same boats. There had been wealthy students at Gonzaga, but no real social hierarchy—if you were Catholic, then you were pretty much in. But the rowers at Vesper had summer homes. They had graduated from Ivy League colleges with elite rowing programs that offered a glide path to the national rowing team. Monica wasn't part of that world, but as outsiders went, she was special. The West had romance to it. The other rowers liked having her around. They asked her about cowboys and horses. They stopped calling her Flipper and started calling her "Montana."

That year, the national coach for the US rowing program stopped by Vesper on a scouting visit. He gave Vesper's top rowers a timed test on the ergometer rowing machine. Although Monica was more of a hanger-on at that point, someone said that Montana should take the test, too. She sat down on the erg machine thinking she'd pull as hard as she could without dying. When she got off the erg, the coach told her she had just pulled the fastest time in the country.

Monica was full of raw talent, but unfocused. She was invited to an elite training camp for the American national team, but once she got back to Philadelphia, she trained when the spirit moved her and bagged early morning practices when it didn't. She did dumb things, like going out drinking the night before a race.

That changed when she met Fred Michini, a rower eight years her senior who won bronze in the lightweight men's four at the 1985 world championships. Fred had found focus and discipline in rowing after a chaotic childhood. "When I started dating him, I got serious about my rowing. It became a different thing," Monica said. "Whether he brought me to it, or that's what I was ready for, I don't know." She committed to her training and began winning races. Monica and Fred married in 1993—the year she won a place on the US national team.

The 1995 world championship in Tampere, Finland, was a prelude to the Atlanta Summer Games. The American women took the lead from the start, their racing shell knifing through the chop on Lake Kaukajärvi. A pair of British rowing experts called the race. Untidy bladework perhaps, said one, noting the water flying off the Americans' oars. But tremendous power. They took it by the scruff of the neck off the start, and no other boat could catch them. The US crossed the finish line a full two seconds ahead of Romania, to blasts of air horns, whistles, and cheers. Monica yanked off her hat and flopped back in her seat, shrieking with elation. She and her teammates were now world champions.

Rowing is not a spectator sport. Long stretches of a two-kilometer race take place out of view. Unlike basketball or gymnastics, there's no opportunity for a breakout move or a virtuosic play by any individual athlete. The choreography is monotonous, and the whole thing is over in about seven minutes. Monica and her teammates were used to competing in obscurity. No one was dreaming of being on a Wheaties box.

But America loves a winner. The American women's eight were the best on earth, and that put them in the spotlight. The speed with which they inhaled bagels during training breaks was news, reported by an awestruck writer for *Time* magazine. So was the rib that Monica broke in training, a painful but common stress fracture that inspired feverish speculation from a *New York Times* sportswriter. "As with other Olympic athletes in the final weeks of preparation," he wrote, "there is a question about just how much the body can take."

When Monica and her teammates were locked in, working in sync, an electric current seemed to ripple from one oar to the next, a steady flow of power without static or friction. But the current became erratic once the American women got to Atlanta, pulsing strong one moment, thready the next. They finished nearly four full seconds behind Belarus in the first qualifying round, then squeaked out a win in the second-chance repechage to make it to the final with Canada, Belarus, Romania, the Netherlands, and Australia.

The race for gold in the women's eight was televised live by NBC one muggy Sunday afternoon. A neighbor recorded it for Monica on his VCR. Cameras captured the race from every angle: high overhead by helicopter, alongside the rowers on motorboats. Seen from the sky, the race was serene, orderly. Six yellow boats glided across the water in chalk-straight lines, with six sets of oars tracing a flurry of white commas on its gray-green surface. Close up, it was all punishing labor: biceps, triceps, and deltoids straining, teeth bared, faces twisted with effort, as though the oars were pickaxes and the women were breaking rocks.

Any home-court advantage the American women had going into the race was lost within the first five hundred meters. They briefly shot ahead, then fell back, as Romania took the lead. At the thousand-meter mark, the US was still in medal contention, in third place, ahead of Canada. The 5 on the American bow seemed to inch closer to Belarus's 4, but was then overtaken by both boats.

The cameras skimmed alongside the women as they toiled at their oars, sucking air and casting split-second sidelong glances at the boats nosing ahead of them. At 1,500 meters, the cameras pulled back for a long shot as the Americans' boat came within view of the grandstands, trailing the competition. And then, at six minutes, nineteen seconds, and seventy-three milliseconds, it was all over. Romania crossed the finish line for gold, with Canada and Belarus taking silver and bronze. The American women had finished fourth, nearly seven full seconds behind the gold medalists.

Jennifer Dore, the team stroke, clung to the sides of the boat, chest heaving. In the bow, Anne Kakela leaned back on her hands, grimacing in pain. Only Monica was still gripping her oar. It was clenched in her right hand, her knuckles white, as she stared down into the water. No one said anything. Apart from their ragged breath, the women were silent. They were silent on the bus back to the Olympic Village, and for some hours after that. Everyone knew how every other woman on the team was feeling. There was nothing to say.

Hours after the race, Linda Wertheimer interviewed Monica on National Public Radio's *All Things Considered*. "I still believe that we are the best-trained athletes in the world and that we were the best-trained athletes in that race," she said softly, her voice cottony with tears. "And that makes the pill even more bitter to swallow, because I know we lost, not on our best day, but on our worst." In some ways, she said, this loss had more meaning to her than her victories.

President Bill Clinton and the First Family hosted a reception for the US Olympic Team on the South Lawn of the White House that August. Monica tied her Team USA jacket around her waist and danced with her rowing teammate William Carlucci, who won bronze in the men's lightweight four. The bronze medal slung around Carluccci's neck glinted in the August sunshine as they danced. Afterward, Monica told Virginia that the only thing she had to show for her years of hard work and sacrifice was a jacket.

Twenty-four years after the race, almost to the day, I asked Monica the same question Wertheimer had: What went wrong? "I think to this day, if you set all eight of us down, you would get a different explanation from each one of us," she said. "We were the defending world champions. We were just really fast. And we finished fourth." It was a life-defining failure, she said. "It's like you can put your whole heart and soul into something and you're not necessarily going to win just because you are totally committed."

With an eye on the 2000 Olympics in Sydney, Australia, Monica began to train again. Her focus had shifted from the eight to the single. If she made it to rowing's world stage again, her success or failure wouldn't depend on anyone but herself. Monica and Fred moved to Missoula, where she clerked for a federal judge and rowed her twenty-seven-foot-long Kevlar single on the Milltown Dam, a Superfund site contaminated with decades of toxic mine tailings that had been washed downstream from the copper mines of Butte and Anaconda. When she wasn't dodging beavers on the arsenic-laden waters of the Milltown reservoir in her scull, she built up her endurance by running up and down past the concrete M on Missoula's Mount Sentinel.

Fred supported Monica's second Olympic bid, but their marriage was troubled. Fred was volatile, with an explosive temper. Monica's father took her aside and said that in his professional opinion as a psychologist, she was in an abusive relationship. Monica shrugged it off. Fred was the one who showed her that you could channel all your energies into athletics—the good and the bad. She had been an outsider on Boathouse Row until she met him. Fred had given her entrée into the world of elite rowing—*her* world now. "And then he started throwing things at me," she said. "I was like, 'Well, that could actually hurt at some point.' I'm a big woman, but . . ."

Fred Michini, a retired software consultant, still lives in Missoula. I asked him if he threw things at Monica during their marriage. "Occasionally. A TV remote, things like that," he said. "She was not bad at that stuff, either. You could say that not only one of us had a temper."

In September 2000, the Tranel clan boarded planes to Australia and headed to the Sydney International Regatta Centre to cheer Monica on as she raced her single in the Summer Olympics. Monica advanced to the semifinals, only to finish dead last in the qualifying race. She didn't make it to the final. After the race, Monica's brother watched Fred smash his binoculars against the railing in frustration.

"If that's all you were going to do, why did you waste our time?" Fred asked Monica after the race. (Michini does not remember saying this.) The marriage, and the rowing career that had defined it, were over. While Fred was away on a work trip, Monica moved out of their house in Missoula. The next time he saw her was at an attorney's office.

Monica worked as a staff attorney at the Public Service Commission, focusing on telecommunications issues, then went to Washington, DC, to work as a legislative counsel for Montana Republican senator Conrad Burns. She moved back to Helena and married a lawyer. They had two daughters and went into practice together, but dissolved the partnership when they divorced in 2012.

Monica took on a broad range of clients and cases. The clients who hired her had no idea that their lawyer was a two-time Olympic rower. But the medal that had eluded her was embedded in her psyche. She wrote a poem called "On Finishing Fourth in the Olympics" and put it in a drawer.

Monica did find meaning in her work as a litigator, even though the courtroom wasn't the setting for high drama people thought it was. That *Perry Mason* "gotcha" moment? That never happened. It was her job to guide her clients through a murky process where wins and losses weren't thrown up on a scoreboard; to fight for them, but also be able to accept a mixed outcome if it gave them what they needed—to settle, in other words. There were no photo finishes in the legal profession.

"I think that's the value of having this fourth-place finish sort of embedded in my heart," she said. "I don't define the outcomes by the external label. You can settle a case and feel like you didn't really get what you deserve, but you have peace. So, that's what you value—that thing that allows you to walk away."

She was a single parent in her mid-forties when she joined the office of Montana's Consumer Counsel, a state agency that advocates on behalf of utility customers in matters that come before the Public Service Commission. Monica liked fighting for ratepayers and their pocketbooks. It engaged her sense of fairness—it wasn't right for a utility to take more than its share of its customers' maraschino cherries.

In 2014, the Public Service Commission was asked to approve the costliest utility deal in state history: NorthWestern Energy wanted to spend $900 million on a passel of eleven hydroelectric dams. If the commissioners preapproved the purchase, as the utility was requesting, that $900 million would be folded into the rate base for electricity and passed on to the ratepayers.

That April, the PSC commissioners left the cozy confines of the Bollinger Room to solicit feedback from Montana ratepayers about the Big Dam Deal, holding listening sessions at C'mon Inns, chamber of commerce halls, and senior centers. On behalf of the Consumer Counsel, Monica gave them an earful. "Your rates are going up by $400 million in the next eight years. That's a given," she told the crowd at a public meeting at Stevensville's North Valley Public Library. She pointed out that the investor-owned utility that was selling the dams, PPL Montana, and the investor-owned utility that wanted to buy them, NorthWestern Energy, shared the same pool of shareholders. Those shareholders—hedge funds like BlackRock and the Vanguard Group—would benefit twice over from the sale and the ratepayers would be stuck with the bill.

The PSC held nine days of hearings at the state capitol that summer. Over objections from NorthWestern's attorney, Monica questioned the utility's chief financial officer, Brian Bird, about its other high-priced ac-

quisitions, like Colstrip Unit Four, a problem-plagued coal-fired generator whose outages had cost Montanans tens of millions of dollars over
the years. The PSC had already ruled that the utility's monthly trackers,
which showed evidence of those cost overruns, could not be admitted as
an exhibit. Monica asked Bird about them anyway.

"I'd like to just take a run at it," she told the commissioners. "Are you
aware that in this filing, NorthWestern is asking for approximately $20
million in recovery related to a period of time when Colstrip Four was
out for seven months?"

"I'm aware that we asked for recovery of those costs," Bird replied
tightly.

When he equivocated about cost overruns at the Dave Gates generating station—another costly acquisition that had gone straight into the
utility's rate base—Monica's response was withering.

"Mr. Bird, you're the CFO of NorthWestern, correct?" she asked.

At times, she reached for a broadsword when a scalpel might have
been better suited for the job. Untidy bladework, perhaps, but tremendous power. The hydro hearings were widely covered. If you were a
wind developer who'd been burned by NorthWestern, watching the
Consumer Counsel lawyer's takedown of the utility's suave CFO made
you want to get popcorn.

That October, the PSC voted four to one to approve the Big Dam
Deal, with only the contrarian Commissioner Kavulla dissenting. Monica had fought hard to make the case that ratepayers shouldn't have to
pay $900 million for those dams. Now it was time to walk away. It wasn't
about winning or losing. At least that was what she told herself.

Then, in the spring of 2016, Marty Wilde called.

Months after he sent NorthWestern a signed power purchase agreement
for Crazy Mountain Wind with the demand that it honor its legally enforceable obligations, Marty was still in the boxing ring.

The giant utility had refused to negotiate, insisting that it could not
do business with Crazy Mountain Wind, QF, because it was still in a
contract with Crazy Mountain Wind, CREP. That contract had not been
officially terminated, even though the PSC had denied the wind farm its

CREP certification, effectively killing it. Crazy Mountain Wind was a zombie CREP. Like the Outcasts said to haunt the Crazy Mountains, it was alive, yet not alive; a CREP, yet not a CREP, trapped in the bureaucratic purgatory of the Bollinger Room.

But Marty had somehow succeeded in getting the monopoly to the negotiating table for Greenfield Wind—the other twenty-five-megawatt project he'd been developing, in Teton County. The utility grudgingly agreed to honor the legally enforceable obligation (LEO) of the draft PPA Marty had fired off—though it fought him on the price. After months of back-and-forth, the monopoly and the wind prospector arrived at a tentative agreement and appealed to the Public Service Commission to stipulate the terms for a contract for Greenfield Wind in November 2014.

The PSC responded by scuppering the whole deal at a work session that December. Chairman Gallagher had just watched Robin Williams in *The Angriest Man in Brooklyn*. The movie really spoke to him. "There's a theme phrase in there—'What the hell?' And that was the phrase that came to mind as I considered this," Gallagher said, sounding like the angriest man on the Public Service Commission.

The chairman's strict-constructionist hackles had been raised by Greenfield Wind's insistence that NorthWestern had a legally enforceable obligation to buy its power because it was a renewable-energy project. The notion of a LEO was bogus—"an artificiality," Gallagher declared. "The legislature says, 'We're going to give certain producers an advantage.' Clearly, the Constitution is designed to avoid that very thing," Gallagher thundered. "What the hell!"

Two months later, Marty was back in the Bollinger Room, watching his lawyer implore the commission to reconsider its decision. Even NorthWestern's own attorney conceded that Marty had won this round. The monopoly had to give Greenfield a contract, because PURPA gave it no choice. "We still have a 1978 law driving many of these processes," he said ruefully.

The lawyer for the Montana Consumer Counsel was there to make sure that ratepayers didn't get caught in the crossfire between NorthWestern and Marty Wilde.

"Mr. Chairman, I would request probably forty-five to sixty seconds of your time," she said in a flat eastern Montana drawl. Marty recognized her from the Big Dam Deal hearings that summer; the lawyer who tied NorthWestern's CFO up in knots. Now she was directing the commissioners' attention to the eighth page of a staff memo, Section B. It recommended that any agreement insulate ratepayers from unanticipated costs related to the integration of Greenfield's wind power with NorthWestern's grid. "The Consumer Counsel would ask that the commission adopt that recommendation from its staff. Thank you." That was it. In a chamber known for soliloquizing and speechifying, the lawyer may have set a Bollinger Room record for brevity.

Once the meeting was over, she didn't waste time on small talk. The commissioners had yet to rise from their comfy high-backed chairs by the time she had slung on her long brown parka and headed out the door, kicking her chair back into place with the toe of her chunky black boot. She was tall and broad-shouldered, with a fall of thick, wavy brown hair and a jock's loose-hipped gait. Marty watched her lope by and made note of her name: Monica Tranel.

Monica knew who Marty Wilde was. Marty's friend and frequent partner Dave Healow was good friends with her father, Ned; the two men met and bonded in Alcoholics Anonymous. Monica knew that Marty was also in recovery. He reminded her a lot of her dad, who had died that April. Both men were high-octane personalities who would take whatever you threw at them and keep going.

Wind developers were a sketchy bunch. They operated just a little outside the bounds of sanity, living on a wing and a prayer. Marty was no exception. He was paranoid, slow to trust, quick to judge. He was also an old-school male chauvinist.

"I'm not going to let some blonde bimbo tell me what to do with my money," Marty fumed, when a would-be investor—female—asked for assurance that her money would go toward a wind project and not Marty's mortgage payments. Dave Healow later explained that the woman had reminded Marty of someone he used to date. "Marty has a problem with estrogen-powered life forms," he said. Marty didn't get the money.

Marty came to see Monica at her law office. It was April 2016. She had just returned to private practice and was six months pregnant with her third child, at the age of fifty. The surprise pregnancy was the product of a new relationship with Greg Lind, a hospital anesthesiologist and former Democratic state senator. Monica and Greg were trying to squeeze in a wedding before the baby was born in July.

Marty didn't tell her about Crazy Mountain Wind at first. He had a more immediate crisis. Two wind projects he had developed from the ground up in Teton County, Fairfield Wind and Greenfield Wind, were being sold out from under him by his financing partner, which had cut him out of its negotiations with potential buyers. Fairfield had already been sold—over Marty's objections—for over $19 million. WINData, Marty's company, was owed $2 million, but he'd only been paid a measly $22,000. Now they were about to pull the same maneuver with Greenfield Wind, a project that was expected to generate nearly $80 million in revenues over the life of its twenty-five-year contract.

After spending years developing these projects, battling for power purchase agreements with NorthWestern Energy, wooing the commissioners on the Public Service Commission and living out of his car, basically, Marty was about to be cheated out of his long-awaited payday. He had filed lawsuits against his ex–financing partner, an outfit called Foundation Windpower, but they were stagnating in appeals. Now Foundation Windpower had sold its 90 percent stake in Greenfield Wind to Greenbacker Renewable Energy Corporation—a Big Wind outfit with offices in New York City—and Greenbacker was quietly negotiating a deal to flip the wind farm to US Bancorp and Firstar Development. With each downstream corporate transfer, Marty's chances of ever getting the money he'd originally been promised became more remote.

Marty had seen Monica in action, and he liked what he saw. She was a bit of a maverick, like he was. Marty didn't usually work with women, but his other lawyers were getting nowhere with this case, he told her. He didn't mention that he owed them money. Michael Uda, the attorney who represented Marty in the successful FERC complaint and other cases, was still waiting on an unpaid $8,000 bill.

"Right before he hired Monica, he called me. And I said, 'I'm happy to represent you, but you know, you still haven't paid me for that last case,'" Uda recalled. "He said, 'Fair enough,' and that was that."

Which is how Marty found himself in Monica's law office, asking if she wanted to take a run at these wankers. "I need to do something extreme," he said.

"What do you want me to do?" she asked. She wanted to know how far Marty was willing to go. Did he want to see the wind farm he had spent years fighting to develop get built, or did he want to get paid, even if it meant a scorched-earth battle that might kill Greenfield Wind? Marty didn't hesitate: "Fuck 'em. I want to get paid. I'll take the project down."

Monica drafted a sweeping motion asking for a temporary restraining order against the wind farms' LLCs, their parent corporation, and the large financial institutions that were about to acquire them—over a dozen defendants in all. In the interest of expediency, Monica decided to file the motion herself and invited Marty to drive over to the courthouse with her. He recoiled when he opened the passenger door of her car and beheld the riot of toys, juice boxes, and half-eaten snacks.

"It's a minivan. Shut up and get in," Monica said.

When they got to the courthouse, the clerk said that the judge was in his chambers and that she'd bring the motion to him. Marty and Monica followed her up the stairs and took a seat in the back of the courtroom. The judge read the motion and granted a temporary restraining order on the spot. Marty went home to Great Falls and told his girlfriend, Annette, that he had a new lawyer—a woman lawyer. He thought she might be pregnant.

Processes were served, and a settlement conference was held. Attorneys in expensive suits flew in from New York, from San Francisco. The judge would dismiss the case, they said. The whole thing was absurd. It was a case Monica and Marty couldn't win.

"We may. We may not. Let's see," Monica said, leaning her palms on the table and resting her heavy belly against it. "What else are you going to put on the table?" Marty wanted $10 million. The suits offered $2 million. Marty said, "Let's leave," and got up. Monica said it looked like they were done and followed her client out the door.

It was a risky move, but Marty liked his odds. The wankers had already bought the wind turbines—they were loaded up and ready to be shipped to Montana. With the restraining order and the threat of an injunction, Monica had those guys tied up in barbed wire.

"They'll pay," Marty said. "They're going to pay." Monica got the call soon after. "We want to get this settled," the lawyers said.

They agreed on just under $4 million. It was the first real payout Marty had gotten in nearly thirty years of scraping by. In the space of the month that Monica had been Marty's lawyer, she had made him a very wealthy man. When Marty got the check, he called Monica and said he felt like he was using cocaine again.

Monica and Greg got married just before the baby was born and took the girls with them on their honeymoon. Marty called Monica while they were on their getaway at a resort in the Cascade Mountains. "I want you to do Crazy Mountain Wind," he said.

Marty had been hammering away at Northwestern ever since Crazy Mountain Wind's CREP contract was officially declared dead. It was the same old story: Marty insisted that the utility had a legally enforceable obligation to buy his wind power—waving that signed power purchase agreement, updated to reflect current QF-1 rates—and the utility ducked and weaved. This time around, they were deflecting his overtures by offering unworkably low rates. For Crazy Mountain Wind to be financially viable at those prices, it would have to get bigger; he'd have to sell more power. So, Marty added more turbines to his schematics. NorthWestern responded by dropping the rate again. He bumped the size of the Crazy Mountain to forty-five megawatts, seventy-two megawatts, seventy-eight megawatts; each time, NorthWestern Energy dropped the price still lower.

Marty hadn't had the money to fight NorthWestern in court, but the Greenfield settlement had replenished his war chest. What's more, Crazy Mountain Wind had captured the interest of a Big Wind outfit—Pattern Development in San Francisco. Marty liked the guys at Pattern; they seemed to know how to get stuff done, unlike the Spaniards. If he could lock down a power purchase agreement with NorthWestern—at a price that would make it worthwhile—Crazy Mountain Wind would finally be in business.

Marty called Monica every day during the honeymoon. Greg took the girls for bike rides and ate french fries with them at the lodge bar while Monica spent hours talking to Marty on the phone. It wasn't a classic honeymoon, but Greg didn't begrudge her any of that. It was exciting stuff. Monica was taking on big, bad guys and winning. Greg enjoyed watching her fight them. "She's no fun to fight with, I can tell you that," he told me.

Monica and Marty hashed out a plan. She would file a motion with the Public Service Commission, a petition to set the terms and conditions of a power purchase agreement between Crazy Mountain Wind with NorthWestern Energy. If the commissioners denied Marty's motion, they'd take the PSC to court. Marty liked that idea. Monica came back from her honeymoon, filed the petition, and gave birth to her third daughter five days later.

The plan worked. The PSC accepted Marty's petition, and after several months of procedural back-and-forth, the date for a public hearing was set in November.

Monica had worked hard for over twenty years to find meaning in what she did, undistracted by scoreboards and medals. But this was a big win. The little guy had taken on a couple of multibillion-dollar corporations and won—*she* had won. Independent wind and solar and hydro developers across the Northwest were calling her and asking her to take on their cases. Monica had never used cocaine, but she knew what Marty meant: winning was a huge high.

NorthWestern and the PSC would throw up hurdles, but Monica was ready to take a run at them, for Marty and Crazy Mountain Wind. That fourth-place finish at the Olympics would always be embedded in her heart, but it was a relic from a past life. Monica had come so far from that moment that it was almost possible to forget that you could put your whole heart and soul into something—to commit everything that you had—and lose.

11

WHAT WOULD YOU DO?

February 20, 2019
Park County Courthouse
Livingston, Montana

RICK JARRETT, *Cross-examination*:
Q: Isn't it true, sir, that you believe you have more rights to your property because you're from Montana, than the folks who have come from out of state?
MR. JARRETT: Absolutely not.
Q: And you're jealous of their wealth, aren't you?
MR. JARRETT: I'm absolutely not jealous of their wealth.
Q: . . . And you heard the testimony of the plaintiffs in this case, right?
MR. JARRETT: I have.
Q: And how much land they have purchased.
MR. JARRETT: Yes.
Q: And that they intend to keep that preserved and conserved. You heard that, right?
MR. JARRETT: Yeah, I heard that.

SEPTEMBER 2015
CRAZY MOUNTAIN CATTLE COMPANY
BIG TIMBER, MONTANA

Jami was sitting with Rick at his cluttered kitchen table when the phone rang. Russell Gordy was on the line.

There had been sporadic calls and emails between Gordy's lawyer and Rick's lawyer about a possible buyout of the Jarretts' wind development rights over the past year, but the two men had never spoken—until now. From what Jami could pick up from her dad's side of the conversation, the Texan wanted to cut a deal. Gordy wanted to put a stop to this deal with the windmills. And Rick Jarrett needed money.

Ranchers get one payday a year—when they sell their calves. For the other 364 days, the cash flows out of the ranch in a steady stream. That made bank loans an inescapable fact of life for ranchers like Rick Jarrett. The bank gave you a line of credit, and you drew from it each month to cover your operating expenses and buy feed and pay for your groceries and put gas in your truck. That was your operating note. Your line of credit was backed up by another loan from the bank—the land note. The land note was a guarantee on the ranch itself, which took the form of a mortgage.

In a good year, Rick would clear enough of a profit when he shipped his calves to make good on his land note, repay the money he had borrowed that year, and replenish his line of credit. But there were so many forces beyond his control. If a frigid winter killed off some of his calves or a drought shriveled his alfalfa crop, forcing him to buy hay instead of selling it, then he wouldn't be able to pay off his operating note. The bunkhouse guests and the pheasant preserve had all been efforts to supplement the ranch income so that Rick could keep up with his bank payments.

When Rick couldn't meet his operating costs, he had to borrow more money on his land. The loans that Rick was taking out now were ones he knew his calves would never repay. In May, he signed a pair of mortgage agreements with a bank in Deer Lodge for a total of $882,500 on his 2,300 acres. If Crazy Mountain Wind didn't get built, Rick didn't know how he'd make good on those payments. The prospect of losing the land that Jarretts had ranched for over a century was something Rick lived with all the time. It was like the wind: the worry was always there, but some days you noticed it more than others.

Tentative discussion about a deal to acquire Rick's wind rights began in the months after Gordy, Engwis, Chesnoff, and MacMillan filed their Valentine's Day lawsuit against Sweet Grass County back in 2014. Rick's lawyer, Michael Begley, reached out to Gordy's Montana lawyer, Kyle Nelson, to see if the Texan would be willing to parley, and was encouraged by his response.

"Our solicitation of an offer was well received," Begley emailed Rick and Jami. He told Rick to work up some hard numbers that they could throw at Gordy. Rick came up with $1.2 million, which was promptly rejected. "The $1.2 million demand (for lack of a better word) is too high and is respectfully declined," Gordy's lawyer wrote in the fall of 2014.

Begley took pains not to offend Gordy the second time around. In the summer of 2015, he asked the Texan's attorney to review a draft of a letter inviting his client and the other members of the litigious anti–wind farm group to negotiate a buyout. "Please let me know if you see anything that would be viewed as counterproductive. We don't want any unintended consequences, particularly with Mr. Gordy whose participation in the negotiations is very much appreciated," Begley wrote.

Gordy's lawyer had discussed the possibility of "our 'Group'... crafting a potential counter-offer." But the group, such as it was, existed in name only. Little united Gordy, MacMillan, Chesnoff, and Engwis beyond a common aversion to wind turbines. The men had never sat down together, or even spoken much. Begley's carefully worded invitation to join Rick Jarrett at the bargaining table landed with a thud. Through his attorney, Engwis declared himself "not agreeable" to paying Rick Jarrett anything for his wind development rights. "That guy is very emotional about this place," Gordy would say of Engwis. "I don't really know him, to be honest. I don't know any of them."

Whitney MacMillan was equally disinclined to partake in whatever deal Texas was cooking up; Jarrett's invitation was respectfully declined. Betty and Whitney did not know Rick Jarrett, though they were friendly with his silent partner, Penny Bell Hatten, whom they'd known since she was a child. Wayzata was a small town, especially if your last name was MacMillan, Pillsbury, or Bell. I asked Penny, who supported Rick's decision to lease his land for Crazy Mountain Wind, if the wind farm had ever come up in conversation with the MacMillans. "Whitney always said, 'Sell the ranch to me,' but that was about it," she said.

In the summer of 2015, MacMillan's attorneys were preoccupied with another problematic neighbor. The family of Darlene Fahrenbruch— the woman at the Coyote Wind hearing who told the story of how her family's ranch was left off the power grid after her father banned utility poles—had announced plans to open a seasonal trailer park on land they owned in the high foothills of the Crazies, on Alkali Creek. It was rugged, remote, and just over the fence from Wild Eagle Mountain Ranch. There'd be thirteen lots for RVs, five campsites, a hospitality building with a restroom and showers, and an RV sewer dump site.

A public hearing was held in late July about the Fahrenbruchs' subdivision application to build their trailer park, but it didn't attract much attention, perhaps because it was a small project in an isolated location. But the MacMillan family did not relish the prospect of RVs parked in their corner of the Crazies, stressing out the Yellowstone cutthroat trout. By mid-November, the Darlene C. Fahrenbruch Living Trust had sold the two sections of land that would have been the Alkali Creek RV Park to Wild Eagle Mountain Ranch for an undisclosed sum, with a down payment of $692,474.25.

Only Gordy continued to negotiate with the Crazy Mountain Cattle Company. Rick's wind lease with Marty expired on July 15. He didn't tell Marty that he was in discussions with Gordy about a possible buyout. In the eleven years that they'd been in business together, Rick had only collected a couple thousand dollars from those wind leases.

Rick and Jami had a lot of kitchen-table conversations about money that summer. The weight of the ranch, and the looming question of how to preserve its legacy for her children, was something that Jami carried around with her every day, just like her dad did. When Rick set his mind on getting some wind on his ranch, the fight for Crazy Mountain Wind became Jami's fight as well. She saw the project as something that would benefit not just her own family, but the county, by bringing in millions of dollars in tax revenue. "We had cursed the wind in Sweet Grass County all our lives. Finally, something good could come out of it," she said.

Rick had a lot of faith in Marty; Jami never did. Marty was a smooth operator. He knew his shit about wind, she gave him that. But Marty was a wild card. He was also a misogynist, a womanizer. Not that Jami was his type, not at all. Marty liked them young. He wanted to feel young, that was his deal.

Rick was a bit of a lothario, too; Marty and her dad had that in common. Rick's new girlfriend, Lois Huffman, who ran Big Timber's Farmers Market, had moved in with him at the ranch. But Rick continued to see other women, cleaning himself up and driving to Billings to see a lady friend he had up there, some Friday evenings.

Rick's love life was not Jami's business, except that it was, because the ranch and its future were her business, and Rick was the ranch. Every gallon of gas he put in his beat-up Cadillac, every dinner he treated his girlfriends to in Big Timber or Billings, anything he used or drove or ate went on the ranch credit card or was paid for with the ranch checkbook. Jami didn't begrudge him that. But it added up to a fuck-ton of money.

Years back, after Rick's hired man handed in his notice, Jami floated an idea: What if she quit her job and became his hired man? Rick didn't take a minute to think about it: no. He told Jami he needed someone who would help him, not be a hindrance.

Her dad didn't mean to be hurtful, Jami understood that. She understood that what he was saying was that he needed someone mechanical, someone who could fix a busted tractor engine. But it was a wholesale dismissal all the same, of her time and effort and the sacrifices she had made. Jami had grown up knowing how to ride and move cows and shoot gophers, but Rick never taught her how to operate heavy farm machinery or how to do the shop work essential to running a ranch. Those lessons had been reserved for her older brother, Jay, while Jami was left with a bunch of recipe cards and loads of dirty laundry. The unfairness of it killed her.

For years, Jami had spent all her free time working on the ranch, worming sheep, irrigating, haying—often with two little kids in tow—and she'd never drawn a paycheck or asked for any compensation for her labor. All that time, her father had been daydreaming about the day his son would come home and take over the Crazy Mountain Cattle Company. Now Jay was a firefighter living nearly three hours away in Great Falls with no plan of returning to the ranching life, and Jami was an unpaid ranch hand who couldn't figure out how to back up the hay truck. Rick got mad as she struggled to put the thing in reverse. He couldn't believe she didn't know how to do it. "How the fuck would I have learned how to back up a hay truck? I was doing your laundry," she yelled back.

When the lease on a two-thousand-acre parcel of land next to Jami's home on the Boulder River just outside Big Timber became available in the early 2000s, she saw an opportunity to prove herself to her father.

More land meant you could run more cows and raise more calves; by working that land for free, Jami could increase their profit margin. She helped secure the lease and took charge of overseeing the ranching operation there.

After JV moved out, Jami had to do everything on her own. On top of her job at the county and taking care of the kids, ranching the new sections of land—it was a lot of work. She'd pack up the kids in the side-by-side when she got home from work and head out to salt the sheep and irrigate the fields and fix fence. Rick would come over and clear ditches. If Jami needed a culvert, he'd put one in for her. But when she got home late, with dinner to make and kids to put to bed, and saw that a gatepost was busted, she'd have to fix it then and there. Otherwise, she'd be the one who got the phone call at ten o'clock at night from someone complaining that her livestock was wandering around on Old Boulder Road. More than a few times, she had roused the kids from bed in their PJs and packed them in the side-by-side to chase down some dumb-ass cow or a bunch of sheep.

When Rick partnered up with Marty to get some wind on the ranch, Jami assumed another responsibility. Rick kept away from a lot of the public discussions that went on about his wind farm at the Sweet Grass County annex building. Jami was there for all of them, representing Crazy Mountain Wind and acting as an informal go-between for Marty and the county commissioners. When Jan Engwis got red in the face and started yelling, Jami was the one sitting opposite him at the conference table, taking the heat.

The wind farm opponents complained to Jami's boss, Pat Dringman, the county attorney. Why was a county employee attending meetings on behalf of her family's wind farm, on the county's dime? Dringman defended Jami, who worked late or skipped lunch to make up the time she spent at the commission meetings. But she knew the appearance of a conflict made him uncomfortable. After the public meeting wrapped up, Pat would go into a closed-door session with the commissioners to hash over the latest developments in the lawsuit. Then Jami would switch hats, joining them in her capacity as a county employee. She felt guilty about all the time and energy and money the litigation was costing the county.

But in an unexpected turn, that litigation had opened a narrow window for her family to negotiate a settlement. Jami was more open to the idea of taking a buyout from the rich neighbors than Rick was—a bird in the hand and all. But it wasn't her decision to make. It was Rick's ranch, and Rick wanted the damn wind farm because he believed in it and because he was stubborn. If there was a chance that Marty could push Crazy Mountain Wind over the finish line and get Rick those turbines, then he would take that chance.

Gordy offered $300,000. Rick turned it down. Gordy upped it to $400,000—with strings attached. In addition to the Jarretts' wind rights, Gordy wanted all their subdivision rights, to prevent Rick and his descendants from breaking up the property or developing any part of it. He wanted their feedlot rights, too. Maybe Gordy was worried they'd put in a hog trough somewhere he could smell it. Rick bristled at these conditions. The Texan wanted control over what a Jarrett could do on Jarrett land, now and for years to come. It was no secret that Gordy wanted to swallow up the small ranches that bordered his land. Over the years, he bought a 600-acre tract here, a 1,280-acre tract there. This wind rights deal was just another way of planting the Lone Star flag on Jarrett ground. Rick refused the $400,000 and told Begley he wasn't interested in negotiating with Gordy anymore.

Just before Labor Day weekend, Gordy made a surprise final offer: $655,000.

Jami thought $655,000 was a lot of money. But Rick measured that $655,000 against all the restrictions and encumbrances it was sure to entail, and decided it wasn't worth it. If he took Gordy's money, he'd need to ask Gordy's permission to take a shit on his own ground, as it were. So, fuck no, Rick wasn't selling to the Texan.

Begley communicated this to Gordy's lawyer, "as delicately as possible." "I don't think that you will be able to resume negotiations with Mr. Gordy if you continue with the wind project—but that is a business decision you have made," he wrote Rick, all but wringing his hands over his client's obstinance.

In fact, Rick had already gone ahead and signed an extension of his lease with Marty. The wind prospector had paid one of his periodic visits to the ranch a few weeks before. Invigorated by the FERC ruling against the PSC's discriminatory policies against wind farms, Marty was scheming up fresh strategies for advancing Crazy Mountain Wind. But first Rick needed to re-up the wind lease. Marty's confidence was contagious. Rick signed on the line.

When Gordy heard that Mr. Jarrett had turned down his money and didn't want to negotiate anymore, he decided to take it upon himself to call the man and ask him if there was a number that he would agree to. In hindsight, doing the negotiating through attorneys had probably been a mistake, Gordy would say. Shoulda just went and met with Mr. Jarrett and made a deal.

Gordy was ready to go to great lengths for his Montana ranch. "I just love that country," he told a reporter in 2002, after news of his epic land purchase became public. He swore he'd never subdivide the place, or drill for gas or coalbed methane. This ranch was his legacy. It would be there long after he was gone, same as it ever was, for his children and his grandchildren.

Gordy thought a lot about legacy. Land was one kind of legacy; his businesses were another. He was willing to make bold deals to secure those legacies, and build generational wealth for his family.

Around the time Gordy turned fifty, he heard a rumor: US Steel was considering selling off its minerals division. The steel giant owned enormous tracts of land in Illinois, Wisconsin, Minnesota, and Nevada, close to 1.5 million acres in all, with attached mineral rights to reserves of coal, iron ore, dolomite, limestone, and copper. Some of those holdings dated back to the company's founding in 1901. By the early twenty-first century, they didn't seem very valuable: the coal was cheap, high-sulfur coal, the iron ore was low-grade and difficult to extract with conventional mining techniques.

But Gordy had a genius for harvesting profits from hard-to-get, undervalued resources like coalbed methane and shale. And he wanted the land. Three decades in the oil and gas business had taught him that if you drilled a well and it was prolific, you'd make money. If it was a dry hole, you'd lose a bunch of money. But if you owned the mineral rights to that piece of land and leased it to others to drill and explore, you'd make money no matter what. There was no risk. The owner was guaranteed a percentage of any profits and was insulated from any loss. "It really goes to my background of wanting land and coveting that," Gordy said.

After scrutinizing all the public information he could find, he felt confident he could do something with US Steel's unloved minerals division. "I called the chairman out of the blue and made an offer," Gordy recalled. "He had never heard of me. He told me they had just done a strategic analysis and this property wasn't strategic anymore. They were thinking of an auction. I said, 'If you tell me what you want for it, I may just buy it on the spot.' He did, and I said, 'Okay.' Then he said, 'Who are you again?'"

Neither Thomas Usher, who was US Steel's chairman and CEO at that time, nor his successor, John Surma, who headed the company until 2013, could recall having any phone conversations with Gordy, let alone one that matched the great story he told me. ("I don't remember the guy's name," Gordy said, when I asked. "I know he was on the board. I could have swore it was the chairman.") The way Usher and Surma remembered it, word percolated up to the C-suite that a Texas oil and gas tycoon wanted to buy the stagnating minerals division to form the bedrock of a family trust. The holdings that Andrew Carnegie and J. P. Morgan had amassed over a century ago would become a treasured legacy for Gordy's children and generations to follow.

"I said, 'Yeah, that sounds great. As long as he's got the money, we can sell it to him,'" Surma recalled.

In 2004, US Steel sold its minerals division to Gordy for about $150 million after an extended negotiation and some Texas-style bare-knuckle bargaining. Gordy insisted on rights to any coalbed methane he might discover, "which our operating people weren't real happy with," said Usher, who was CEO at the time. But Gordy got his way. "The steel business was going through a tough time and we were anxious to raise money. We may have taken a little less than it may have been worth at a different time," Usher said. "He got a good deal."

Gordy formed RGGS Land & Minerals to manage his new portfolio. The initials stood for Russell, Glenda, and their sons, Garrett and Shaun. Gordy viewed RGGS Land & Minerals' holdings very differently than his beloved ranches. This was land he wasn't afraid to mess up.

Within a year, he had entered into a leasing agreement for a coal mining operation called Sugar Camp Energy on 37,644 acres he now controlled in Illinois. Gordy's partner in the deal was Chris Cline, an up-by-the-bootstraps billionaire like Gordy. The descendant of Appalachian coal miners, Cline had worked his way to the summit of his own mining empire, Foresight Energy. He built himself a mansion in Palm Beach, Florida, bought a chain of islands in the Bahamas, and tooled around them in a 164-foot yacht with five staterooms and its own submarine. He called it *Mine Games*.

The land that Gordy leased to Cline for the Sugar Camp Mine was in Franklin County, an agricultural region in the southern part of the state with more than a billion tons of coal below its corn and soybean fields. US Steel had owned the rights to Franklin County's Number Five and Number Six seams since the early twentieth century, when mules stabled deep below ground pulled wagons of coal to the surface, to power the nation's steel mills.

By the late twentieth century, the region's coal industry was pretty much a thing of the past. The high sulfur content of Franklin County's coal made it less valuable than the lower-sulfur coal mined in the Appalachian basin. But Cline, foreseeing that the federal government would eventually require power plants to install scrubbers to reduce pollutants, regardless of the kind of coal they burned, saw an opportunity: if the coal had to be scrubbed anyway, might as well dig up the cheap stuff. And Cline's Foresight Energy would extract every ton of it through an aggressive new technology called longwall mining.

Deep beneath the earth's surface, the continuous miner, a shearing machine with whirling drum cutters sixteen feet wide and nearly six feet high, advanced on a drivetrain alongside the wall of the coal seam, slicing off thick panels of coal. Those panels were chewed up, crushed, and fed back up to the surface, cascading onto automatic conveyors like rattling coins pouring out of a slot machine. Hydraulic jacks on the continuous miner were raised like colossal arms to support the ceiling of the mine while the shearer was at work, but as its whirling blades advanced to the next section of the coal seam, those arms would retract, allowing the mined cavity behind it to collapse and fill up with crushed coal waste and rock, called gob.

Gordy's renewable twenty-year lease with Cline ensured him an un-disclosed production royalty on every ton of coal Foresight sheared out of his coal seams, as well as royalties on Sugar Camp's gob gas and hori-zontal borehole gas—a form of coalbed methane released by the collapse of the broken and fractured underground mines. Foresight Energy, in turn, had the right to dump the waste and gob byproducts from all its mining activities on RGGS land.

Sugar Camp became one of the nation's biggest producers of coal, with two longwall mining complexes and an overall productive capac-ity of fifteen million tons a year. It was one of Gordy's best deals yet, with a cherry on top: an all-expenses-paid share in Cline's fully staffed superyacht, *Mine Games*. Russell took Glenda on a cruise through the Bahamas. They marveled at the twenty-four-karat inlay on the furniture in their stateroom, the baby grand piano in the lounge. "We were like the Beverly Hillbillies," he chuckled.

Sugar Camp was good for the Gordys, but not for the residents of Franklin County. Longwall mining bore little resemblance to the room-and-pillar mining that some of their grandfathers had done. The con-tinuous miner left chaos in its wake. Seismic waves rippled hundreds of feet upward to the surface, causing the ground to sink. Farmers, who saw their fields drop by six feet or more and then flood with disturbed groundwater, called it the bathtub effect. It killed crops and ruined fields for cultivation, disrupted streams and underground aquifers, cracked the foundations of homes and split roads.

Dark gray mountains of mining waste—gob—rose above the fields of corn and soybeans. Sometimes those gob piles flooded their ditches, coating acres of crops with black gunk. Coal slurry was released into streams and other waterways, ruptured pipelines spilled toxic waste-water laden with aluminum and manganese, coal dust from the waste impoundments polluted the air. Sugar Camp was charged with scores of environmental violations and cited for multiple health and safety vio-lations. Three miners were killed in accidents at the mine.

In addition to the coal seams themselves, Gordy's deal with US Steel included century-old farmland leases. Under the terms of Gordy's deal with Cline, those antique contracts now belonged to Sugar Camp En-ergy.

Don Webb, whose family had farmed in Franklin County since the early 1800s, had inherited a seventy-five-acre parcel of land with one of those old leases attached to it. One day, a landman for Sugar Camp Energy paid Webb a visit. He told him Sugar Camp wanted to claim that seventy-five-acre parcel under the terms of a mineral rights deed, which a long-dead landowner had signed for one hundred dollars in 1910. The Sugar Camp landman told Webb that under the terms of that deed, the mine had the right to force him to sell. Sugar Camp needed Webb's land for a new gob pile.

Webb didn't want to sell his land. It was good farmland, with some history to it. There was an Indian burial mound on it, an ancient landform that rose a good twenty feet above the flatlands around it. Webb told the Sugar Camp landman about the burial mound. "But that wasn't anything they wanted to hear," he said. The landman threatened to take him to court if he refused to sell. Webb held out for four years before he finally submitted to Sugar Camp's demands.

"The coal mine excavated us out, basically. They surrounded it with gob piles. I figured I may as well sell it to them before they out and out took it," he said. The ancient Indian mound was now buried under a mountain of gob.

In 2010, Gordy did another deal with Cline, leasing him nearly twenty-two thousand acres in northern Wisconsin's Penokee Range. The Penokee Hills sat at the head of the Bad River watershed, near Lake Superior. The Bad River Band of Lake Superior Chippewa, whose tribal lands abutted Gordy's acreage, hunted, fished for sturgeon, harvested wild rice, and foraged for morels and Juneberries there, as Indigenous people had done for millennia.

In 2005, Matt Dallman, director of the Nature Conservancy in Wisconsin, flew to Houston to try to persuade Gordy to sell the Penokee Hills to the conservancy. He invited Gordy to come fishing for smallmouth bass in the Penokees' Chequamegon Bay. Those bass were the size of footballs, he said. Gordy passed on the invite. The Penokees contained another natural resource, far more valuable to Gordy: taconite, a hard rock containing magnetite, a low-grade iron ore.

For most of the last century, nobody had much wanted taconite, which had to be processed and concentrated into pellets before it could be used for steel: a costly and resource-intensive process that involved pulverizing tons of rock into powder, mixing it with water, and separating out its ferrous content with powerful magnets. It generated tremendous amounts of waste material, which filled vast tailing basins and tailing ponds and formed high, ashy mountains. But in the mid-2000s, the global market for iron ore tightened. The price for taconite pellets quadrupled, then quintupled.

The Penokee Hills are part of the Gogebic Range—an eighty-mile belt of iron ore–rich rock that stretches from Wisconsin to Michigan. Gordy partnered up with Cline on a plan to turn the Penokees into a four-and-a-half-mile-long open-pit mine. Cline called the $1.5 billion operation Gogebic Taconite—G-TAC for short. He launched a multi-year, multimillion-dollar campaign to persuade Wisconsin governor Scott Walker and Republican legislators to enact a new mining bill that would bypass the state's environmental laws so he could build it. Cline got his mining bill in 2013. But the following year, iron ore prices fell, and plans for G-TAC were shelved. Foresight would eventually declare bankruptcy.

Dallman continued to reach out on behalf of the Nature Conservancy to negotiate a deal for the Penokees. Gordy ignored the standing invitation to come fishing in Chequamegon Bay. The price the environmentalists were offering wasn't high enough. "I just like to jack with them," he said with a wink in 2017. "That land has probably got $5 billion in iron ore in it. What would you do?" Potential production royalties from that ore—his share of the take—could amount to two or three billion dollars. It would be irresponsible to his family not to act on an opportunity like that, Gordy said.

As the G-TAC debacle unfolded, Russell and Glenda were putting the last touches on their new family compound in Montana: a seventeen-thousand-square-foot complex with a baronial lodge, interconnected homes for their two sons, artificial ponds stocked with trout, and its own heliport. Greg Dennee of Locati Architects had never heard of the Gordys when they wandered into the firm's Bozeman office. Russell had made an appointment at a rival firm down the street, but when he and

Glenda were kept waiting in the reception area, he became annoyed and decided to leave.

Dennee met them in the conference room. Gordy, who was dressed in shorts, a T-shirt, and a vest, looked like he'd been called away from bird hunting. He told Dennee that he and Glenda had been staying in a little old ranch house on their property. They wanted to create something where the whole family could be together. "He started very slow, talking about building a home in Montana. When he got to the part where he said, 'I have forty-four thousand acres,' my ears pricked up a bit," Dennee said.

Gordy's Double Arrow compound was completed in 2014 at a cost of $15 million. Every detail had been considered. The posts, beams, and trusses of its high vaulted ceilings were antique timbers reclaimed from old buildings. The stone walls were built from Montana moss rock—weathered fieldstones gathered from the ground—because it was more organic-looking and pleasingly timeworn than quarried stone. At the heart of the house, a nineteenth-century homesteader's cabin with dovetail corners had been painstakingly restored and reassembled to serve as a butler's pantry. There was one just like it on Rick Jarrett's ranch. He used it as a sheep pen.

Double Arrow had everything: a concealed gun room for Gordy's collection of rare firearms, a gym with a speed bag and a heavy bag for Glenda, who liked to box. There was a mirrored saloon, and a wine cave with its own tasting room. Russell had an entire room for his hunting clothes, grouped by camo pattern.

The only thing missing was a view of the Crazy Mountains. Tucked in the low foothills, the compound had knockout vistas of the distant Absaroka-Beartooth range, but its back was turned to the Crazies. It was a concession the Gordys had made—a more sheltered location, so the lodge would be out of the wind. "There's a practical side to the Gordys and the way they think," Dennee said.

Now Gordy was doing the practical thing and reaching out to Mr. Jarrett himself. He'd bought this thing, these seven ranches that he himself had put together, because it was a wild and beautiful piece of Montana, with beautiful mountains and a beautiful river—the Yellowstone River, the greatest river in America. Gordy wanted to protect the land;

that's why he bought it to start with. He knew how people talked. They said, "He's a rich guy and he just wants to do what he wants." Well, Gordy probably grew up poorer than any of those people. Anyone who had a ranch growing up had had a lot more than Gordy did.

Jarrett picked up the phone after the first or second ring. Gordy introduced himself and, after a short preamble, got to the point: I don't want windmills, you want money. Can we negotiate something?

Rick sat at his kitchen table, contemplating his domain. His sweat-stained Stetson hung on a peg above a sideboard piled with work gloves and loose change, a socket wrench, a portable weather station, and a collection of novelty salt-and-pepper shakers—two ears of corn, a pair of bashful lambs. Rick thanked Gordy for the call. But he couldn't really consider any new offers. He had just signed a lease extension for a new wind project. "I'd like to see where it goes," Rick said.

Recalling the conversation, Gordy shook his head. Mr. Jarrett decided he'd found a better deal. "I think Marty Wilde convinced him he could get a lot more by doing the wind farm," he said.

12

CROW COUNTRY

February 20, 2019
Park County Courthouse
Livingston, Montana

RUSSELL GORDY, *Direct Examination*:

Q: Was this going to be a special and unique thing for you and your family?

MR. GORDY: Yes. I mean, this is kind of a once in a lifetime thing to be able to do. I mean, this is really a historic place. I mean, I went to all the newspapers, I had a guy go and get every article about Hunter Hot Springs, and there was so many. He did it from 1870 to 1932 in ten separate binders. So, we read all of those, and it was very interesting. I mean, at one time, there were five hundred tipis along the Yellowstone River, right there, at the hot springs.

JUNE 28, 2014
WILSALL, MONTANA

Under a steady rain that shrouded the Crazies in a gray veil, a group of people gathered at the base of a sandstone cliff by Flathead Creek. Thomas Larson Medicine Horse, an Apsáalooke medicine man and Sundance leader, wafted smoke from a bundle of smoldering sweetgrass over the small black box that Sarah Anzick held tight against her chest, brushing it with white feathers as he prayed. The box contained the tiny, ocher-stained skull and bones of the Clovis child.

Mel Anzick, stooped but hale in his blue rain poncho, stood alongside members of the Apsáalooke, Blackfeet, Salish-Kootenai, Yakama, Umatilla, and Yavapai Apache tribes—some draped in blankets, others holding umbrellas, all linked by a fragment of code to the child whose earthly remains rested in that tiny casket. Archaeologists and scientists who had studied the boy bowed their heads as honor songs were sung for him, this child of woolly mammoth hunters.

Medicine Horse nodded at Sarah Anzick, who lowered the box into a deep grave. An elder from the Blackfeet Amskapi Pikuni tribe sprinkled it with red ocher, and everyone present took a turn shoveling in some dirt, including cameramen from two documentary television crews. Then the sun came out, and the Anzicks invited everyone to join them for a pancake breakfast at a community park.

The Clovis child's reburial, and the homecoming it represented, were the work of a slim, soft-spoken man in his early forties who hung toward the back of the group, hands clasped in front of his red windbreaker. His name was Shane Doyle, and he was an adjunct professor of Native American studies at Montana State University, a drummer in MSU's intertribal Bobcat Singers, and an enrolled member of the Apsáalooke tribe.

Doyle's personal history, and, increasingly, his career, were intertwined with the Crazy Mountains. Born on Crow Agency, nearly two hundred miles to the east, Doyle didn't know much about the lost homeland that lay beyond the reservation's borders when he was growing up. He would compare himself to Marlow, Joseph Conrad's narrator in *Heart of Darkness*, drawn to a white spot on a map to find what was there. Doyle's map had brought him here, to the Crazy Mountains.

Like every Crow kid, Doyle knew the story of Plenty Coups's dream. Plenty Coups was the last of the great Crow warrior chiefs, born sometime around 1848. He made the first of several medicine fasts in the Crazy Mountains as a boy, after his mother, Otter-Woman, died of smallpox. The tribe was under constant threat. A crier rode through his village, calling on the young men to dream. "Are you afraid of a little suffering? Go into these mountains and find Helpers for yourselves and your people, who have so many enemies!" The boy answered the call. After purifying himself with a sweat bath, he climbed Crazy Peak, where he built a bed of rocks and lined it with cedar leaves and sage. He lay in his fasting bed for days, his body raked by fierce winds, but no Helpers came. Sensing that a sacrifice was required, he cut off the tip of his index finger and bashed his finger until it bled. That night, he dreamed.

Many decades later, when he was an old man, Plenty Coups described what he saw on Crazy Peak to his biographer, Frank B. Linderman. He saw the bison vanish from the plains, replaced by herds of strange spotted creatures. He saw a dark forest and a gathering storm. "The sky was black with streaks of mad color through it. I saw the Four Winds gathering to strike the forest, and I held my breath . . . I heard the Thunders calling out in the storm, saw beautiful trees twist like blades of grass and fall in tangled piles where the forest had been . . . Only one tree, tall and straight, was left standing where the great forest had stood . . . Standing there alone among its dead tribesmen, I thought it looked sad."

A voice told him that the last surviving tree was the lodge of the chickadee. The chickadee was small and powerless, but strong in mind, and a good listener. "There is scarcely a lodge he does not visit, hardly a Person he does not know, and yet everybody likes him, because he minds his own business, or pretends to," the voice said. Wind was the strongest thing on earth, but the little bird withstood it.

Tribal elders interpreted the boy's dream. The Four Winds were the white men; the twisted, fallen trees of the forest were the tribes of the Great Plains. The last sad tree was the Crow people. The white men would take over Crow Country, the elders said. They told the young man to be like the chickadee—to listen and learn from the mistakes of others. If the Apsáalooke were to survive, they'd have to turn their faces another way. They'd have to prove their friendship to white men.

Plenty Coups's dream shaped Apsáalooke history, and the history of the United States. "We traveled by that dream," Plenty Coups's old friend Coyote Runs told his biographer. Under Plenty Coups's leadership, the Crow nation adopted a policy of cooperation with the yellow eyebrows—Plenty Coups's name for government factotums and army officers. Like Iron Bull, whom he had looked up to as a boy, Plenty Coups sought strategic military opportunities that aligned with Crow interests. "We had always fought the three tribes, Sioux, Cheyenne, and Arapahoe, anyway and might as well do so now," he said.

Crow warriors pointed their guns with the white men's guns against their longtime foes in the Battle of the Rosebud, and again in the Battle of the Little Bighorn. Apsáalooke scouts—called wolves, for the wolf pelts they concealed themselves in to track the enemy—alerted General George Custer to a vast encampment of enemy Sioux and Northern Cheyenne on the Little Bighorn River. The wolves advised a visibly inebriated Custer to get away with the blue horse soldiers of the 7th Cavalry while he could, according to the Crow medicine woman Pretty Shield, who heard all about it from her man, a wolf called Goes Ahead. There were more enemies than the bullets in the soldiers' belts, they warned Custer. "They were like ants on a freshly killed buffalo robe that is pegged to the ground," Pretty Shield recalled. "But he only said, 'Go on again,' and then drank from a straw-covered bottle that was on his saddle. Tst, tst, tst! He would not listen."

So many proofs of friendship, to no avail. Decades later, when those wolves were old men, they were still waiting for the government to fulfill its promises to them. "The White Chief never paid us when we were his soldiers, never even paid us for our dead horses," Plenty Coups's comrade Plain Bull said.

In 1880, President Rutherford B. Hayes summoned Plenty Coups, Pretty Eagle, and four other Crow leaders to Washington, DC. The Crow Country was good country. The Great Father wanted more of it. Pretty Eagle described their summit at the White House to a Crow tribal council on their return to Montana:

> We went into his house and he said, "My children, I want to tell you something. I want a little piece of your land." He wanted from the Boulder to the Mountains and all the mountains, and a road cut through our land to drive cattle, and a Railroad to run through our land. Then the whites got together and talked until it made my heart feel dead.

Government officials prolonged the Apsáalooke delegation's stay to wear them down. There were trips to Mount Vernon, a tour of the Capitol, a visit to the zoo. Pretty Eagle, Plenty Coups, and the other delegates were each given twenty dollars to shop for souvenirs. In the end, the Crow leaders agreed to sell 1.5 million acres of land and to allow the Northern Pacific Railway a right-of-way through what remained. They wanted to go home.

By 1882, railroad work crews and herds of cows ranged across the Apsáalooke's ancestral hunting grounds. Plenty Coups' prophetic dream had come to pass. The bison were gone, wiped out. The period from 1883 to 1884 was a starvation year for the Crow. Crow Agency was pushed eastward, first to the Stillwater Valley, then to the Powder River Basin. Government agents distributed food ration tickets, divided land into allotments, and told the Apsáalooke to plant wheat, oats, and hay. Plenty Coups settled down on a farm and opened a general store. In 1924, he became an honorary member of the Kiwanis Club. Crow Country, which had once spread across the Mountain West, had been reduced to an irregular shape on a state map, 160 miles away from the Crazies.

Today, Crow Agency is the largest of Montana's seven tribal reservations. Its 2.3 million acres encompass the Pryor Mountains, Bighorn Canyon, and the Little Bighorn battlefield site, where reenactments of Custer's Last Stand are staged every June. In August, hundreds of tipis sprout on Crow Agency for Crow Fair, a three-day powwow that draws over fifty thousand spectators for dancing, parades, and an all-Indian rodeo.

Over fourteen thousand enrolled tribal members live on Crow Agency, according to the US Bureau of Indian Affairs; many live below the poverty line. In 2015, Tribal Chairman Darrin Old Coyote told a Senate Bureau of Indian Affairs panel that the reservation's official unemployment rate was 47 percent—four times the national average—though he thought the true rate was about six times that, once you factored in people who had given up looking for work.

The tribe's economic mainstay is the Absaloka Coal Mine, a fifteen-thousand-acre open-pit coal mine built on a prehistoric bison kill site. Since the mid-1970s, the tribe has leased a portion of its coal reserves to Westmoreland Resources, which sells the coal to Midwestern power plants. Royalties and taxes from the mine have accounted for as much as two-thirds of the tribe's non-federal budget.

Many tribal members lease their homes from the Apsáalooke Nation Housing Authority: dilapidated single-level houses that are identical but for the faded blue, green, or tan paint on their exteriors. In 2013, Old Coyote complained that the houses were falling apart faster than the housing authority could maintain them. But housing stock is in short supply on Crow Agency, and there's a long waiting list for those below-code houses. It's not unusual for two or three families to share a two-bedroom home.

Shane Doyle's family history traced the arc of the reservation era. Born in 1972, he grew up on the last remaining piece of the 38.5-million-acre expanse that had been granted to the Apsáalooke by the 1851 Fort Laramie treaty. Doyle's great-great-great-grandfather, an Apsáalooke chief named Four Times, was part of the Crow delegation that witnessed the treaty signing.

The Apsáalooke had lost more than two-thirds of the land it was promised in that treaty by 1875, when Four Times' sixteen-year-old daughter Strikes the Gun married Tom Shane, the waggish fur trader who lived among the Crow and acted as their interpreter in treaty negotiations. Windham Wyndham-Quin, the Earl of Dunraven, had been much impressed by Shane's skills on his visit to Crow Agency, looking on as his guide engaged in an animated conversation in Apsáalooke with an amply endowed female, "which, to judge by her wriggling and giggling, must have been highly complimentary."

Strikes the Gun changed her name to Sarah on her wedding day. She raised eleven children with Shane on a 320-acre allotment on the second Crow reservation in the Stillwater Valley, which was called Absaroka Agency. After Shane's death in 1901, Sarah married Rattlesnake Jack Williams, a murderous cowboy with designs on her land. While traveling by train to Salt Lake City with her new husband, Sarah overheard him plotting with another man to kill her. She got off at the next station and walked three hundred miles home. Then she drafted a will directing that if her daughters married white men, they would be disinherited. Sarah's daughter Margaret was already married to a white man named Tom Doyle. But Sarah's will was unyielding. Margaret Shane and Tom Doyle, Shane Doyle's great-grandparents, were cut off from the family.

Doyle didn't know anything about this family history when he was a kid. His mother, one of ten children, was a quiet, intensely private person who hadn't finished high school. His grandfather was an alcoholic who disappeared for months at a time, leaving Doyle's grandmother to raise the children in poverty. As for his own father, Doyle didn't know anything about him—not even his name. "I thought my life was like the

Immaculate Conception," he said. Years later, he learned that his father was a married man. His mother never told the man that he had a son, named for the stoic gunslinging hero of her favorite Western—*Shane*.

Growing up on Crow Agency seemed like the greatest thing in the world when Doyle was little. He had a big extended family, with lots of cousins. His aunts and uncles looked out for him and loved him, and he was very close to his grandmother. But when adolescence hit, the darker realities of life on the reservation became inescapable. To be born on Crow Agency was to be born into a community in despair. The weight of all that depression crept into your system in ways you couldn't understand. It was just too much, too overwhelming for a young person to process.

"The community that I was growing up in was very much impoverished and traumatized, through all kinds of different things," Doyle said. "I mean—disease, death, boarding school. Unemployment, alcoholism, despair, depression. Poor health care, poor nutrition. High infant mortality, high vehicle death rates . . . To grow up in and among that—you don't really get it, you don't really understand it when you're right there in the midst of it. It's not until you're away from it—if you ever are away from it—that you begin to see."

He and his mom moved around a lot, trading one ramshackle home in Crow Agency Upper Housing for another, on streets without names. Doyle watched television; that was his thing. He learned everything there was to know about white people from TV. In high school, he got in the habit of reading the newspaper from cover to cover. He wanted to know everything.

Growing up on Crow Agency was like being stuck behind a one-way mirror. Doyle could see the whole world through the shows he watched on television and the books and newspapers he read. But the world did not see him. He was invisible, his family and his community were invisible. He couldn't learn anything about his own world through his TV or the newspapers in the school library. For that, he'd have to leave Crow Agency.

Doyle went to college at Montana State University in Bozeman. He struggled to fit in at first, drank too much. But that changed when he joined the Bobcats and learned how to drum and sing tribal music. There were kids from across Indian Country at MSU. Doyle found a sense of connection with them—they shared so much, regardless of what tribe they were from. He wanted to learn more about the old traditions. He joined the powwow committee, went to the sweat lodge.

After graduating college, Doyle taught in the public schools on Crow Agency. He had always thought he'd spend his life on the rez. But after his grandmother died, something shifted. Doyle went back to Bozeman to pursue a doctorate in education, eventually becoming a professor at MSU. He would never live on Crow Agency again.

"Remarkably, the 200 miles of road between the sleepy reservation village and the bustling college town is almost entirely located within the boundaries of my tribe's original reservation," Doyle wrote in his doctoral dissertation. Two hundred miles isn't far by Montana standards, but this particular stretch of highway crossed cultural and historic time zones that Doyle would become adept at navigating. The phrase "walking in two worlds," which some Indians use to describe the experience of living in twenty-first-century America, was more than just an expression for Doyle: it was his own "peculiar reality."

For his thesis project, Doyle designed a series of collaborations between Crow tribal members and archaeologists studying the site of the razed Absaroka Agency in the Stillwater Valley—the reservation where his ancestor Strikes the Gun became Sarah. Not far from the excavations, an old wagon that had belonged to Doyle's great-great-grandfather Tom Shane still stood on a cutbank of Shane Creek, its wooden wheels disintegrating into the scrub.

Doyle chartered a bus to bring Crow elders to the dig site. The lead archaeologist showed them the foundations of the razed compound and some of the artifacts his team had uncovered. The elders were mostly silent. Then a woman asked the archaeologist if he would be willing to make a symbolic apology on behalf of his culture for the injustices that had taken place there. He was, and did. Afterward, a Crow Sundance chief who was among the elders offered a prayer of thanks and reconciliation.

"My tribe, through colonization, has been through a meat grinder. That's what it feels like," Doyle would say. "We need to get back to where we were." At Absaroka Agency, he regained a sense of connection to his heritage, to his great-great-grandmother and great-grandmother. Now

Doyle would be drawn into the spiritual epicenter of Crow Country—Awaxaawippíia, the Crazy Mountains—by its most ancient resident, the Clovis child.

In 2013, Doyle was contacted by Larry Lahren, an archaeologist and MSU instructor who had spent decades studying the Anzick site. Lahren wanted to introduce Doyle to Eske Willerslev, a Danish palaeogeneticist who was about to publish a paper in *Nature* about the nuclear genome of the Clovis-era skeletal remains. Willerslev was filming an episode about the discovery for his Danish television show, *DNA Detektiven*, in which he played himself, a famous palaeogeneticist traveling the globe in pursuit of ancient DNA.

Doyle didn't know anything about the Clovis child, discovered years before he was born. But he knew the place where the child had been found, and he knew all about the people who had once lived there. The Clovis child came from the Crazies—the spiritual heart of Crow Country. Doyle agreed to meet with Willerslev, Lahren, and Sarah Anzick at the rocky sandstone cliff. A Danish television crew captured him getting out of his minivan, then zeroed in for a close-up on his face as Willerslev declared that the child was a direct ancestor of between 80 and 90 percent of all Native Americans.

Overwhelmed, Doyle didn't say anything. Then he went back to his minivan and got his drum. Closing his eyes, he sang an honor song for the boy at the foot of the cliff. Sarah Anzick wept behind her sunglasses. She had always known the child was important, but the full significance of what he represented didn't hit her until that moment.

Willerslev asked Doyle what he thought they should do next. "Speaking from the heart, I think you should put him back now," he said. Doyle urged Willerslev to visit Montana's tribal communities to share what he had learned and ask for guidance on how the child's remains should be handled. "I believe that it is an important thing to do," Doyle said, and offered to accompany him.

The two men spent over a week driving from one Montana reservation to another, trailed by the Danish camera crew. Doyle brought Willerslev to meet Medicine Horse at his home on Crow Agency. The house was rundown, with a refrigerator on the porch. A hand-drawn poster for the Asshitchite Big Lodge—Medicine Horse's clan—was tacked to a corkboard on the bare plywood walls of the main room, where the seventy-three-year-old Sundancer sat in a wheelchair with a mug of coffee. Willerslev asked him about the Clovis child. "I will tell you that the skeleton is no longer with the spirit," Medicine Horse said. "The spirit is what I deal with." The boy needed to be returned to his burial place in the Crazies.

Doyle took the lead on the repatriation of his ancient ancestor. There was considerable resistance from officials on the state Burial Preservation Board, who argued that burying the remains would destroy an artifact of incomparable scientific and historic value. Some scientists saw it as a dangerous precedent that could jeopardize the very nature of their professions. "Everybody hates you," a colleague told Willerslev.

But not Shane Doyle. The reburial of the Clovis child bathed him in a flattering spotlight. The camera loved him. He had a warm smile and an air of plainspoken sincerity. He brought an emotional immediacy to a story about old bones, mitochondrial DNA, and genome sequencing. Doyle was featured prominently in a PBS *Nova* documentary about the Clovis child, banging his drum and singing soulfully at the burial site.

Although Doyle didn't hold any official position within Apsáalooke tribal government, his role in the ancient child's return to the Crazies established him as a kind of free-range ambassador for Indian Country. The Smithsonian invited him to speak at a symposium about Native peoples and genetic research. The History Channel hired him as a consultant for *Custer: The Final Mystery*, a reality show about a treasure hunt for lost 7th Cavalry rifles. Doyle was supposed to be a behind-the-scenes consultant, but the producers were soon asking him to appear on camera.

It snowballed from there. Schools and museums asked Doyle to design cultural programs. He appeared atop a forklift in an open-air performance piece about Indigenous people and climate change, delivering a monologue about Plenty Coups's dream as performers in black leotards danced with lodgepole pines strapped to their backs. Conservation groups invited him to join their boards and made him the spokesman for their causes. Doyle's face stared down from giant billboards in Whitefish and Missoula, urging Montanans to "Hold Our Ground" after President Donald Trump moved to eliminate federal protections for national monuments like Montana's Upper Missouri Breaks. A billionaire paid Doyle a thousand dollars a day to talk about the ceremonial traditions of the Crow people at gatherings he hosted for his top executives on his ranch near Billings. People liked Doyle. He was easygoing, a good listener. The billionaire invited him to stay for dinner. Shane Doyle was welcome in everyone's lodge.

"In Crow culture, the number one thing is, you have to show up," Doyle told Willerslev that September day at the sandstone cliff in Wilsall. By showing up—by taking on these projects and causes—Doyle was making visible what had been erased or gone unseen. He stood in the white spots on the map where the Apsáalooke had been and sang songs to honor them. And the more he showed up, and the more prominent he became, the more Doyle began to see the Crazy Mountains as an essential piece of this process of restoration and repair.

Doyle saw the Crazies for the first time when he was seventeen. He and his mom were driving to Bozeman. Stunned by the island of mountains that popped up off the plains, they pulled off the highway in Big Timber and got out of the car. It was December, and the wind was fierce.

"It's still in my mind's eye—this fortress, a splendorous piece of ground that just rose up off the prairie into the heavens," Doyle said.

He made his first fast in the Crazies when he was twenty-one. His uncle gave him cedar leaves, bear root, sage, and a ceremonial pipe with tobacco, for praying. It was spring, and the mountains were covered in snow. Doyle and a friend hiked for hours, ascending over glacial moraine past alpine lakes and snowfields high into the interior of the mountain range. His friend pitched a one-person tent, but Doyle, who wanted to go hard-core in the tradition of his ancestors, fasted out in the open. Then night fell and it began to rain.

"We should have checked the weather," Doyle said.

Cold, wet, buffeted by the wind, Doyle was in the early stages of hypothermia when his friend brought him inside the tent and zipped him into his sleeping bag. The next morning, a full-circle rainbow hung in the sky. The experience had been hard, possibly life-threatening. But it gave him something intangible: good medicine that he would draw on all his life.

Doyle's ancestors had climbed into the Crazies to find out who they were, what life was all about—what they should truly value. He believed that the Crazies still had the power to inspire and restore Apsáalooke people, but their connection to the mountains had been severed. And then something remarkable happened: an old dude ranch high in the Crazies called the Lazy K Bar Ranch went up for sale in 2012.

The ranch had been in the Van Cleve family for generations. Paul Ledyard Van Cleve arrived in the Montana Territory after the Battle of the Little Bighorn to settle the affairs of his distant relative, the late Jonathan Jordan Crittenden. Crittenden was a West Point dropout who lost an eye in a hunting accident, a streak of bad luck that continued after he became a second lieutenant with the 20th Infantry, attached to Custer's 7th Cavalry Regiment. Crittenden was killed at Little Bighorn with the rest of Custer's troops, his remains so badly mutilated that they could only be identified by the shards of his glass eye. An 1877 photograph shows a man with large ears who looks a lot like the young Van Cleve, painting Crittenden's name on a wooden cross at the site where he fell at Little Bighorn.

After seeing to his unfortunate relative, Van Cleve took a look around and decided he liked what he saw. He arrived in Big Timber in 1885 to take a post as station agent for the Northern Pacific Railway, but soon realized there was more money in cattle ranching. When the Northern Pacific began selling off its checkerboard squares in the Crazies in 1887, Van Cleve started buying. Over several decades, the Van Cleve family amassed a sprawling ranch that encompassed Crazy Peak, Conical Peak, Granite Peak, and a huge chunk of Big Timber Peak, and all the canyons, glacial lakes, and alpine forest in between. They called it the Lazy K Bar. It was less a ranch than a small national park. In the space of Plenty Coups's lifetime, Crazy Peak—the Notre Dame of the Apsáalooke—had become the private property of a station agent.

Paul Ledyard Van Cleve Jr. founded the Lazy K Bar dude ranch in 1923. It drew an elite clientele from the beginning—people much like the Van Cleves themselves, whose ancestors included a Union general, an early trustee of Princeton University, and Jan Van Cleef, a Dutch patroon who arrived in New Amsterdam in 1653. East Coast blue bloods spent their summers at the ranch gadding about in chaps and spurs, watching the cow punches brand calves, or playing polo on toppy mounts from the Lazy K Bar's stables. Spike Van Cleve—Paul Ledyard Van Cleve III, a Harvard and prep school–educated cowboy—would reminisce about trail rides into the Crazies with full-bosomed English girls more accustomed to fox hunts.

When Spike's elderly children listed the Lazy K Bar for $9 million in 2012, Doyle saw an extraordinary opportunity. What if the tribe could buy it? Apsáalooke people could hold retreats there. They could hunt elk and deer and gather medicinal and ceremonial plants in the alpine forests and meadows. Above all, they could protect the Crazies as a sacred landscape, ensuring that no one ever built roads there or developed them in any way. Crow Agency didn't have the $9 million, but there might be private foundations and philanthropists with deep pockets willing to help finance such a bold plan.

But in 2012, Doyle was an untenured college professor. He didn't have the influential connections in cultural, political, and philanthropic circles that he would develop later on. And he had no standing in Apsáalooke tribal government; he didn't even live on Crow Agency. The reservation was a political place. Some tribal officials and influential community members judged you based on your degree of traditionality—whether you grew up in an extended clan where people called you by your Indian name, for example, or if you spoke Crow as a first language. Doyle hadn't grown up within that tradition. There were those who looked down on him as a half-breed, an upstart. Some of the older community members, who liked Doyle and approved of the work he did, questioned if he went about it the right way.

"It's nothing against Shane. But his perspectives are maybe too far-thinking a lot of times for us. I see so much of the good he does, but there is no protocol," Rachel Sue Old Coyote said. "To me, a lot of what he does is not right because he's not speaking about it to elders first, which is customary."

There were so many more urgent concerns on Crow Agency. The schools and health services were underresourced, overtaxed. The tribal police force had just five officers overseeing a reservation nearly twice the size of Delaware. Big Horn County, where Crow Agency and the

Northern Cheyenne Indian Reservation are located, had the highest rate of missing and murdered Indigenous people in the state. Almost everyone who lived on Crow Agency had been touched by trauma in some way. On January 1, 2020, Selena Not Afraid, the sixteen-year-old niece of then-Crow tribal chairman A. J. Not Afraid, became the county's twenty-eighth Indigenous woman to go missing; she was found dead of hypothermia three weeks later near a highway rest stop.

Doyle was resigned. "When you take over as chairman of the Crow tribe, you're taking over a community in crisis. From day one you are putting out fires," he said.

The Lazy K Bar sold that September. Doyle learned that the new owner of Crazy Peak was a billionaire named David Leuschen. A former partner and managing director at Goldman Sachs, Leuschen was the cofounder of Riverstone Holdings, a private equity firm with billions of dollars invested in the energy sector. Leuschen, a third-generation Montanan, had been born into the energy business: his father, Don Leuschen, a World War II veteran who got his start as a lineman climbing utility poles, had been the president of the Montana Power Company, a precursor to NorthWestern Energy.

Around the time that Shane Doyle was singing an honor song for the Clovis child at the foot of the sandstone cliff, Leuschen was telling a group of business students at Dartmouth, his alma mater, how to make it in the energy business. *Forbes* magazine had just ranked him seventh on its 2013 list of the nation's top dealmakers.

"Decades ago, I was told, 'You're a middle-of-the-pack, nice, fun guy, but you're not that bright. You're from an energy state. Why don't you focus on energy?'" Leuschen said. He told the students that the real secret to his phenomenal rise was luck. "I was very lucky to be born where I was in the year I was."

A humblebrag, maybe, but true. The American shale revolution meant it was a great time to be working in the energy investment sector. Riverstone poured investment capital into shale gas plays and made buyout deals that gave it a controlling interest in the companies that fracked them. It also invested in traditional oil and gas exploration and development, coal mines, and power plants. (In a full-circle Leuschen family moment, a Riverstone subsidiary would acquire an ownership interest in Colstrip, the complex of coal-fired power plants that David's father, Don, expanded as president of the Montana Power Company.)

In 2007, Riverstone Holdings invested $600 million in Foresight Reserves, becoming a part owner of Chris Cline's longwall coal mining empire. Riverstone's capital made the Sugar Camp mine possible. Without it, Don Webb's Indian burial mound might still rise up from fields of corn and soybeans.

Leuschen hit a speed bump in 2009 when he came under investigation in connection with a corruption scandal at the New York State Common Retirement Fund. The investigation, led by the state's then attorney general, Andrew Cuomo, was a hydra-headed beast, but in a nutshell: the AG claimed that Riverstone and its employees had given thousands of dollars in campaign contributions to the pension fund's former state comptroller—and paid millions of dollars to his top political aide to act as an agent on its behalf—in an effort to win hundreds of millions of pension fund dollars. After the state pension fund plowed $150 million into a Riverstone joint venture with the Carlyle Group, Leuschen invested $100,000 of his own money in *Chooch*, a 2003 movie produced by the brother of the fund's then-chief investment officer. Perhaps the movie's title—slang for "jackass"—should have been a red flag. Leuschen paid $20 million to settle the case, on top of the $30 million Riverstone Holdings paid in restitution.

That year, Riverstone acquired the wind energy portfolio from an insolvent investment firm that went belly-up during the global financial crisis. Riverstone turned that portfolio into a renewable-energy company called Pattern Energy Group and committed $400 million to it. This was not motivated by a desire to save the planet. By 2017, renewables would constitute a $250 billion global market. Riverstone began sniffing out investment positions that would enable it to grab a piece of that market early on. In September 2013, Pattern launched an initial public offering—the first IPO in history for an American wind power company. The IPO far exceeded market expectations, raising $352 million as Pattern's share prices leaped 10 percent. By the end of trading, Pattern was valued at $1.24 billion.

Leuschen, fit and athletic well into his sixties, approached his work with a certain swagger. The key to understanding the energy business, he told the Dartmouth students, was that everyone in it was driven by a high libido. Leuschen had risen to the apex of the energy food chain: the students could fill in the blanks. For a TEDx Talk at Big Sky, he pulled up a large chart with an *S* curve to explain the rate of adoption for new technologies. The bottom line of the *S* showed how exploratory tech started out—flat, slow—before swelling upward as demand grew. The middle of the *S* was the inflection point, when desire peaked. The flat top of the *S* was the level-off point when you had reached saturation. It was just like sex, he told his audience. "The upper flat part is the cigarette in bed."

As Leuschen prospered, he indulged his favorite hobbies. He developed a passion for sailboat racing and bought a few yachts. An accomplished skier, he became an owner of the umbrella group that owned Montana's major ski resort complexes, including the ultraexclusive Yellowstone Club, a gated ski community with the largest concentration of billionaires anywhere outside New York City. Leuschen enjoyed hanging out in the club's Boot Room, a grungy bar with sawdust on the floor and TVs in every room, where you might rub elbows with Jeff Bezos, Bill Gates, or Mark Zuckerberg over a craft beer.

He bought houses. A Gilded Age mansion on New York's Fifth Avenue designed by McKim, Mead, and White, for $42 million. A $23 million oceanfront compound on Southampton's Meadow Lane. A private island in Maine's upper Penobscot Bay.

And then there was Switchback Ranch. Leuschen was enthralled by the West. Unlike most members of the Yellowstone Club, he actually knew something about ranching. His father Don was raised in a dugout cabin on a ranch in eastern Montana, an experience that left him with a lifelong aversion to cattle. Leuschen liked to say that his father never met a cow he liked. Fortunately, young David had plenty of aunts and uncles who liked cows, and thirty-three cousins who did, too.

In his junior year, Leuschen took a break from his studies at Dartmouth to work on his cousins' cattle ranch in the Yukon territory. Leuschen described the experience in a privately published book about Switchback Ranch that he wrote for his children during the COVID pandemic. The Yukon ranch had no electricity. The roofs were covered in bear hides and dinner was hacked from a moose haunch that dangled from a meat hook in the kitchen, dripping blood into a pan.

Leuschen fed and vaccinated cows in sixty-below temperatures, learned how to light a fire under the ancient tractor to warm its frozen block engine enough to start, and got drunk on his cousins' homebrewed rotgut—fermented dandelions and corn silage, aged in detergent bottles. Once a month, they drove into town and paid seventy-five cents for a shower. Leuschen loved it. He decided that if he ever got the money, he'd buy a cattle ranch.

He would spend decades creating Switchback Ranch, a collection of six distinct ranch properties spread across Montana and Wyoming, with a total fifty-seven thousand deeded acres. The ranch was named for the twenty-three narrow switchbacks leading to the first ranch that he bought, a pristine inholding on a high plateau in northern Wyoming's Sunlight Basin. The place was so remote that the building materials for his lodge had to be flown in by helicopter, one load at a time—four thousand loads in all.

The main unit of the ranch was a thirty-five-thousand-acre expanse on the edge of the Beartooth Mountains in Roscoe, Montana. It was here that Leuschen built one of the top commercial cattle operations in the northern Rockies, running two thousand units of Black Angus cows and stabling over a hundred horses. Everything was top of the line, starting with the beautiful curvilinear corrals and scales designed by Temple Grandin. Leuschen bought semen from the world's best bulls and got a license so he could artificially inseminate his cows himself. This process took place in a mirrored trailer with a stereo. Leuschen, who enjoyed telling people that he had fathered more than three thousand babies this way, blasted the B-52s' "Love Shack" as he worked.

When he wasn't moving cows from one sun-washed alpine pasture to another, Leuschen fly-fished for trout on his private eighteen-mile stretch of the Clarks Fork of the Yellowstone, hunted elk and bighorn sheep in his private forests and canyons, and skied his private slopes, a can of bear spray tucked in his ski jacket. Grizzly bears frequented his ranch, which delighted Leuschen. He loved grizzly bears. He never went fishing without a Smith & Wesson large-caliber revolver on his hip.

After his first wife ran off with his ranch manager, Switchback became Leuschen's romantic testing grounds. He invited a series of lady friends to join him there for a week of fly-fishing and horseback riding. Aware that a competition was underway, some would leave a little something behind at the end of their visit to stake their claim: a pair of lacy panties under the bed, perhaps, or a single earring in the shower. In a scheduling snafu, two of Leuschen's girlfriends were once booked for the same week. The more enterprising of the two crammed a chewed-up Ex-Lax square into a freshly baked brownie and somehow managed to get her rival to eat it; the next morning, she enjoyed a solo horseback ride with Leuschen while the competition writhed on the commode.

Leuschen's father died in the summer of 2012. The day before his father's memorial service in Bozeman, Leuschen was at Switchback's Roscoe unit, where he had an office in a handsome white building that housed a double rows of horse stalls, an indoor riding arena, and an old-fashioned saloon. He was married again by then, with a little daughter. Leuschen collected his thoughts, reflecting on the stories he'd tell about his father as the occasional whinny issued from the stables. Before he left, he idly clicked on the website of Hall and Hall, a leading ranch brokerage firm. This was something he liked to do from time to time, checking ranch listings the way other people trawl shopping websites for shoes. A new listing popped up: the Lazy K Bar Ranch.

Leuschen's cattle operation was well established by then. He didn't need more cows. He already owned superb hunting and fishing properties, teeming with twenty-inch-long cutthroat trout, record-book elk, grizzlies galore. But the Lazy K Bar was iconic. It was one of the most storied ranches in Montana. The Van Cleves were selling the whole thing—the dude ranch, the alpine meadows and glacial lakes, and the mountains—all of them, including Crazy Peak, the highest mountain in Montana north of the Beartooths.

On his way to Bozeman to join his family for the memorial, Leuschen made a detour and drove up Big Timber Canyon to see the Lazy K Bar. The cabins were dilapidated. A public road cut right through the ranch, so close to the main lodge that you could reach out and shake hands with whoever was driving by. But the landscape was staggering—like something out of *The Sound of Music*. The four highest peaks on the eastern range of the Crazies towered over the ranch like magnificent sno-cones. This was the true West. Leuschen thought how much his dad would have loved the place.

He had heard the legend about the Crow chief Plenty Coups, how he climbed to the top of Crazy Peak and had a vision that foretold the future of his tribe. As he took in the grandeur of the scene before him, Leuschen had an epiphany, his own vision into the future: if he didn't move fast, someone was going to buy this place and ruin it forever. He figured he could pay to reroute the road.

Leuschen called his broker on the spot and told him to make an offer, for the full asking price. When he got to Bozeman and his wife asked him what had taken him so long, Leuschen said something about needing extra time to pull his thoughts together. He did the whole thing without telling her—went to Big Timber and subjected himself to interviews with each of the four Van Cleve siblings to prove his worthiness, plied them with wine over dinner at the Grand, and signed the contract. He bought the Lazy K Bar; it was his, and his alone. Leuschen's wife was pissed off when he finally told her about it. But when she saw the place, of course, she thought it was the most beautiful place on earth.

The new Mrs. Leuschen was an interior designer. She took on the restoration of the old dude ranch and its thirty-odd buildings. In the main lodge, a taxidermy eagle spread its moldering wings above a stone fireplace high and wide enough to spit-roast a pronghorn. The log cabins had names that were spelled out in nails hammered into their doorsteps—Plenty Coup, Pick Axe, The Ditch. Most hadn't been touched since they were built in the early 1920s. By the time Mrs. Leuschen was finished with them, the cabins were tone poems of high alpine style: whitewashed chinked log walls, kilim rugs, high iron bedsteads, bentwood chairs, clawfoot tubs. The rundown store where the Van Cleves once sold bags of Sun Chips to the dudes was transformed into a play store for the Leuschens' two young children, its shelves stocked with apothecary jars of candy, stacks of cowboy hats, cap guns, and toy bow-and-arrow sets.

Leuschen built a landing strip for his toys: his ten-seat Pilatus PC-6 and his Short Tucano—a turboprop plane with a bubble canopy and a vertical air brake for steep descents. There were landing strips at all four

Switchback units. Leuschen, who got his pilot's license while he was in business school, liked to hop between ranches with the same ease that he bounced between his homes in New York City and the Hamptons. After a botched landing in his Aviat Husky two-seater sent him plowing through a barbed-wire fence—flipping the plane and shearing off its propeller—he hired a Swiss test pilot named Eric to fly with him full time. His piloting skills improved significantly.

Leuschen peppered remote beauty spots on the ranch with cabins—retrofitted shipping containers, air-dropped by Chinook helicopter—so he could spend days horseback riding and hiking to its farthest reaches. One cabin was set nine thousand feet above sea level at Druckmiller Lake, a glacial lake that was covered in ice well into July. The cabins were stocked with bedrolls, stoves, food, medical supplies, fishing rods. Snow shovels were lashed to the exterior so that they could be dug out in the winter and used as warming shacks, while skiing.

The ski terrain on Leuschen's Lazy K Bar—LKB for short—was amazing, better than Big Sky. He could heli-ski on his private mountains. This was not an everyday thing, and required a high degree of advance planning, to avoid triggering an avalanche. Leuschen would bring in guides to do snow studies. Then he'd go up in a helicopter with a seasoned pilot to find a line down the couloir he wanted to ski. Once everything had checked out, the pilot would deposit Leuschen and his friends high on the flank of one of his peaks. Then they'd ski down the mountain across the checkerboard of private and public land, acres and acres of virgin snow. It was perfectly legal: after all, Leuschen was a member of the public like anyone else.

The demand for more access to the Crazies and all its tantalizing recreational possibilities was building. Bozeman was growing faster than almost any small metropolitan area in the country. The people moving to Bozeman loved mountains. They wanted to go hiking and climbing and fishing and camping, and there were only so many mountains where you could do all those things within an hour or so of town. The Crazies beckoned, a spectacular and largely inaccessible wonderland. People wanted to play up there. But the public wasn't always the best steward of public land. "Don't plan on a pristine campsite," an online message board for climbers warned of a public campground in the Crazies. "Axe wielding fire builders have pretty much trashed the area."

Which explains, perhaps, why some ranchers in the Crazies balked at letting the public use access roads and trails that ran through their land to get to the national forest beyond it. The Lazy K Bar fired the first salvo in this battle back in 1940, when Paul Ledyard Van Cleve Jr. began locking a gate to a road through Big Timber Canyon during hunting season. By 1943, the gate was locked year-round. The government sued Van Cleve over the public's right to use the road. The case dragged on for years. It was ultimately resolved out of court, presumably in exchange for a financial settlement with the Van Cleves, who granted a deeded public right-of-way through their land in Big Timber Canyon in 1953.

But other access points remained blocked, including a road that wound through another piece of the Van Cleve land holdings in the Crazies: Sweet Grass Ranch, a guest ranch owned by Spike Van Cleve's daughter Shelly Carroccia and her family. Shelly's daughter Page Dringman and her husband, Pat Dringman, the Sweet Grass County attorney, spent their summers on the dude ranch, which they ran with Page's brothers Rocco and Tony.

The Carroccia Family Partnership took down a Forest Service trailhead sign on Sweet Grass Creek and replaced it with a sign that said, "This Is Not a Trailhead." Hikers and hunters who wanted to pass through Carroccia land to national forest trails were directed to sign in at the main house. When Alex Sienkiewicz, the Forest Service's district ranger for the Crazies, instructed his staff never to ask permission to access public land through traditional routes across private land, a group of landowners—Page Dringman among them—leveraged their political contacts in Washington to have him removed from the post and reassigned.

Now that he owned LKB, Leuschen had been drawn reluctantly into this conflict. Hikers and horseback riders could use a rocky trail along Big Timber Creek that traversed a section of his land to get to the national forest beyond. There was even a small picnic area where they could pause for a snack and take in the view. But that was it. Members of the public didn't have the right to leave the trail or the picnic area and wander onto his land. They weren't allowed to fish in the creek or camp there overnight. Of course, people did those things all the time, in full view of the signs asking them not to. If Leuschen wanted to be a prick about it, he could threaten to revoke the easement across his land. Not that he would. Now, *that* would be a shit show.

The public always wanted more: more trails, more campsites, more access for mountain bikes and ATVs. Leuschen, who gave money to a host of conservation groups through his philanthropy, wanted less. He could have dropped a couple of ATVs in the backcountry he owned and torn around on them—built roads there if he wanted to. But he didn't. When Forest Service rangers asked his permission to use mountain bikes on the trail through his land, he said no. There should be some places that were never marked by the tread of a mountain bike, he thought. Keep it Western.

As for his mountains, Leuschen made a point of climbing one every summer. If you own it, you climb it, and he had climbed them all: Crazy Peak, Granite Peak, Conical Peak, Big Timber Peak. Leuschen preferred not to encounter random members of the public on his mountains. If you wanted to climb one of Leuschen's mountains, you'd do well to call the ranch and ask permission. Nice people did.

Over the years, various entrepreneurs had approached him about a commercial heli-skiing operation in the Crazies. They wanted to lease his high-altitude landing zones. Leuschen turned them all down. If he wanted to indulge in the occasional heli-ski on LKB's peaks, that was his prerogative. They were his mountains, he owned them, and he should be able to do what he wanted on them. But he wasn't about to compromise their unspoiled majesty for profit.

Those mountains were Leuschen's legacy, his gift to his children. One day, LKB would be theirs, and they would become the stewards of Crazy Peak. Which is why he winced during a business meeting with some of the guys from Pattern, the wind energy company Riverstone had acquired. The guys were telling him about an eighty-megawatt wind project they wanted to build in Sweet Grass County, Montana.

"Please don't name it Crazy Mountain Wind," he told them. "The Crazy Mountains, that's like a sacred place."

Shane Doyle had never asked permission to climb Crazy Peak. The idea made him laugh. Crazy Peak was an island of rock and ice eleven thousand feet in the sky. It was really hard to get to. He couldn't understand why anyone would want to personally own it.

Since his first harrowing fast, Doyle had climbed to the top of Crazy Peak several times, even bringing a pair of filmmakers on one occasion. Traversing the ridgeline of the mountain was like walking on the edge of a knife. The land just fell away as you ascended. There was a narrow gap with a five-hundred-foot drop; you had to jump over it to get to the summit. And then you were in the stratosphere. You could see everything—all the way to Crow Agency, across the great expanse that once was Crow Country. The filmmakers launched a drone at the summit, which swooped above Doyle's head, capturing the amazing views and filming him as he sang and prayed. Then the sky went dark and a thunderstorm swept over the peak. Lightning bolts spiked the spine of the ridge as the three men scrambled down it, striking so close that you could hear a buzzing in the air.

"No matter how you do it, religion is kind of hard," Medicine Horse had told Doyle and Willerslev when they visited him on Crow Agency. Getting to Crazy Peak wasn't meant to be easy. When you stood at the summit, you stood where Plenty Coups fasted for days on end, where he cut off the tip of his finger and bashed it till the blood came. All in pursuit of a dream. Plenty Coups understood that when you went up to Crazy Peak, you had to be ready to sacrifice something of yourself.

The possibility that someone, someday, might prevent Crow people from being in this place—or might leave their mark on it, permanently altering a sacred landscape—was profoundly troubling to Doyle. Stone fasting beds built by his ancestors still stood on windswept ridges. These were ceremonial sites of profound importance. They needed to be protected. But there were no protections for any part of the Crazies. Reagan's veto of the Montana wilderness bill in 1988 had eliminated that possibility. The Crazies' tens of thousands of acres of national forest were pristine—a true wilderness. But the federal government didn't recognize it as wilderness. Absent that federal designation, there was nothing to prevent roads from being built in the high elevation or cell phone towers from going up on its ridges—even oil and gas exploration was a possibility.

But suddenly, Doyle found himself in a position to help change that. In 2016, the US Forest Service announced that, for the first time in thirty years, it would reexamine its land management plan for the Crazies and begin looking at ways to update it. Even though the Forest Service could only set the policy for public land in the mountain range—the pine-green squares in the checkerboard pattern—the new plan would have profound implications for the entire Crazy quilt.

The Montana Wilderness Association—the conservation group that put Doyle on its Hold Our Ground billboards, and which is now known as Wild Montana—hired him to act as a liaison with the Forest Service. The conservation group felt a special obligation to ensure that Native voices were part of any conversation about the Crazies' future. National parks and forests had been taken from Indigenous people. The creation of America's public lands—the very origins of the American conservation movement—sprang from historic injustice. The more buy-in the Apsáalooke had for a new plan for the Crazies, the better, from the association's perspective. And Native involvement would give added weight to its own calls for rigorous environmental protections for the mountains.

Doyle reached out to Crow leadership. Then he began working the media. "Although our tribe lost our legal ownership of the Crazies in 1868, we have not forgotten their power and the sacred role they have played," Doyle declared in an open letter coauthored with Crow tribal chairman A. J. Not Afraid and Adrian Bird Jr., the lead monitor for Crow Agency's historic preservation office. "We must be able to fast and pray in ceremonial solitude as we have since time immemorial . . . That's why we're asking the Forest Service to not expand mechanized and motorized travel in the Crazies . . . to not allow mining, the building of any new roads, construction of any new energy or utility corridors, or development of any recreation sites."

Landowners like Page Dringman looked on warily as the public conversation about the future of the Crazies played out. Maybe the Crow thought it should all be untouched wilderness; many of the Crazies' current residents disagreed. "Generally, residents think there should be multiple uses," Dringman told the *Billings Gazette*. "In the Crazies, wilderness seems inappropriate." Forest Service land was pocked with private land—their land. Any attempt to restrict uses of public land would inevitably impact them as well. New federal protections could infringe on their mineral rights, maybe even their water rights. The Crow tribe's talk of ceremonial sites and historic cultural practices also made them nervous. Some of those sites were on private property, land the Forest Service had no business trying to manage.

A reporter joined Doyle and Bird in a Cessna for an aerial tour of the Crazies organized by the Montana Wilderness Association. Bird had never visited Awaxaawippíia before. Looking down on the mountain range from the Cessna's tiny window was the closest he had ever gotten to the sacred place of his ancestors. "That's not just a pile of rocks to us," he said. "How much more is going to be taken from us?" Doyle spotted what looked like tipi rings, vestiges of ancient seasonal villages. They were all over the mountains. He understood the ranchers' desire for freedom, but wondered why they couldn't respect the land that they had inherited, land with a long and important history for so many people. The Crazies—the Apsáalookes' cathedral—were locked up because a handful of landowners wanted to keep everyone off their property.

Doyle went up in the Cessna several times that day, with locals and different members of the media. He never tired of telling the story of Plenty Coups's fast on Crazy Peak, how the vision he had there led to a policy of nonviolence toward white settlers that influenced the course of American history. Crazy Peak belonged to a billionaire now.

Doyle would never compare himself to Plenty Coups. He had never been visited by a dream on Crazy Peak. But Doyle had his own vision of what could be. Staring at the Crazies through the windows of the Cessna, it seemed so obvious. That billionaire should give Crazy Peak to the Apsáalooke. "If I could have my dream, that's what he would do," Doyle would later say. "He would say, 'This belongs to the Crow tribe,' and he would hand it over to the tribe. And that would signify a new dawn of a new era for the Crow tribe in the Crazy Mountains."

13

EARTHQUAKE

February 21, 2019
Park County Courthouse
Livingston, Montana

WARD MARSHALL, Senior Director of Business Development,
  Pattern Development, *having first been duly sworn, testified as follows*:
Q: Ward, how did Pattern come to be involved in this project?
MR. MARSHALL: It's probably back in late 2015 that the developer
  of Crazy Mountain Wind, a guy by the name of Marty Wilde, had
  approached my boss. Actually, it was a smaller project at that time.
  I think it was about forty-five megawatts, is what he was looking
  at. And we were not interested, it was just a little bit on the small
  side for Pattern. And then at some point, either it was in late 2015
  or possibly early 2016, Marty basically came back with a project
  that we are looking at today, which is around eighty megawatts, a
  good-sized project. So we entered into discussions with Marty, did
  our due diligence, and by the end of 2016, we purchased the project
  from Marty Wilde . . . Crazy Mountain Wind, LLC.
Q: And who—just to give a little more background—who is Marty
  Wilde?

NOVEMBER 9, 2016
BOLLINGER ROOM
PUBLIC SERVICE COMMISSION
HELENA, MONTANA

The public hearing on docket D2016.7.56 got underway approximately
eight hours after Donald J. Trump had been declared president-elect of

the United States of America. The mood in the Bollinger Room was buoyant. Compounding the excitement of Trump's surprise victory, Commissioners Lake and Koopman had both won their reelection campaigns, cementing the Republican lock on the Public Service Commission. NorthWestern Energy's attorney Sarah Norcott hurried over to offer her congratulations to the commissioners as they took their seats. Monica Tranel, dressed in a brown pantsuit and nursing a large coffee, didn't get up from the counsel table.

The subject of the hearing was Crazy Mountain Wind's petition to set the terms and conditions for a contract with NorthWestern Energy. Twelve years after Marty, Jaffe, and Rick had raised the first white-and-orange meteorological tower on the Jarrett ranch, Crazy Mountain Wind was inching closer to reality. The holy grail of Montana wind development—a power purchase agreement with the state's monopoly utility—was just within reach. Marty's dogged insistence on the brilliant moneymaking potential of Rick Jarrett's wind had never wavered. Now Monica's legal maneuvering had brought NorthWestern to the negotiating table.

Marty had driven to Helena in his new silver Porsche 911, purchased with Greenfield money—$100,000, cash down. He took the witness stand right around the time that Hillary Clinton was making her concession speech in a Manhattan hotel. Marty hadn't voted. A hard-core Bernie Sanders supporter, Marty thought Trump was an asshole, but he hated Hillary, whom he saw as the embodiment of a corrupt establishment, a political hack in the pocket of Big Oil and the big banks, an enemy of progressive ideas. #NeverHillary, #CrookedHillary, and #ClintonMilitaryIndustrialComplex hashtags punctuated his Facebook posts from that time, along with the occasional misogynistic cartoon, like one that showed the secretary of state as a jaded whore in fishnet stockings, soliciting johns on Wall Street. "My ideals are too strong to remain a party to this corrupt bullshit," Marty wrote in a Facebook post that summer. "Vote For Hillary Clinton and Sell-Out Everything I Believe In???"

Marty couldn't vote for Bernie in the general election, so he sat it out. He rolled the dice and the asshole won. So, America had gone to the dark side—well, maybe Trump was the president they all deserved.

Sitting at the microphone to the left of the commissioners' long table, Marty fielded questions from NorthWestern Energy's lawyer about Crazy Mountain Wind's growth spurt. Since his last visit to the Bollinger Room nearly three years ago, Crazy Mountain Wind had mushroomed from a humble twenty-five-megawatt CREP to a seventy-eight-megawatt project with twenty-two turbines, capable of powering twenty-six thousand Montana homes.

The turbines were substantially taller than the ones that Marty had planned to use for Coyote Wind—about five hundred feet from ground to blade tip. The diameter of the rotors' blades was four hundred and fifty feet. Taller turbines could harvest more electricity from the air, which meant you didn't need as many. Crazy Mountain Wind had half the number of turbines of Coyote Wind. About ten of them would be on land that belonged to Rick's neighbor Alfred Anderson. Marty had paid a visit to the old Norwegian to re-up their wind lease agreement, which had been dormant since 2007, just the week before.

For the project to be viable, Marty had to scale up. The cost of developing a wind farm of any size was enormous, he told the commissioners. A twenty-five-megawatt project cost him as much in attorney fees as one four times its size. Meanwhile, the price that NorthWestern Energy would agree to pay for wind power kept dropping. At current rates, only big projects that generated more megawatt-hours of electricity would turn a profit. There was also the federal production tax credit to consider. It was impossible to get the attention of tax equity investors who would finance Crazy Mountain Wind—very big folks with very big tax bills; banks, in other words—unless the project would guarantee multimillion-dollar tax credits to match.

"I'm a businessman," Marty said, "and I think it's just a basic principle of business that you want to have a profit in the thing you do."

Like his hero Bernie Sanders, Marty was just being honest. His answer was like red meat thrown to the fiscal conservatives of Montana's PSC.

"It is not the responsibility of the utility or the utility ratepayer, and it's certainly not the responsibility of the Commission to guarantee your project's profit and profit for its financiers," Commissioner Koopman scolded.

Koopman had campaigned hard through the summer and fall, handing out his "Firepower for Rate-Payers" flyers at the Bozeman gun show, tossing candy to kids at the Manhattan Potato Festival, and marching in MSU's Homecoming Parade with a "Stand Up for Our National Anthem" banner as a country band played patriotic music on a "Roger Koopman for Public Service Commission" float, decorated with a giant red-white-and-blue crepe-paper eagle. But listening to Marty Wilde explain QF megawatt thresholds—as he was now doing, in response to Koopman's comment—seemed a bit too much for the newly reelected commissioner to take in that post-election morning.

"So, we're in an evolving market," said Marty, coming up for air. "I might be losing your point. Am I answering what you asked me?"

"I'm not as familiar with wind projects to fully understand where those thresholds are, but we can move on," Koopman said, looking for an off-ramp.

"There's bound to be businessmen among us here," Marty insisted. "Internal rate of return is the metric, right? And if I have a robust internal rate of return, I can get the interest of some really strong financial types."

In fact, he already had. Marty was deep in negotiations with Pattern Development, a wing of the San Francisco–based Pattern Energy Group—one of the biggest renewable-energy companies in America. Impressed by the years of wind assessment data Marty had amassed, along with his environmental reports, interconnection studies, and real estate leases with local landowners, Pattern was ready to buy Crazy Mountain Wind. The price was right, and the project was a good fit for its portfolio. There was another seventy-eight-megawatt project under development in neighboring Stillwater County that Pattern also had its eye on, called Stillwater Wind. The two projects complemented each other, and one facility manager could oversee both.

During a break, Marty ambled over to Koopman, whose district was home to Crazy Mountain Wind, for some targeted schmoozing. As it happened, the commissioner had another question about Crazy Mountain Wind, one he preferred to ask off the record: "Do you find there are local folks that object very much?"

"It depends on where they hail from. You know, billionaires from Texas who have made money off oil tend to want pristine little ranchettes in Montana," Marty said dismissively. He pointed to Rick Jarrett, who had just taken a seat in the back of the Bollinger Room, having driven 160 miles from Big Timber. Marty had asked Rick to speak at the hearing. "For folks like these folks here—Rick is fifth-generation. His great-granddaddy used to chase Indians out from camping on his land. And those folks, the local folks that are trying to scratch a living on that windy, gravelly, dry land, are all for it."

Koopman knew all about Big Timber; he used to hunt around there. "The wind up on those ridges, up on those flats—man, there were times of year you could barely stand up. It was always blowing," he said with a laugh.

When the hearing resumed, Don Reading, a utility industry analyst who was testifying as an expert witness for Marty's WINData, took the stand. Reading had used statistical models and NorthWestern's own pricing structure to calculate the full avoided cost for each megawatt-hour of energy that Crazy Mountain Wind would produce: $49.83, which included a ten-dollar carbon emission adder.

The carbon adder had become a standard feature of renewable-energy contracts with NorthWestern Energy. It was a bet on a greener future, one in which carbon-emitting coal and gas-fired power plants would become subject to fines and penalties. As the market phased out fossil fuels, the reasoning went, they would become more costly than renewables. The carbon adder represented the money that the utility would save in future fines and penalties over the twenty-five years of the wind farm's contract. Crazy Mountain Wind's positive environmental attributes had market value. Those environmental attributes could even be sold or traded in the form of renewable-energy certificates.

Far from rejecting the concept of the carbon emissions adder, North-Western had embraced it. The utility factored a $14.63 carbon adder into its rate calculations for the clean energy generated by the passel of hydroelectric dams it acquired in 2014. During hearings at the state capitol, the utility's executives had made the case that if the carbon adder were removed from its pricing model, the Big Dam Deal would not be financially viable. Take out the price for avoided carbon emissions, they argued, and you will blow up the deal. The Public Service Commission approved the carbon adder, and the Big Dam Deal went through.

But there was a sunbed-tanned elephant in the Bollinger Room that morning.

Reading cleared his throat. "I haven't heard it mentioned here, but the earthquake that happened with the new election—I don't know where EPA and carbon is going—but it is generally assumed that there will be some kind of penalty for high-carbon-producing generation plants," he said.

The somnolent late-morning fog that had descended during the discussion of incremental integration costs suddenly lifted. Commissioner Kavulla, an owlish fellow whose thick-framed glasses and receding hairline made him seem a good decade older than his thirty-two years, straightened in his high-backed blue swivel chair.

"I guess I would have to say, Dr. Reading, that up until twelve hours ago, I would have agreed with the idea that society in the United States seemed poised to further ratchet down carbon emissions," Kavulla said. "But now the person who is the executive above those relevant agencies, you're aware that he said that this isn't real?"

On the campaign trail, Trump had made many statements about climate change: climate change was a hoax; climate change was natural, not manmade; climate change would boost the US economy. Trump had called for a greater reliance on coal and vowed to pull the United States out of the Paris Climate Accord, an international pact to curb greenhouse gas emissions. Trump loved coal mines and hated windmills, hated them with a passion. This aversion was rooted in a long, bitter, and ultimately unsuccessful fight to block an eleven-turbine offshore wind development from going up within eyeshot of his Trump International Golf Links in Aberdeen, Scotland.

"I am building what many are already considering to be the greatest golf course anywhere in the world. I don't want to see it destroyed by having eleven monstrosities built, looming over it literally one mile away," Trump said in a 2012 diatribe before the Scottish Parliament that ticked every box on the anti-wind agenda. Wind farms didn't work without massive subsidies. They killed massive amounts of birds and wildlife. And there were lots of other reasons. "Most importantly, they are so unattractive, so ugly, so noisy, and so dangerous that if Scotland does this, I think Scotland will be in serious trouble. I think you'll lose your tourism industry to Ireland and lots of other places that are laughing at what Scotland's doing."

Great Britain's highest court rejected Trump's lawsuit, and construction of the North Sea wind farm went forward.

"Do you think it would be reasonable for the Commission to consider the possible effect on carbon price of what has only lately happened in the political arena?" Kavulla now asked Dr. Reading.

Reading was sad to say that he did think that might be prudent, although he urged the commissioners to let the dust settle before they made any decisions.

But Commissioner Lake was in no mood to wait. The former feed mill owner hated the carbon adder—hated how it made the ratepayers pay for environmental regulations and penalties that did not yet exist, and which now might never exist, thanks to soon-to-be-president Trump.

"Given the earthquake we've had in the last twelve hours—and we still haven't seen how many buildings are collapsing and how many bricks are still going to fall—have you seen in your experiences a separate clause?" Commissioner Lake asked Marty's expert witness.

Perhaps an amendment could be added to the power purchase agreement to strip out the carbon adder, given the uncertainty about whether the president-elect would choose to follow federal laws, Lake suggested. He was something of a stickler about rules and protocols himself. As soon as this hearing wrapped up, Lake planned to head home and take down all his campaign yard signs, which any self-respecting politician did late election night or first thing the next morning.

After the commissioners had asked all their questions, anyone who wanted to make a public comment was invited to come take a seat at the microphone, push that white button, and have at her. Rick, who had dressed in a clean button-down shirt and his usual jeans and suspenders, made his way unsteadily to the front of the room.

Although he had spent the better part of his life on the back of a horse, Rick stopped riding that year. He'd had a couple of falls. Somehow, he couldn't stay in the saddle anymore. "I don't know what's going on with me, but I'm just getting old too quickly," he told Jami. He was forgetting things. It got to the point where his girlfriend, Lois, started going to county commission meetings with him, to help him remember what got said about the wind farm. Within the year, Rick would be diagnosed with Parkinson's disease.

"I'm interested in this project because I'm a landowner where some of the turbines go," he said into the microphone. "Our cattle prices were down 40 percent this year. A wind farm would enable me to pass my ranch down to future generations, where right now that's not possible because there's just not enough money." Rick told the commissioners that he and Marty had come close a couple times to getting their wind farm built, but somehow they hadn't gotten the job done. "We just keep coming back and struggling. And I guess I would like your help in that struggle," he said.

Rick was followed at the microphone by a burly man in a flannel shirt with a shaggy red beard. "My name is Harv Van Wagoner, H-A-R-V, V-A-N-W-A-G-O-N-E-R," he said, voice shaking as he spelled it out for the commission stenographer.

Harv was Jami's partner. He had been working full time on the Crazy Mountain Cattle Company for almost a year by then. Harv and Jami lived together in the house on Old Boulder Road, and though they weren't married, he was considered part of the Jarrett family. Only a family member would work the long hours that Harv did for the low wages that Rick paid him. Harv saw it as a kind of sweat equity he was investing in the place, for himself and Jami and for Jami's kids, whom he cared for as his own.

Harv grew up in Midway, Utah, where his family raised dairy heifers and owned a meat-cutting business. He'd always wanted to ranch; the only reason he went to college was so he could learn how to preg-check cows. After graduating from the University of Utah with an ag degree, Harv earned a master's in cattle reproduction at the University of Montana in Bozeman. He spent six years working on a study of grazing behavior as a university research assistant. When his friend Brian Engle started his own meat-cutting business in Big Timber, Harv came to give him a hand.

Brian's family owned the Boulder River ranch where Robert Redford shot *The Horse Whisperer*. While his dad and uncle Keith were busy with the producers, Brian was behind the scenes, trying to keep up with all the ranch work. He had warm memories of the catering tent. "That was a lot of fine foods," he said.

In 2002, Russell Gordy's ranch manager, Dave Gibson, called Engle and asked if he wanted to come work for the Texan. Gordy employed six or seven full-time workers who lived with their families in farmhouses and trailer homes dotted across the ranch, overseeing different units of his Lone Star cattle operation. Engle, who had two small children, jumped at the chance to manage the cows on the Hunter's Hot Springs unit. His dad and Uncle Keith paid $650 a month; Gordy was offering $2,000. "I was excited. We wouldn't be strapped for cash every month," he said. "Working for an absentee landlord was always my dream job, because you knew you were getting paid."

Some of the air went out of the balloon when Engle saw where his young family would have to live. The farmhouse at Hunter's Hot Springs was in bad shape, with black mold in the basement. Gibson assured Engle that the Texan planned to replace the house with a new double-wide mobile home. Brian and his wife, Kary, should go pick out one they liked, he said. But that double-wide never materialized.

Engle never spoke directly to Gordy about the black mold or the new three-bedroom mobile home he and Kary picked out; all communications went through Gibson, who died in 2020. In the two years that he worked on the ranch, Engle saw Gordy twice, maybe three times. One autumn, he went hunting on Rick Jarrett's place with a friend who shot a stag mule deer. The calving barn by Hunter's Hot Springs was nice and cool, so Engle hung the deer in there to skin it. It was one of the rare occasions that Gordy stopped by. According to Engle, the boss didn't like what he saw in his calving barn. Despite Engle's insistence that the buck hadn't been shot on his ranch, Gordy bristled at the sight of the mule deer and its handsome rack.

"He said something like, 'You had to take the biggest deer,'" Engle recalled, still affronted by the unfairness of it all. "I don't like eating mule deer, they taste like shit." Engle, who hunted white-tailed does and cow elk, had never been one to care about big racks. "You can't eat the horns," he said.

Engle quit working for Gordy in 2004, after a miserable winter when both of his kids came down with serious respiratory infections. "The moldy house was the crux of it all," he said, convinced that mold spores in the basement were activated when he turned on the furnace. Engle moved his family out of the farmhouse to a home in Big Timber, then drove back and forth to Gordy's ranch all through calving. He stayed on the job until June, once the cows and calves were out on grass and had salt and all the fences were fixed, so there was nothing left hanging. Engle paid his children's medical costs out of pocket; Gordy didn't provide health insurance. "I didn't even ask him to pay," he said. The farmhouse was torn down not long after he quit.

Engle salvaged a refrigerated trailer from a wrecked semi and converted it into a cutting room for wild game. During hunting season, Harv would spend his weekends in the semi-reefer helping Brian process the elk and deer that hunters brought in, breaking them down into steaks and grinding them into sausage. When Brian's business, Pioneer Meats, expanded into lamb and beef, Harv went to work for him full time.

That's how Harv met Jami—she and Brian had known each other since they were kids at the Bridge School, a one-room schoolhouse near the Greybear Bridge over the Yellowstone. Brian was four years older than Jami, but when there's only ten or twelve kids in your entire school, you play together sometimes. When Jami's marriage was on the rocks and JV moved out, money was tight. She worried about making her mortgage payments. Brian offered her a part-time job cutting meat, on top of her courthouse job.

On nights when the kids were with JV, Jami would work from six in the evening till two in the morning in the semi-reefer alongside Brian and his friend Harv, packaging meat, mixing sausage, and making pepper sticks. It was tight quarters in that reefer; you got to know who you were working with a little bit. Harv was strong and smart. She'd never seen anyone work so hard. In Jami's experience, it was tough to find a man who was more of a man than she was. Jami and Harv started dating after her divorce from JV was finalized in late 2005; the following summer, he moved in.

Harv worked for Brian for about eight years. A rancher would bring in a cow that had come up dry to be harvested. They'd put her in the knock box, shoot her between the eyes with a .22, then break down the animal with bone saws and knives. It was hazardous, messy work. Once, Harv shot a hog in the knock box and the magnum bullet went through its skull and ricocheted off the concrete floor pad, tearing through his clothes and grazing him in the stomach. It didn't break the skin, which was fortunate.

He wasn't so lucky in 2014. A blade in the meat saw broke while he was processing an animal, severing the first finger on his right hand. Brian wrapped his friend's hand in duct tape and drove him seventy miles to the emergency room in Billings. Jami packed Harv's severed finger on ice and followed them in her truck, flooring it past the ninety-mile-an-hour speed limit, but the surgeon told her he only did thumbs.

For all the hazards involved in harvesting animals and process-ing them in a wrecked semi-reefer, it was nothing compared to the gut-churning stress of trying to keep a small family cattle operation afloat. As Rick became more unsteady, Harv picked up the slack. After a year or so, he was pretty much managing the place. Harv had minored in ag business in college, which he soon realized hadn't prepared him for shit. The real way you learned the ranching business, whether it was when to ship calves or buy grain, was when there were tens of thou-sands of dollars riding on your decision and you were saying, "What did I just do?"

Addressing the Public Service Commission and a roomful of peo-ple in suits was stressful in a different way. Harv's voice trembled and cracked as he told the commissioners that Crazy Mountain Wind would help diversify Sweet Grass County's tax base and bring in needed rev-enue. "So, I hope that's kind of in the back of your guys' mind. And I don't know if I should touch on this, but I'm going to anyways because I found it interesting. I've heard a lot about risk in this proceeding today, but I've not heard a lot about potential benefit . . . all I hear is negative in looking at things today."

Marty, who was sitting behind Monica, nodded approvingly.

The commissioners met shortly before Christmas with a staff attorney and two of the PSC's in-house analysts to hash out the details of Crazy Mountain Wind's contract with NorthWestern Energy. It was at these work sessions that the nuts and bolts of power purchase agreements were put in place. The staff made recommendations based on their knowl-edge of the utilities and the regulatory issues involved, but it was up to the commissioners whether to heed them or not.

Neil Templeton, an analyst in the commission's regulatory division, knew that the carbon emissions adder had become a flashpoint in the Bollinger Room. But the staff's recommendation was to keep it in Crazy Mountain Wind's price rate. There was strong precedent: Templeton pointed out that NorthWestern Energy itself had incorporated such costs in setting rates for its hydro facilities, rates the commission had approved. Not even NorthWestern was contesting Crazy Mountain Wind's carbon adder.

This made Commissioner Koopman unhappy. In a newspaper opinion piece earlier that year, he had complained that renewables hooked on "the subsidy narcotic" were being forced on ratepayers over cheap, reliable coal by the Environmental Protection Agency, "a power-obsessed federal agency that apparently believes burning the US Constitution is an acceptable CO_2 emission." Better science was needed to determine the earth-greening benefits of carbon emissions, Koopman thought.

Now, with President-elect Trump about to take office, it seemed time for a course correction. "Right now, it appears that the political climate has shifted," he declared. "I don't think CO_2 has a negative impact on the environment, I truly don't. To coin a term this season from Ebenezer Scrooge, I think it's bah humbug."

Koopman liked to compare himself to a batter stepping up to home plate. There were times you wanted to smack a home run over the left field wall, but the best you could do was bunt down the third base line and hope for a single. That was how he felt about the carbon adder. He'd like to do away with the thing entirely, but his own staff was insisting that the extra charge for avoided emissions had to stay. It was illegal under PURPA to discriminate against wind projects, and taking out the carbon adder would look a lot like discrimination.

So, Koopman bunted. He made a motion to delay the carbon adder for the first three years of Crazy Mountain Wind's contract. This delay would be built into the levelized price rate for the project's megawatt-hours of electricity. Kavulla seconded the motion, and it passed three to two, with Commissioners Lake and Bushman voting nay. They wanted the carbon adder killed off altogether.

The PSC order, issued in early January, made no mention of climate hysteria or Ebenezer Scrooge, but it did refer to Trump's election six times. The seismic shift in the political landscape had given the commissioners an excuse to give Crazy Mountain Wind a haircut. The delayed carbon adder would take a 2 percent bite out of Crazy Mountain Wind's total profits—a loss of $10 million. Monica read the order in disbelief.

Even so, it was a good day for Crazy Mountain Wind. The wind farm was going to get its twenty-five-year power purchase agreement at a good enough price—$36.36 per megawatt-hour. And best of all, Pattern had put a ring on it. The San Francisco wind corporation bought Crazy Mountain Wind in November, before the commissioners met for their work session. It was another win for Marty Wilde. He would collect a $750,000 developer's fee, to be paid in installments, with the big payday still to come: $2.39 million when the wind farm's turbines started spinning up electricity.

When all the paperwork was finalized that summer, Rick would collect a one-time execution payment of $10,000. There would be additional payments during construction, set to begin in late 2018. But it wasn't until Crazy Mountain Wind went into operation that he'd see any real money. Although their agreements were structured a little differently, both Jarrett and Anderson would receive 3 percent of Crazy Mountain Wind's annual gross revenues from the megawatts generated on their ranches, an earnings percentage that would gradually scale up over the twenty-five-year life of the project.

That money would help pay off mortgages and debts. It would buy more cattle and sheep. It would enable the Jarretts and the Andersons to do what they needed to do so the land would be there for their children and their grandchildren. Crazy Mountain Wind would spin air into gold.

In January, George Hardie III, vice president of Pattern Development, reached out to NorthWestern's legal counsel to hash over some fine points in the power purchase agreement. Hardie's letter was entered on the PSC's website in late January as part of the Crazy Mountain Wind docket. Which is how Jan Engwis, on one of his periodic PSC website trawls, learned that Crazy Mountain Wind had been bought by a Big Wind company out of San Francisco valued at over $1 billion.

For a long time, it had seemed that Rick Jarrett's wind farm was stuck in bureaucratic purgatory. Marty Wilde was a thorn in Engwis's side, a pebble in his shoe. Engwis had been fighting him almost as long as he'd been in Montana. But Wilde was a known quantity. Now a billion-dollar corporation had picked up the mantle of Crazy Mountain Wind, and it would be a far more formidable opponent than the wildcat wind prospector.

Engwis would wait for the right opportunity to sue, his weapon of choice against Rick Jarrett's obsessive wind development efforts. In the meantime, he worked the media. In late March, a local television news program ran a feature on the prospective wind farm in Big Timber. "This is what the area looks like now," the on-air reporter for *Wake Up Montana* said, pointing to a picture of the Crazy Mountains. The image was replaced by a photo simulation that showed the mountains fenced behind a phalanx of wind turbines that stretched as far as the eye could see. "This is what Big Timber residents might see looking out their windows if the project is approved," he said. It bore no resemblance to any site plan from Crazy Mountain Wind's various incarnations.

The reporter interviewed only one Big Timber resident—local ranch owner Jan Engwis, who showed off the views from a rise on his ranch while complaining that wind turbines would drive away all the tourists. "They come here to visit this beauty, this pristine nature," Engwis said. "They come to float the river, they come to do fly-fishing. They don't come here, however, to see massive windmills." The reporter reached out to Rick for comment and got an ornery response: "Jarrett says as far as he's concerned, it's the landowners' right to decide what they want to do with their land."

The *Wake Up Montana* feature didn't mention that all the land that lay between the Yellowstone and the Crazy Mountains—the view that Engwis showed off for the cameras—was privately owned. Engwis had no plans to allow tourists to fly-fish his three private miles of the Yellowstone, and neither did his neighbor David Chesnoff, who posted No Trespassing signs to dissuade rafters from beaching on his private riverbanks for a picnic. The maximum exposure most tourists would have to Rick's and Alfred's windmills would occur during their drive to Big Timber on I-90.

Engwis would eventually shift the focus of his anti–wind farm rhetoric from the tourists to the locals—specifically, the golden eagles and bald eagles that inhabited his ranch and built nests the size of treehouses in its cottonwoods and sandstone ledges. The Engwis ranch fell within a 1,200-mile swath of south-central Montana where golden eagles had been studied on and off since the 1960s by Craighead Beringia South, a conservation nonprofit in Kelly, Wyoming.

The Engwises first welcomed Ross Crandall, a research biologist with Craighead Beringia South, to the ranch in 2011. Crandall was tracking golden eagle nesting behavior and eaglet survival rates. Jan and Karen took him to see their golden eagle nest and allowed him to trap and tag select adult eagles for his research. Every spring during the nesting season, Crandall and his research partner would drag a roadkill carcass onto a promising piece of rugged terrain as bait. Then they'd spend hours hiding just out of the raptors' line of sight, waiting for the target eagle to come within reach of a remote-controlled net launcher.

Crandall looked forward to his annual visits to the Engwis ranch. Jan and Karen had so much enthusiasm for his research. They'd throw him in the side-by-side and drive him out to their golden eagle nest, or look on with interest as he tagged the eagle he had netted, outfitted it with transmitters, and drew blood for his various studies, including one on lead exposure. Karen took lots of pictures.

Participating in the research study was a thrill for Jan. He was proud of his golden eagles and their fledglings—it was immensely enjoyable, observing them, watching those eaglets being raised and learning to fly. He felt like he provided for them. The Engwises' sense of connection to these wild creatures went beyond anything a random motorist spotting a golden eagle from I-90 could understand, Jan would say. The Engwises didn't just see the mule deer, pronghorns, bears, and eagles, they lived with them, *experienced* them.

The Engwises' attachment to their wildlife may have been infused with extra intensity given the isolation of life on their 5,500-acre ranch. Building a new life in Big Timber wasn't easy, however beautiful the scenery or photogenic its raptors and ungulates. The climate was harsh, particularly the winters, with bitter cold and blowing snow. The social climate could be equally inhospitable—there was no welcome wagon in Sweet Grass County.

The Engwises made an effort in the beginning. They donated to the local food bank and the Big Timber Volunteer Fire Department, and they helped sponsor an FFA summer program for local teens. Jan became an officer of the local irrigation company, the Hunter's Hot Springs Canal Company, often hosting its meetings at his home, which sat atop the six-thousand-square foot workshop where he did maintenance and displayed his classic cars and trucks, his collectibles.

Unlike many recreational ranch owners in Big Timber, who might spend as a little as a month or two there all year, Jan and Karen lived on the ranch full time, rarely leaving for more than a day here or there. Karen's adult son, Mikey, who had cerebral palsy, lived in a home attached to an indoor riding arena with his two shih tzus, Buddy and Peanut.

But after less than a decade in Montana, Jan and Karen listed the Engwis ranch for sale. Jeff Bollman, the Montana Department of Natural Resources and Conservation staffer who led the state's effort to partner with Marty on Coyote Wind, stumbled across a listing for the Engwis ranch on a ranch brokerage website in 2010. It got his attention, because Engwis was in the process of suing the DNRC over Coyote Wind. "Just kind of interesting," Bollman noted, forwarding the listing to his colleagues.

Karen hired Tom Morse, a ranch broker based in Durango, Colorado. Morse was accustomed to working with wealthy people who had found that their dreams of owning a Western ranch didn't match up to the realities of living on one. "They say, 'I worked my butt off, I just want to enjoy it.' They want to recreate—to hunt, fish—and what happens is they end up spending all their time taking care of the place," Morse said.

But the situation with the Engwises was a little different. They didn't feel at home in Big Timber. "It's a difficult place to move into and be embraced by your neighbors, that's what they said. [Karen] was very, very clear about how it was difficult, having not grown up there," Morse said. The Engwises had strong opinions on a lot of issues, he said, which might have made it harder for them to fit in.

The Engwises wanted $17.5 million for the ranch, which Morse thought overpriced. The ranch had a decent location—not far from Livingston, where you could go out to dinner—and it had several miles of frontage on the Yellowstone. But sheer cliffs made much of its riverfront inaccessible, and there were no tributary streams to add a secondary fishing component, which many of his recreational ranch clients looked for.

The view of the Crazies was a plus, but most of the ranch acreage was high desert prairie. Ranch buyers in this price range wanted a mix of forest and meadows with their blue-ribbon trout water, not windblown plains. Then there was the problem of the Engwises' main residence. Bottom line, it was a three-bedroom home over a big garage.

The ranch broker did his best. He placed a cover story about the Engwis ranch in *Farm & Ranch*, a glossy publication for high-price land listings. The three-page article was studded with pictures of pronghorns romping in the sagebrush, the sparkling Yellowstone, a brown bear in a tree. The prose was of the purple-sage variety. "Follow the ever-present heartbeat of the roaring Yellowstone to a place where nature still reigns," it read. "Those who share in the conservation philosophy . . . will see the Engwis Ranch for what it is: a last stand in the 'last best place.'"

But it was a hard sell. More than once, Morse drove a client out to see the ranch, only to be told to turn the vehicle around before he even got to the main residence. It just wasn't the setup his clients were looking for.

Frustrated that more people weren't coming to see the ranch, the Engwises fired Morse. They decided they could do a better job marketing the place themselves. Karen made a twenty-minute video compilation of her wildlife photographs, scoring it with plaintive penny whistles and classical guitar. *Engwis Ranch Adventure* went up on YouTube in September 2015. "Along the Yellowstone River in Big Timber, Montana . . . Preserving Nature's Bounty," floated across the screen, like the opening credits of a movie. A baby goat frolicked in a meadow; a herd of deer bounded in slow motion past Jan's center pivot. The Crazies rose up from a snowy winter landscape. Jan himself made an appearance, fly-fishing on his private stretch of the Yellowstone.

Karen's YouTube video had a link to the engwisranch.com website, where interested buyers could click on pictures of the main residence, the guest house, the indoor arena, and the expansive workshop where Jan displayed his collectibles. There were pictures of the old steel windmill framed by a dramatic sunset, and an entire section dedicated to eagles, with pictures of Ross Crandall and his research partner drawing blood from an eagle hooded with a red-white-and-blue blinder. "Come tour the ranch with us and see the unique opportunities it presents," the website urged. "Email Me."

Jami wasn't surprised when she heard that the Engwises were trying to sell. It happened all the time in Big Timber. She called it the "Fifteen-year Plan." Rich people came out, bought a ranch, and were just enamored with the place for the first three years. You'd see them at church and at the Big T, doing their grocery shopping. They'd donate money to local causes. And then, gradually, somewhere around year five, you'd stop running into them at church or the Big T. On year ten, they'd put the ranch up for sale. It was fun, but it was such a long drive to the store. It was cool, but the wind blew so hard. And then they were on to a newer something, somewhere else. The last five years of the Fifteen-year Plan? That was how long it took to sell the place. If they were lucky.

In the run-up to the 2016 presidential election, Karen began spending less time photographing the ranch's eagles and antelopes and more time on the internet, posting memes on Facebook calling for Hillary Clinton to be indicted and accusing her campaign chief, Huma Abedin, of "direct terrorist ties to 9-11." Karen posted throughout the day, ten and eleven times or more. Apart from the occasional picture of Peanut and Buddy romping in the shallows of the Yellowstone in their shih tzu–sized life jackets, there were no animal photos. In December, in a nod to the holiday season, Karen posted a picture of Santa Claus's sleigh tangled in a wind turbine, reindeer dangling from its blades.

Monica filed an appeal on the PSC's decision to delay the carbon adder, and in late February the commissioners heard oral arguments on the issue. This time, Marty had company in the Bollinger Room. George Hardie III, Pattern vice president, flew in from Texas for the hearing, along with Michael Thompson, the Pattern developer from Vancouver who would oversee the construction of Crazy Mountain Wind, and Ward Marshall, Pattern's senior director for business development. Marty introduced them all to the PSC commissioners with the air of a proud new father handing out cigars.

Marshall, who was based in Houston, had worked in wind for decades. He built Texas's first multi-turbine wind development in 1994. Marshall got a kick out of Marty. He wasn't bashful about taking on the man, Big Brother, whatever you wanted to call it. And it was clear that he had developed close relationships with the landowners, Anderson and Jarrett. Marty was in it for himself first and foremost, but he was fighting for them, too.

Marshall didn't realize he had been drawn into that fight himself until the day Russell Gordy called him at his Houston office.

Pattern's acquisition of Crazy Mountain Wind was the second piece of bad news to cloud Gordy's quail season. In mid-November, the Bureau of Land Management canceled twenty-five oil and gas leases in Colorado's Thompson Divide, eighteen of which were held by Gordy's SG Interests. There had been vocal opposition to drilling in the divide from across the political spectrum—hunters and hikers, farmers and ranchers, local officials and business owners.

The BLM ruled that the federal leases should never have been issued in the first place. Vowing to fight the decision in court, Robbie Guinn, SG Interests' vice president, accused Obama-era officials in the bureau of colluding with environmental groups to cancel the leases, and expressed faith that its right to drill the public lands would be restored under the new Trump administration.

Peter Kolbenschlag, a public lands and conservation activist based in Paonia, Colorado—an agricultural community on the western edge of the Thompson Divide—read about the BLM's decision in the online edition of his local newspaper, the *Glenwood Springs Post Independent*. Kolbenschlag thought Guinn's remarks were outrageous. In the reader comments section, he posted a link to a Justice Department statement on SG Interests' non-compete bidding arrangement with Wild Bill Koch's Gunnison Energy Corporation in the Thompson Divide.

"While SGI alleges 'collusion' let us recall that it, SGI, was actually fined for colluding (with GEC) to rig bid prices and rip off American taxpayers," Kolbenschlag wrote. "Yes, these two companies owned by billionaires thought it appropriate to pad their portfolios at the expense of you and I and every other hard-working American."

A few months later, a sheriff's deputy in full uniform showed up on Kolbenschlag's porch and handed him an envelope. "You've been served," he said. SG Interests was suing him for libel. Kolbenschlag, it appears, hadn't just been served; he had been SLAPPed.

The acronym stands for strategic lawsuits against public participation. It seemed that SG Interests wanted to discourage the Paonia environmental activist, and others, by suing him for the comment he had left on the *Post Independent*'s website. The oil and gas company sought unspecified damages for the harm it claimed Kolbenschlag had done to its reputation. "Reasonable people reading this assertion would be likely to think significantly less favorably about SGI than they would if they knew the true facts," the lawsuit alleged.

Kolbenschlag set up a crowdfunding site to raise money for his legal defense. A friend shot a YouTube video of him in downtown Paonia, bundled up in a black ski cap and a Carhartt jacket amid a crowd of townspeople carrying signs bearing slogans like "Oil and Gas Won't Shut Us Up" and "We the People" and "Pete Speaks For Us!"

SG Interests pursued the case against Kolbenschlag aggressively. When a judge ruled that the activist's comments were substantially true and dismissed the case, SG Interests appealed. The ruling was upheld, and SG Interests was ultimately ordered to pay Kolbenschlag's attorney fees. But the case dragged on for two and a half years.

"It cost me a lot of time and money I'll never get back. I was able to fight it, but it was intimidating. I'm not a billionaire," Kolbenschlag said. (His case inspired the Colorado legislature to enact an anti-SLAPP law to protect advocates and journalists from retaliatory lawsuits.)

Gordy did not comment publicly on the Kolbenschlag lawsuit, and his name never appeared in news coverage of the case. He did complain about the canceled leases, though. "It's tough when people tell you what to do on your own land," Gordy told Bloomberg News, though the BLM land in the Thompson Divide had never belonged to him. Privately, as SGI's lawsuit against Kolbenschlag worked its way through the appeal process in the summer of 2017, he groused that Colorado had been taken over by liberals. "It's not a pleasant place to be," he told me at the time. "If I had it to do over again, I would have stayed in Texas or Oklahoma."

Gordy was stewing over the lost leases and the recent insults to SGI's reputation when he learned that Crazy Mountain Wind had a new owner. The windmills he had thought mostly dead were suddenly rising up from the purgatory of the Public Service Commission. Like Engwis,

Gordy saw the wind farm as a threat to the things he held most dear. It would kill the birds he loved to hunt, the Hungarian partridges and sharp-tailed grouse. He hadn't told Glenda yet, but he was building kennels in Montana for his bird dogs.

The windmills would also spoil a pet project of his: a boutique hotel and spa at Hunter's Hot Springs. Gordy had toyed with the idea on and off for years. It would be small, just twenty or thirty rooms, but high-end. There'd be an indoor pool and a spa, shuffleboard courts, a terraced dining room with an outdoor bar. It would be a fun project, he thought. A legacy for his grandkids and a great thing for the community of Big Timber.

Locati Architects, which had designed the Gordy compound, drew up some handsome sketches of a spa with stone arches modeled on those of the long-gone Dakota Hotel, and put Gordy in touch with a water law attorney who could do the work necessary to reestablish old water rights to the springs. He spent about $100,000 in all.

Gordy would later say that he shelved his hotel project when he learned that Rick Jarrett's wind farm was back in play. But it was already on a back burner by then. Gordy had another legacy venture in the works in the winter of 2017, one much closer to his heart than hot tubs and shuffleboard: Gordy & Sons, an opulent rod and gun shop set to open that spring in Houston.

Russell Gordy had long dreamed of building a world-class hunting store, stocked with the finest firearms money could buy. Gordy & Sons would be the fulfillment of every fantasy he'd had as a boy, mooning over the guns in his grandmother Ocie's Sears & Roebuck catalog—the wish book. "Life doesn't always turn out like you want," Ocie used to tell her grandson. Gordy & Sons would be proof that it had—every wish in that tattered book coming true—and he was prepared to spend unlimited funds to make it happen.

"I told my wife, 'Sweetheart, it's just one offshore dry hole,'" Gordy said, recalling the first time Glenda saw the place while it was still under construction. He showed off the hand-pressed copper tile ceilings and floors of antique longleaf pine, the eighty-foot casting pond he planned to stock with Amazonian peacock bass. "She looked around and said, 'I think it's two holes.'"

Gordy hadn't applied for a building permit for his hot-springs hotel and spa. Once he heard that the wind farm was back, he decided not to bother, he'd say. Who'd want to come to a boutique hotel to soak in a hot tub and stare at a bunch of windmills?

In early 2017, Gordy called Ward Marshall and asked if Pattern would be interested in selling him the wind farm project it planned to build next to his ranch. Marshall told him that Pattern was confident that they could attract investors and was committed to Crazy Mountain Wind. Gordy listened politely. His tone was cordial. But before he hung up the phone, he made an odd comment.

"It might have been in jest, but it was, 'You know, maybe I'll just build my own wind farm around you and suck away all your wind,'" Marshall said.

As the cold war over Crazy Mountain Wind heated up, Marshall would remember that joke and realize that it had been a warning. The Texas oilman would make Pattern regret ever trying to build Crazy Mountain Wind.

Now that Crazy Mountain Wind was in Pattern's hands, Marty could take off his boxing gloves at long last. He committed himself to having an excellent time. He flew to Greece that January, trading Montana's screaming winter winds for sun-washed villages on the Ionian Sea. At an AA meeting in Greece, he met and befriended a young filmmaker. In May, he flew to the French Riviera for the premiere of his new friend's short film at the Cannes Film Festival. Marty walked the red carpet in Ray-Bans and a tux like a Hollywood player.

Back in Montana, he worked on his music—songs about lust and lost chances and darkness and despair, which he posted on SoundCloud. "Some stupid draft stuff from my new album 'Get on with it Muther-Fucker,'" he wrote on Facebook, with a link to his latest. He paid $40,000 to restore an 1880 Steinway he owned. He rebuilt a 1966 F-100 pickup truck and took the engine of his Porsche apart because he didn't think it was driving perfectly. Then he put it back together and drove 1,100 miles to the Minnesota Men's Conference, part of Marty's ongoing process of confronting his demons, of walking through his fear to heal himself. He drag-raced through downtown Fargo against a Plymouth Barracuda on the way there.

"Hope life continues to be an epic adventure and that you are a happy and contented man," an old friend wrote on his Facebook page that September. "Yes I am," he replied, and invited her to join him at the regular 12:30 AA meeting in Great Falls.

But a month later, Marty was back in the boxing ring, swinging at the two-headed monster he called the leviathan: NorthWestern Energy and its pliant regulator, the Public Service Commission. Marty filed a sweeping lawsuit that October against the monopoly utility, the PSC, and all five PSC commissioners, accusing them of colluding to kill green energy development in Montana.

Wind and solar projects had always had a target on their backs in the Bollinger Room, but it had ballooned under the Trump administration. At a work session in June, Commissioner Koopman made a motion to kneecap the independent renewable-energy projects known as QFs by chopping down contract lengths from twenty-five years to ten and slashing the price rate. "We are told, Mr. Chairman, if we don't have long contracts with fixed rates, these QFs can't get financing," Koopman said. "It is not our job to guarantee someone else's business success."

It was as though he was speaking directly to Marty, who was watching the live stream of the meeting on his laptop. Koopman's measure wouldn't affect Crazy Mountain Wind, whose contract was close to being finalized. At Pattern's insistence, Marty had dropped his appeal over the carbon adder. The guys at Pattern wanted nothing to do with it. They wanted to build Crazy Mountain Wind, not lob grenades at the PSC. Litigation was toxic to project financing.

Now, with Koopman's motion up for a vote, it was looking like Crazy Mountain Wind's PPA might be the last decent contract any wind developer would see in the state of Montana. Short-term contracts would be an effective death knell for new wind and solar projects. Koopman's motion passed, with the enthusiastic backing of the newest commissioner, Tony O'Donnell, a free-market warrior who had worked at a Lowe's home improvement store before his election to the PSC.

Having hit a home run for anyone who thought climate change was climate hysteria, Koopman and his fellow commissioners broke for lunch. No one turned off the cameras. Marty kept watching as Commissioner Lake returned to the Bollinger Room and began chatting with Neil Templeton, the PSC staffer who advised the commissioners on regulatory issues.

The microphone turned back on in time to catch Templeton saying that the new rates the commissioners had just enacted would probably kill off QF development completely, to which the snowy-headed Lake responded, "Well, actually, the ten-year [contract length] might do it if the price doesn't . . . just dropping the rate that much probably took care of the whole thing." Then he noticed the blinking light on the camera. "We're live," he observed.

Marty called Monica. "You'll never believe what just happened," he said.

The hot-mic moment had exposed the commissioners' naked animosity toward small wind and solar projects. Financial analysts, concerned that short-term contracts would drive up energy prices, recommended that investors consider selling or reducing their stock in NorthWestern Energy. That prompted the rare spectacle of the utility's own government affairs director beseeching the Montana legislature to rein in the PSC. "The Montana Public Service Commission, or at least a majority of the commissioners, have lost their regulatory minds," he said. "They're destroying existing law and they're out of control."

Marty wanted to sue for discrimination, collusion, and the violation of his constitutional rights. "I'm throwing harpoons at these fuckers until they turn around," he told Monica, and didn't blink when she said it could cost $100,000 in legal fees. Marty wanted every public service commissioner to be held accountable. He started tracking their whereabouts on Twitter, so the process server could find them.

Marty called and texted Monica every day to hash over the case—sometimes texting and then calling, irate, when she didn't text back right away. He complained about all the money he was paying her. He complained about his neighbor, a young game warden who lived a quarter mile from his home. The guy's dog barked all night; it drove Marty crazy. He asked Monica to write his neighbor a threatening letter on her law office letterhead. The dog kept barking.

Once, Monica made the mistake of asking Marty how he was doing. "You don't want to know how the fuck I'm doing," he said. "Let's talk about the law." But there was little he didn't talk about with Monica—the BMW motorcycle he was rebuilding, his opinion of Audis (pieces of shit), his thoughts on marriage (not for him). "Monica is like my girl-friend who I don't fuck," Marty told his girlfriend, Annette.

He met Annette in AA six years before, when she was in the first stages of her sobriety. She was a real estate agent, fifteen years younger than Marty. They lived sixty miles apart, which Marty thought was just about perfect. Annette loved Marty, but she was careful around him. One night, they went out to dinner. There was a stretch of straight high-way where he liked to test his Porsche, to see how fast it could go. "So, he gets up to 150 miles an hour," Annette recalled. "I said, 'Marty, will you please slow down?' and that made him mad, because I was full of fear, and he didn't like it when you were full of fear." There were rumble strips in the road, which made him even angrier.

That was pretty much how Marty did relationships. He wasn't speak-ing to Jaffe. They'd had one of their periodic blowups that spring. Jaffe was earning an architecture degree, paying his own way through MSU by working construction on weekends. Marty had called to say he'd be coming through Bozeman, and they should meet up. Then it was finals week and Jaffe stayed up three nights straight. He conked out the night his dad got into town and missed his call. Marty left a message telling Jaffe how rude he was, that he was done trying to reach out to him. Jaffe called Marty back and said something along the lines of listen, bro, it's finals week, you should get over yourself. "And then I said, 'I don't want to turn this into something where we don't talk for six months,'" Jaffe said. He didn't hear from Marty for six months.

Marty's lawsuit was covered by local news outlets. Every segment featured a clip of Commissioner Lake's hot-mic moment. On the Friday before Veterans Day weekend, Monica sent Marty a draft of his testi-mony. Marty was moving house that weekend. A couple from Seattle had made a surprise offer on his log house near Augusta. Marty had always talked about buying a ranch and building something nice. Maybe this was the kick in the ass he needed. He accepted the offer.

"I have a couple young dudes and a couple old dudes who think they're young dudes coming over to help me move," he told Monica. He had to move several motorcycles, a pickup truck, and a 1972 Massey Ferguson tractor to a place he was renting. The Steinway was already in a climate-controlled storage facility. That week, he had finally broken his silence with Jaffe, to tell him he was moving and to ask if he wanted to pick up some music equipment.

Jaffe was working at a residential job site that Saturday when he saw Annette's name flash on his phone. He had been up to his dad's house to get the equipment earlier that week and they'd hung out. Marty spent the whole time talking about himself.

"Your dad," Annette said, and that was enough for Jaffe to intuit the situation. He heard it in her voice.

Marty and his buddies had been loading the Massey Ferguson, which had a mower hitched to it, onto a flatbed truck that morning. The Massey had huge back wheels and a skinny red nose; Marty liked that old, vintage shit. As Marty started driving the Massey Ferguson up the flatbed ramp, towing the mower, its front wheels lifted up—too much torque. The tractor did a full wheelie, flipping off the side of the flatbed. Marty, who was crushed beneath the seat, didn't even have time to yell. By the time Jaffe got to Marty's house, the tractor was wrapped in a tarp. A crane had been brought in to lift it off his father's body.

But that dude Marty Wilde, he was a hard-core fucker. He had wired Jaffe since he was a little kid to handle a situation like him dying. Jaffe tried to comport himself accordingly. He was the one who broke the news to his sister and his mom and his grandparents—Marty's parents. He resolved to be strong for them. Jaffe spent that night by himself in his father's house on the Rocky Mountain Front in the middle of nowhere, the wind nuking across the plains. It was scary, being alone in a place he'd only ever been with a man who was gone.

Once, when Jaffe was little, Marty told him, "You don't have to love me, but you will do as I say." It wasn't gentle. It wasn't kind. Jaffe's whole life, Marty had been that way. But the moment he died, all that shit made sense. That's what it took to see the whole picture, to realize in an instant that everything that seemed negative or harsh, everything he ever did, was about love. Marty wanted his son to be tough. He wanted to make him hard. Because Marty knew the world would kick your ass.

14

GOOD NEIGHBORS

February 19, 2019
Park County Courthouse
Livingston, Montana

DAVID CHESNOFF, *Direct examination*:

Q: Now the defendants allege that you waited until the last minute to file this lawsuit. Do you have anything to say about that?

MR. CHESNOFF: Yeah, I have a lot to say about that. The defendants, never, one time, contacted me, by text, by email, by phone, by letter, by smoke signal, nothing. It was radio silence. And when I found out it was Pattern, I did some research. I discovered who the Chairman of the Board of Pattern was, he lives in Connecticut. I reached out to people who knew him. So, I called him at home, in Connecticut. I got his home number, and I said, "Sir,"—I explained my relationship to the person who introduced me to him—and he said "I'd be glad to talk to you." And I said, "Do you realize that you have a project that's going up in the middle of the most beautiful spot on the Yellowstone River?" And of course, I don't believe he had a clue about it.

JULY 27, 2018
SWEET GRASS COUNTY FAIRGROUNDS
BIG TIMBER, MONTANA

Charles Shawley, Pattern's man on the ground in Big Timber, had spent the day walking around the Sweet Grass County Fair, looking at pigs. Having grown up in a small farming community in Eastern Washington, Shawley knew something about swine. He also knew something about county fairs, where kids dressed in starched white shirts and ties showed off their livestock—lambs, steers, goats, and hogs that had been scrubbed, brushed, blow-dried, and sprayed with show sheen till their coats and hooves gleamed. As Shawley watched the hogs trot around the show ring, the kids tapping them with pig whips to demonstrate their handling and presentation skills, he wasn't assessing the pigs so much as the kid each pig was attached to—figuring who they were, who their parents were, and where they stood in the circles of influence in Sweet Grass County—before the auction that night.

Fair Week had kicked off with small animal showmanship, poultry judging, and a dog agility contest, gradually building up to sheep, goats, hogs, and steers. The Friday night livestock auction was the climax of Fair Week. The animals would be sold off to the highest bidder, marking their apotheosis from hand-raised pets to pork butt, lamb chops, and steak.

The pre-auction Buyer Appreciation Dinner in the Ag Pavilion was the same every year: brisket, scalloped potatoes, and coleslaw, followed by cookies and sliced watermelon. Shawley paid five dollars for a plate laden with food and sat down at a picnic table with the chairwoman of the high school's board of trustees—one of several county officials he had befriended since moving into the Super 8 on Big Timber Road earlier that month. It was time to get the lowdown on Big Timber's 4-H and FFA animals before the bidding began.

Shawley had been to enough livestock auctions to know the rules. You didn't try to outbid someone for a kid's pig if that someone happened to be the kid's grandfather. You *did* try to outbid everyone under the tent for the pig raised by a kid whose family was facing a medical crisis or had lost their hayfields in a lightning strike. You would bid up that pig for an obscene amount of money and then donate it back so it could be auctioned again. Shawley's brief was to bid on strategic swine, to pay generously for pigs whose sale would create a ripple effect of goodwill in Sweet Grass County in the name of Pattern Development and Crazy Mountain Wind, LLC.

A wind industry veteran turned independent consultant, Shawley had been hired by Pattern to smooth Crazy Mountain Wind's path through the county's various approval processes. Shawley's success in securing tax abatement for the project, and in locking down tedious but essential agreements on construction-related impact fees and weed control, would depend on his ability to create a sense of trust and goodwill among the citizens of Big Timber. Shawley thought of his work as social engineering. It was less about permits than about insinuating yourself into the community, becoming someone that people saw at school board meetings and Herders football games.

The Sweet Grass County Fair was a banquet of opportunity for a social engineer like Charles Shawley. He could talk pigs with anyone. His in-laws owned a large hog farm in Ephrata, though he'd never been an FFA kid himself, not seeing the point. As a teenager, Shawley had preferred to spend his time experimenting with resins and polymers in a national lab on a science fellowship that enabled him to skip high school every Friday afternoon.

He had already done some preliminary research over lunch with Rick Jarrett and his daughter, Jami, at the Thirsty Turtle, a low-slung bar and hamburger joint near the railroad tracks. As Shawley saw it, there were two kinds of hogs: those raised by kids whose parents he wanted to win over, and those raised by kids whose parents he wanted to neutralize. The latter were people who opposed the wind farm and could kick up a stink if they chose, but with careful handling, might do their grumbling in private.

As the auction began, Shawley bid on Trevor Halverson's lamb, because Halverson's mother was the weed coordinator for Sweet Grass County, and Pattern needed her approval on its plan to curb the spread of noxious weeds during construction. Coulter Rein's 4-H market hog was a good pig for Pattern; the Rein family had ranched in the eastern Crazies since 1893 and were influential in the county. Coulter's dad, Chuck Rein, a Century Club member of the Sweet Grass County Farm Bureau, was rumored to be in the anti-wind camp. As auctioneer Jimbo Logan started the bidding on Coulter's pig, calling out numbers in a brisk singsong, Shawley raised his hand.

By then, people sitting in the auction tent had noticed the clean-cut out-of-towner who was bidding on 4-H livestock. Some started bidding against him for fun, driving up the price just to see how much the man from the wind company was willing to pay for that hog. But that was all right. Once the auction was over, those kids would have to come over and shake Shawley's hand and say thank you—it was a Sweet Grass County Fair tradition. Their parents would have to shake his hand, too. If you dropped over a grand on a pig from the "Antis," as Shawley privately referred to them, they had to be nice to you for at least a day.

Harv recommended that Shawley bid on Gracie Lou Fleming's hog. Gracie was the daughter of Rob Fleming, who ran Whitney MacMillan's haying operation on his thousand-acre ranch on the Yellowstone— the River Ranch, they called it. Fleming answered to Jim Hogemark, the MacMillans' longtime ranch manager. Shawley knew that the Hogemarks were among the most outspoken wind farm opponents in Big Timber, and the MacMillans' Wild Eagle Mountain Ranch had been involved in past litigation against the wind farm.

So far, Rob Fleming had kept out of the public debate over Crazy Mountain Wind. Word was that he didn't like it, but he had strong feelings about private property rights. The Fleming family would be directly affected by Crazy Mountain Wind, particularly during construction. The River Ranch abutted the project site, with the laydown yard for the turbines on the far end of Alfred Anderson's fields—not far from the River Ranch property line. The Flemings were in a tough position. Shawley resolved to be extra nice to them. Gracie, a freckled teen with strawberry blond hair pulled back in a tight French braid, was showing a pink Yorkshire pig as clean and spotless as her white collared shirt. He outbid everyone for that hog, then donated it back so she could sell it a second time. He also gave back Coulter's pig and Trevor's lamb. Later on, when he met Gracie's parents and learned that she hoped to play college softball, he offered to arrange a call with his wife, who had played college softball herself and knew a couple of coaches and recruiters.

By the time the auction was over, Shawley had spent $3,391 of Pattern's money on Sweet Grass County–raised pork and lamb, then generously donated the livestock back to the youth of Big Timber. The kids all sent him thank-you cards with pictures of their animals. Shawley forwarded them to his bosses at Pattern.

The irony of Shawley's role as chief tactician in the ground game for Crazy Mountain Wind was not lost on him. He had passed on Crazy

Mountain Wind back when he was the managing director of Gaelectric North America, a Dublin-based wind company seeking to develop projects in Montana. People in Big Wind thumbed their noses at wildcat prospectors like the late Marty Wilde, and Shawley had been no exception. Marty's projects always had a lot of hair on them. There were gaps in his wind measurement studies, his data rooms weren't great, his met towers looked like they they'd been cobbled together from used parts. Marty never had the money to check all the boxes on his projects. He tried to flip them before they were shovel-ready—when he ran out of money, basically. And the man was unpleasant. If you asked him what kind of anemometer he was using for his wind measurements, he'd take it as an insult—like you were knocking his secondhand equipment—and then you were in a fight.

A company like Gaelectric was trying to make much bigger plays than some little twenty-five-megawatt project put together out of the back of a truck. The only time Shawley got in bed with Marty Wilde, it was to sell him a hundred-meter met tower he didn't need anymore. He was still waiting to be paid for that tower.

But here he was in Big Timber, playing midwife to an eighty-megawatt project that Marty had managed to sell to Pattern, one of the biggest players in the American wind industry. Charles Shawley was used to being the smartest person in the room, but even he had to admit he'd been a little bit wrong about Marty, because Marty had achieved the near-impossible: he got NorthWestern Energy to sign off on a decent power purchase agreement for an eighty-megawatt QF.

Pattern initially hired Shawley to spend every other week in Big Timber for several months. They'd have put him up at the Grand, Big Timber's nicest hotel, but from a social engineering perspective, Shawley preferred the Super 8. If you were living at the Super 8, people felt sorry for you. They'd invite you over for dinner and weekend barbecues and introduce you to their friends. After a few weeks living at the motel, even the Super 8 staff started feeling sorry for Shawley. The housekeepers baked him cookies and stocked the freezer with ice cream for him.

Shawley did the rounds. He met with the county's public works director, the planning director, the school superintendent. One county official spent an entire meeting telling him about influential people in the community who were vehemently opposed to wind development—the Antis. Shawley took notes. Another warned him that Commissioner Faw was dead set against Crazy Mountain Wind. This, Shawley already knew; Pattern had worked up dossiers on the county commissioners, which he had studied before arriving in Big Timber.

Sweet Grass County was down to just two commissioners: Bob Faw and Bill Wallace. Susie Mosness, who beat back a challenge from Cindy Selensky to win reelection in 2016, resigned the following October. Susie was hard of hearing and it had become increasingly difficult to follow what was said at meetings. Serving on the commission had become difficult in other ways, too. "One thing I hadn't thought about, is who you work with—who the people elect to work with you," she said privately. "That was challenging."

The Sweet Grass County Republican Committee, which was chaired by Bob Faw's wife, Judy, put together a list of three possible candidates to fill Susie's vacant seat until the 2018 election and submitted it to Wallace and Faw. But Wallace and Faw didn't see eye to eye on much these days, and they couldn't agree on a replacement for Susie. The committee came up with another three names: Wallace rejected the ones that Faw liked, and vice versa. Whenever Faw and Wallace disagreed on an issue, the commission, and effectively the county, became locked in a stalemate. Not much was likely to get done until a third county commissioner was elected that November.

In the meantime, there was plenty of social engineering to be done. Shawley delivered the same message at every chamber of commerce and school board meeting he attended: Pattern was a good neighbor. It wanted to invest in the community. "I understand Montanans are very proud and don't like taking money, but I've got money to spend," he'd say. It wasn't long before he got a call from the superintendent of the Reed Point schools; the 107-year-old elementary school was infested with termites and bats and she was scrambling to find temporary classrooms for the kids. Shawley said he'd see what he could do.

Shawley spent a lot of time with the Jarretts and the Andersons. Now that Marty Wilde was gone, Shawley was the ranchers' liaison with Pattern. He'd drop by the Andersons' with documents to sign, and stay to visit. Their home was cluttered, with too many dogs and not enough places to sit, but they were the sweetest people he'd ever met. Dorothy was so animated and full of stories. She asked Shawley lots of questions about himself and where he was from. Washington State had a lot of huckleberries, didn't it? Dorothy loved huckleberries. After that, Shawley had several pounds of fresh huckleberries shipped to the Andersons. Delighted, Dorothy asked Shawley what his wife's favorite color in the kitchen was, and knitted her a bright yellow pot holder.

He met Rick for lunch or coffee a couple times a week. Shawley admired Rick's enterprising spirit, how he was always trying different ways to make money, and had so many lady friends. There was Lois in Big Timber, who ran the farmer's market on Fridays at Lions Club Park, and Geri in Billings, who worked at a hospital. Shawley called Rick "The Compass." When Rick set off in his beat-up Cadillac on a Friday afternoon, Shawley would razz him, asking which lady he was off to visit, so they'd know what direction he was headed. You could see that Rick and Marty had been kindred spirits, these two older single guys who behaved the way some older single guys did.

But sometimes—more often, as the summer progressed—Shawley had to give Rick a pep talk. Rick had shouldered the load of Crazy Mountain Wind for a long time, and it was weighing on him, particularly now that Marty was gone. It was only a matter of time before his neighbors sued to stop him, he'd say in his low moments. Shawley told Rick to leave the worrying to him—that was his job now. And Pattern's.

Rick's neighbors had been on Pattern's radar for some time. Russell Gordy was a rich man with the power to make trouble, and he'd made no secret of his distaste for Pattern's latest acquisition. That spring, George Hardie III, Pattern's vice president, reached out. Hardie worked out of Pattern's office in Houston, where Russell's splashy hunting emporium had opened for business. The Vault at Gordy & Sons was the talk of Houston. Tucked behind an eighteen-thousand-pound steel door from an old bank, the Vault was a wood-paneled room filled with some of the rarest and costliest firearms in the world. A set of handcrafted shotguns by James Purdey & Sons was priced at $550,000—more than five times the amount Gordy had invested in his abortive boutique spa at Hunter's Hot Springs.

Gordy took Hardie's call. He seemed very familiar with the details of Crazy Mountain Wind's power purchase agreement. He asked Hardie if they were just doing this thing for the tax credits. By the time Hardie got off the phone, it was clear that his courtesy call had not earned Pattern any brownie points.

When Marty Wilde was alive, Pattern had taken pains to distance itself from his slash-and-burn tactics. Now that Marty was gone, Pattern had no choice but to pick up where he'd left off. He wasn't there to advise them on how to deal with the Texas guy who owned half a township. But maybe his lawyer could.

The day after the accident, Monica called Marty to go over his testimony in their lawsuit against NorthWestern and the PSC. Jaffe answered his phone. He was at Marty's house, waiting for family members to arrive. "My dad was killed yesterday," he said. Monica hung up the phone in shock. Marty had been her mentor, the person who taught her about the wind industry and showed her how the money worked. They had been throwing spears at the leviathan together.

Monica called Jaffe back. "I feel like if your dad was around right now, he'd want me to help you guys out." She handed the baby to Greg, grabbed her breast pump, and drove to meet Jaffe and Chloe at an Applebee's in Great Falls. Marty's girlfriend, Annette, organized a celebration of Marty's life at a funeral home a few days later. A lot of people from his regular AA meeting came. "Hi, I'm so-and-so, and I'm an alcoholic," they'd say, and everyone said hello to them. They told stories about Marty's impact on their lives. How he spent hours on the phone with anyone who was struggling to maintain sobriety. How he'd drop everything to meet a guy who had just been released from jail into a prerelease community program and take him out for tacos.

After the memorial service, Monica walked Jaffe through the details of Marty's business. In addition to the money Jaffe and Chloe would inherit from the Greenfield settlement, Marty's company, WINData, would be paid $2.39 million when Crazy Mountain Wind became operational. As he contemplated the big stack of money his father had left him and his sister, Jaffe felt like he was gambling for his allowance again. He and Chloe could walk away, buy homes and cars, and be set for life. Or he could use his inheritance to pick up where his father had left off, which is what Jaffe decided to do.

"From day one, it was just, like, chasing my father," Jaffe said. He arrived for meetings with Monica in Marty's silver Porsche, wearing clothes and shoes from Marty's closet—literally stepping into his father's shoes.

Now Pattern was stepping into the wind prospector's shoes. Days after Marty's memorial service, Monica dialed into a conference call with Pattern executives and in-house counsel. Pattern was worried about the neighbors—Gordy in particular. They wanted to strategize about possible angles of attack he might take against Crazy Mountain Wind.

Monica thought Gordy's likely opening move would be to file a nuisance claim. But how could a renewable-energy project, authorized by Montana statute, constitute a nuisance? That would be Pattern's best defense if it ended up in court, she said. She didn't see how Gordy could prove that the wind farm would harm him or his ranch. His ranch compound was three miles from the wind farm site. What damages could he claim, other than some subjective impact on his personal experience?

David Chesnoff, meanwhile, had been flipping through his Rolodex and working his connections. The chairman of Pattern Energy, the parent company of Pattern Development, was Alan Batkin, a former investment banker and managing director at Lehman Brothers. In Batkin's world, as in Chesnoff's, if a friend asked you to speak to a friend, you said you'd be glad to, of course. Chesnoff began the conversation by saying he was a big proponent of renewables. It was essential to move toward renewables, but not on the most beautiful spot of the Yellowstone, where he had his ranch. The gentleman farmer made it clear to Batkin that he did not want to look at wind turbines.

Batkin listened politely. There was a certain protocol when one influential man reached out to another. He offered to put the gentleman farmer in touch with Pattern's general counsel. "He was a very pleasant, professional person," Chesnoff would recall. "And I said, 'Well, do you realize that you've never done a neighborhood visit?'"

Pattern wanted to be a good neighbor, to do what it could to allay the gentleman farmer's concerns. The team would make a neighborhood visit, just as Chesnoff suggested. And to demonstrate just what an exceptionally considerate neighbor Pattern would be, the team would create detailed photographic simulations that would show Chesnoff and Gordy what their actual views of Crazy Mountain Wind's turbines would be, from a variety of locations on their ranches. Maybe they'd be mollified when they saw that the wind farm wouldn't block their views of the mountains or the Yellowstone.

On August 7, Ward Marshall and Allen Wynn, a senior environmental manager, paid a visit to Chesnoff's imposing timber-framed lodge on the Yellowstone with a team from NewFields, an environmental engineering consulting firm. As he stepped inside the high arched portico and beheld the great room with its tree-trunk columns and clustered antler chandeliers dangling from the rafters, Marshall felt as though he had walked inside a Bass Pro Shop.

Even here, during his rare time off at his retreat on Sanctuary River Lane, Chesnoff was working. Charles Oakley, the retired NBA power forward and Chesnoff's occasional poker buddy, had been arrested at the Cosmopolitan in Vegas that July while playing Texas Hold'em. TMZ reported that the casino's eye in the sky allegedly caught the basketball great clawing back a hundred-dollar chip from his pile when he realized he had lost a hand, then sneaking more chips onto his bet when he had a winning three of a kind.

Committing fraud in a casino is a felony that can result in prison time; Chesnoff made it go away. The charge was dropped and the former New York Knick pleaded no contest to a minor misdemeanor, with a $1,000 fine. Just before the Pattern team arrived, Chesnoff and his partner, Richard Schonfeld, had issued a statement expressing Oakley's appreciation for the professionalism of Las Vegas DA Steve Wolfson and the Cosmopolitan "in resolving the event." Chesnoff had donated $10,000 to Wolfson's 2018 reelection campaign the previous year.

Chesnoff and his wife, Diana, invited Marshall and his colleagues into the kitchen, just off the great room, with its wall of windows overlooking the Yellowstone. The NewFields photographer spent a long time walking around the ranch, taking pictures. Elizabeth Greenwood, a lawyer based in Pinedale, Wyoming, who was representing Chesnoff and Gordy, was also present. As they sat at the kitchen island, Chesnoff asked Marshall how much of the wind farm he'd be able to see from his lodge. Guesstimating, Marshall said that maybe he'd see the tips of two or three turbines, off to the west, toward I-90's Springdale exit. But nothing that would interfere with his sightlines of the Yellowstone River or the Crazies.

"Okay," Chesnoff recalled. "I said, 'Well, I guess the picture will speak a thousand words.'"

Two days later, Wynn and Michael Thompson, the project manager for Crazy Mountain Wind, drove high up Convict Grade Road to Double Arrow, the Gordy compound. Gordy gave them a tour of the place and took them out to the helipad where he kept his Eurocopter AS-350 helicopter. Gordy had an automated tug, a kind of dolly that made it easy to move the helicopter in and out of the hangar. He demonstrated it for the Pattern executives, towing the shiny blue helicopter out onto the launchpad. He asked if they'd like to go up for a ride so they could see the property. They said no, thanks. "That's probably smart," Gordy said, and made a joke about how he'd have dumped them out of the helicopter so they could *really* see the place.

From his command post at the Super 8, Shawley was keeping tabs on Gordy and his helicopter, whose flights he occasionally tracked on FlightAware. He knew the tail numbers of Gordy's Gulfstream, too. Shawley knew when the Gordys were in Montana, and when they had guests to stay. Some of the housekeepers at the motel moonlighted at Double Arrow when extra staff was needed to help clean and do laundry. Shawley was on excellent terms with the housekeepers at the Super 8.

There were plenty of people in Big Timber who had worked for the Gordys at one time or another, either as part-time maids at the ranch compound or as hired hands for the Lone Star Land and Cattle Company, which ran between 1,000 and 1,200 cow-calf pairs, and 100 bulls. Big Timber was a small community; everybody pretty much knew everybody. So, pretty much everyone knew Feliciano Orlando Chavez, Gordy's longtime cow boss.

Chavez, who went by Orlando, emigrated from Mexico at the age of seventeen. He was hardworking and soft-spoken, with a gift for working with animals. He started as a ranch hand on the Sheep Mountain Ranch when the place belonged to John Moreland. Orlando and his wife, Kim, moved into an old farmhouse there with their three young children in the mid-1990s. After Moreland sold the ranch to Gordy, Orlando agreed to stay on. He eventually became Lone Star's cow boss, overseeing the crew of ranch hands and the care of the cow-calf pairs.

The farmhouse was infested with mice. Unlike Brian Engle, who quit over a moldy house, the Chavez family put up with the mice for years. When Gordy decided to raze the old farmhouse and replace it with a triple-wide modular home, Orlando was overwhelmed. He asked his pastors, Ron and Kathy Countryman from Big Timber's Church of God, to come bless his new home and dedicate it to the Lord.

"He said, 'I don't deserve this, I haven't earned this'—that's the kind of humble man he was. He didn't have one proud bone in his body," Countryman told me. "This is the gospel truth—I never knew a person that met Orlando that didn't just like the guy."

Orlando was a man of faith. He loved Jesus; the Lord was his number one. He loved his family. He loved the mountains, and the horses and the cows. When he became cow boss, Orlando vowed to care for those cows better than if they were his own. He loved to ride and rope and break colts. The Chavez kids were on horseback before their legs were long enough to clear a saddle. Orlando put the tiniest ones on an old, steady horse, and they'd tag along behind him while he moved cows all day. When the kids got older, they pitched in to build corrals and brand calves and drive the cows up into the Crazies. Everyone worked. The ranch was a wonderful place to raise a family. The Chavezes had graduation parties there, and weddings. Two of the Chavez kids got married on the ranch.

Every August, Chavez led a team of ranch hands from Gordy's Lone Star Land and Cattle Company in the Crazy Mountain Stockgrowers Ranch Rodeo, where working cowboys got to show off their skills at gathering stray steers, or cutting out calves from a herd and loading them in a trailer. Team Chavez came in fourth in 2016, winning a hundred-dollar check and a set of new halters donated by Yellowstone Feed. Chavez beamed and held up his halter like it was a golden trophy.

He had been experiencing pains and a persistent cough for some time by then, but the way Orlando was, he just kept working.

A few weeks after the rodeo, Chavez was diagnosed with thymus cancer. He underwent major surgery to remove his right lung, thymus, and thirty lymph nodes early that fall. Part of his pericardium, the fluid-filled sac that surrounds the heart, was cut away. The medical bills were staggering. Chavez would require ongoing treatment, including chemotherapy and radiation. But he didn't have health insurance; Gordy didn't provide it.

Gordy told me that in lieu of health coverage, he allowed every ranch hand to run up to fifteen of his own cows on his ranch, for free. (This practice was instituted sometime after Brian Engle quit in 2004.) They had to buy the cows, but Gordy let them graze his grass and eat his hay and be serviced by his bulls—essentially covering all the costs of a miniature cow-calf operation. It was a generous benefit. A bunch of cows, acquired over time, can function as a savings account for a cow punch who's living paycheck to paycheck. Come fall, he can sell some calves and collect a few thousand dollars free and clear.

But the Chavezes didn't own enough calves and cows to pay Orlando's medical bills. "Ranching doesn't pay real good," Countryman said. "Kathy and I both shed some tears, just because of the difficulty of the situation. I told Kathy, 'We've got to do something to help them.'"

The Countrymans and members of their church organized a fundraiser for the Chavez family that November on the county fairgrounds. More than five hundred people filed into the Ag Pavilion to pay ten dollars a plate for a tri-tip steak luncheon with all the fixings; many dug into their pockets and paid a lot more. There were so many people that some ate standing up, elbow to elbow. The caterers donated all the food and refused to take any money for their costs. Lunch was followed by a bake sale and a live auction for donated items: six Angus heifers, a pair of tickets to a Tim McGraw–Faith Hill concert, one hundred gallons of propane, free processing on a side of beef at Pioneer Meats. The Chavezes put a group of young cows they owned on the block. A local rancher bought them, then stood up and announced he was donating them back to the family. The Chavezes got to sell those cows twice over.

In all, the event raised nearly $63,000, Countryman said. The outpouring of generosity from the people of Big Timber reduced Kim Chavez to tears. "It kind of makes you think that it'll be okay to go ahead and get treatment and do what we need to do to get him well and get him through all of this," she told Lindsey Kroskob, now editor of the *Pioneer*.

Gordy donated a ride on his helicopter.

"I don't want to say too much about their boss. He's in oil in Texas. He's a multi-multimillionaire. There are people that are wealthy that want to help others, and there are people that are extremely wealthy that want to get more wealth," Countryman said. "I'm not saying the man's that way, but [Chavez] coulda, shoulda had health insurance. The man could have done that."

But Gordy paid Chavez a full salary during the long months that he was too sick to work and assured him that his job would be waiting for him. Orlando got back on his horse while he was still recovering from surgery. "The joke was that they took out one lung, so now maybe the hired hands would be able to keep up with Orlando—he worked so hard," Countryman said. "His hardest thing was to sit in the house and look out the window and watch others work when he couldn't."

At shipping time the following autumn, Orlando and his ranch hands were rounding up the calves when he saw that ten pairs of mother cows and calves were missing. The Gordys were bow-hunting elk in the mountains, and the ranch workers had been told to stay away. But Chavez couldn't imagine shipping off the calves minus ten head—it went against his ethos as a cow boss. So, he set out looking for them on horseback. He didn't go high into the mountains, he'd later say. He kept to the lower elevations, hoping maybe those pairs would drift down a bit.

The phone in the Chavezes' triple-wide started ringing as soon as he got home. It was the ranch manager who oversaw Gordy's cattle operation, calling from Wyoming. He was furious. Chavez and his dogs had disrupted the Gordys' hunt, and Russell's son had missed his elk because of it. The man called Chavez every bad name in the book, using profane language. Then he told him that he was fired. Orlando listened quietly. He didn't yell or get upset. He didn't try to defend himself. That wasn't his way. "How long do I have?" he asked. Ten days, the man said. The

Chavezes had lived on the ranch for twenty-two years. They had no idea where they would go.

"Orlando was a really good ranch hand—a very good cowboy, very good, honest guy, a very hard worker—and they were a good family," Gordy said, when asked about Chavez's firing. "But he wasn't a delegator. And he kept running the cattle in the same area every year, which was not good for the grass." His ranch manager had complained about it, Gordy said, but Orlando was hardheaded. The Chavez family denies this; Orlando was obsessed with the grass on Lone Star and most of his time on horseback was spent rotating the cattle between pastures so they wouldn't become overgrazed.

But both Gordy and the Chavez family agree on one thing: Orlando was fired because he spoiled the Gordys' elk hunt. "That was kind of the straw that broke the camel's back," Gordy said. "We had a bunch of guests up there hunting . . . and he came through there with quite a few cattle and just basically ruined their hunt."

The Chavezes packed up their belongings and prepared for their move to an abandoned farmhouse owned by a family friend. They'd be taking a cow with them. Every fall, after the heifers had been pregtested, Gordy let his ranch hands claim a head of beef from the ones that had come up dry. Employees like the Chavezes relied on that benefit to fill their freezers and feed their families. Orlando had been fired, but he had earned his beef for the year; the Chavezes had already claimed their dry heifer and penned her under a lean-to behind the machine shop. It's against state law to take a cow off ranch property or across county lines without a brand for livestock inspection, so before their departure, the Chavezes put their brand on her shoulder—a heart bar 5.

Next thing they knew, a brand inspector from the state's Department of Livestock was on their doorstep with a warrant. He said he was following up on a complaint that the Chavezes had stolen a head of beef; a ranch hand had just shown him the branded heifer in the pen under the lean-to. The inspector gave Kim and Orlando a choice: he could arrest them both for cattle rustling, or they could write a letter of apology to the ranch and hope that Mr. Gordy wouldn't press charges. The Chavezes wrote the letter of apology. They surrendered the heifer with the Chavez heart branded on its shoulder. The brand inspector even had them fill out a bill of sale for that head of beef to Lone Star, to make it official. Then Orlando and Kim finished packing their belongings and left the ranch. "They wouldn't even let him walk away with his integrity," a family member said.

Gordy told me that according to his ranch manager, the Chavezes were given till the end of the month to move out, not ten days. He didn't recall receiving their letter of apology.

Orlando's cancer returned not long after he left Lone Star. He died in 2020, at the age of fifty-two.

An announcement appeared in the *Big Timber Pioneer* in August, inviting everyone in the community to an open house at the Grand Hotel: "Come for appetizers and refreshments and have all your questions about the Crazy Mountain Wind Project answered by the team at Pattern Development." An identical notice appeared in the *Livingston Enterprise*; an open house would be held there two days later.

That day, the *Big Timber Buzz*, the community Facebook page, posted its own announcement about the open house, accompanied by a picture of a phalanx of wind turbines. "Here are a couple of ideas for the community to consider asking Pattern Development before they build a windfarm on the Jarrett Ranch," the post began. It was written by the *Buzz*'s creator and administrator, Beccy Stolte Oberly.

Oberly and her husband, Dale, had once owned the *Big Timber Pioneer*. Dale was the paper's publisher and Beccy was its editor-in-chief, with her own column, "Little Splinters from Big Timber." In 2008, the Oberlys sold the *Pioneer* to a regional newspaper group.

The *Buzz* was a community mainstay. People posted photos of missing sheepdogs and updates about dangerous driving conditions on I-90. They used it to ask if anyone had local honey to sell or a candy mold they could borrow. The Countryman family posted updates about Orlando's benefit and solicited auction items on the *Buzz*.

But Oberly wanted the *Buzz* to be more than a message board. She spent hours managing the page and posting newsy items to stimulate discussion. When Oberly heard a rumor that a mural of the Crazy Mountains in Big Timber's nursing home, the Pioneer Medical Center, was going to be painted over, she rallied the *Buzz* community to save it. "UPDATE! UPDATE! UPDATE!" her post declared. "A petition is circulating throughout the Big Timber community to save this painted mural." She urged anyone who cared about the mural and the "Save the Crazies cause" to contact a PMC board member and "voice your stand."

It all came as news to nursing home administrators and board members, who were planning to replace the dining room curtains but had never discussed—or even contemplated—painting over the Crazy Mountain mural. Oberly's post generated over fifty outraged comments before anyone had a chance to set the record straight.

No matter. Controversial posts, Oberly noticed, garnered more *Buzz* members. "Human nature being what it is, those are the most popular threads," she told a reporter from the *Billings Gazette* in 2015.

Crazy Mountain Wind was a clickbait bonanza for the *Buzz*. After Jan Engwis's appearance on *Wake Up Montana*, Oberly posted a picture of the Crazies rising above a photoshopped valley of wind turbines. "What do you think?" she asked. The post garnered seventy-nine comments, overwhelmingly negative. When a helicopter was spotted flying low over the Yellowstone, conducting a Pattern-commissioned avian study, the *Buzz* lit up. "They were definitely chasing and harassing an eagle—flying so low . . . with an eagle flying for its life with all its might right in front of it!" Cindy Selensky posted. Karen Engwis urged "anyone who saw this helicopter harassing Eagles" to call the federal game warden, adding, "If you think this helicopter is harassing wait for the 500 ft. turbines."

With Pattern headed to Big Timber for a meet-and-greet, Oberly suggested a list of *Buzz*-y discussion topics. Would Pattern Development compensate neighboring landowners for the damage to their property values? Would the Jarretts? "Come get the facts, Rick Jarrett's friend Lois Huffman urges. It has been my experience over the last 40 plus years that proponents of projects like this windfarm seldom disclosure the facts, or more correctly, at least not all the facts," Oberly wrote.

Lindsey Kroskob followed the wind farm chatter on the *Buzz* with rising frustration. Although the *Pioneer* had covered every tax abatement and road-use hearing in the wind farm's long and complicated history, a newspaper that appeared once a week was no match for the daily churn of rumors and inaccuracies generated on social media. "Beccy Oberly would very clearly state her opinions and rile people up and share misinformation in an attempt to get people going," Kroskob said. "We were doing really good work and people were reading it, but we didn't have eight hours a day to spend on Facebook." Kroskob eventually left the *Pioneer* to become a victim advocate for the county. She no longer followed the *Buzz*: Oberly blocked her after she questioned the *Buzz* administrator's ethics for blocking people who disagreed with her.

At a Saturday barbecue at Jami and Harv's home on the Boulder, Charles Shawley urged Rick and Jami to stay off the *Buzz*. If they insisted on reading it and wanted to bitch about it to him, great, but he didn't want to see their names on any posts. "We're not engaging with anything on social media," he said.

Shawley himself, of course, was constantly on the *Buzz*, following what was being said about Crazy Mountain Wind. After Oberly's latest post, he made a note to reference the 2013 study by Lawrence Berkeley National Laboratory—the one that analyzed fifty thousand home sales in close proximity to sixty-seven wind projects across nine US states and found no impacts to local property values—in a "frequently asked questions" brochure he was putting together.

The weekend before the get-together at Jami and Harv's, Rick had attended a Clean Energy Fair in Bozeman, where he had been the headliner at the screening of a Sierra Club–produced movie called *Reinventing Power*. To the event's organizers, Rick Jarrett was a dream spokesman: a salt-of-the-earth rancher whose family had ranched in Sweet Grass County for generations. Here was an obvious Republican—a Trump voter, no doubt—eager to join the renewable energy revolution. They put him on a discussion panel following the screening. Lois, who came with Rick, was delighted. One of Big Timber's few registered Democrats, Lois wrote a regular column for the *Pioneer* called "Trash Talk" that gave advice about the best way to recycle plastics and compact fluorescent light bulbs.

Lois had been one year behind Rick in high school. She'd had a big crush on him back then; he took her to the winter formal one year, before he started going steady with Susan. They reconnected online many years later, when Lois was living in Portland, Oregon, and going through a nasty divorce. By 2014, she had moved onto the ranch with Rick and was spending her days in muck boots. Lois knew there were other women; Rick didn't make a secret of it. But he was kind and smart and absolutely fearless. The man could drive a vehicle anywhere, straight up a cliff or straight down it. And he loved that ranch. It was so deep in his blood, he couldn't walk without it sloshing.

When Rick started forgetting things, Lois thought maybe it was due to stress, the constant worry about whether he'd get enough money for his calves to pay for hay and renew the loan at the bank. Then he started shouting and thrashing in his sleep. One night, Lois woke with Rick's hands around her throat. He had no memory of it at all the next morning. She moved out in the spring of 2016. Rick was diagnosed with Parkinson's the following year. Even though they lived apart now, Rick and Lois were still close. They were dating, was how Lois put it.

Rick kept his dirty Stetson on as he fielded questions from Bozeman liberals in shorts. He took a dim view of the fair, with its workshops on electric vehicles and off-grid living, and of his fellow panelists—true believers from Harvest Solar Montana and the Montana Renewable Energy Association who wanted to shut down Colstrip and fill the world with windmills and solar panels. Environmentalists had no fucking business talking about anything, Rick thought. If they did everything they were trying to do, they'd starve half the people in this country. Rick didn't know if he believed in climate change, but he did believe in doing what he could to make money. And once again, he was being blocked in this fundamentally American pursuit by people who wanted to control what he did on his land.

"I don't have millionaires for neighbors; I have billionaires," Rick told the audience. He estimated that the odds of the project actually going forward were fifty-fifty.

In between pep talks, Shawley had begun to wonder, with some impatience, when those rich neighbors of Rick's were going to make their move. Elizabeth Greenwood, the Wyoming-based litigator who had met the Pattern team in Chesnoff's kitchen, had requested copies of the photo simulations. "My firm has been retained to consider the ramifications of your development and consider possible avenues to protect my clients' valuable property rights," Greenwood wrote. The letter was courteous; the threat of legal action unmistakable.

All through the summer, that threat hung in the atmosphere like a thunderhead over the Crazies. Shawley's weeks at the Big Timber Super 8 turned into months. It was a fairly bleak existence. He brought a large duffel bag of food back from his visits home so he could eat meals in his room, and rose hours before dawn to work out in a gym that had opened in the old firehouse on McLeod Street. Sometimes, he'd unwind by playing a round of golf by himself at Big Timber's public golf course. As he chipped balls, he'd mull over the most delicate part of his social engineering mission: triggering the lawsuit against Crazy Mountain Wind.

It was in Pattern's interests to deal with any legal challenge to Crazy Mountain Wind as soon as possible. There was an ironclad condition in its power purchase agreement with NorthWestern Energy: a guaranteed commercial operation date of December 31, 2019. Crazy Mountain Wind had to be up and running in a little over a year. If the wind farm was not fully operational on that date, Pattern would be on the hook for damages, and its contract to sell power to NorthWestern Energy would be terminated within ninety days.

If the wealthy foes of Crazy Mountain Wind sued now, there would still be time—time for Pattern to go to court and shred their baseless nuisance complaints, then build Crazy Mountain Wind and get its turbines spinning by its guaranteed commercial operation date. But if a late-breaking injunction shut down construction, it could be fatal to the project. Pattern wouldn't be able to close financing for a project tied up in litigation—lenders got spooked by lawsuits. And no one expected NorthWestern Energy to grant an extension on the guaranteed operation date. If the monopoly utility could wash its hands of Marty Wilde's wind project thanks to a blown deadline, it would do so, happily.

As Shawley contemplated how best to provoke the rich neighbors into filing their lawsuit, he and his bosses at Pattern were working hard to spread warm fuzzies through the county. A few days before Pattern's open house at the Grand in late August, the *Pioneer* reported that Pattern was donating $100,000 to the Reed Point Elementary School, whose students had been displaced by termites and bats. The money would pay for modular classrooms with clean new desks to replace ones stained by dripping bat urine. A Pattern press release showed a beaming Reed

Point superintendent receiving a giant cardboard check and expressing her thanks to Pattern—"a great neighbor."

About fifty people attended Pattern's meet-and-greet in the banquet room off the Grand's bar. Site plans were laid out on tables showing where the twenty-two wind turbines would go. There'd be ten on the Anderson ranch, twelve on Rick Jarrett's Crazy Mountain Cattle Company. From the ground to the tip of its highest blade, each turbine measured 495 feet. Crazy Mountain Wind's turbines would be nearly twice the height of Montana's tallest building, the twenty-story First Interstate Center in Billings.

The windmills were not arrayed in rows in front of the mountains, like the simulation Beccy Oberly had posted on the *Buzz*, but in an irregular wavelike pattern spread over three miles. It would be impossible to see all twenty-two turbines at once, given the distances between them.

Alfred Anderson helped himself to a plate of food from the buffet and found somewhere to sit to enjoy the good meal Pattern had put on. Dorothy had stayed home. She was having trouble with her feet and didn't get out much anymore. Rick and Jami made a quick appearance and left, as Shawley had instructed. He wanted to give people space to air their grievances without feeling inhibited by the Jarretts' presence.

The Pattern team, wearing name tags, circulated through the room, answering questions. There would not be a formal presentation. This disappointed some of the Antis, who had been planning on getting a few things off their chests in front of an audience, town-hall meeting style. Elizabeth Greenwood, the lawyer who had been at Chesnoff's lodge during Pattern's visit, buttonholed Allen Wynn. It wasn't enough to invite people for some food and shake hands, she told him. Pattern should put on a program to educate the public, and then open it up to questions. Shawley noted Greenwood's designer sunglasses and purse. You could tell she was from Rich Town.

A man with a neat gray beard in a Sitka hunting jacket stood on his own, taking in the scene with a squinting expression. People didn't wear

Sitka unless they had money to spend. Shawley figured this must be Russell Gordy. He made a mental note to compliment him on his jacket.

It was just a few days till September, and one of Gordy's favorite times of year: Hungarian partridge season. Huns were small, round-bellied birds with gray-brown feathers, a rust-colored face, and a jerky, chicken-like gait. They were partial to grasslands and fields, hunkering down in little bunches called coveys. When your bird dog flushed a covey of Huns, they'd burst upward in a cloud of chirps and whirling wings. Though dogs rarely got the chance. Those birds were skittish. They'd see you coming from sixty feet.

Huns weren't as flashy as pheasants, but they were fun to hunt—an unpredictable, elusive bird. Gordy understood that hunting Huns demanded patience, and stealth. If you gave away your position and flushed them too soon, you'd miss your shot.

15

FIRE SEASON

February 20, 2019
Park County Courthouse
Livingston, Montana

JIM HOGEMARK, *having first been duly sworn, testified as follows*:

Q: Mr. Hogemark, what are your job duties as part of being the ranch manager?

MR. HOGEMARK: A ranch manager is not what it's cracked up to be in my part of the world. I manage to do most of the work on the place. Like I said, I've been there for forty-some years. It is—that's what it is, it's a working ranch and always has been. That's what the owner wants it to continue being is a working ranch, and that's what my job is—to make it that way, or keep it as they want. Satisfy their wishes, I guess.

AUGUST 27, 2018
THE GRAND HOTEL
BIG TIMBER, MONTANA

Most people couldn't take the isolation of life on a thirty-thousand-acre ranch in the mountains. Wild Eagle Mountain Ranch was twenty-five miles from Big Timber—the last nine a rocky dirt road that rose and fell like a roller-coaster track. You could go weeks without seeing anyone up there if you were lucky; that's how desolate it was. Therefore, Jim Hogemark wasn't real fluid in his talk, because most days, the only things he talked to were his wife, Roxie; his dog, Jack; and his cows.

There had been a time when the prospect of going into town for a meeting would have made Hogemark sick with nervousness. He was content to stay on the ranch when Roxie went into town to shop or get her people fix. She likes her people and I like my cows, he'd say. But the windmills changed that. When their daughter said there was a meet-and-greet going on about the wind farm at the Grand, well then, Jim said, he and Roxie would try to be there, even though they were haying and Jim was up at all hours, going around in circles on the round baler.

He had seen the signs of activity and stuff all summer from the Mac-Millans' lower ranch on the Yellowstone River. The River Ranch, as it was called, shared a boundary with Alfred Anderson's ranch and Rick Jarrett's Crazy Mountain Cattle Company. Wild Eagle kept about a hundred fifty replacement heifers down there, and it was where they grew their hay.

In August, Hogemark might make eight or nine trips a day in two trucks, hauling that hay eleven miles up the county road to Wild Eagle. That was time enough to observe that more white-and-orange met towers had gone up on Jarrett and Anderson ground. Rob Fleming, Jim's hired man on the River Ranch, said the windmill people were in Big Timber, getting ready to build this thing. Like it was a done deal and they'd just have to live with it.

Some people thought Jim and Roxie opposed the wind farm because of who their landowners were—that they took their stand because of the MacMillans. Well, that wasn't it. Jim Hogemark had lived on Wild Eagle Mountain long before Whitney MacMillan bought the place.

When his father, Ken Hogemark, came to work as Roger Whidden's hired man in 1959, Jim was eighteen months old. The family lived in a ramshackle house with rooms that had been cobbled onto it over the years. Snow blew in through the cracks, forming drifts on the stairs to the unheated second floor where Jim and his younger siblings slept. When he wasn't in school or playing football, Jim helped Kenny dig post holes for fence or irrigate the hayfields. In the winter, they'd load the truck with small square bales of hay to toss off the back to the cows—a couple hundred bales on, a couple hundred bales off. When Jim graduated high school in 1976, Whidden hired him full time.

Jim knew every part of that place. An abandoned one-room school-house set off in the sagebrush still had the blackboard in it and stuff. There were homesteads all over the ranch, log cabins sinking into the earth, decaying buckboard wagons, old ditches where they'd tried to run a little water to irrigate. Most of them had starved out. One homesteader cabin still had an old piano in it. You could see how desperate it had been, trying to make a go of it on that dry, windy ground.

The sheer ruggedness of the place made it popular with outlaws. Jim's great-uncle had been a lawman back in the old days, and he told stories of escaped prisoners and shootouts in the Kelly Hills at the southern end of the ranch. A madam had a pretty fancy house in those hills. To the north was Kid Royal, a peak named for a local horse rustler who lit up there after he broke jail at Big Timber. Kid liked that peak, because of the panoramic views. He could spot a sheriff's posse riding out to get him from any direction—Big Timber or Livingston.

The Hogemark family left the ranch every Sunday to square dance with the Big Timber Trippers at the Moose Lodge, an 1892 sandstone building at First and McLeod, one of the few that survived the great fire. Jim and Geraldine Hagberg brought their daughters, Roxie and Kristi. If you were old enough to tell your left from your right, you could dance a few tips at the Moose Lodge, so Jim and his younger brother Danny spent their Sunday evenings do-si-do-ing and squaring through with the Hagberg girls. The Trippers were a tight-knit group. When Jim Hagberg's leg got crushed in a swather while he was haying, the square dancers held a benefit dance to help pay his hospital bills.

Jim and Roxie got engaged in 1979, the year the MacMillans bought the ranch. (Their younger siblings, Danny and Kristi, paired off a few years later.) Whitney and Betty were nice people, ordinary-type people. You'd never recognize who they were—what they had. They didn't want you to call them Mr. and Mrs. To Jim and Roxie, they were always Whitney and Betty.

In the first years of their marriage, Jim and Roxie lived in a small trailer home; when the babies started coming, Jim propped an old bunkhouse against one side of the trailer, and that's where the little ones slept. The MacMillans built them a new house in 1986, after their third daughter, Julie, was born—a tidy ranch house near the barns. It might have been nicer had it been set away from the ranch buildings and paddock, but that was where the work was. It just made sense to have it in the same yard, so to speak, instead of having to drive half a mile to the barn or whatever.

Jim replaced his father as Wild Eagle's ranch manager in 2002. It was Whitney's decision. Kenny wasn't ready to step aside, even though he was hobbled by back pain from all those decades of ranch work, the hundreds and thousands of square bales he had lifted. It got to where he couldn't hardly get out of the truck, he was just so crippled up, though Kenny would always say that he'd feel pretty good once he got on a horse. Jim's dad was bitter about Whitney's decision, but that was the Cargill way. Once you got a certain age, it was time to make way for the new generation, just as Whitney himself had done, stepping down as CEO after he turned sixty-five.

Whitney was a year older than Jim's dad, but spry. He and Betty enjoyed taking walks on an old trail that led from their house to the corrals. He chided the Hogemarks for getting in the truck whenever they had to go someplace. Montanans never took walks the way people in Minnesota did, he'd say, not understanding that a ranch manager had too much to do to spend his time walking from here to there, just to turn around and walk back. A man in Whitney's position, he'd not done much manual labor.

Jim ran the ranch basically the same way it had been run forever, so the MacMillans wouldn't see any changes. He bought top-of-the-line bulls, $10,000 to $15,000 apiece, because he considered natural service superior to AI. He kept a stable of well-trained horses, because they could navigate the steep coulees and rocky creek bottoms better than four-wheelers when you were moving the cows and their calves from the pastures to the mountains for summer grazing, or vice versa. But when Whitney and Betty came out to Wild Eagle, Jim set ranch work aside. "I've got one thing, would you mind?" Whitney would say, as he asked Jim to mow a lawn or tend to the walkway around the fishpond or move some books from here to there. Piddly little tasks, just to show his authority, which was fine. It was Whitney's place, after all. Jim tried to anticipate these requests. Get it done before they ask, that was his and Roxie's motto.

The bosses' grandkids, who were all grown now, loved the place. They'd nicknamed all the peaks, and some of them had proposed to their wives there. Jim would saddle up the horses for the little kids—the great-grandkids—and lead them around to the barn and back so their parents could take pictures. That was their big thing, taking pictures. It took Jim longer to saddle the horses than for the kids to ride them, but that was fine. They were there so rarely. He could take an hour once a summer to saddle up some horses.

The MacMillans only had so much time to enjoy what they had there on the ranch. That was their biggest deal, time. They'd spend two weeks, or ten days, there in the summer, entertaining people. That's what their lifestyle was all about. Jim would ask Whitney if he could run up to the house after supper to catch him up on what needed doing on Wild Eagle, or take him to see some project he'd been working on. Whitney would ask how long it was going to take, because they only had fifteen minutes before they had to be in such-and-such place to meet so-and-so for dinner. It seemed a sad thing, to own all this and not even know what you'd got.

Whitney took charge of selling the steer calves; that was his contribution. Sometime around the third week in August, he'd call the buyer and say he was thinking of selling his calves that week, and what would he give him for them? Then they'd dicker back and forth. When cattle prices were down, Hogemark would worry that maybe they should scale back their operations. But MacMillan took it in stride. He'd tell Jim to take the long view. You might have a bad year, or even two bad years, but you had to look at the ten-year picture, the way they did in the grain business.

With working ranches, it was pretty hard to come out on top. But the MacMillans could afford to run Wild Eagle at a loss. In some ways, it was the best part of Jim and Roxie's situation. They ran the place like it was their own, lived the lifestyle, and had the view, and someone else paid the bills. You didn't have to worry if a machine broke or the roof blew off the barn. When Jim needed something, he called back East and they'd shuffle things around and make it happen. You could sleep well even when beef prices were down a quarter.

A cousin once remarked that if Jim lost a calf during calving, what did it matter? These cows aren't yours, he said. It stung. Jim lived with those calves nearly twenty-four hours a day. Once, at shipping time, when they were down at the River Ranch with seven hundred of them bawling in the corrals, Jim turned to Roxie and said, "I just don't feel they're all here." They went back to the pasture and found three more calves that had gone astray.

He guessed that's why he had this job as long as he'd had it, because he cared so much. Because as good as the MacMillans had been to his family, and as generous as they'd been, he and Roxie had been good to them, too. They had given the ranch their all, which in Jim's case, was his whole life, just about. He didn't know anything different. This was it.

At the Grand Hotel, Pattern had some of their individuals walking around, and there were maps lying out that showed where the wind towers would go. Jim took a close look. The River Ranch was right in the thick of it. He thought of Rob Fleming out there in the fields, trying to work with those things whistling and sputtering and queering around, or whatever the heck they did. Russell Gordy was looking at the map, too. The MacMillans did not socialize with the Texan, but Hogemark had seen him at one or two wind farm meetings. He sidled up alongside him. "Isn't this purty?" he said. Gordy gave him a sour look. "I'll sue you, too," he said. Jim sputtered that he was with Wild Eagle, the Mac-Millan place. They were on the same side of this! But Gordy had no clue who Jim Hogemark was.

The stress of that encounter would have been enough to discourage Jim from setting foot off Wild Eagle again for months. And yet, the very next day, he and Roxie headed out down the rough dirt road to Big Timber for a county commission meeting about a road-use agreement for Crazy Mountain Wind.

The road-use agreement obligated Pattern to leave the county's roads in the same condition it found them, or better, after construction of the wind farm. They were public roads, and Pattern's trucks could drive on them without a formal agreement, but doing so would expose it to potential lawsuits. From a practical standpoint, Pattern really couldn't start construction without nailing down a road-use agreement with the county first. The Pattern team was eager to sign; they had already inked a similar agreement with Park County. They wanted to break ground on Crazy Mountain Wind on October 1, before winter set it. It took at least eight months to build a wind farm this size. Construction would grind to a halt sometime in November, until March, so that didn't leave much room for delays if Crazy Mountain Wind was to be up and running by the end of 2019.

As the hearing got underway, Chairman Faw made it clear that if the people from Pattern were expecting a rubber stamp, they'd come to the wrong county. "I actually went to your open house last night, just with all ears," he said. "And there was some concern about this road agreement."

Faw was not running for reelection in November. When he first campaigned for county commissioner, Faw vowed to serve only one term. He didn't want to make government bigger; he wanted to make it more efficient. But county government wasn't like the car business. At the dealership, if Faw wanted to do something to make his business more efficient, he'd just go ahead and do it.

Cory Conner, the county's public works director, had a few minutes to explain how he had drafted the road-use agreement, and then Faw opened it for questions. The first hand up belonged to Greenwood, who introduced herself as an attorney for Russell Gordy and David Chesnoff, whom she called "David Chernoff." Greenwood wanted the public to have a chance to read and comment on the road-use agreement before it was voted on. "It just seems that it would only be fair," she said. "And it would seem that there is the possibility that it could be improved upon." Then the commissioners could have a public meeting—on a weekend, so more people could come—and everyone could ask questions.

"The thing of it is, this is a very good road-use agreement," Conner said. "It covers our county, our citizens. I will say right now, I'm going to be very reluctant to alter this agreement."

Jan Engwis told Conner that he had become a very good bureaucrat, and he didn't appreciate bureaucrats telling him how things were going to be.

"Well, I don't appreciate being called a bureaucrat, so," Conner replied.

Faw said he would not put up with name-calling from anybody, and to keep it civil.

"I was at the so-called gathering last night," said Jim, who thought it was time someone spoke up for Wild Eagle Mountain Ranch. At the meet-and-greet, one of Pattern's individuals had told him they'd be hauling in their heavy equipment on the same roads where Hogemark trucked his hay. "They pretty much give me the assumption that I was to cease and desist. I gotta deal with it, is what it comes down to." Jim threatened to get a big semi and stop it on the road. Then watch those Pattern trucks try to get by.

Michael Thompson, the project construction manager, was a native Briton who worked out of Pattern's Vancouver office. He assured Hogemark in his broad Yorkshire accent that sometimes their pilot car would let his hay trucks go first. Jim snorted.

Bill Wallace hadn't said much, other than to point out that the county had signed similar agreements to keep the roads in good shape and cover their butts, without controversy. But he reluctantly agreed to table a vote until mid-September. Faw thought Pattern should hold an open house first, where people could ask questions.

"We did one last evening," Thompson protested.

"The complaint is nobody knew about it, they didn't pay any attention to it or something," said Faw.

Pattern held a second meet-and-greet the next day in Livingston. Although Jim would rather be going in circles on his round baler, he and Roxie made it their business to attend. They needed to know what was happening, so they could pass it along to the MacMillans.

Though there'd been a big turnout at the Grand, only a handful of people showed up for the Livingston event, at a community food bank and bakery. Elizabeth Greenwood was there. Alfred Anderson filled a plate with salmon and steak from a generous buffet.

The Hogemarks had known the Andersons forever. Jim was the same age as Dorothy and Alfred's son Kevin, and Alfred still called him Jimmy. Jim and Kevin went to the one-room schoolhouse in Springdale together, and high school after that. The River Ranch shared a border with the Andersons' ranch. The Hogemarks had always gotten along with them, even after water from one of Alfred's irrigation ditches ran into the River Ranch's stackyard and ruined some hay.

But their long friendship had sundered over the wind farm. The crux of it was a phone call. Dorothy called Roxie to tell her their sheep were coming through Wild Eagle, and they got to talking about the wind farm. Roxie heard Dorothy say that once they got the wind farm in there, she and Alfred would move out. Well, gee, thanks, Roxie thought. Wasn't that neighborly, reaping the benefits but not being there to view it? Alfred and Dorothy Anderson would deny ever planning to move off their ranch, but Roxie knew what she'd heard.

Roxie made a point of ignoring Alfred. She was waiting for their new neighbor Kelly Engel to arrive. Engel, who owned a doggie daycare and dog-training business in Bozeman, lived in a circa-1900 farmhouse that had once belonged to Alfred Anderson's family. The Andersons had sold it many decades ago. The house and its five acres of land occupied a neat, bite-sized square cut out of the section of land that the Andersons had leased to Pattern.

Engel, who was forty, had bought the property in a private sale the year before. It was her dream home, a place where she could escape the stress of running her own business while living close to nature with her pack of eleven dogs, two horses, a flock of homing pigeons, and one umbrella cockatoo. The property was surrounded by tens of thousands of acres of private land, with views of the mountains. Engel's only neighbors were the Andersons' sheep. She rode her horses into the hills and hunted rattlesnakes with her compound bow. "It had this amazing, super Wild West feel to it. It was straight-up Daniel Boone," she said.

When Roxie looked at the wind farm maps at the meet-and-greet at the Grand, she saw that Kelly Engel's house was practically at ground zero. There were two or three windmills backed up behind it, no more than two thousand feet or so away. That little gal probably didn't have a clue, she thought. Roxie's daughter Julie found Engel on Facebook and got in touch with her, to tell her about the open house Pattern was hosting in Livingston. Betsey Greenwood, a lawyer who was representing the neighbors, would be there.

Engel walked into the Livingston food bank that night, thinking she'd just say a quick hello to Julie and the lawyer. There was a large photograph mounted on posterboard that showed where the wind farm would be. Engel walked up to it and saw that whoever made the photo mockup had put a green blob where her house should have been. The blob was surrounded by wind turbines.

A Pattern guy dressed in khakis was talking about the project and how it would benefit the community. Engel was a professional person, a business owner, but she had trouble controlling her emotions in that moment. She pointed at the green blob that was her dream home, the property that she had spent her life's savings to buy. "This is me, and you're fucking me," she said, and asked when Pattern had planned to let her know about the wind farm it was building in her backyard. Then she started to cry.

"I'm screaming at them, and then Betsey swoops in and hugs me and says something dramatic, like, 'Look what you've done, you're ruining her life,'" Engel recalled.

A flustered Thompson asked for Engel's phone number and told her Pattern wanted to make things right. After the hugs and drying of tears, Greenwood got her number, too. By the time Engel got home to her dogs that night, her phone was lighting up with calls and text messages from Pattern Development and Greenwood Law, LLC, both trying to arrange meetings as soon as possible.

Looking on as he ate his salmon, Alfred thought that gal Kelly sure had put a monkey wrench in it. Charles Shawley, who had organized both meet-and-greets, was thinking much the same thing. After the big turnout at the Grand, he'd been expecting a lot of people at the Livingston event, and had ordered way too much food. Watching Kelly Engel dissolve in tears, Shawley was relieved that he had been wrong. This had the makings of a full-blown PR disaster: a spirited young dog trainer who'd bought her dream house, only to end up in a thicket of wind turbines. Fortunately, the *Livingston Enterprise* hadn't sent a reporter and the room was practically empty. Shawley would donate the uneaten salmon and steak to the food bank and hope that Thompson got to Engel before Greenwood did. She'd be a much more sympathetic figure than a Texas oil billionaire on the witness stand when the lawsuit went down.

But there was no lawsuit, not yet. The Antis continued to hold fire through the dog days of August. It was hot and dry—fire season. It didn't take much. A horse's shoe could strike a spark off a rock that would smolder in the sagebrush for hours, waiting for a gust of wind to whip it into a brushfire.

With the October start date fast approaching, Shawley began contemplating various actions Pattern could take to provoke the Antis. Maybe they could expand the entrance to the project site—bring in a few trucks, spread some gravel around. The project's enemies would become alarmed by the signs of construction and spring into action, filing their injunction while there was still time to resolve it in court.

Just after Labor Day weekend, Greenwood submitted twelve pages of objections to the county road-use agreement on behalf of her clients— Russell Gordy, David Chesnoff, and Jan Engwis, who had thrown in with the other two landowners. Hogemark passed on regular updates about the windmill meetings in his phone calls with Whitney, but he hadn't been able to persuade him to get involved. Whitney was determined to stay neutral. The MacMillans liked to stay in the background and live their lives without a fuss.

It was like that summer a few years back, when Hogemark got a call from the sheriff, telling him to keep things locked up. A fugitive had escaped from jail and was on the loose. He had ditched a truck in a coulee west of Sheep Mountain, then set out for the Crazies on foot. As it happened, Whitney and Betty were about to make one of their rare visits to Wild Eagle. Roxie called Betty to tell her maybe they should postpone it, or stay in a motel. But Betty, an energetic, no-nonsense woman with a white pixie cut, pooh-poohed the idea, and the MacMillans arrived as planned.

Whitney was in the shower when Betty heard a knock on their door. A man, disheveled and exhausted, was asking for water. Betty told him to wait a moment, closed the door, and called the police. Then she called Jim to report that the outlaw had just shown up on their doorstep. She sounded a little excited.

Hogemark stopped baling hay on the River Ranch and drove there straightaway, pulling the truck over just within sight of the MacMillans' house. If he confronted him, the fugitive might run away, he figured, and then where would they be? Jim hunkered down, got out his field glasses, and trained them on the yard. The man was lying on the grass, in pretty sad shape. Another a day or two out in those hills and he'd be a bone pile.

Soon enough, the law came racing up Duck Creek Road, lights flashing. Jim put down his binoculars and drove up to the MacMillans' house, figuring it was safe to do so. Betty brought the outlaw a glass of water before the sheriff took him away in handcuffs. Whitney came outside in his slippers, his snowy crest of hair still damp from his shower, and sat heavily in a lawn chair. "Oh, it was no big deal," he told Jim. Even with all that excitement on their doorstep, Whitney and Betty still went out to dinner that night. The MacMillans didn't make a big deal over things; that's how they were.

Same with the windmills. Whitney told Jim the wind farm would never happen, because of all the eagles. The bird people would never allow it, Whit said. He and Betty spent Labor Day weekend on Lake Minnetonka, attending a benefit gala for Global Minnesota, a nonprofit dedicated to advancing international understanding that was vice-chaired by his niece Muffy.

Lightning struck a few nights later on Wild Eagle Mountain Ranch, setting off a string of grass fires in the hills near Duck Creek. Harv and Jami were clearing a beaver dam from an irrigation ditch at their place on the Boulder when they got a call from Big Timber's volunteer fire department, asking the best way to get up to the school trust section they leased on Duck Creek, which was the nearest access point to a fire on Wild Eagle. Jami told them to drive straight up past the farmhouse. Then she and Harv raced up there in their truck.

When there was a fire in Big Timber, your neighbors showed up and did what they could to put it out. It didn't matter whose land it was on; you set aside your differences. Fire didn't respect fences or boundary lines. "We might not be the best neighbors to each other, but if there's an emergency, we're going to help each other out," Harv said.

Jim and Rob had Wild Eagle's firefighter unit and were spraying water on the burning grasses alongside volunteer firefighters from Big Timber, Melville, and McLeod. Taylor Davis, the ranch manager from Lone Star, was there, too, with one of their ranch hands. Jami and Harv got out their shovels and rakes and went around the perimeter, stamping out hot spots, raking up the grass and turning the dirt over it so it wouldn't burn. When sagebrush caught fire, it could work its way down to the roots, so they used spades to uproot the smoldering brush and smothered that, too.

After all the fires and hot spots were smothered and banked, there was no chitchatting. Everyone got in their trucks and went home. But the following week, a boxed announcement appeared in the *Big Timber Pioneer*. It was from Jim Hogemark at Wild Eagle Mountain Ranch, thanking firefighters and "All the Neighbors, for their quick response to the fire that was on us last Thursday! A Great Crew! Thank you *So* much." Rick, Harv, and Jami expressed their own thanks to "all the neighbors who responded so quickly & competently" a few pages later.

On September 13, the Hogemarks and the Jarretts were once again on opposite sides of the conference table in the county annex building, as Wallace and Faw met to vote on whether to accept the road-use agreement. After introducing herself as the attorney for Engwis, Gordy, and "Mr. Chesnot," Betsey Greenwood read her lengthy list of objections aloud, into the record.

The vote on the motion to adopt the road-use agreement went as expected: Wallace for, Faw against. "The motion didn't pass," Faw announced, in case anyone was confused.

Rick had seen it all before. He knew the Antis would use the road agreement as a tool to block the wind farm. "You can spend all the time you want," he had said at the commissioner meeting in August, "but this won't end till you stop the project." He told Jami he was afraid Pattern would drop Crazy Mountain Wind and run off—go looking for an easier project in a friendlier county.

The struggle was wearing on him, or maybe it was the Parkinson's. Depression was one of the disease's symptoms. Rick's body betrayed him a little more each day. His world was getting smaller. The Frosty Freez had abruptly closed. For more than thirty years, Rick had been a regular at the Frosty Freez, a coffee shop with gingham curtains and a NO POTTY MOUTH sign on the wall. It was where he met his friends in the afternoon to drink coffee and tease the waitresses. Now where was he supposed to go?

Shawley met Rick and Lois for lunch at the Thirsty Turtle. Rick was morose. They had gotten to this point before, only to see the project die, he said. Shawley assured him that Pattern wasn't running anywhere. There'd be a new commission in a few months. He urged Rick to go to the candidate forum at the Sweet Grass County Farm Bureau to show support for his former son-in-law J. V. Moody—retired regional commander for the highway patrol, current head football coach for the Herders, and soon-to-be Sweet Grass County Commissioner. JV had won the Republican primary for Faw's seat, which made him a lock for November. The talk in the Anti camp was that Jami had pushed JV to run. With Rick Jarrett's ex-son-in-law on the commission, they muttered, the wind farm would be a done deal. There was no denying that Jami and JV's children, Jordan and Jess, had an interest in the ranch's future. But Jami wasn't happy about her ex-husband's political ambitions. "He and I had a fairly substantial fight about him running, in which I asked him not to," she said. JV confirmed this. "She was livid," he said. Back in the days when they were still married and JV was with the highway patrol, Jami and her husband had worked across the hall from one another in the Sweet Grass County Courthouse. During the bitter time that their marriage was disintegrating, Jami became convinced that JV was having an affair with a county employee, an affair she had no choice but to watch unfold from her office across the hall. It was fifteen years ago, but it still rankled.

"Once he had finally retired from the patrol and was gone, I was like, 'Thank fuck,'" Jami said. "And then, when I heard the mutterings that he was going to run, I was like, 'Oh my God, can you not let me have my own fucking life?'" Jami had always worked closely with the commissioners in her capacity as assistant to the county attorney. That wouldn't be possible once her ex was elected. It would make everyone too uncomfortable. JV ran into Rick at a local Republican committee dinner. "Even her dad told me that she was pissed at me," he recalled. "But he said, 'I think you'll do a good job, and she just needs to get over it.'"

Shawley urged Jami not to pick any more fights with her ex-husband. Shawley was on excellent terms with JV, himself. The night that Pattern's road-use agreement died in a deadlocked vote at the county commission, they sat together in the stands at a Lady Herders volleyball game. Pattern was planning to make a donation to the high school to pay for new weight-room equipment. Shawley told JV that Pattern would downplay the contribution, to avoid any appearance of trying to buy off the Herders' head football coach and future Sweet Grass County Commissioner. No giant cardboard checks this time around.

JV's Democratic opponent didn't even show up at the candidate forum at the farm bureau; that's how much of a shoo-in JV was for the commissioner's seat. Asked about Crazy Mountain Wind, Moody said he supported the project because it would strengthen the county's tax base. "We have to be inviting to outside businesses," he said. "I don't see a lot of negatives toward wind farms."

Moody's words of support for Crazy Mountain Wind appeared on the front page of the *Pioneer* alongside a story, planted by Shawley, about how the wind farm was gearing up for construction with some advance roadwork. "Pattern Preps for Project," the headline read.

The fuse had at last been lit. The next day, Jan Engwis's R. F. Building and Engwis Investment companies, Diana's Great Idea, and Rock Creek Ranch, Ltd., filed a complaint in Montana's Sixth Judicial District seeking to put a stop to Crazy Mountain Wind. "The harms are real, grave, and practically certain," it charged. "The construction and operation of the Project will cause injuries to Plaintiffs' and neighbors' health, is indecent or offensive to the senses, is an obstruction to the free use of property, and thus interferes with the comfortable enjoyment of life or property of the Plaintiffs and the rights of the community at large."

On October 2, Rick Jarrett was met on the door of his farmhouse by a process server from the sheriff's office, who handed him a lawsuit with his name on it, then headed down North Yellowstone Trail Road to serve Alfred Anderson. Rick's neighbors were suing him personally, by name. Pattern had an entire legal department to fight this lawsuit. Who would stand up for the Crazy Mountain Cattle Company?

16

ANACONDA

February 19, 2019
Park County Courthouse
Livingston, Montana

MONICA TRANEL, *Opening statement*:
The Legislature explicitly created an interest in wind energy and
granted to Mr. Jarrett and Mr. Anderson a property interest in the
wind that flows over their land and the ability to develop that . . .
These statutes immunize Mr. Jarrett, Mr. Anderson, and Crazy
Mountain Wind from the claims that the plaintiffs bring. As a matter
of law, nothing that is done or maintained under the express authority
of a statute can be a nuisance.

OCTOBER 20, 2018
CHARLES RIVER
BOSTON, MASSACHUSETTS

Every October, Monica Tranel competed in Boston's Head of the Charles
Regatta, a three-day series of races that draws top-ranked rowers from
around the world. An Olympic teammate from the 2000 Sydney Games
lived in Boston, and he lent Monica his scull for the Women's Grand
Masters Singles. Greg and the girls cheered her on from a bridge over
the Charles as she powered upstream in her borrowed Ultimate Shark
Predator. She finished tenth, which made her wonder if any of these
women had actual jobs or just spent all their time training.

Monica was back at the Hyatt, riding the elevator to her room, when
Jami called. Monica had met Jami at the Public Service Commission the
day Rick and Harv Van Wagoner testified in support of Crazy Mountain

Wind. Marty's ranchers. She remembered them. They were being sued by their rich neighbors.

"We need a lawyer," Jami said. "Will you represent us?"

"I guess I could—I mean, I've represented everybody else, why not you?" Monica said.

Monica had advised Pattern in the weeks after Marty's death, and she continued to represent Marty's company, WINData. WINData's big payday wouldn't come until Crazy Mountain Wind was built and operational. Marty would have hired Monica to take those wankers to court in a heartbeat for trying to stop him from getting his money.

Jaffe was running WINData now. He had stepped into Marty's shoes knowing little about his father's work, only that he was a tenacious fucker. Jaffe considered himself a tenacious fucker, too, but navigating the intricacies of interconnection agreements and power purchase negotiations with NorthWestern Energy was overwhelming. It gave him some insight into his dad—the burden he accepted with this work. Jaffe spent less time with his friends, doing the things he used to do. He needed time alone now, to think things through.

Monica told Jaffe that WINData could file a counterclaim against Crazy Mountain Wind's antagonists—to sue them back for obstructing a lawful wind project that his father had invested so much to develop. But Jaffe had inherited a whopping legal bill from Marty's hot-mic lawsuit against NorthWestern and the PSC, which would be dismissed with prejudice in 2019. He passed.

"I just got my ass handed to me," Jaffe said, "so I didn't want to mess with the court system anymore."

WINData was out. Monica wondered about Pattern. It wasn't unreasonable to think that Pattern would ask her to represent Crazy Mountain Wind, given that it had sought her advice in the past. But Pattern hired W. Scott Mitchell, a partner at a large Billings law firm who specialized in environmental litigation. Monica supposed she shouldn't have been surprised.

So, she was free to represent Marty's ranchers, though they'd need to sign waivers acknowledging that her past work for Pattern could constitute a conflict of interest. Under the terms of a confidential joint defense agreement, Pattern would pay the ranchers' legal fees, but it would have no say over how Monica handled their case. Later, Monica would wonder if the arrangement had created an inescapable power dynamic from the beginning. Rick and Alfred had a unique stake in the future of Crazy Mountain Wind, but this was Pattern's show. Monica wasn't driving the bus, their fancy lawyers were. Her clients were the straphangers in the back.

The stakes were high for Pattern. If the judge granted the plaintiffs' motion for a preliminary injunction, it would hit the pause button on Crazy Mountain Wind. All work on the project would stop, pending a civil trial—a trial that wouldn't happen for months. If the judge denied the plaintiffs' motion, Crazy Mountain Wind could still break ground in late March or early April. That would give Pattern a solid ten months to finish the build in time to meet the project's guaranteed commercial operation date—December 31, 2019.

But if the judge granted the injunction—well, that would be a death warrant for Crazy Mountain Wind. An injunction would create insurmountable construction delays and repel potential investors. Crazy Mountain Wind's power purchase agreement could become null and void before the case ever came before a jury.

Pattern had invested a lot of money in Crazy Mountain Wind—nearly $10 million. In a few months, a $59 million bill for twenty-two General Electric turbines would come due. But Pattern was a billion-dollar company. Win or lose, Pattern would go on doing business as usual.

For Rick Jarrett and Alfred Anderson, the stakes could not be higher. The ranchers were depending on the revenue from Crazy Mountain Wind to pay their bills and meet their debt payments. If Crazy Mountain Wind didn't get built, they might lose their land.

Monica went to Big Timber to meet her new clients. "There's no money in ranching," Rick told her as they sat at his kitchen table. "The money's in the land." He saw the land as a trust. It represented a commitment that past generations had made to the ranching lifestyle, and to the generations who'd come after them. The land wasn't really his, he told Monica. He was borrowing it from his kids and his grandkids.

Monica got in her minivan and drove to the Andersons' farmhouse. Dorothy asked Monica what her favorite color in the kitchen was, so she could knit her a pot holder. Monica had grown up around ranchers like Alfred Anderson, whose quiet stoicism was sometimes dismissed as hayseed simplicity. The man was eighty-seven. His hands trembled as he drank from his cup of coffee. But he got up every morning to feed his herd and do whatever else needed doing, and he did it without complaint. Alfred seemed pained by the lawsuit. "We used to be able to talk to each other," he said, thinking of other neighbors and other times. When Monica asked if he had a chance to look over the legal documents she had sent him, Alfred shook his head with a little laugh. He only collected his mail on Tuesdays and Thursdays.

Pattern's first order of business after its disastrous open house in Livingston was taking care of Kelly Engel, the feisty dog trainer. Engel, who had hired herself a lawyer, was a step ahead of them. She booked back-to-back meetings with Elizabeth Greenwood, the plaintiffs' lead attorney, and Pattern's Michael Thompson. Each urged her not to talk to the other.

Greenwood paid a visit to Engel's home and they walked the property with her dog pack. Engel was curious about Greenwood and asked the lawyer a lot of questions. A fourth-generation Wyoming native, Greenwood had gotten her start working for the state's most famous attorney—Gerry Spence, a self-styled Lone Ranger of the legal profession who wore ten-gallon hats to court and once sent a silver bullet to the opposing counsel in a lawsuit.

Greenwood wasn't a cowboy. She was poised and incisive—imperious even, at times. Her nickname among Facebook friends was the Queen. She was also a fearsome Scrabble player, the champion of Sublette County's first-ever Scrabble tournament. When Greenwood told Engel who her clients were—a Texas oil billionaire and a famous criminal defense attorney—the dog trainer was impressed. Betsey really had balls to represent those guys, she thought.

Unlike Greenwood's high-octane clients, Engel wasn't rich or powerful, which made her all the more useful to their case. To use a Scrabble analogy, she was a ten-point letter tile, like a *Q* or a *Z*, with high strategic value in the game that was unfolding in the foothills of the Crazy Mountains. "Betsey really wanted me on their side," Engel said. "If we went to court, I was the one who was most affected, being a single woman who bought her dream property."

Thompson met Engel at a Bozeman café near her doggie daycare business, Know Thy Dog. As Engel saw it, working with dogs was all about the owners—showing them how their dogs' behavioral issues were a lens on their lives. Though she rarely got the chance. Most of her clients were wealthy people from Big Sky who just wanted someone to train their goldendoodle while they went skiing. Thompson seemed jittery, ill at ease. "They send in this English guy in a plaid shirt. His knee was shaking the table," Engel said. "The tension between us was quite hostile."

The tension eased significantly after Pattern offered to buy Engel's dream house for a generous sum, more than she had paid for it. "I will say, they did right by me in the end," said Engel, who signed a nondisclosure agreement. The threat of the wind farm and the unexpected financial windfall had been a kind of weird blessing, she reflected. "I loved it so much, but I was struggling with my commute to Bozeman every day. And the wind wore me out. I'm a pioneer woman, but it was just too much."

Pattern had won that round. But Greenwood was pursuing other avenues of attack. In September, she requested a meeting with Julie Johnson, executive director of Big Timber's chamber of commerce, to discuss the boutique hotel and spa that her client Russell Gordy hoped to build on the site of Hunter's Hot Springs.

Johnson and Monte Koch, the chamber's president, met with Greenwood in a conference room at Opportunity Bank on McLeod Street, where Koch was a commercial loan officer. Greenwood showed them several large leather-bound albums filled with antique postcards and newspaper stories about Hunter's Hot Springs. Then she spread the pen-and-ink renderings of Gordy's spa across the conference table. The new resort would create tax revenue—and new jobs, she said. But if Crazy Mountain Wind was built, there would be no spa; Gordy would shelve the project.

Koch was skeptical. "I'm not even sure the ink was dry on the renderings," he recalled. "I mean, she just thought we were the local rubes."

The chamber of commerce had already spent hours that summer discussing Crazy Mountain Wind. The chamber's board members were excited at the prospect of expanding the county's tax base beyond the Sibanye-Stillwater Mine, which accounted for about half of its tax revenues. Charles Shawley, who attended every chamber meeting, told the board that Sweet Grass County would reap $10.6 million in property taxes over the life of the project, and another $1 million in impact fees. After the mine and NorthWestern Energy, Crazy Mountain Wind would contribute more tax revenue than the next eight highest taxpayers combined.

Johnson wasn't worried about the impact of a wind farm on tourism. "No one driving by it on Interstate 90 at eighty miles an hour is going to say, 'Oh, look at these windmills,'" she said. Tourists weren't spending that much money in Big Timber to begin with. Every two years, Montana's Institute for Tourism and Recreation Research released a report on visitor spending in the state's six primary travel regions, factoring in revenues from hotels, restaurants, gas stations, and park entrance fees, with a breakdown by county. Sweet Grass County ranked at the bottom of the list. It just didn't have as many hotels and restaurants and tourist attractions as other places in the state. Sweet Grass County collected $69,388 in so-called bed taxes—the 7 percent tax on hotels and campgrounds—in 2018. By comparison, Park County—the gateway to Yellowstone Park—reaped $2.4 million.

The chamber had nothing against Gordy's spa hotel, but its economic benefit to the county would be negligible. Hunter's Hot Springs were just over the county line, so Park County, not Sweet Grass, would collect any property tax revenues.

Two nights after Greenwood's meeting with Johnson and Koch, the board's nine members voted to draft a statement of support for Crazy Mountain Wind. "Even though there might have been individual board members who didn't like the idea personally, in the end, everyone agreed that as the chamber, it was the right move to support the project," Johnson said.

Sweet Grass County needed money. Its social services couldn't keep pace with its problems. Rates of substance abuse, mental illness, and suicide were on the rise—a subject that the county's prospective new commissioner, J. V. Moody, had addressed at the farm bureau's candidate forum.

"It takes a ton of money away from the county," he said. "Just flat trying to deal with people who have mental issues that we are not prepared to take care of."

Moody knew all about Big Timber's cinematic beauty and its mesmerizing effect on visitors. Back in his days on the highway patrol, he had been the one writing Robert Redford's speeding tickets when he was filming *The Horse Whisperer* on the Engle ranch. But mostly what Moody saw in his work in law enforcement was the impact of untreated mental illness on the community. Sweet Grass County just didn't have the resources to handle it. One of Moody's reserve deputies once had to drive a guy seventy-six miles to a facility in Great Falls.

Recent cuts to state health and human services had made it worse. Big Timber was set to lose its sole mental health counselor that January. County social services were underfunded. So were its schools. Susan Metcalf, the Sweet Grass County school superintendent, faced budget shortfalls every year. To avert program cuts, the school system dipped into the county's Metal Mines Fund, established with tax revenue from the Sibanye-Stillwater Mine. But there wasn't enough money to hire a school safety officer for the high school, or to install a secure entry system. Metcalf couldn't replace aging computers or buy new welding equipment. The rural elementary schools were always short-staffed; if she could boost salaries, she could attract more teachers. Crazy Mountain Wind would be a game changer for Sweet Grass schools. Metcalf had done the math. "It was a lot of money," she said. "I mean, big money."

As the controversy over Crazy Mountain Wind heated up, a school board member told Metcalf that he had been approached by Gordy's ranch manager. Metcalf should put together a wish list: new technology for the schools, or whatever she was hoping to buy with tax revenue from the wind farm. Gordy would follow through and see that she got it, the ranch manager said. Metcalf made a wish list and passed it along through her middleman on the school board. "Nothing ever happened," said Metcalf, who retired in January 2023. "Crickets."*

The filing of the lawsuit marked the end of the Gordys' Montana season. Russell and Glenda returned to Houston and a busy circuit of country

---

* In February 2024, the *Big Timber Pioneer* reported that Russell and Glenda Gordy had donated $100,000 toward a $1 million playground renovation at the Big Timber Grade School, which their ranch manager's children attend.

club luncheons and charity galas. In late September, Gordy made head-lines with a $15 million gift to Texas Children's Hospital for research into pediatric cancer—one of Glenda's pet causes—in honor of his friend and longtime partner Lester Smith. Meanwhile, Chesnoff was closeted with the Portuguese soccer star Cristiano Ronaldo, who had been ac-cused of raping a woman in a Las Vegas hotel nearly a decade before.

With his fellow plaintiffs thus occupied, Jan Engwis had the front page of the October 11 *Big Timber Pioneer* all to himself, in a story on the lawsuit against Crazy Mountain Wind. The *Pioneer*—under new editorship—dived right into the lawsuit's most sensational claims. "The complaint cites multiple studies that have found a negative affect [sic] on the health of people living in proximity to wind turbines as a result of the noise they emit," the reporter wrote, referring to a 2013 article "pub-lished by the National Institutes of Health."

That article, "Adverse Health Effects of Industrial Wind Turbines," was cited five times in Engwis, Gordy, and Chesnoff's lawsuit as evidence of the health risks Crazy Mountain Wind posed to county residents. But the attribution to the National Institutes of Health was misleading: the paper was not written or published by scientists at the nation's medical research agency. The article's only connection to the NIH was that it could be found on PubMed Central, an online clearinghouse of scientific and medical citations that can be accessed through the NIH website.

Coauthored by an Ontario family physician, a retired pharmacist, and a certified management accountant, "Adverse Health Effects of Indus-trial Wind Turbines" relied on "a community-based self-reported health survey" to draw its conclusions—chief among them, that the noise from wind turbines could be "expected to result in a non-trivial percentage of persons being highly annoyed."

The *Pioneer* reporter reached out to Rick Jarrett, who contributed an ornery comment about his neighbors: "Their concerns with their prop-erty are not my problem." The reporter told Shawley that Rick hung up on him.

Some damage control was in order. Shawley set up an interview with Rick on his ranch, so the reporter could get a fuller understanding of his point of view. Jami thought it was a good idea, so Rick agreed to let the man in his kitchen. Shawley sat at the table with them as Rick talked about his ancestor Cyrus Mendenhall and the generations of Jarretts that had ranched in Sweet Grass County. Leasing his land for wind development seemed like his best chance at hanging on to the ranch long enough to pass it on to his grandkids. He could still run cows and sheep. The wind farm would make him a better rancher, Rick said, because he wouldn't have to push the land harder than anyone should.

The article that ran in the *Pioneer* the following week was sympathetic, but when he got to the jump, Shawley winced. It was just one line: "Jarrett said the extra income would allow him to temporarily scale back operations in order for his land to recover from decades of aggressive grazing."

The reporter had interpreted Rick's comment about not pushing the land harder than anyone should as an admission that he had overgrazed his land. No self-respecting rancher would ever admit to that, any more than he'd boast about trying to starve a profit out of his cows. It was as though Rick had confessed to gross mismanagement of a sacred family trust.

Throughout the fall, motions, notices, and answer briefs piled up like autumn leaves in the docket for Case No. DV 2018-161 in Livingston's Sixth District Court. Monica called the plaintiffs "the Oligarchs." The Oligarchs' attorneys wanted to see Pattern's contracts with Jarrett and Anderson. They demanded their tax returns and decades of medical records—every colonoscopy and prostate exam—"due to Jarrett and Anderson's purported claims that without the contract they could not pay for the[ir] health care and medical needs."

Jami hoped that the district judge, Brenda Gilbert, would be sympathetic to their case. Judge Gilbert was a cattle rancher. The Gilbert ranch in Clyde Park, west of Big Timber, had been in her husband's family for four generations.

Judge Gilbert had indicated a progressive stance on environmental issues with her ruling in a high-profile mining case that spring. Local conservation groups sued the state's Department of Environmental Quality for issuing an exploratory drilling permit to Lucky Minerals, an outfit that wanted to mine for gold in Paradise Valley, north of Yellowstone National Park.

Gilbert faulted state environmental regulators for giving Lucky Minerals the green light without fully considering the impact of mining on the valley's wildlife and its water sources, which could be contaminated by drilling waste—always a risk with drilling and fracking. Just a year before, the BLM cited Gordy's SG Interests for improper drilling after it spilled some two thousand gallons of wastewater, foam chemicals, and drill cuttings on federal land a few miles southwest of Colorado's Thompson Divide. Instead of containing the waste from its drilling in a tank as required, BLM officials said that SG Interests had tried to burn it off through a flare stack.

But Judge Gilbert's thoughts on the case against Crazy Mountain Wind would remain a mystery. In November, Elizabeth Greenwood, the lead attorney in Gordy, Chesnoff, and Engwis's legal offensive, moved to have Judge Gilbert removed from the case. No reason was given, and none was required. Under a curious statute in Montana's legal code, each party to a legal action—be it civil or criminal—is entitled to one substitution of a district court judge, for any reason.

The rule is a relic from the War of the Copper Kings, when Gilded Age tycoons fought for control over the Anaconda Copper Mine in Butte—once the largest source of copper in the world. The mine was named in tribute to the Anaconda Plan, the US naval blockade of southern seaports and the Mississippi River, which choked off the Confederacy's access to goods and trade. Anaconda strangled the seceshes' economic lifeline like an enormous and implacable snake.

Augustus Heinze, a wily Brooklyn-born copper magnate, took on William Rockefeller's Amalgamated Copper Mining Company in the battle for Anaconda. Heinze bought the claim to an overlooked little triangle of land that sat between three monstrously productive shafts and preceded to tunnel down into the rich tangle of veins below, straight into copper mines owned by Amalgamated Copper. Heinze's team of thirty-seven lawyers tied up Rockefeller and his other rivals in lawsuits while he stole their copper out from under them.

Heinze had an ally in this campaign: Judge William Clancy, a slovenly jurist known for wearing yesterday's eggs in his beard. Amalgamated sued to stop Heinze, but Judge Clancy found in his friend's favor, time and again. In frustration, Amalgamated exploded one of its own mines to keep Heinze from getting its copper. When that didn't work, Rockefeller and company resorted to a scorched-earth campaign. In October 1903, Amalgamated shut down all its mining operations, laying off ten thousand workers in a single day, and thousands more over the following month.

Amid the growing misery of a vast unemployed workforce and their hungry families, Amalgamated issued an ultimatum: the mines would reopen only if the governor called a special session of the state legislature to enact a "fair trials" bill allowing a change of venue if either party to a lawsuit thought the judge was corrupt or prejudiced. The governor and legislature submitted. Amalgamated's bill was swiftly passed and signed into law.

Amalgamated's grievances were legitimate. Clancy *was* corrupt. But, as the historian C. B. Glasscock wrote in his 1935 history *The War of the Copper Kings*, "the fact remained that a combination of corporations had, through the threatened starvation of one hundred thousand persons, forced the unwilling governor of a sovereign state to call a legislature to enact laws for its benefit. That the laws themselves happened to be just was ethically beside the point." Victorious, Amalgamated renamed itself the Anaconda Copper Mining Company. The great snake had once again constricted its prey and swallowed it whole.

The fair trials law lives on in Montana's legal code as Section 3-1-804. Plaintiffs in a civil case have thirty calendar days after the first summons has been served to move for the substitution of the judge. Greenwood made her motion on November 7, twenty-seven days after the summons to Rick Jarrett and Alfred Anderson was served. To Monica, it looked like a play to slow-walk the legal proceedings to the detriment of Crazy Mountain Wind and her clients.

Judge Jon Oldenburg of Montana's Tenth District Court in Lewistown was assigned the case. In a conference call with all three sets of attorneys, two sets of court administrators compared court schedules, searching for a two-day window in which Oldenburg could hear the case. His courthouse was a good 130 miles from Livingston, so they had to factor in about three hours of drive time each way. There were only two days in December that worked for the court: the twelfth and thirteenth. Otherwise, the hearing would have to wait till February.

Pattern's attorneys pushed hard for December. If Crazy Mountain Wind was going to be up and running by the end of 2019—as the terms of its power purchase agreement with NorthWestern demanded—construction had to begin that March or April. And before construction could begin, contractors had to be hired and the financing for the project had to be locked down, a process that ordinarily took three months.

But Greenwood had another trial scheduled on December 14, in Rock Springs, Wyoming—"roughly an eight-hour drive from Livingston," she said—which would make it impossible for her to be in Livingston on December 13. Over Pattern and Monica's protests, Judge Oldenburg set the hearing for February 19 through 21.

A few days after the hearing date was set, lawyers for Wild Eagle Mountain Ranch filed a motion to intervene in the case against Crazy Mountain Wind. Whitney MacMillan had at last gotten off the sidelines. It was the River Ranch that decided it, his ranch manager, Jim Hogemark, thought. "He said, 'It will never happen,'" Hogemark recalled. "I said, 'Whitney, it's going to happen and you're going to be affected. The River Ranch is right there.'"

Whitney MacMillan's name did not appear anywhere in the motions filed by his attorneys. Even as he threw in with the Texan, his complaint communicated a certain empyrean remove from the other litigants. "In this case, there are other landowners already involved, but the facts and circumstances of their situations are different than Wild Eagle's," MacMillan's attorneys wrote. They stressed the threat that construction of the wind farm posed, not only to Wild Eagle's "unobstructed pristine views," but to its creeks and streams, which could become clogged and sullied by "fugitive dust"—so lethal to MacMillan's beloved Yellowstone cutthroat trout.

David Leuschen had warned the guys at Pattern. It was just common sense. You don't name a wind farm after a majestic mountain range that people hold sacred. Name it Sweet Grass Wind, he told them.

But the name stuck. Crazy Mountain Wind. And sure enough, the guys at Pattern got into a fight with Russell Gordy and Whitney MacMillan, and just which side of that fight was Leuschen supposed to be on?

Pattern Energy was owned by Riverstone Holdings, Leuschen's private equity firm. He sat on Pattern's board. So Crazy Mountain Wind was his project, in a sense. But Leuschen owned a ranch in the Crazies, just like MacMillan and Gordy. Crazy Peak was Leuschen property, along with Granite Peak, Conical Peak, and a good chunk of Big Timber Peak, all part and parcel of twenty square miles of high alpine country as magnificent as a natural park. Leuschen was the steward of those mountains. So, he was on all sides of this thing.

When Leuschen wasn't skiing his mountains or artificially inseminating his cows—or sailing in Maine, or weekending in Southampton or racing his one-hundred-foot yacht *Galateia* in Sardinia or St. Barths—he could be found in a Fifth Avenue skyscraper across the street from Trump Tower. Riverstone's corporate headquarters were like a chunk of Montana reimagined as a Chelsea art gallery: blackened steel beams offset by roughhewn timbers. The reception desk was a polished stone monolith. The Riverstone logo was seared on a barnwood slab, like a cattle brand. And at the heart of Riverstone were the Crazy Mountains. The entire island mountain range was etched onto the glass walls of the conference room.

Riverstone had started out as a conventional energy fund, its profits powered by fossil fuels. But these days, Leuschen's private equity fund was all about saving the world. Riverstone had pivoted. Carbon-generating energy sources had lost their sex appeal. To evoke the *S* curve from Leuschen's TEDx Talk, that cigarette had been smoked. It was a cold pile of ash. The whole world wanted to invest in decarbonization technology; that's where the money was going.

Riverstone Holdings was going to ride that wave, surf it straight toward pure decarb and a trillion-dollar market. It was investing in companies that produced hydrogen fuel cell–powered trucks with zero carbon emissions, advanced fast chargers for electric vehicles, and solid-state batteries, which had higher energy density than the lithium-ion batteries Elon Musk put in his Teslas—and didn't spontaneously combust, like his sometimes did.

Above all, it was investing in large-scale renewable-energy development. Pattern Energy was one of the biggest wind developers in America, and Riverstone was financing its expansion, committing more than

$800 million in growth capital from its institutional investors. The goal was to double Pattern's energy portfolio to five gigawatts by 2020—to enable the company to build enough wind farms to light up five midsize American cities. Pattern Energy had projects in the pipeline in the US, Chile, Canada, and Japan. The company's CEO, Mike Garland, was a true believer. To hear him talk, wind energy was going to save the world. Wind turbines everywhere.

But the problem with wind turbines was that when you wanted to put them someplace, you got into arguments with the locals. Turbines transformed rural landscapes, lit up dark night skies. If you went up a hill on Leuschen's Switchback Ranch in Roscoe, you could see the winking lights of Stillwater Wind, now under construction some sixty miles away in Reed Point. Stillwater was a Pattern project. That one sailed through county approval processes and would be completed in September 2019.

Crazy Mountain Wind, different story.

Leuschen didn't know Gordy, other than in passing. Whenever he saw Whitney MacMillan at the Grand, he'd stop and chat. If those guys were against Crazy Mountain Wind, he wasn't going to try to convince them it was a good thing. He wasn't sure he'd like those turbines sticking up near his ranch, either, though it was most unlikely that he'd be able to see the lights of Crazy Mountain Wind from the Lazy K Bar's backyard—not with all his mountains in the way.

Crazy Mountain Wind was a minor project, one-thirteenth the size of Western Spirit Wind, a 1,050-megawatt project that Pattern was developing in Central New Mexico. Western Spirit Wind would be the largest renewable-energy facility in US history. It was one of the crown jewels of Pattern's portfolio. Crazy Mountain Wind wasn't a crown jewel. It was a headache. Let the guys in San Francisco do what they thought appropriate; Leuschen would recuse himself.

In December, the Crazy Mountain Neighbors Coalition began a petition drive on Facebook. A statement on the coalition's website described it as "a pro-property rights, pro-preservation group dedicated to protecting our small-town communities from the growing threat of industrialization." Its hashtag was #StopCrazyMtWindFarm.

"Our iconic Crazy Mountains need your help. Out-of-state developers want to build a wind plant in our mountains. Join your friends and neighbors. Sign the petition to protect the Crazy Mountains from commercial wind exploration," the Facebook post urged. There were testimonials from "Brandon from Big Timber," a friendly-looking guy hiking with a toddler on his back, and Jessie, an attractive young mom, also with a toddler, who was "concerned about the danger wind plants pose to wildlife, including the eagles and bats who call this area home."

The testimonials, along with the coalition's website and petition drive, were the work of Chris Puyear, a consultant with Strategies 360. The Seattle-based lobbying and media relations group had been hired to create an astroturf campaign against Crazy Mountain Wind. Before becoming a lobbyist, Puyear had been the communications director for the Public Service Commission. "Most people see lobbyists as a dirty word, but ultimately your job is to represent clients who are too busy making a living to engage in the political process," he declared in a profile on his gym's website, upon being named its CrossFit Athlete of the Month.

There were no testimonials from the plaintiffs in the lawsuit against Crazy Mountain Wind on the coalition's Facebook page. Gordy restricted his appearances on social media to the curated images on Gordy & Sons' Instagram and Facebook pages—climbing a hunting tower with Glenda in matching camo, or teaching his grandson Rio how to handle a shotgun. "Our children: We give them roots so they can take flight," the caption read. "#quail #hunting #grandparents."

The plaintiffs tried to win the support of bona fide grassroots organizations—conservation groups like the Park County Environmental Council, which had led the legal challenge to block gold mining in Paradise Valley. Erica Lighthiser, a director for the Park County Environmental Council, was immersed in the campaign against Lucky Minerals when she got a call from David Chesnoff that summer. He invited her to come out to his ranch, to learn about a wind farm development that was being proposed on a neighboring property.

"They toured me around in a little quad that was nicer than my car," Lighthiser recalled. Chesnoff showed her the guest house on his ranch and explained that its views would be spoiled by the wind turbines. He told her about the many eagles that nested along the Yellowstone.

The Park County Environmental Council declined to enter the fight over Crazy Mountain Wind. As Lighthiser saw it, the real issue at stake wasn't wind development or eagles—it was zoning. Her group advocated for proactive land use planning that balanced the needs and interests of ranchers and other landowners against environmental concerns. "These types of neighbor-versus-neighbor conflicts come up all the time when you have no rules," she said.

While Gordy, Chesnoff, and Engwis's lawyers prepared for the February injunction hearing, their lobbyist worked to nudge public opinion in their favor. Mass mailers with the coalition's white-and-purple logo flooded every mailbox in Big Timber. One showed a tiny farmhouse dwarfed by towering wind turbines: "Tell Sweet Grass County Commissioners: NO 500 FT TURBINES IN OUR CRAZIES. Sign the petition today!" Puyear flagged every upcoming county commission and county planning meeting on the coalition's Facebook page, urging like-minded neighbors "to show up and voice our opposition to rubber stamping this project without any public input or local review!"

"It was well-publicized: 'We gotta go to this meeting and be annoyed,'" Brandon Droeger—aka "Brandon from Big Timber"—told me. "The whole banding-together thing happened more on Facebook then it did in person."

Droeger, a finish carpenter and amateur photographer, had recently moved to Big Timber from Colorado with his wife, Jessie—the same Jessie who was worried about Big Timber's eagles and bats. That was the same toddler they were holding. Droeger loved photographing the Crazy Mountains. On his way to and from his carpentry job in Bozeman, he would get off the interstate at Springdale and take pictures of the Crazies, then post them on the *Buzz*. They got so many likes that he began selling matte prints in hand-built frames for $225 apiece.

Puyear reached out to Droeger to ask if he could use some of his photographs in the coalition's campaign, which is how he found out about Crazy Mountain Wind. "You can't just go sticking crap like that in front of the mountains—that's going to be right in the middle of one of my best picture spots," Droeger said. He posted a new ad on Facebook for his framed Crazies photographs: "Quick! Get your landscape photos . . . Before there is a big stupid windfarm in front of them!!!"

Droeger got an idea. He went on Pattern's website to see what kind of wind towers they'd be using. Then he got busy on Photoshop, filling one of his landscape photos of the Crazies with skyscraper-sized GE turbines.

"Wherever there was a high spot, I stuck one—they're not going to stick them in the low spots, they're going to stick it on a hill," Droeger reasoned. He started out with a Crazies-in-winter shot, but the turbines didn't stand out enough against the snow—too much white. He used a summer scene instead. When he was finished, Droeger posted his photo simulation on the *Buzz* with the tag "For the people who are visual learners." Then he forgot about it, until it turned up in his mailbox as the latest flyer from the Sweet Grass Neighbors Coalition.

The flyer showed a split-screen view of the Crazies. In the first image, the mountains towered over the Yellowstone in their snow-mantled majesty as a BNSF freight train chugged past, its cars loaded with coal. The second image was identical to the first, but filled with wind turbines, massive turbines that rose so high and were so thickly clustered, it was hard to see the eleven-thousand-foot mountain range behind them. "Save the Last Best Place! We need your help!" the flyer read.

Monica went on the coalition's website to figure out who was behind it. She remembered Puyear from the PSC. "Neighbors," she snorted. It sounded so friendly. "Well, I'm not so sure I'd call 'em *neighbors*," said Alfred, who had brought home the flyer from one of his twice-weekly trips to the mailbox.

The Crazy Mountain Neighbors Coalition petition gathered just under five hundred signatures. Shawley cross-checked the list. There were five fake names and thirty-one duplicate registrations. Out-of-state residents accounted for seventy-five signatures. Of the 352 Montanans who had signed the petition, fifty-two lived in Big Timber—so, 3 percent of the town's population. Elizabeth and Whitney MacMillan had signed; so had Bob Faw and Beccy Oberly.

The names Gordy, Engwis, and Chesnoff were nowhere to be found on the petition to stop Crazy Mountain Wind. But they did appear on a new lawsuit against Sweet Grass County, filed just hours before a scheduled vote on Crazy Mountain Wind's road-use agreement in January. After more than a year of deadlock, the county had three commissioners again: Bill Wallace, J. V. Moody, and Melanie Roe, a construction company owner and past president of the Park Electric Cooperative. In their complaint, Gordy, Engwis, and Chesnoff charged that the county was ceding too much control over its roads to the wind farm. The vote was delayed. But on February 1, the commissioners unanimously approved the road-use agreement—despite the lawsuit.

"We didn't do this for Pattern. We did it for the county," Moody told the *Pioneer*. He had seen the chatter on the *Buzz*, read the mean comments that he was supporting Crazy Mountain Wind out of greed— because his kids would cash in on their granddad's wind farm. Moody didn't mind being unpopular. He was stationed in Jordan during the height of the Montana Freemen movement in the mid-1990s. The Freemen were heavily armed white supremacists who led an anti-government movement from a farm they called Justus Township. They issued phony checks and fake arrest warrants and harassed local officials, judges, and sheriffs. One night, the Freemen nailed a warrant to Trooper Moody's door, threatening to hang him from a bridge. So, he wasn't going to lose sleep over some nasty remarks on Facebook. But bringing his kids into the mix—that pissed him off.

It was Super Bowl weekend. With Crazy Mountain Wind's injunction hearing just two weeks away, the citizenry of Big Timber took a break from fighting over windmills to focus on the one thing everyone could get behind: football.

Moody was at home, watching the New England Patriots play the Los Angeles Rams, when the Budweiser commercial came on. Ears flapping in a stiff breeze, a dalmatian sat atop a wagon of beer pulled by the famous Clydesdales through golden fields of grain. "The answer my friend, is blowin' in the wind," Bob Dylan sang, as the camera pulled back to reveal scores of turbines arrayed before a majestic mountain range, blades slowly turning, white nacelles emblazoned with the red Budweiser logo. "Now brewed with wind power for a better tomorrow," Moody read, and almost died laughing. The Budweiser Clydesdales were trotting through a wind farm.

17

SHOW PONIES

February 19, 2019
Park County Courthouse
Livingston, Montana

W. SCOTT MITCHELL, *Representing Pattern and Crazy Mountain*
Wind, LLC:
The issue in this case, and more particularly the issue before the Court
in this preliminary injunction motion, is whether four landowners who
don't want a windfarm built on their neighbors' property can veto that
and put an end to it before it is even constructed. And the answer to
that question is unequivocally, no.

FEBRUARY 18, 2019
HILTON GARDEN INN
BOZEMAN, MONTANA

Monica spent Presidents' Day weekend skiing with the girls in Big Sky,
where her brother Dan had a condo and they could take advantage of the
family discount. After a day on the slopes with their cousins, the girls went
home to Missoula in the minivan with a babysitter, and Monica rented a car
and drove to the Bozeman Hilton, where Pattern had set up its war room.

It was late, around 6 p.m., when she found the Pattern guys in a conference room with Scott Mitchell and Shane Coleman, litigators from the
Billings law firm who'd be arguing their case. They had converged on
Bozeman from all points of Pattern's corporate empire. Daniel Elkort,
executive vice president and chief legal officer of Pattern Energy Group,
had flown in from San Francisco; Jeremy Rosenshine, assistant general
counsel, was there from New York to work with the local defense team.

The lawyers were huddled with Allen Wynn, Pattern Development's chief environmental manager, and Ward Marshall, its senior director of business development, both from Pattern's Houston office. The last time Monica had seen Ward was at Marty's memorial service.

"Hey everybody," Monica said as they turned in their seats, a bunch of pasty white guys who looked like they hadn't seen the sun in weeks.

Coleman was practicing his direct examination with Ward, lobbing softball questions about Crazy Mountain Wind's layout. Charles Shawley sat the conference table with them, correcting Ward, providing additional information about the rules on turbine setbacks, and generally annoying the lawyers. Pattern's man on the ground had traded his room at the Big Timber Super 8—where he'd been pretty much the only guest since January—for the sybaritic luxury of the Hilton Garden Inn. He would be on hand all week to provide the Pattern team with whatever it needed.

Ward Marshall had never testified in a court proceeding before. The lawyers prepped him on how to answer the opposing lawyers' questions. Just tell the truth, was the main thing. The opposing counsel would try to fluster you, to tie you up in knots. Clear, concise answers were good. "Correct," or "Yes" or "No," were even better.

Monica dropped her backpack on a chair and shook off her brown duffel coat, listening as Coleman badgered Marshall a bit to prepare him for the opposing counsel's cross-examination.

In the months leading up to the hearing, Monica had exchanged emails with the Billings lawyers to discuss strategy. They hadn't seemed very interested in her take on the case. Monica wanted to strike back against the Oligarchs. She suggested filing counterclaims against Gordy, Chesnoff, Engwis, and MacMillan for obstructing a lawful project.

"I was like, 'Screw these bastards, let's sue them back. You've got a $100 million contract,'" she recalled. Elkort, Pattern's head legal honcho, threw a bucket of ice water on that plan. He told Monica they weren't that kind of company.

Pattern wasn't about to get in the trenches and lob grenades. It was walking between a narrow set of lines throughout this litigation, defending its interests while maintaining the role of responsible corporate citizen. Pattern was a good neighbor, and it wasn't neighborly to trash-talk the plutocrats next door. Elkort was fond of quoting Michelle Obama: "When they go low, we go high."

Sitting in the conference room at the Hilton, Monica felt like a hick. It was like her first days rowing at Vesper, when the suave Ivy Leaguers called her "Flipper" and she was killing fish with her oar. Everyone on the Pattern defense team was respectful, but she had been sidelined. Monica decided not to take it personally. Mitchell and Coleman were experienced litigators. Elkort and Rosenshine were corporate lawyers at the top of their field. These guys were the pros; they knew what they were doing. Monica figured her clients would be okay.

Mitchell's strategy was to keep Pattern's defense focused on the law and the science. The plaintiffs had brought a nuisance case riddled with baseless claims against a state-of-the-art renewable-energy project that would provide electricity to twenty-six thousand Montana homes and benefit the local economy. The case, as Team Pattern saw it, boiled down to one question: whether the project's opponents should be allowed to effectively shut down a lawful, economically beneficial development just because they didn't like it.

Gordy, Chesnoff, Engwis, and MacMillan were bringing in a boat-load of expert witnesses. The next two days would be dominated by eagles, owls, songbirds, bats, prairie dogs. Wild Eagle Mountain's attorneys were petitioning the judge to make a site visit. They wanted him to experience the beautiful scenery for himself, and to see the met towers—"a haunting foreshadow of the dramatic change to the viewshed certain to occur if the development of Crazy Mountain Windfarm proceeds."

The Pattern team would not indulge in such theatrics. Marshall and Wynn would guide the judge through the details of the project and the extensive environmental studies that had been conducted. Then Pattern would call two expert witnesses: Mike Hankard, an acoustical consultant, and Christopher Ollson, an environmental scientist who specialized in health issues related to the energy industry. Both men were leaders in their fields. Pattern's defense team was confident their testimony would dispel the miasma of misinformation that had surrounded Crazy Mountain Wind. Their experts were going to hit it out of the park.

But the main reason that Pattern's defense team wanted to keep it tight was the calendar. It was now late February. Construction on Crazy

Mountain Wind had to begin in early April if they were going to meet the guaranteed operation date in their power purchase agreement. Everything hinged on that date: it was the contract's bright-line. They couldn't cross it if they were to hang on to their deal with NorthWestern Energy.

Pattern needed to wrap up the hearing as quickly as possible. The defense team would urge Judge Oldenburg to make a decision from the bench, as soon as both sides in the hearing had made their case. They had faith that he would see through the plaintiffs' motives and they didn't want to spend added weeks waiting for a written opinion. If the judge dismissed the lawsuit—which, given the strength of their case, they thought was a reasonable assumption—then they could hire contractors, close project financing, and complete all the final steps needed to get Crazy Mountain Wind up and running by the start of 2020.

But as Monica listened to Coleman going over Marshall's direct testimony with him, asking technical questions about the project, burrowing into the nitty-gritty details—Shawley jumping in with extra details—she thought it all sounded so dry, so emotionless. The longer she listened, the more frustrated she became. Where was their fire? If Marty was alive, he'd have been breathing fire and brimstone. She'd have put him on the stand to tell the judge about the nonstop war of litigation that these wankers had waged against her clients. If it was me and Marty, she thought—but it wasn't. It was just her.

"I'm going to give an opening statement," she announced.

Crazy Mountain Wind was Pattern's project, but it was Rick and Alfred's ground—the judge needed to understand that their basic property rights were at stake. Rick and Alfred's neighbors—some of the richest people on earth—were trying to control the fraction of land that they didn't own. This case was about Jarrett and Anderson and their families. It was about the future of Montana ranches that generations of Jarretts and Andersons had worked so hard to hang on to.

Mitchell and Coleman hadn't planned on making an opening statement—too time-consuming. But they liked Monica's idea. Rick and Alfred should be front and center. The old ranchers would appeal to the judge's sympathies.

"Everybody was using them," Monica said. "We were going to be the show ponies."

OPENING STATEMENTS
February 19, 2019
Park County Courthouse
Livingston, Montana

INGA PARSONS, *for the plaintiffs*:
The plaintiffs are not against wind, Your Honor, and they're not
against wind in Montana, but they are against wind, as any Montanan
and certainly anybody in these counties who live here would want.
They're against a commercial wind development in the jewel—the
crown jewel, if you will, Your Honor—of Big Timber, near the
Yellowstone River, in front of the Crazy Mountains.

The first day of the hearing was scheduled for 1 p.m., to allow Judge
Oldenburg enough time to drive the 136 miles from Lewistown after a
morning of hearings in his own courtroom. Monica, who liked to get to
court early, piled her exhibits in the jury box and dumped her brown duffel coat on one of the twelve seats. She had spent a fitful night in a hotel in
Livingston, cross-examining witnesses in her sleep. That morning, when
she was getting ready, she impulsively put her hair in a braid. Monica
never wore braids, but it seemed more Montana. She wanted to show the
court that her clients were the real Montana, unlike these millionaires and
billionaire interlopers. She'd be the cowgirl of the defense team.
    They were calving around the clock on the Crazy Mountain Cattle
Company, and Harv was occupied with the mother cows, so Jami drove
to Livingston on her own. She pulled up in front of the courthouse just
as Gordy arrived in his shiny black sport utility vehicle, his ranch manager at the wheel. She stared at him, realizing that Gordy had zero idea
who she was.
    Once inside the big double doors of the courtroom she thought
of as the Royal Blue Disaster—the whole building was an ode to the
seventies—Jami saw that the room had divided itself down the middle:
plaintiffs on the left, defendants on the right. Jan and Karen Engwis
were sitting up front, staring straight ahead, not even glancing across the
aisle where Lois and Rick had taken their seats, behind a row of Pattern
executives. Jami was relieved to see Rick had on his good suspenders,

not the ones that were held together with baling twine. As nervous as she was, her dad was in his element. Having all his enemies assembled in one room energized Rick.

He'd always taken pleasure in being excessively polite to people who hated him, crossing the street to say hello instead of looking the other way. When Karen Engwis drove down the county road in her John Deere Gator at fifteen miles an hour, refusing to let him pass, he'd tool along patiently behind her. When she finally turned off the road, he'd honk his horn and wave. All those county commission meetings where he'd sat opposite Jan, watching him argue and get red in the face—it never bothered Rick. He kind of enjoyed it. Jan was an asshole. It felt good to fight Jan.

Being in court felt very good. Rick was excited for the hearing that was about to begin, ready to enjoy the whole spectacle of it. Wrong was wrong and right was right. Every rancher should have the right to develop their resources, and wind was a resource. It was like he had a gold mine on his place, and these sons of bitches had kept him from digging it. They were used to buying their way through everything, but some things couldn't be bought. Pattern was standing up to the millionaires and billionaires. It was going to be fun to see those guys get what was coming to them.

Lois gazed with open curiosity at Russell Gordy as he entered the courtroom. She and Rick weren't dating anymore. They were better as friends, she had decided. Since the Frosty Freez had closed, Rick had gotten in the habit of stopping by Lois's home on the Boulder River for coffee. As his Parkinson's got worse, Lois went with him to meetings and helped him where she could. That was her role that day at the courthouse: to support Rick. But honestly, she wouldn't have missed the hearing for anything.

Gordy sat down in a back row, stony-faced, keeping to himself. David Chesnoff arrived with his wife, Diana, in her dark sunglasses. Her face didn't have a wrinkle on it; Lois wondered how the poor woman could close her eyes at night. Chesnoff wore a tailored navy suit. He had tucked his trouser cuffs into a pair of gray Ugg ankle boots. Lois had never seen a man in Uggs—they were something high school girls wore. Maybe he had a sore foot and couldn't put real shoes on, she thought.

Alfred arrived with his granddaughter, looking like he had come straight from the sheep shed. He nodded at Jimmy Hogemark's wife, Roxie, who was sitting on the opposite side of the aisle with a notepad in her lap. Roxie was going to write down everything that happened that day, so she could report it to Jim when she got home.

Elkort and his team were seated up front. They had done a little digging into Oldenburg after the plaintiffs had Judge Gilbert removed from the case. The judge, who was a few years from retirement, wasn't a well-known quantity. None of Oldenburg's rulings had grabbed headlines. But he had the reputation of being a judge's judge—even-handed.

Judge Oldenburg called the case to order and asked all the attorneys to introduce themselves. The plaintiffs' table was crowded. Elizabeth Greenwood was joined by her cocounsel, Inga Parsons, and by Stephen Woodruff, Engwis's longtime attorney. Greenwood and Parsons would argue the case and cross-examine the witnesses. Woodruff's role was limited. Mostly, he made objections, which Oldenburg would invariably overrule.

Wild Eagle Mountain Ranch, the latecomer to the lawsuit, was represented by a pair of young lawyers: Nicholas Lofing and Andrew Person, a former army officer and one-term Democratic state representative who graduated law school in 2015.

"Let's get going on the motion for the preliminary injunction," Oldenburg said.

Monica began her opening statement by displaying a topographical map of the land north of the Yellowstone River that she'd had blown up and mounted on foam board. The map was blanketed in colorful squares. Monica gave the judge a tour. The sea of yellow squares extending from the Yellowstone all the way up into the Crazies represented the sections of land that Russell Gordy owned. The right side of the map was a wash of blue squares—that was Whitney MacMillan's Wild Eagle Mountain Ranch. Engwis's red squares didn't cover as much ground as Gordy's and MacMillan's did, but they still dwarfed the small pink-and-green block wedged in at the base of the map. The pink was Alfred Anderson, the green was Rick Jarrett. Combined, their land added up to just four and a half squares.

The Montana legislature had expressly authorized wind projects, explicitly encouraged wind development, with powerful incentives such as tax abatement. These statutes—Monica had come prepared with copies, which she now handed out—immunized Mr. Jarrett and Mr. Anderson from the nuisance claims that the plaintiffs had brought against them.

"Could I interpose an objection?" Woodruff said. "This is lengthy legal discussion. Ms. Tranel presented this as a brief opening of about five minutes. We have a number of witnesses to call."

"Overruled. Keep it short, Ms. Tranel," Oldenburg said.

"I think I have about two and a half more minutes," Monica said.

Jaffe had slipped into the gallery. He planned to attend all three days of the hearing. Even though WINData hadn't entered the lawsuit, he and Chloe had a lot at stake. If Crazy Mountain Wind didn't get built, they would lose out on Marty's $2.39 million payout.

"Mr. Jarrett and Mr. Anderson have private property rights to have this wind project built on their ground. No zoning prohibits it," Monica said, and urged the judge to rule quickly. "If this project is enjoined it won't get built, and my clients are at risk of losing their ground."

In his brief opening statement for Pattern, Mitchell asked the judge to consider the time crunch that his client was under. His client had spent close to $10 million on Crazy Mountain Wind. The wind farm had to be delivering electricity to the grid by December 31, 2019—just a hair over ten months away. "If this motion is granted, or if this motion languishes, this project is dead. It's that simple, because of the PPA," he said.

Greenwood's cocounsel, Inga Parsons, delivered an impromptu response. A former clinical law professor and assistant federal defender in New York's Southern District, Parsons divided her time between Marblehead, Massachusetts, where she had a law office, and Pinedale, Wyoming. Like Greenwood, she was a Wyoming native. The women had another thing in common: both were quite tall. Greenwood posted a picture of herself with Parsons on Facebook and captioned it "Twin Towers."

Parsons' style was forceful, emotional—dramatic, even. "Our clients actually came here for the purpose of being in a quiet, undisturbed, dark skies, beautiful area, where the eagles run free," she told the court. If the wind project was built, those eagles would not fly free. "They will fly into five-hundred-by-three-hundred-foot turbines, Your Honor. They will be Cuisinarted."

Parsons appealed for sympathy for her clients. For Mr. Gordy, who wanted to build his spa but couldn't, because no one would come to a tourist attraction to look at five-hundred-foot turbines that spun all day and flashed all night. For the Engwises, who bought their land in order to conserve and preserve it. "Then you have Mr. Chernoff and his wife, Diana's Great Idea. And it was a really great idea then, but it's not looking so much if this project comes through." A flicker of annoyance passed across Chesnoff's face when Parsons got his name wrong.

All Montanans—and actually, all Americans—would be impacted by the irreparable damage that was about to be done, Parsons declared. "This is the last great place on earth. Let's keep it so. Thank you, Your Honor." As she took her seat, Parsons seemed on the verge of tears.

The plaintiffs called their first witness: Ross Crandall, the wildlife biologist who had spent years tracking the eagles on Jan and Karen Engwis's ranch. Crandall, now executive director of Craighead Beringia South, had driven from Wyoming to testify in the hearing. He wasn't being paid; Crandall was glad to be able to share his knowledge about eagles for the plaintiffs' cause.

The wind farm site was home to a lot of golden eagles—an unusually large number, he told the court. There were twenty-seven golden eagle nests within a ten-mile buffer of the project area that Crandall and his research associate had documented, and he had observed seventeen distinct pairs of eagles. Crandall feared that the wind farm would not only kill eagles, but permanently disrupt an important habitat.

Golden eagles suffered higher levels of mortality from wind turbines than other birds. They had that in common with another avian species: Hungarian partridges. Crandall had attached four studies on wind turbines and avian mortality to his affidavit, including a 2008 paper on the Altamont Pass wind farm—the sprawling complex of thousands of latticed turbines built in Northern California in the 1980s.

Monica kept her cross-examination brief. "Helicopters, do they kill birds?" she asked. She intended to ask Gordy about his helicopter when he was on the stand.

Crandall said he was sure that helicopters had killed birds.

"I don't have any further questions," she said.

Coleman brought up the eleven-year-old Altamont study Crandall had referenced. Would he agree that lots of things had changed in the wind energy industry since the early 1980s? Did he know that at least half of those Altamont turbines had been replaced as a result of the very study that he had cited? Would he agree that there was a difference between twenty-two turbines and 5,400 turbines?

"Yeah, of course," Crandall said.

Coleman did not ask Crandall about a prime focus of his research: lead poisoning. The wildlife biologist had spent years tracking lead exposure in eagles. Almost every autopsy he did on a dead eagle revealed toxic levels of lead in its blood. Crandall's theory was that hunters and their ammunition were the culprit. The golden eagles and bald eagles of Big Timber were facing an immediate threat that had nothing to do with renewable-energy development and everything to do with one of the plaintiff's favorite pastimes.

Most hunting ammunition contains lead—lead-core bullets, shotgun shot, pellets. At the time of writing, Gordy & Sons sold 354 different kinds of ammo on its website; only three were lead-free. Lead ammo fragmented in an animal's viscera. When a hunter disemboweled an elk or deer in the field, lead-flecked gut piles were left behind for eagles—voracious scavengers as well as apex predators. Bird hunters didn't always recover every partridge or grouse shot. In that case, entire pellets of bird shot could be ingested by carrion birds.

Crandall had done a multiyear study on lead exposure in a group of bald eagles and ravens in Wyoming, drawing blood during elk season and again in the off-season. The findings were striking: year after year, the raptors' blood lead levels shot up during hunting season. Privately, Crandall estimated that between 2.5 percent and 4.5 percent of eagle mortalities could be attributed to lead—a far greater percentage than the 1.5 percent of eagles killed by wind turbines. The evidence was everywhere: Two of the golden eagles that Crandall and his associates had been tracking in the Craighead Beringia South nesting study—the same study that the Engwises participated in—had died of lead toxicity. One of those dead eagles was recovered in the vicinity of the Engwis ranch. A few days after the injunction hearing, the *Journal of Raptor Research* would publish Crandall's findings in a paper titled "Survival Estimates and Cause of Mortality of Golden Eagles in South-Central Montana."

None of this came up during Crandall's time on the witness stand.

From her blue bench, Jami thought Crandall had probably made an impression on the judge. The eagle guy knew his shit. But the expert witnesses that followed him were a sideshow. There was an owl guy who had spent the better part of a day driving around with Jan Engwis, looking for owls on his ranch. He didn't find any. Nonetheless, he returned to conduct a five-day raptor survey. Greenwood made the owl guy go through seventeen photographs in detail, naming every raptor species and describing where it had been photographed.

Next up was a songbird expert. The fact that wind turbines killed fewer birds than power lines or cars or cats was nothing to boast about, the songbird guy declared. "It would be like the ninth guy out of ten on the FBI most-wanted list saying, 'Go after the other guys.'"

"Your Honor, I see no reason to examine this witness," Coleman said.

"No, thank you," Monica echoed.

The final witness of the day was David Chesnoff, who had been sitting in the row directly behind his attorneys, occasionally scribbling notes on yellow sticky notes and passing them to Greenwood. After being sworn in, he made a point of spelling his surname. "C-H-E-S-N-O-F-F," he said, enunciating each letter.

Greenwood asked what had been important to David and Diana when they bought their ranch. Chesnoff, staying on theme, said it was the eagles, owls, hawks, songbirds, and owls. "We, also, have a lot of bats," he said. He told the court how much he and Diana enjoyed the dark night skies.

When Greenwood asked about the Pattern team's visit to his ranch that August, and the photo simulations they subsequently sent him, Chesnoff's tone morphed from rhapsodic to outraged. "I got them and almost fell off my chair," he said. The Pattern team had told him he would only see a few windmills. "They basically lied to me or deceived me," he said. "When I got the pictures, there's—I don't remember the exact count, but it's a lot and they're tall and they're visible."

Chesnoff told the court that he and Diana were thinking of bequeathing their Montana ranch to the Wounded Warriors organization, for veterans to enjoy after they were gone. "I can't imagine that someone suffering with PTSD wants to hear 'swoosh, swoosh, swoosh,'" he said. "That was, for the court reporter, a swishing sound."

Before his cross-examination, Coleman put up a large exhibit. It was a photo simulation of the view from Chesnoff's lodge, looking east toward Springdale. The turbines were not immediately apparent; on closer inspection, they appeared as distant white toothpicks against the bright blue sky—entire turbines, blades, and blade tips. It looked nothing like Brandon Droeger's photoshopped mass mailer.

Coleman displayed two more simulations—more distant, thin white lines—and asked if these were the same pictures that had almost toppled Chesnoff from his chair. "I can't say this one is what I was surprised by, but I'm still surprised by this," Chesnoff replied, adding that he still saw far more than two and a half turbines. Coleman had no further questions.

Greenwood objected. Maybe they were different pictures than the ones Chesnoff had received, she said. Perhaps someone from Pattern went and took those pictures when he wasn't there. They must have done something to the colors, to make it look weird.

Oldenburg excused Chesnoff from the stand. "Nice to meet you," Chesnoff said, as though they'd just been chatting at a professional gathering. "Nice to meet you, sir," the judge replied. "Given the time of day, let's break for the afternoon."

The defense team was dismayed. The plaintiffs' first four witnesses had taken up the entire afternoon, with six more expert witnesses still to come. And Judge Oldenburg was still mulling over their motion for a site visit—another giant time suck. Monica told the judge that Jarrett and Anderson objected to the proposed site visit.

"So noted," Oldenburg said.

TESTIMONY

February 20, 2019
Park County Courthouse
Livingston, Montana

JAMES ESPERTI, PARTNER, FAY RANCHES, *having first been*
duly sworn, testified as follows:

Q: What is the reality of the effect of an industrial wind development
being placed in the location where Pattern Energy is proposing to
place it?

MR. ESPERTI: You know, everybody certainly has their own view of
what reality is, but you know, from my perspective, and you know,
what I've been asked to do is market and sell the ranch . . . it's just
my opinion, but from my experience, I really think if someone had
a choice of investing in an asset like a ranch, they'd much prefer not
to have a wind farm next to it. I think, if they had their choice, they
would, in my opinion, a hundred percent of the time say, "I'll take
the ranch with no windmills in sight."

Judge Oldenburg began the second day of the hearing by announcing
the court's intention to make a site visit. He wanted to see the lay of the
land. They would break for the day at four o'clock and drive there in
his Chevy Traverse—the judge and his law clerk, John, with one lawyer
from the defendants' side and one lawyer from the plaintiffs' side. "We'd
need a bus to take all the lawyers out there," Oldenburg said.

Now that the field trip was inevitable, Monica insisted that Jarrett
and Anderson needed to be represented in the judge's Chevy Traverse.
She'd ride in the wayback if necessary. "We've got two seats in the back.
My wife says you don't know how uncomfortable they are, because you
never ride back there, but if you're willing to, then we'll certainly accommodate you," Oldenburg told her.

The first witness of the morning was the Engwises' real estate agent,
James Esperti. Back in 2001, Esperti had sold the ranch to Jan and
Karen. Sixteen years later, after working through another broker and

then trying unsuccessfully to market the ranch on their own, they hired him to sell it again. The Engwis ranch was back on the market for $19.5 million. Esperti was a partner with Fay Ranches, a luxury brokerage. He showed off the glossy multipage sales brochure he had created for the Engwis ranch.

"If you flip through this, the main focus is on the wildlife and the recreation, and the beauty of the land, of course," Esperti said. "So, really, we are marketing to the folks from their emotional side." The prospect of a wind project next door had dampened the emotional appeal of the Engwis ranch, Esperti said. His top-tier buyers were holding back, waiting to see what happened.

Greenwood submitted the Engwis ranch brochure as an exhibit.

Alfred Anderson arrived with his granddaughter a little late, after feeding and watering his herd. He'd be taking the stand that afternoon. As he settled himself on his blue bench, Greenwood was questioning a bat expert from Springfield, Missouri. MacMillan and Gordy and the rest of them, they had a lot of million-dollar witnesses, Alfred thought.

The bat witness described the importance of bats and their value to agriculture. Citing a list compiled by the Montana Heritage Project, he said there were possibly a dozen different bat species near the wind farm. And yet Pattern hadn't searched for bat roosts in the trees and rocky bluffs.

Alfred listened to the man go on, saying stuff about red bats and brown bats and hoary bats and silver-hair bats. He supposed some of those bats would have to move out a little when the windmills came, but they'd come right back again soon enough. There'd always be bats, he guessed. Alfred was not fond of bats. A bat once found its way into his bedroom and bit Dorothy as she slept. Alfred killed it right away. It came back rabid, and Dorothy had to get a full course of rabies shots, which was news in Big Timber. "Shades of Dracula," the *Pioneer* called it.

During his cross-examination for Pattern, Mitchell pointed out that the list the bat expert had referenced included some species that lived four hundred miles from the Crazy Mountain Wind site, in places like Sidney and Glendive. He asked the man if he could tell him where Sidney was—or Glendive. "I cannot," he replied.

"Sir, how many times have you been to Montana?" Mitchell asked.

"This is the first time," the bat man replied.

Greenwood asked the court for a short break so that they could set up for their next witness: Dean Apostol, a scenic impact assessor from Portland, Oregon, who would present a slideshow. Mitchell objected. "This is irrelevant and a waste of all our time to be going through this," he said. He was overruled.

Apostol described his work as a blend of art and science. His team, which included a photographer and a mapping expert, had spent several days doing field analyses. Their guide was Jan Engwis, who showed them around the various ranches in his pickup truck, capping off the tour with a visit to his antique car collection.

Although it had been cold and gusty as hell, Apostol couldn't help noticing that this was a very scenic landscape. It had naturalness—very important. It had mountains and cliffs and outcrops. It had complex vegetation in the form of shrubs and trees. And to top it all off, it had water—an actual river running through it, just like the book by Norman Maclean. That was a big plus.

Apostol asked the court to douse the lights. The first slide showed a profusion of flowers, with a hand-painted "Healing Garden" sign. There was also a picture of a river and a quote from a *A River Runs through It*. Greenwood handed Apostol a pointer and asked him to describe the benefits of a scenic landscape.

"Life enhancement, identity, stability, calming, imagination, adventure, stimulation, illustrated by Montana being called 'the last best place.' Why is it called the last best place?" Apostol asked. "Scenery."

Clicking past the idyllic vistas, he moved on to images of wind turbines—phalanxes of thickly clustered towers, in daytime and at night, glowing an infernal orange. An illustration showed a Boeing 747 standing on its nose next to a wind turbine. The turbine was taller. Another slide showed a picture of the First Interstate Center in Billings—Montana's tallest building. The hub of the turbine was almost as tall as the bank headquarters; when you added in the blades, it was taller.

There were many scenic issues with wind energy. Turbines were impossible to hide. They were very tall, and they were very white, which clashed with the earth tones of the landscape. And then there was the problem of how turbines were arranged. Wind farms were chaotic, with turbines everywhere, blades overlapping. Or they were too orderly, which was even worse.

"Like, they're in straight rows in a very natural landscape, so they're introducing kind of an order to a disorderly landscape," Apostol explained.

That was wind energy for you—everything against it, Jaffe thought from his spot in the gallery. Green is good. Go green, recycle. Everyone driving Teslas but no one wanting to see a wind farm.

Monica objected. The wind farms Apostol had shown were nothing like Crazy Mountain Wind. "There was a lot of material in there that wasn't relevant at all."

"Overruled," Oldenburg said.

"Your Honor, the plaintiffs would call Jan Engwis," Parsons said. Once he had been duly sworn, she asked if it was true that his ranch was up for sale.

"Unfortunately, that is correct," said Engwis. "I need to move on. I'm getting old."

The fiery inquisitor of the Sweet Grass County annex had been replaced by a mild-mannered senior citizen, worn down by his neighbor's relentless wind development efforts. His wife had a debilitating illness. After six challenges from these wind farms and his neighbors, Jan and Karen and their handicapped son had had enough. The wind farmers were tearing their hearts out, tearing the heart out of the Yellowstone Valley. Yes, he had put up the ranch for sale. As yet, he had not been approached by the type of buyer who he believed would sustain the environment that they had created—that the good Lord had provided for them.

Engwis described a ridge on the western edge of his ranch, a beautiful piece of land with spectacular views in every direction. There was a buildable area on that ridge where a future owner of the ranch might want to create a home, he said. That magnificent piece of land overlooked the wind farm site. To mar that landscape with wind turbines would be a desecration, Engwis said. Once that viewscape was gone, it could never be obtained again.

"It's built of unobtanium, to pick a word," Engwis said. "You simply cannot reacquire it. I don't know why people don't understand that."

During his cross-examination of Engwis, Mitchell returned to the subject of wildlife. One of Pattern's main arguments was that the plaintiffs had no business suing them over the wind farm's alleged threat to eagles and the other creatures they loved to photograph and observe, because wildlife was a public resource.

"You understand that just because those animals, that wildlife, is on your property, that's not something you own. You understand that, correct?" Mitchell asked. The landowners had no claim over those creatures; Montana's department of Wildlife, Fish, and Parks did.

"Well, only ostensibly," Engwis said. "You'll see that the landowner is the ultimate manager."

Listening to Engwis put Jaffe in mind of his father's rants about Californians—Marty's catchall term for wealthy out-of-staters who moved to Montana. He blamed Californians for the hundreds of miles of rumble strips the state DOT had started installing on the highways. They'd be driving to a project site—Marty speeding, using all the pavement as he went around a turn—and then he'd hit that rumble strip. "Fucking Californians, gotta move here and fuck everything up," he'd say. Jaffe imagined Marty up there on the stand, shredding these assholes who thought the eagles were their fucking eagles.

Monica showed Engwis a copy of an easement agreement that a previous owner of his ranch had signed with a wind developer and asked him to read it. "It's so small, I can't determine what it is," he said. She offered to enlarge it.

"That would be very helpful, thank you. I'm too old to see very well," he said. Monica asked the judge for permission to approach. "Don't worry about me, I'm harmless," Engwis assured her.

Monica switched tack. Didn't Mr. Engwis sue Sweet Grass County over the wind project back in 2014? And didn't he sue the Department of National Resources and Conservation before that? Wasn't it true that he had sued Sweet Grass County again, just last month, over a road-use agreement for the wind farm?

Monica wanted to show the judge that the plaintiffs had used litigation as a weapon against Crazy Mountain Wind for over a decade. "Our argument here is there's a strategy of delay that has been successful," she said. But she struggled to gain traction. Judge Oldenburg wouldn't allow her to submit a timeline that she had created, which began with the installation of Rick Jarrett's first met tower in 2004 and led up to the plaintiffs' recent lawsuit against Sweet Grass County. And Parsons gave her no quarter, objecting and interrupting as she questioned Engwis about his various lawsuits.

"Counsel, we are not here for you two to argue," Judge Oldenburg scolded.

Parsons was getting in Monica's head. Monica had been flabbergasted by her emotional opening statement. All that poetry about the dark night skies of Montana from this out-of-towner in designer clothes. Parsons reminded Monica of that Baby Ariel music video the girls watched over and over. "I've got Gucci on my body," she hummed to herself as she washed her hands after crossing paths with Parson in the courthouse lady's room.

Monica wished she had delivered a rebuttal to Parsons' opening statement. She could have given her own speech, about growing up on a ranch in eastern Montana. How the school bus would drop her off at the end of the drive, and she'd walk three miles to the ranch house under those dark Montana skies, hearing the coyotes howl.

Engwis's vision seemed to deteriorate with each new document Monica produced. "Sorry to bother you again, I just can't see that," he said. "Now what am I looking at?"

"Mr. Engwis, your testimony, as I understood it, was that your first notice of the wind development was quite late. Is that true?" she finally asked.

"I'm sorry, I don't understand your question. I don't know what 'quite late' means," he replied.

Jami shifted on her royal blue bench, frustrated. Jan seemed so meek on the stand, going on about that ridge and how beautiful the lookout was. She wished that Monica would needle him some more, get him to lose his cool. Judge Oldenburg wasn't seeing the belligerent, empurpled, name-calling Engwis that Jami knew. One row over, Shawley was thinking the same thing. Who is this guy, and what has he done with Jan Engwis? he wondered.

Court recessed for lunch. The Jarretts and Andersons met Monica at the Stockman, a local place with plastic green tablecloths, worn laminate floors, and Christmas lights roped around the rafters. When you ordered the steak, that's what you got: a big slab of meat reposing in its own reddish-brown juices, with a chunk of Texas toast on the side. They figured they'd be safe there from the Oligarchs and their top-dollar attorneys.

Rick and Alfred would both take the stand that afternoon. Monica had worked with them on their testimony. She took some pride in her preparation of witnesses. It was her job to show them how they fit into the case—to help them understand what the overarching story was, and their part in it.

But Rick and Alfred were challenging witnesses. Both men were hard of hearing—Alfred extremely so, not to mention practically blind. And Rick had a chip on his shoulder. Monica thought there was a distinct possibility that opposing counsel would be told to fuck off during Rick's cross-examination.

"Dad, don't get defensive, you got nothing to hide," Jami said. At the Sweet Grass County Courthouse, she worked with witnesses who would testify in criminal proceedings. People got flustered on the stand. Even police officers. She'd tell them to be sure to mention something important. Then, sure enough, they'd be sworn in, start answering questions, and forget.

There was really just one thing each man needed to tell the judge: "You want this wind farm because you need the money to keep your ranch." Monica went over it with them again. She asked Alfred why he needed the wind farm, what he would do with that money. Alfred said he thought he'd improve his livestock. He could buy a bull with better genetics, one that threw offspring with better slaughter value.

Monica asked Alfred to please not talk about the bull. "You want this wind farm because you need the money to keep your ranch," she told him. "You need to say that you will be harmed if it doesn't get built."

After lunch, the plaintiffs' attorneys raised an issue with the judge. Monica had subpoenaed Chris Puyear, the lobbyist behind the Crazy Mountain Neighbors Coalition. She wanted to get him on the stand so she could expose the neighbors coalition for what it was: a well-financed propaganda campaign paid for by the plaintiffs. Unsurprisingly, the plaintiffs objected. Strategies 360 had been hired to aid in the counsel's representation of her clients, Greenwood argued. Therefore, Puyear's work for them was legally privileged.

The Pattern team didn't want Monica to call Puyear, either. They didn't understand what she hoped to accomplish. It was a distracting sideshow that would just eat up more valuable minutes. Mitchell and Coleman were already in a state of high anxiety about the time that would be lost to that afternoon's field trip.

"Judge, I can make this easy," Monica said, and withdrew the subpoena. At least she had put Texas Inc. on notice, she told herself.

Gordy took the stand. He had been very fortunate in life, he told the court. He had been looking for a special piece of land that stretched from the river to the mountains, and he'd been lucky enough to get it, by amassing seven different ranches and putting them together. One was the site of the famous Hunter's Hot Springs resort. Greenwood showed the judge the Hunter's Hot Springs album that Gordy and his wife, Glenda, had put together. Then she showed him the architectural renderings for Gordy's boutique spa and hotel.

"If we are successful in our preliminary injunction and subsequently at trial, would you proceed to build that project?" Greenwood asked.

"Absolutely." Gordy was emphatic. "No question."

Listening, Alfred wondered how much was on the up and up with Gordy. To end up with so darn much, he must have tromped on somebody's feet, getting those oilfields going.

In her cross-examination of Gordy, Monica tried to weave a story for Judge Oldenburg, about a rich outsider who was trying to control his neighbor, a fifth-generation rancher. She submitted an aerial photograph of Gordy's sprawling compound—just one of his homes, she noted—and pointed out the helipad. She quoted from Gordy's interview with a local newspaper, that he never intended the ranch to be his permanent home.

"I still never intend it to be my full-time home," he told Monica. "My wife can't take the cold."

During his initial testimony, Gordy told the court he'd had a guy go out and get every article about Hunter's Hot Springs ever written. He had ten binders full of old newspaper stories and had read them all. Gordy loved history.

"Do you know that Mr. Jarrett's great-great-grandfather owned Hunter's Hot Springs?" Monica asked. The courtroom became very quiet.

A year later, Gordy would recall his interrogation by Monica Tranel with a mirthless chuckle. That gal was something. Definitely a go-getter. He wasn't going to say anything more.

"I did not," he said, in answer to her question.

Coleman cross-examined Gordy for Pattern. He displayed another photo simulation Pattern had created, showing the view of the wind farm from his helipad. Gordy's blue helicopter was down in the right-hand corner, its rotors catching the light. Coleman asked Gordy where he saw windmills. Gordy pointed at a few almost imperceptible lines over the horizon, off to the left. Coleman asked if those were fence posts. "Yeah, there's fence posts right there and the windmill tops are right behind them," he insisted.

Jim Hogemark sat down on the bench next to Roxie. He was in the calving barn day and night this time of year, with some 250 new calves on the ground and another thirty expected that day. But the MacMillans' lawyers had asked Hogemark to testify. Whitney and Betty were in Florida for the winter. They needed him, the lawyers said. Hogemark was their chosen representative.

Hogemark said he'd do it, but he was nervous. Oh ho, he was nervous. What were they gonna ask? he wanted to know. The attorneys told him not to worry, they'd help him through it.

So, here he was. He had agonized for half a second about his beard that morning. When it got cold on Wild Eagle, Jim fuzzed up, was how Roxie put it. He stopped shaving before the calves started coming and let his beard grow till spring. It was the only way to protect himself from the lacerating winds. Remembering the painful spots of frostbite he had gotten on his cheeks one winter, Hogemark put down the razor.

After he was called to the stand, he'd hardly had time to state his name when the lawyer for Jarrett and Anderson objected.

"Judge, if I may be heard?" Monica said. "I object to the testimony of this witness."

Wild Eagle Mountain's owners were the plaintiffs, not Jim Hogemark. He had no business testifying. He didn't own any part of Wild Eagle.

"He's the wrong guy," she said. "I believe he just testified that he's an employee, and that's all he said."

"I understand. That doesn't disqualify him from testifying," the judge said.

So, Jim told the court what it was like being ranch manager on Wild Eagle, and how he'd been calving since the twenty-sixth of January. "I do this for about eighty days this time of year. I'm out day and night, so I see all aspects of the weather, of the beauty of the outside and stuff. So, that's hence why I wear my beard this time of year."

Monica objected when Lofing asked him how the MacMillans enjoyed using their property. "He can't testify about the plaintiffs' experience," she said.

"Overruled, counsel. He can testify to what he sees. He can't testify to what they think," Oldenburg said.

So, Jim told the court about his ranch tours. How the MacMillans enjoyed taking guests around the place, as it was their pride and joy. "Some of that country up there, they've never seen before, or maybe seen once or twice, and I try to show them those places for their enjoyment or their pleasure, just to let them know what they've got," he said. He told a story about a professor friend of Betty and Whitney's, an uppity-up from back East who had been just amazed at all the birds he saw on one of Jim's tours. This time of year in particular, there were eagles all over the place, just flying the ridges and stuff, eating, enjoying life.

Lofing asked Hogemark to try to imagine how the area would change if something like the Judith Gap wind farm got built across the border from the River Ranch. He asked him to imagine what it would be like having forty-four First Interstate Center towers—

Oldenburg interrupted with a scolding.

"Counsel, come on. You know that's not proper argument."

Pattern's lawyer, Mitchell, promised not to keep him long. "It sounds like you're a busy man who needs to get back to tending your mother cows this afternoon," he said. Mitchell asked about the open house Hogemark had attended at the Grand, and his concerns about traffic on the county road where he hauled his hay. "That's a public road you're driving on," he said. It wasn't owned by the MacMillans, was it?

"Nope," Hogemark said.

The ordeal was over in a few minutes, and then Hogemark was back in his seat next to Roxie, who thought he did very well—of course he did.

There was a ten-minute break before the defense called its first witness. When Monica came over to talk to Rick, Lois decided to stretch her legs. David Chesnoff was standing just outside the courtroom, talking to Apostol, the scenery expert from Portland. Thinking maybe she'd say hello to Apostol and chat about Portland, where she'd lived so many years, Lois stopped about four feet away from the men. She stood there in the hallway, just looking at them, waiting for a break in the conversation—or for either of them to pause and notice her. But neither man looked in her direction. They just chatted away.

Chesnoff told Apostol that he was a lawyer. Then he said something about property rights. That got Lois's attention. Chesnoff knew that the property rights issue won out in Montana, he said. Then, with Lois standing right there in front of him, he said something that sounded like "We are just hoping to delay this long enough—four or five months—to kill it once and for all."

Lois was stunned. It was so blatant. Monica had been saying all along that Rick's neighbors filed this motion for a preliminary injunction as a stalling tactic, that they had no intention of actually seeing it go to trial. They just wanted to delay things to death. Now Chesnoff had gone ahead and admitted it in front of her. Lois couldn't believe it. Then she realized that he hadn't even noticed she was there. "I'm in invisible mode for sure," she would later say. Lois, a sixtysomething woman who was five feet, one and three-quarters inches on a good day, was a nonentity to important men like Chesnoff. Suddenly, that seemed like a superpower.

Lois found Monica and started to tell her what she had just overheard. Monica stopped her. "Don't tell me, write it down," she said. Which is what she did. Lois always kept a journal with her. Standing in the doorway to the courtroom, she wrote down everything she had heard, noting the time—2:45 p.m. She could barely read her own writing, her hands were shaking so hard. She tore out the page and gave it to Monica. She offered to clean up the note, to rewrite it, but Monica told her to leave it the way it was.

When Judge Oldenburg called the court back into session, Monica asked to be heard. The plaintiffs had no case, she declared. Mr. Chesnoff had testified that he only spent sixty days a year in Montana. Mr. Engwis had testified that he was planning to leave Montana, because of his wife's health. Mr. Gordy was only here part time. "And with respect to Wild Eagle, they didn't even show up . . . ," she said. "So I ask the Court dismiss this case completely."

"The motion is denied," Oldenburg said. "Call your first witness, please."

Alfred took the stand. Monica asked him the question they'd re-hearsed at lunch: Why did he decide to lease his ground to Crazy Mountain Wind?

"Well, I started out, I wanted more income for the ranch, and I thought there would be extra money for the county. That's why I started out, in the first place," he said.

She nudged him a bit. "Okay. What do you gain by having these wind turbines on your property?"

Alfred had trouble hearing the question, so she repeated it.

"Well, it would be financial gain there," he said.

Monica tried again.

"Can you tell the judge why you want this wind farm here?"

Alfred said primarily he thought he needed it for the extra income, for the ranch. He could put some of it on insurance and taxes, and machinery repairs and fuel and irrigation expenses. He could maybe re-build the corrals, which were kind of rundown. "And then, after that, I think there'd be enough I could probably buy a $10,000 bull," he said. "And then, like she said, retire would be the ultimate goal, I guess."

Monica had gone over this with Alfred: If the wind farm doesn't get built, you will be harmed. When you are on the stand, you have to say, "I will be harmed." It all came down to that one moment.

"How will you be harmed if this isn't built?" she finally asked.

"We'd probably be back to just doing what we're doing, welding machinery up and putting another plank on the corral," Alfred said.

Remembering that moment, Monica would drop her face in her hands and groan. It had been a mistake, trying to get Alfred to say he'd lose his ranch. He was an eighty-seven-year-old Norwegian who would probably die on his feet shearing a sheep. A man like that was never going to say that he was about to lose everything he ever had, because he'd never allow himself to believe it.

Parsons cross-examined Alfred. His property was worth millions of dollars, was it not? More than enough to pay for a little corral work.

"Yah," he replied.

"And you inherited that land," she said.

"No," Alfred said. "Purchased it from my folks."

"And you talked about this being helpful for the community, for the county," Parsons said.

"I can't hear so good anymore," Alfred said.

Parsons repeated the question. "Well, yah, tax-wise," Alfred replied.

But when she asked if Pattern told him to say that—that the project would benefit the community, with the tax revenue and all—Alfred heard her just fine.

"No, no. That's what I decided. That's what I thought," he said firmly.

"And you understand, after having sat here, that these projects are going to block or go up in front of the Crazy Mountains," she said. "You understand that."

Alfred said it depended on your point of view, yah.

"And eagles are going to die."

"That's what they say, anyway."

"And bats are going to die."

Alfred said yah, he supposed.

"No further questions, Your Honor," Parsons said.

The judge told Anderson he could step down.

Returning to his seat, Alfred felt uneasy. It had been different, maybe, than what he was used to. He thought he couldn't hear every question the lawyer asked him. She got kind of passionate about the eagles and bats. Then he was excused. Maybe Alfred hadn't told them everything they wanted to know. He wasn't up there very long, it seemed.

Rick was up next. Monica wanted to show the court a video that his granddaughter Jordan—Jami's daughter, an undergraduate at Cornell—had made. It was about the ranch and the family's history on it, and what sustaining that legacy meant to her.

Parsons objected. The video was hearsay. It was not relevant. It was a sentimental journey. "It's done in a baby doll voice," she said. "I think it's clearly aimed at trying to appeal to the emotions of the Court."

Oldenburg said the court would review the video in chambers.

After Alfred's $10,000 bull, Monica wasn't taking any chances, so she put the question to Rick as bluntly as she knew how: "Can you tell the Court how you will be harmed, if this project isn't built?"

Rick knew what he wanted to say. He had thought a lot about it in his head.

"Well, I won't be able to achieve my goal of passing the ranch down to the next generation, which is really very important to me. The two best crops I've ever raised on the ranch are my grandkids and my kids, and I want to conserve that for the next generations."

Monica, who had promised Pattern's lawyers that she'd get Rick and Alfred on and off the stand fast, in five minutes, said she had no further questions. Rick got up from the witness stand, then sat down again. "I was wanting to be done worse than you," he said, as Parsons rose from the plaintiffs' table to begin her cross.

Parsons observed that generations of Jarretts before Rick had been able to maintain the ranch as a working cattle ranch, without building an industrial wind project on it. She asked about his interview with the *Big Timber Pioneer*, the one that said the wind farm would allow Jarrett's land to recover from decades of aggressive grazing.

"One of the reasons you can't keep your land, Mr. Jarrett, is because you've overgrazed it. Isn't that right?" Parsons said.

"I don't think I told the reporter that. I think he put that in there," Rick said.

Parsons suggested that Rick was building his wind farm to stick it to the rich outsiders. He had bad blood with his neighbors, didn't he? He hadn't contacted Mr. Engwis or Mr. Gordy to tell them about the project.

"Did you contact Mr. Chernoff?" she asked. "Or Mrs. Chernoff?"

"CHESNOFF," Chesnoff said loudly, from his seat in the gallery.

Parsons suggested that Rick's neighbors cared more about the land than he did, because they were preserving their land and he was transforming his into an industrial site by leasing it for wind development.

"You would agree that it changes the area to a commercial use," she said.

"No," Rick said. "It's a crop I can raise on my ranch."

"Well, it's a crop that has five-hundred-foot steel turbines," Parsons said. With spinning blades and lights that flash 24/7, she added.

Monica objected.

"Sustained," Oldenburg said.

"Your Honor, I should be allowed to impeach his notion that this is some kind of crop," Parsons protested.

"Counsel, you're arguing with him," Oldenburg said. "I don't know what we're going to gain by arguing with him."

"Fair enough," said Parsons, switching tack. "In fact, you don't even care what happens to your neighbors, do you?" she asked Rick, quoting another *Pioneer* article. "Isn't it true that you said, 'Their concerns with their property are not my problem, I'm doing things with my property, it has nothing to do with their property'?"

"I was in the middle of a hayfield, trying to put up hay, and this goddamn reporter from some paper started pestering me, and I just finally got tired of it, and I got him to shut up by telling him that, and hung up," Rick said.

Watching from the gallery, Jami wished her dad wouldn't act so defensive and owly. Parsons was being condescending and rude, but cranky didn't play well on the stand. "Fake news," he said, in response to another one of her questions.

When Parsons had finished with him, Monica returned to repair the damage.

"I didn't escape when I tried," Rick said, as she approached.

Monica asked Rick if he had been misquoted in that newspaper article, and if he had in fact aggressively grazed his property.

"In the eighties, sometimes, I aggressively grazed my property. To turn a cow out on it was to aggressively graze it," he said. Owly, Jami thought. She also thought that she'd never seen so many really tall, seriously statuesque women in one room before. Monica, Greenwood, Parsons—they were Amazons. Jami felt like a little Lilliputian.

Parsons cross-examined Rick a second time. She asked why he didn't put his land in a conservation easement instead of causing all these problems with the turbines.

Conservation easements were land trust agreements; ranchers agreed to permanently restrict development on their land in exchange for tax breaks. The Jarretts took a dim view of conservation easements. What good was a tax break when you weren't making any money to start with?

"I don't think I'm causing the problems," Rick said airily, in response to Parsons's question. He had decided to respond to her the same way he did to Karen Engwis when she blocked him on the county road with her Gator—with a toot and a wave.

"But the turbines are," she replied.

"I don't think the turbines are," he replied, pleasantly.

"Well, we'll let the judge decide that," Parsons said.

Oldenburg excused Rick, who said he'd try not to take the chair with him this time.

"I believe, given the time, it's time for our tour," Oldenburg declared.

Plaintiffs, defendants, and a small army of attorneys filed out of the courthouse. It was cold and dreary, with heavy gray skies. Monica whipped her head around, scanning the street for the judge. She was determined not to let him leave in his SUV without her.

Shawley said he'd follow in his car with his cell phone on speaker, in case Monica had any questions. He had just met Jaffe, who said he'd carpool with Rick and Lois. Jaffe seemed laid-back, nothing like the combative Marty Wilde. Shawley told Jaffe that his dad might have stiffed him on a met tower he sold him.

Inga Parsons and Betsey Greenwood emerged from the courthouse in mink coats. Parsons had a matching mink hat. Greenwood picked her way across the ice and slush on East Callender Street in court-heeled leather pumps, swathed in black fur to her ankles. After all that talk about saving the birds and bats and Cuisinarted eagles, Lois thought, glaring at Parsons's hat.

Monica squeezed into the narrow back row of Oldenburg's Traverse. Like a body in a trunk, she thought. Greenwood and her mink took a spot in the middle row, next to Mitchell. The judge got in the passenger seat; his law clerk, John, would drive.

A convoy of seven vehicles assembled at the Springdale exit, including Engwis's truck and Chesnoff's massive Ford F-450, a turbo-diesel with dual rear wheels that bulged out from flared wheel wells. John drove first to the Hunter's Hot Springs site, pausing so the judge could get a good look at the cow pasture the once-famous resort had become. The caravan proceeded to the house where Gordy's ranch manager lived, then turned around in their driveway and headed east. Chesnoff had to make a multipoint turn to navigate the circular drive in his dually truck.

On the judge's instructions, none of the lawyers said much, though Greenwood pointed out the location of the Engwises' magnificent overlook, as well as the house where Mikey—"their handicapped son"—lived. Monica was having trouble seeing anything at all from her spot in the wayback: flashes of low brown hills thinly carpeted with snow, utility poles, barbed-wire fences flying past. The Crazies had sunk below a chill white fog. "Where are we?" Monica texted Jami, who was following in her Dodge Ram. "Whose property line is this?" A meteorological tower went past at twelve o'clock. Oldenburg asked Monica how tall it was.

When they reached Sanctuary River Lane, Chesnoff peeled off from the caravan in his F-450 and headed home to his sprawling lodge. Chesnoff had heard the jokes comparing his place to Cabela's. It made him laugh. "I wish I had Cabela's," he said.

Monica's phone vibrated with a text from Jami: "Do NOT go down our drive."

But the site visit concluded after it reached Chesnoff's place. Judge Oldenburg had no interest in driving down the dirt road to Rick's farmhouse.

Later, Monica asked Jami about her text. What was going on in the driveway? "She said there were, like, twenty bald eagles sitting there."

REBUTTAL
February 21, 2019
Park County Courthouse
Livingston, Montana

ELIZABETH GREENWOOD, *for the Plaintiffs*: You heard their
    testimony that they enjoy roaming the entirety of their property,
    free of industrial development. Is that correct?
WARD MARSHALL: I heard that they roam all of their property.
MS. GREENWOOD: Did you not hear them say that they enjoy it?

As the final day of the hearing began, Monica said there was a matter she wanted to bring before the court. "So, if I may, I would like to call David Chesnoff to the stand."

Monica had only gotten a few hours of sleep, strategizing about the best way to get Lois's bombshell on the record. Chesnoff's casual comment that all they needed to do to kill Crazy Mountain Wind was to delay it a few more months confirmed what Monica had been arguing from the very beginning.

Monica told the Pattern team what she intended to do, and they didn't like it. "They were like, 'We can't afford the time to do that. It's going to be a whole shit show,'" she recalled. They were eager to get their experts on the stand. The experts were going to win this thing.

But Monica wouldn't budge. "I'm calling him," she said. She promised to keep it short. Chesnoff, with the air of one colleague to another, reminded the judge that he was still under oath as he took his seat on the witness stand. Monica asked if he remembered speaking to Mr. Apostol during the break. Chesnoff needed to be reminded who Apostol was. Irritated, he pushed his wavy silver hair back from his brow with both hands.

"Do you remember saying words to the effect that you know that private property rights are primary in Montana and they will win out and—"

Chesnoff interrupted her. "Never, never. Absolutely not." He knew that private property rights would prevail because the public nuisance argument would prevail, he explained.

Monica read him the rest of the statement. "'We're just hoping to delay this long enough, four to five months, to kill it, once and for all.' Did you make that statement?"

"I don't think I said we're just—" Chesnoff said. "I said a delay would certainly be in our interests."

Monica said she had no further questions, then called Lois Huffman to the stand. Clutching a copy of the note she'd torn from her journal, Lois told the court what she had heard.

"Thank you. I have no further questions," Monica said.

Greenwood greeted Lois as "Mrs. Huffman" and asked if she was Rick's girlfriend.

"It's not 'Mrs.,'" Lois said. "Rick Jarrett and I are good friends."

"What does that mean, good friends?" Greenwood pressed.

"It means that we help each other remain independent," she said.

"Do you date him?" she asked. "Do you have intimate relations with Mr. Jarrett?"

Monica objected.

"Sustained," Oldenburg said.

Greenwood homed in on the note, dissecting the words that Lois thought she had heard. "'We are just hoping to delay this, long enough, four or five months, to kill it once and for all'—you heard that, you claim, exactly. Is that right?"

"Yes, that's why it's in quotes," Lois said. "That was verbatim what I heard."

Go Lois, go, Rick thought. They weren't about to get the best of her.

"You don't know anything that he may have said afterwards, correct? Like 'We're hoping to win this case because of—to save the eagles and our viewshed'?"

"No, they weren't talking about that," Lois said.

When she returned to her seat in the gallery, Lois was steaming. They didn't ask the bat expert or the eagle guy or Russell Gordy about their sex life, or who paid for dinner. And Greenwood kept calling her "Mrs. Huffman," even though Lois told her that it wasn't missus—twice.

It was time for Pattern to call its first witness. Finally, the defense could deliver a cool-headed rebuttal to all the melodramatic testimony about eagles and bats and owls and chaotic turbine arrangements.

Coleman called Ward Marshall to the stand. Just as they had practiced, he led Marshall through the history of the project. He pointed out the locations of the turbines, and showed how distant the plaintiffs' multiple residences were from them. He described the terms of Pattern's power purchase agreement with NorthWestern Energy. Crazy Mountain Wind had to be up and running by the end of the year. In order to meet that deadline, construction had to begin by April 1. If the project was enjoined, he said, construction would not begin on time, jeopardizing its financing.

Greenwood cross-examined Marshall. "You blame the plaintiffs for trying to delay your project," Greenwood asked Marshall. "Is that correct?"

"That is correct," Marshall said.

Greenwood produced a copy of Pattern's power purchase agreement and asked Marshall to turn to page twelve and read Article 5.2, a list of "defined tasks" Pattern was expected to complete by set dates. She began working her way down the list. The first phase of construction had to be completed before September 1, 2018.

"So, that's come and gone, correct?" she asked.

"Correct," Marshall responded.

The date for final unit construction had also come and gone. And yet Marshall was telling the court that Pattern had to begin construction by April 1, 2019, or the agreement would no longer be effective. "Isn't that what you've told this Court?" Greenwood asked.

"Correct," Marshall said.

She moved down the list. Pattern was supposed to submit term sheets showing that they had locked in financing for Crazy Mountain Wind by February 2018—a full year ago. "You don't have your financing in place, correct?"

"We do not," Marshall said. "We are in negotiations with our financing parties, but we haven't closed." He couldn't say who they were; it wasn't his area of expertise.

"You don't really know who you're getting it from yet, do you?" Greenwood asked.

Marshall was following the playbook Coleman and Mitchell had given him: short, simple answers. No one had prepped him for questions about the minutiae of the power purchase agreement. Pattern's attorneys were mostly mute as Greenwood grilled Marshall about the project's apparent construction and financing delays.

The Pattern executives were seated in the front row. This wasn't going quite the way they had expected. They had anticipated questions about birds and bats and shadow flicker—ice throws, maybe, or another emotional speech about eagles. Instead, Greenwood was drilling down on the language of Pattern's contract with NorthWestern, plucking out lines and using them to skewer Marshall like a rotisserie chicken. Nobody had been expecting Greenwood to go through the PPA. And none of them was sure about what it actually said. A current of alarm rippled down the royal blue bench.

Rosenshine, Pattern's assistant general counsel, rose from his seat and found Charles Shawley, who was sitting a few rows back. They stepped out into the hallway. Did Shawley have a copy of the power purchase agreement? he asked. They hunkered down on a bench outside the courtroom and Shawley pulled up the contract on his phone. What Greenwood was suggesting was false, he said. Pattern was in full compliance with the terms of its contract with NorthWestern. The defined tasks were just guidelines—non-binding guidelines. It said so, right there in Article 5.2.

Shawley scrolled down past the defined tasks to show Rosenshine one line: "failure to accomplish any defined task by the scheduled dates will not constitute a default if"—and this was a big if—Crazy Mountain Wind "achieves Commercial Operation by the Guaranteed Commercial Operation Date." That was the only date that mattered. It drove the PPA. December 31, 2019, was do or die.

Back in the courtroom, Greenwood was throwing everything she had at Marshall. She asked about construction permits and eagle take permits and water permits. She accused Pattern of buying off Kelly Engel—who "was very emotionally upset about what you were doing to her viewshed"—and of buying off the Sweet Grass County Commissioners, who had yet to vote on tax abatement for Crazy Mountain Wind. "Do you have a side deal with the commissioners?" she asked.

"No, I do not," Marshall replied.

After Greenwood was done, Lofing took a turn, repeating many of the same questions.

It seemed like an awfully long time that Ward had been on the stand, Alfred thought. The lawyers were grilling him about this and that, and one thing and another. Maybe that was normal, but it seemed to Alfred like Ward was there for several hours. Meanwhile, Chesnoff was passing more notes to his attorneys over the wooden divider. He was pale, with kind of long hair. Alfred supposed he was a city guy, hadn't been out in the country much and got sunlight.

"May I ask one question?" Monica said, when Ward's cross-examination at last came to a close. She asked him to turn to page four of the PPA and read the part about the commercial operating date. "I'm wondering if that is the driver of the milestones that Pattern has to meet?"

"That is the driver," Marshall said.

"Monica tried," Jami said later. "She saw the burning shit."

During his testimony, Allen Wynn, Pattern's environmental manager, did his best to douse the flames. He addressed the issue of eagle incidental take permits, which Marshall had been asked about repeatedly. It's illegal to take or harm eagles. An eagle incidental take permit is a federal authorization to take an eagle or an eagle nest—to literally take it, or to take its life. Native tribes get take permits from the US Fish and Wildlife Service to hunt wild eagles and take eagle feathers for ceremonial purposes. Eagles can be harmed inadvertently by lawful industries like energy development and power transmission. So, the federal government began issuing eagle incidental take permits, to ease potential restrictions on those industries while providing some oversight.

The process of getting an eagle incidental take permit took three or four years, Wynn explained. Before Pattern could even apply to the USFWS for a permit, it had to complete two full years of eagle surveys. Those surveys had just been completed, he said. The next step was drafting a plan to reduce eagle strikes. At Stillwater Wind, biological monitors were brought on during peak seasons; if they spotted an eagle within striking distance of a specific turbine, it would be shut down.

The conservation plan for Crazy Mountain Wind could involve monitors, or it might involve a new camera-based detection system, Wynn said. Pattern would also implement a mitigation program, offsetting potential eagle deaths by spending millions of dollars to retrofit old power poles. They'd save at least 1.2 eagles from electrocution for every eagle that might be killed by one of Crazy Mountain Wind's turbines.

As it happened, the plaintiff's expert eagle witness, Ross Crandall, had come up with his own idea for a wind energy mitigation plan. At the time of the hearing, Crandall was seeking funding for a pilot program to distribute free, non-lead ammunition to hundreds of hunters in southeast Wyoming. Craighead Beringia South would then monitor blood lead levels in their study group of eagles. Crandall was excited by the possibility that such programs, if effective, could be implemented on a wide scale—by wind developers. The wind industry needed to find new ways to offset eagle deaths, Crandall would write in an upcoming newsletter: "A non-lead ammunition distribution program may be it!"

In his time on the stand, Allen Wynn didn't mention that obtaining an eagle incidental take permit before a wind farm was built was all but impossible, because the permitting process involved eagle assessments that had to be conducted during construction.

As Wynn spoke, Jami kept looking at the judge, trying to read his expression. On the first day, he had seemed very engaged, asking Crandall lots of questions about eagles and eagle behavior. He wasn't asking any questions now.

Pattern's first star witness took the stand after lunch. Mike Hankard was an acoustical consultant—"a noise guy"—who had been creating noise control plans for wind farms for nearly thirty years.

Sound impact was measured in decibels, Hankard explained. Absolute quiet was twenty decibels—or, to be technical about it, 20 dBA. Hankard compared 20 dBA to a calm night with no wind. Thirty decibels was the hushed interior of a library. Forty decibels was being outside with some wind blowing, maybe the sound of a highway in the distance, or birds singing and crickets chirping. Fifty decibels was standing on a busy street. On the far end of the spectrum, one hundred decibels was a rock concert.

Turbines made noise when their blades cut through the air. Wind made those blades turn faster, which made them louder. The turbines had a maximum rotational speed of twenty-two miles per hour; even if the wind blew forty miles an hour, the blades wouldn't turn faster, so they wouldn't become louder. When it was blowing hard, Hankard said, the turbine noise would probably be drowned out by the background noise of the wind itself. If it was really gusting, the turbines would automatically shut down, in which case they wouldn't make any noise at all.

Hankard had done worst-case decibel forecasts for turbine noise at all the plaintiffs' homes. None exceeded thirty-eight decibels—a noise level variously compared to a library, a suburban area at night, and bird calls.

Mitchell asked Hankard if he recalled Chesnoff's vigorous whooshing. "Based on your analysis at the location, outside of the Chesnoff home, would a human ever be able to hear sounds like that from the wind turbines?"

"No, the predicted level is just over twenty dBA, that is never going to be audible," Hankard said.

Pattern's final witness was Christopher Ollson, an environmental health scientist who had investigated the project's potential health impacts.

Ollson reviewed the plaintiffs' health concerns, detailed in their complaint. "I won't go through all of them," he said. "Sleep impairment . . . fatigue, depression, pressure in the ears, dizziness, strain, loss of concentration. With respect to shadow flicker, they had indicated that they were concerned about seizures and exacerbation of stress. And overall, a lowering of quality of life."

Ollson was very familiar with this list of ailments. It didn't come from scientific literature, he said. It came from the internet.

However, if a wind farm made enough noise to disrupt someone's sleep, that was a problem. Sleep impairment was a legitimate health risk. Ollson's golden rule was that the noise from turbines should not exceed 50 dBA outside someone's home. All the homes around the wind farm site were well below that range. The plaintiffs might hear the turbines sometimes, Ollson said. They might even be annoyed by them. But their health wouldn't be impacted. Annoyance was not a health risk.

Ollson had visited the project site. He'd been expecting the usual rural noises—cows, combine harvesters, and the like. But the area in question was quite a bit noisier than that. Ollson hadn't expected the loud freight trains, or the dull roar from the interstate highway, which bordered the train tracks. It was so loud that you could hear it from the road bordering the plaintiffs' ranches, he observed.

Next, Ollson addressed shadow flicker, a flashing effect that could happen when the sun was directly behind the turbine blades as they rotated. The plaintiffs charged that the flickering light could trigger epileptic seizures. But multiple studies had established that the light flashes generated by modern turbines didn't occur at a high enough frequency to trigger seizures; their blades didn't turn fast enough.

Even so, shadow flicker could be annoying. So, in the early 2000s, German courts set a limit for the amount of shadow flicker wind farms could inflict on their neighbors: thirty hours over the course of a year.

All the plaintiffs lived a good distance from the turbines. A mile or more from a turbine, the chance of experiencing shadow flicker was nonexistent. It was simple physics, Ollson said. The plaintiffs' homes were all a good mile or more from the nearest turbine, with the exception of two homes that were three-quarters of a mile away. On Ollson's recommendation, Pattern hired a shadow flicker expert to create a predictive model of how much flashing light the people living in those two houses might be exposed to.

The expert had found that just one home—Rob Fleming's house on the MacMillans' River Ranch—was vulnerable to shadow flicker, from one turbine to the west. In a worst-case scenario—with the sun always shining, and the turbine constantly turning—the house would be exposed to a maximum of one hour and twenty minutes of shadow flicker per year—far below the international standard.

The plaintiffs also alleged potential harm from ice throws. If ice built up on the turbines during freezing rain and then warmed up, it could be thrown from the blade tip. But the turbines were 650 feet or more from the plaintiffs' property lines; the maximum distance ice could be thrown was 550 feet. "The ice isn't leaving the property," Ollson said.

Crazy Mountain Wind had been properly sited. It met or exceeded every national and international wind turbine guideline. The noise and the shadow flicker would not cause health impacts, and they were far below international standards that had been established to minimize annoyance.

When it was Wild Eagle's turn to cross-examine Ollson, Person directed his attention to a map that the noise guy had used as an exhibit. It was marked with wavy circles that showed predicted sound levels from Crazy Mountain Wind across a wide area. There was one spot on the MacMillans' River Ranch where the noise from Turbine A04 could reach fifty-one decibels. Person pointed to it: a pinprick of land bordering the county road, at the edge of a field. It looked like it could maybe fit a cowshed. "So, if my client builds a residence here, on his property, would your analysis change?" he asked.

"If they are at the fifty-decibel-or-less boundary, then absolutely, go ahead and build your home," Ollson said. "If they want to move it inside the fifty-decibel boundary, then that's something—and it's a very small line—but at that point I would recommend that they move the house maybe a little further back."

Person asked again. "So, you'd recommend that my client not build where I pointed at the map."

"I would recommend that your client be sat down and actually have a discussion about it," he said. "It's not that they will experience health impacts."

Person asked Ollson a third time. "You just said within a 50 dBA level, you wouldn't advise my client to build, didn't you?"

Ollson corrected him. "What I said was, if your client was going to be over fifty decibels, if he wanted to build in that small—very small— section there, that we would sit down and have a discussion and talk about the fact that he may experience more noise level at that home than what we would typically set back as a very protective standard."

"Do you know anything about what the neighbors do around this site to use and enjoy their property?" Person asked.

"Certainly . . . ," said Ollson. "Coming from a long line of farmers, I certainly know what this area is. For example, when you talk of noise and neighboring properties and that, I heard your ranch manager talk about combining 24/7 throughout the course of the summer, at a sound level that's going to be much higher than at any of the residences." The noise from a round baler can hit one hundred decibels—rock-concert levels.

Any unease that the Pattern executives had experienced earlier in the day was vanquished by the time Ollson got off the stand. Their two experts had crushed it. After two days of NIMBY theatrics, Pattern had given the judge hard science, simple facts, and basic common sense.

"Rebuttal?" Judge Oldenburg asked.

At the start of the day, Greenwood told the court that the plaintiffs would call a rebuttal witness to push back against the Pattern experts. That witness was Dean Apostol, the scenic expert from Oregon. But plans had changed since Lois dropped her bombshell.

"Our rebuttal witness had to leave," Greenwood said.

"Well, I know the defendants wanted an answer today, but I'm not prepared to do that. I obviously have some documents to look at," Judge Oldenburg said.

The Pattern guys headed to a Bozeman brewpub and ordered pizza. There was no high-fiving, but everyone felt pretty good: no major mistakes, and their expert witnesses had been rock stars. Team Pattern was cautiously optimistic that Judge Oldenburg would see through the plaintiffs' scaremongering.

When she got home that night, Roxie reported everything that had happened in court that day to Jim. Now that it was over, Wild Eagle's lawyers didn't seem to have any idea what might happen next. Roxie had asked them what they thought. And they said they just didn't know.

Rick, Lois, Jami, Alfred, and his granddaughter met Monica for dinner at a Chinese restaurant in Livingston. Jami was elated. The hearing had been hard to sit through, particularly the first two days. But then Pattern's two experts had testified, and they blew her away. Ollson, the environmental guy, was clearly the smartest person in the courtroom—it wasn't even close. She thought he ate that attorney from Wild Eagle for lunch.

When Rick got back to the ranch that night, he peeled off his socks, shrugged off his suspenders, unbuttoned his clean shirt and his jeans, and dropped them on the floor. Then he went outside to his hot tub, naked but for his slippers. It was three degrees by then. Rick sank into the bubbling water, exhausted, but feeling goddamn righteous. They'd finally taken the fight to those neighbors of his. Maybe this time they'd get it done.

18

FINDINGS OF FACT

EXHIBIT 3, NOT ADMITTED INTO EVIDENCE:
"What Is Sustainability to Me," 2015 video by Jordan Moody.

RICK JARRETT, *speaking*:
At what point do you give up? Because it oftentimes seems kind of impossible to really make a living, doing what we're doing.

MARCH 13, 2019
BIG TIMBER, MONTANA

When Harv's 911 call came in, Jami was at her desk in the Sweet Grass County Courthouse, an 1897 fortress of rough-edged sandstone that housed the sheriff's office and the county jail.

After days of heavy snow, Big Timber was in the grip of a deep freeze. Temperatures had plunged to thirty-two below. The roadways were clogged with frozen snow; town water lines had frozen. On the ranch, newborn calves were freezing to death, or losing ears and tails to frostbite.

That morning, Jami got up as late as possible, to give the mercury a chance to climb past zero. She dressed for work and did her makeup. Then she pulled on an insulated Carhartt coverall over her courthouse clothes, put on a hat, and stepped into her muck boots. By the time she got outside it had warmed up to two degrees.

When the cows were having their calves, Jami lived alone at the ranch house on Old Boulder Road while Harv stayed with Rick up on Duck Creek, feeding livestock and pulling calves night and day. They had been snowed in for three days, but a break in the weather had given Harv enough time to plow the drive to the county road the day before.

The herd of black-faced sheep that Jami kept on the Boulder had started dropping lambs. She headed over to the barn to see if anything had been born since she'd last checked around midnight, then fed and watered the ewes and their lambs in their jugs—snug little wooden stalls built for two, where the lambs could learn to suck and their mothers couldn't kick them away. Nothing had died overnight, which was good. Sometimes the lambs wouldn't nurse, or they got chilled. You always lost some.

Chores done, Jami got in her truck and surveyed the long, snow-covered drive to the main road. Harv had come by with the backhoe the night before to yank Jami's half-ton Dodge out of a snowdrift, but hadn't had time to plow more than a quarter mile before he had to get back to the calving shed on Duck Creek. Jami would just have to ranch it. She pressed her muck boot to the accelerator and gave it hell, skidding and sliding and spraying snow till she reached Old Boulder Road.

At the courthouse, she entered through a small vestibule at the back of the building, where she peeled off her insulated coverall, shook out her hair, and swapped her work boots, freshly caked in sheep dung, for her office shoes. At the end of the day, she'd repeat this process in reverse, head home, and do the same set of chores all over again.

The sheriff's deputy came and got her as soon as the call came in. There had been an accident up on Duck Creek. Rick was hurt, something about being run over by a cow. They were going to try to land a Life Flight helicopter on the ranch. Jami ran outside in her good shoes, crawled under the Ram, and began tugging the chains off the tires. It was eighty-two miles to the closest major hospital, in Billings. The chains would slow her down on the highway.

There was too much snow and wind for the helicopter to land. The EMTs brought Rick to the Pioneer Medical Center to stabilize him until an ambulance could transport him to Billings. Rick's face and head were bloody. He vomited, drifting in and out of consciousness.

While she waited for the ambulance with Lois, Jami called Harv, who was still on the ranch. Someone had to stay to feed the cows and calve and get the babies in the barn and all those things. Harv was shook up. He told her what happened. They had penned the cows that were ready to calve in a paddock close to the calving barn, so they could get the newborns in there before they froze to death. The cows were standing in about two feet of snow, and one had just delivered. Harv put the slick newborn calf on a plastic toboggan to drag it inside the warm barn, the mother cow following close behind.

A pregnant cow started trailing the mother cow into the barn, trying to claim the baby in a fit of hormonal confusion. It happened sometimes. Rick moved toward the open door of the barn to separate the two animals. Harv was inside the barn with the calf when he heard the mother cow knock Rick down, heard all the air go out of him. By the time he got to him, the cow had straddled Rick, pinning him facedown in the muddy snow and frozen cow shit. Then she started kicking his head with her hind legs. "She was on top of him, kicking the living shit out of him. She just kicked and kicked. I've never seen an animal do what she did," Harv said.

Harv got the cow off Rick, penned it, and called 911. Rick lay facedown, unconscious, his breath a wet gurgle. Harv knelt in the snow and turned him over. Rick stopped breathing and his face purpled. Harv wiped away the muck and blood and cow shit from Rick's face and gave him mouth-to-mouth. Rick stopped breathing twice more before the first responders arrived.

Lois stopped at her home to pack an overnight bag. By the time she got to the hospital in Billings, the emergency room's waiting area was crowded with Rick's relatives. There was a woman talking to Rick's cousin. When Jami came out from the emergency room and said they were allowing one person in at a time to see Rick, the woman hopped up and headed right in. That's when Lois figured out who she was: Geri, Rick's Billings girlfriend.

Rick had suffered a traumatic brain injury. When he was moved to a room, Lois staked her claim to the recliner chair by his hospital bed. Over the next three days, she and Geri did shifts. Geri came to see Rick before she started work for the day and during her lunch hour. Lois would go to the cafeteria and get something to eat while they visited. Or she'd drive back to Big Timber to get a change of clothes, returning in the early evening. It was kind of funny. Rick had always worked so hard to keep the women in his life separate. Apart from Jami, that is. Jami left work early every day to be with him.

Rick was transferred to St. Vincent's, a Billings rehab center where he'd get every kind of therapy—physical, occupational, speech. The doctors said he needed to build new pathways in his brain to make up for the ones that had been damaged. Rick couldn't do anything for himself. He couldn't get himself out of bed or get himself dressed. He didn't remember anything about the accident.

On March 19, Jami left the courthouse in the midafternoon and drove to Billings. Every day that she drove to the hospital, she passed an array of Siemens Gamesa wind turbines north of the highway, their white blades framed against the sky. It was Stillwater Wind, Pattern's other wind farm, under construction near Reed Point. Its grand opening would be that September. Jami had to look at those turbines every day, and still no word on Crazy Mountain Wind. Judge Oldenburg hadn't issued a decision, despite Pattern's pleas for a speedy ruling. The judge had given the attorneys ten days to submit their final arguments. Those ten days had come and gone. Then a week passed. Then another.

Jami had parked her truck and was walking inside St. Vincent's when her cell phone lit up with a call from Monica.

"It's not good news," Monica said, her voice gravelly. "We lost. Oh my God, Jami, we lost."

Jami sank down on a couch in the hospital atrium, clutching the phone. Monica skimmed through Oldenburg's decision, reading parts of it aloud. The judge had rejected the central plank of their defense, that wind farms couldn't be considered a nuisance under Montana law. The Montana legislature had passed statutes to encourage wind development, Oldenburg acknowledged, but there were no provisions that specifically exempted wind farms from nuisance suits.

The court's job wasn't to rule on the plaintiffs' claims, Oldenburg said. It was to decide if they might suffer irreparable injury before those claims could be decided at trial. And they had convinced him: Crazy Mountain Wind would cause irreparable damage.

It was obvious from the way he stated the basic findings of fact in the case how the judge would rule. Facts were objective; beauty was in the eye of the beholder. But Judge Oldenburg's facts were full of beauty. It was a fact that the land where Pattern wanted to build its wind farm was full of "natural beauty." It had "beautiful vistas," dark skies, and abundant wildlife and birds.

It was a fact that Russell Gordy wanted to build a "beautiful historical reconstruction" of a "beautiful medicinal springs and resort." It was a fact that Jan Engwis had a "prime building site" on a ridge that abutted the project site—a ridge that was a prime area for eagles.

"No witness really disagreed that the area contained natural beauty," Oldenburg said. "The Court observed the same on its visit."

And no one disagreed that the wind turbines would be the tallest structures in the state of Montana. Or that they would be visible for miles. Or that the plaintiffs would be able to see those turbines from some areas of their ranches.

The plaintiffs had testified about how hard they had worked to acquire and "accumulate" their properties, how special they were to them, how much they enjoyed them. Those ranches weren't just homes or income-generating agricultural assets. They had recreational value, Oldenburg said. They had environmental value. They had aesthetic value.

"It is at least doubtful," Oldenburg wrote, that Crazy Mountain Wind would "cause irreparable injury to the plaintiffs due to their diminished viewshed, the potential for shadow flicker, the alleged noise associated with windfarms, the golden eagle taking, or the loss of bats."

Judge Oldenburg had bought everything the Oligarchs were selling, Monica said. The Cuisinarted eagles and bats, the light-polluted night skies and the desecrated viewscapes. All the hysteria about turbine noise and shadow flicker.

Worst of all, Oldenburg pointed to the testimony given by Dr. Ollson—"defendants' own expert"—as a key factor in his decision. "When asked what he would tell one of the Plaintiffs if they told him they were contemplating building a home closer to the Wind Farm, placing it near the border of the same," Oldenburg said, ". . . his reply in effect was, 'don't build your house there.'"

Out of everything that Pattern's top environmental health expert had said, the judge had chosen to focus on that one comment, a comment taken completely out of context. Jami couldn't believe it. Sitting in the courtroom that day, she thought Ollson had made Wild Eagle's attorney look like a fool.

It was the court's job to weigh the balance of harms, Oldenburg said. His site visit had clearly shown him the millions of dollars the plaintiffs had invested in their properties. Gordy had invested over $100,000 in his beautiful spa reconstruction before the wind farm derailed his plans. The judge was clearly more impressed by Gordy's renderings than the Sweet Grass Chamber of Commerce had been.

But what about the potential harm to the defendants? The judge considered the question. Pattern *claimed* to have invested $10 million in Crazy Mountain Wind. They *claimed* that the wind project would create millions of dollars in revenue for the counties, and for the ranchers Rick Jarrett and Alfred Anderson, along with $120 million in value. They *claimed* the project would be killed if it was delayed by an injunction.

But Oldenburg was not convinced: "These claims rest entirely on Pattern's assertion that the PPA will be terminated and the project dead if construction has not started by April 1, 2019, or if the project is not online by December 31, 2019."

Elizabeth Greenwood's dissection of Crazy Mountain Wind's contract with NorthWestern had made a powerful impression on Judge Oldenburg. He read the power purchase agreement. "As pointed out by the Plaintiffs, Pattern has not met any of the benchmark dates in paragraph 5.2," he wrote, pointing to Ward Marshall's testimony as decisive in forming his opinion. Marshall said that Pattern hadn't completed its financing or secured all the necessary construction permits. It hadn't received or even applied for a take permit for incidental eagle deaths.

"More importantly," Oldenburg wrote, "there has been no testimony or argument presented by the Defendants that would show that an extension of the PPA, or a new PPA, could or would not be able to be negotiated."

In what now appeared a fatal oversight, Pattern hadn't called anyone from NorthWestern Energy to testify. Would things have turned out differently if one of the utility company's executives had sworn under oath that the guaranteed commercial operation date—December 31, 2019—was the bright-line that Crazy Mountain Wind could not cross? The question would hang over the ranchers, and Monica, for years.

"Based upon the foregoing Findings of Fact and Conclusions of Law, the Court enters the following," Oldenburg wrote. "The preliminary injunction is GRANTED."

Jami sat on the couch in the hospital atrium and cried. She cried for herself and she cried for her father. She cried because she couldn't bear the thought of Rick hearing what she had just heard. "Don't tell my dad," she told Monica. "Whatever you do, don't tell Dad."

The next morning, Jami got up at six, dressed for work, put on her coveralls and muck boots, and tended her sheep. Then she drove to the courthouse, hung up her coverall, swapped out her muck boots, and went to her desk. "I have to keep doing my thing or I'll break," she told Pat Dringman. "I can't break."

It was weeks before Jami told Rick about the judge's decision. His memory was shot; every conversation ran on a ten-minute loop. He couldn't remember why he was in the hospital. Sometimes he would ask Jami about Crazy Mountain Wind, and she'd tell him they couldn't talk about that. "I just thought, 'Nope,'" she said.

Oldenburg's decision sent a shock wave through Pattern's offices in San Francisco and Houston. The company believed it had mounted a strong case for an environmentally responsible, socially beneficial project, bolstered by testimony from some of the best experts money could buy. But Judge Oldenburg had ignored the evidence and chosen to believe the scaremongering. Pattern's executive vice president and chief legal officer, Daniel Elkort, had been around long enough to know an attorney could never predict the outcome of litigation. But he had to admit: this one surprised him.

The outlook for Crazy Mountain Wind was dire. Litigation was fatal to project financing. The judge's opinion sent a clear message to potential tax equity investors that Crazy Mountain Wind might not get built; if the project wasn't built, they wouldn't be able to claim the tax credit on their investment. And the injunction's halt on construction meant the wind farm wouldn't be built in time to meet the terms of its PPA. Oldenburg set a date for a jury trial in November, one month before the guaranteed commercial operation date.

Pattern didn't give up on Crazy Mountain Wind right away. A few weeks after Oldenburg's decision, Ward Marshall and Hunter Armistead, the president of Pattern Development, met with NorthWestern Energy executives to discuss amending the power purchase agreement. They were ready to bargain, to take less favorable contract terms in exchange for an extension of the commercial operation date. It seemed worth a try. Maybe there was a way to keep Crazy Mountain Wind alive.

"Sure enough, they started talking about how cheap their coal power was," Marshall recalled.

In exchange for extending Pattern's contract, NorthWestern wanted to slash the rate for Crazy Mountain Wind's power nearly in half, from $36.36 to $20.00 per megawatt-hour. The new price was so low that the project would no longer be economically feasible—it wouldn't pay to build it. "There were things coming out of their mouths that I'm sure were absolute bullshit. But we didn't have the time to call them on their own bullshit," Marshall said.

Even if Pattern were to accept the unacceptable terms NorthWestern was offering, Crazy Mountain Wind would still be tied up in litigation. Gordy and MacMillan had the resources to drag out the court battle until the end of time if they chose. In the end, it was a simple business decision. As they walked out of the meeting, Armistead turned to Marshall and told him to pull the plug.

The withdrawal was executed with brisk efficiency. By May, Pattern Energy had removed Crazy Mountain Wind from its portfolio of projects in development. On July 1, Pattern asked the court to be dismissed from the lawsuit. Judge Oldenburg granted the motion and said there was no longer cause for a jury trial.

In January 2021, Pattern terminated its leases with Rick Jarrett and Alfred Anderson, formally relinquishing all rights and interests to their ground. Work crews took down the meteorological towers and removed the concrete pads. They filled the deep circular holes that had been dug for the turbine bases with ten feet of dirt, then covered it with grass seeds that the wind blew away.

"There's something called the three Fs of termination: firm, friendly, and final. Pattern certainly exercised the three Fs," Shawley said. About a month after Oldenburg's decision, he packed up his bags and his golf clubs, said goodbye to the Jarretts and the Andersons and his friends at the Super 8, and went home.

Pattern would lose the $10 million it had invested in Crazy Mountain Wind. Developing wind farms was inherently risky; a $10 million loss here and there was just the cost of doing business. The GE wind turbines it had acquired for Crazy Mountain Wind would be allocated to other projects. "We have multiple projects and we understand shit happens," Marshall said.

For Riverstone Holdings, Pattern's equity owner, Crazy Mountain Wind was a blip on a balance sheet. Riverstone had raised over $39 billion in equity capital for its energy sector investments by then. Not all of it was pure decarb, either. The newest asset in Riverstone's portfolio was Three Rivers IV, a Texas oil and gas company. Riverstone committed $500 million to finance the company's oil and gas acquisitions in the Permian Basin right around the time of Crazy Mountain Wind's injunction hearing.

In late April, while Crazy Mountain Wind was lingering on life support, the Sweet Grass County Commissioners met to vote on a tax abatement for the project. They were hopeful that the project might squeak through, that there might somehow be a chance of grasping $11.6 million in property tax revenues and impact fees. All three commissioners voted in favor.

Rick, who came with Lois, sat on his usual side by the window. He had recovered enough from the accident to return home to the ranch. But his mind wasn't working right, it seemed. His memory was shot, and so was his balance. He had trouble getting out of driver's seat of his Cadillac. When he went to open a gate, he fell. He was falling once or twice a week now. Ranch work was beyond him. He was good for watching the paddock gate while Harv fed the cattle and not much else. Rick spent most of the day in his recliner in his socks, watching Fox News. "It's the shits, that's what it is," he said.

Pattern's decision to drop Crazy Mountain Wind was disappointing. That was the strongest expression of emotion Rick would allow himself. Monica calculated that the project would have reaped over $4.8 million for the Crazy Mountain Cattle Company and nearly $4.2 million for Alfred Anderson—at least. (In a prehearing filing, Pattern estimated that Jarrett and Anderson would be paid approximately $13 million in royalties over the life of the project.) That money would have paid off debts and medical bills, bought more cattle and sheep. It would have ensured that the ranch would be there for the next generation and the one after that. It would have been enough.

Pattern didn't have the fight in them, Rick guessed. They had decided it wasn't a good business decision to spend a lot of money on a battle they didn't have a clear chance of winning. Looking back on it, Rick thought the real blow to Crazy Mountain Wind had been Marty dying. No one ever pushed for the wind farm the way Marty did. If Marty were alive, he'd have made those fuckers pay attention. He wouldn't have pussyfooted around the way they all did. Pattern was too busy looking down the road, thinking about what might come next. Better to protect their reputation and not make enemies. They needed to be able to work with people like Russell Gordy.

Jami tried not to be bitter. Pattern was a great company, an ethical company. She enjoyed everyone she met. They had treated her family fairly. But at the end of the day, everyone got to dust their hands and walk away—everyone except Alfred and her dad. The Jarretts and the Andersons were stuck in the same shitty position as before—worse, because no wind developer in their right mind would think of putting a wind turbine on their land now. The Jarretts and the Andersons had been zoned on their own ground.

Accepting what had happened to Rick since the accident and the injunction ruling—events impossible to disentangle—was even harder for Jami. In the months that followed, it seemed like whole parts of her dad had gone missing. Lifelong habits had been just wiped away. He used to love soaking in that hot tub, morning, noon, and night, no matter the weather. After he got home from the hospital, he never got in it again. Seeing how changed her dad was, it broke her heart. Every damn day.

After Pattern asked to be dismissed from the lawsuit, effectively ending the case, Monica filed a counterclaim against the Oligarchs on behalf of the ranchers. The lawsuit accused Gordy, Chesnoff, Engwis, and MacMillan of abusing the legal process in a bid to control Rick Jarrett and Alfred Anderson's land. Crazy Mountain Wind was dead, and the plaintiffs had frozen any use that her clients could make of their property, restricting their rights.

But Judge Oldenburg dismissed the ranchers' counterclaim with prejudice. Jarrett and Anderson's claims weren't timely, he said; he faulted the ranchers for not filing it when they were sued by their neighbors in the first place. Monica gritted her teeth. They hadn't filed a counterclaim because Pattern had talked her out of it. The judge's new ruling effectively closed the book on the case.

"The court left these people with nothing," Monica said. "It was gut-wrenching."

She filed an appeal with Montana's Supreme Court.

"Crazy Mountain didn't get built because there wasn't anybody there to fight for it," she said.

That summer, Shane Doyle was working on a new project—an inventory of Apsáalooke cultural sites in the Crazies—when one of his contacts at the Montana Wilderness Association called him in a lather. Someone had seen a Chinook helicopter flying over the Crazies with a cement mixer dangling from its cargo hooks. It dropped it off somewhere in the vicinity of Twin Lakes, a set of limpid pools in an alpine basin ringed by peaks. The association's field director hiked up to Twin Lakes on a hasty reconnaissance mission and saw that a small building site had sprouted on a private inholding on the far side of one of the lakes. Trees had been cleared by a CAT mini-excavator, and a concrete foundation had been poured on the raw dirt. The land belonged to a billionaire named David Leuschen, who was planning to air-drop one of his container cabins there.

Doyle knew all about David Leuschen. The two were in regular contact by then. In the years since the Lazy K Bar had been sold to the private equity billionaire, the clamor about private landowners and restricted public access in the Crazies had become noisier and more contentious. A coalition of conservation and outdoor recreation groups was suing the Forest Service for abandoning its claim to historic rights-of-way in the mountains—including two trails that wound through the dude ranch owned by Page Dringman's family, the Carroccias. Now the Yellowstone Club—the billionaire-friendly ski resort that counted Leuschen among its members—had stepped in to try to negotiate a land exchange between the Forest Service and ranch owners like the Carroccias and Leuschen himself. (The Yellowstone Club had designs on a piece of prime alpine Forest Service land near Big Sky; Forest Service officials, preoccupied with the ongoing access conflict in the Crazies, told the club that if it could help broker a land exchange there, maybe it would consider a trade for the ski terrain it coveted.) The goal was to unlock a chunk of the Crazies from the rigid parameters of the checkerboard, consolidating an uninterrupted stretch of public land so it would be easier for regular people to hike, hunt, and climb.

A similar exchange had been in the works for years at the southern end of the Crazy Mountains, involving none other than Russell Gordy and Whitney MacMillan. Both Gordy and MacMillan owned isolated checkerboard squares of land they couldn't do much with because they were blocked by Forest Service squares. The Forest Service was prepared to swap three sections of public land—two with Gordy, one with MacMillan—to create a smooth swath of national forest in the mountains' upper elevations. As part of the agreement, the Forest Service would give up its claim to a public trail that ran through the trophy ranches.

Leuschen owned several high-altitude sections in the eastern Crazies that the Yellowstone Club's private consultant, the Western Land Group, had identified as eminently swappable. More to the point, Leuschen owned Crazy Peak. Which is where Shane Doyle came in: Doyle's advocacy for the Crazies had gotten attention. Publicly affirming Crow tribal members' right to visit Crazy Peak was a feel-good gesture that would imbue the exchange with a kind of moral legitimacy—the cherry on top of the Crazy land-swap sundae.

The Western Land Group asked Doyle for a meeting to discuss the Crow tribe's role in the Crazy Mountain land exchange. The private consultants explained that they wanted to do the right thing, and the right thing was to affirm the tribe's connection to the Crazies. It so happened that the Yellowstone Club wanted something from the Apsáalooke, too: tribal support for their land-exchange deal. The consultants hired Doyle to act as a liaison with Crow tribal government in the negotiations.

Doyle's communications with Leuschen were handled through an intermediary. They never spoke directly. It was all very cordial. Leuschen was open to an exchange of a few sections of land. From his standpoint, giving people some of what they wanted seemed like a good thing, if it relieved public pressure and didn't destroy what he had. Leuschen respected the Crow's history in the Crazies, recognized that Crazy Peak was their sacred ground. Any member of the Crow tribe who wanted to climb to Crazy Peak in the tradition of Chief Plenty Coups was welcome to step across LKB's boundary line and continue upward. "It's the least I can do," Leuschen said. Though they'd better be ready to produce Crow tribal ID if any of his people ran into them up there.

So, Doyle knew all about the billionaire who was now building a cabin on Twin Lake. Doyle's conservationist friends urged him to speak out, to mobilize the Apsáalooke tribal government in protest. The mountains were becoming a private playground for the ultra-wealthy. What was next: a ski hut on Crazy Peak?

Doyle said he'd help. Privately, he didn't think the cabin was that big a deal. That summer had given Doyle other things to worry about. The West was in the grip of a worsening drought. Montana, like other high-latitude regions, was warming faster than the global average. Summers were hotter and drier, and wildfire season now lasted well into the fall. Doyle and his wife, Megkian, had five children. Their eleven-year-old daughter, Ruby, had been diagnosed with asthma. The smoke made it hard for her to breathe, forcing her to stay inside for days at a time. The changing climate was upending family traditions, like dancing in full regalia at Crow Fair every August—too hot and smoky—or going chokecherry-picking. Chokecherries were an Apsáalooke mainstay. The Doyle kids liked to mash them up and boil them into syrup to pour on their pancakes. That summer, they'd found hardly any chokecherries at all. The ones still on the branches were shriveled and dry.

Doyle spoke out about his fears for his children's future at a climate rally in Bozeman that September. Afterward, an MSU undergrad asked him if Ruby and her little sister Lilian, age eight, would be willing to join a children's climate lawsuit against the state of Montana. The lawsuit was one of several such legal actions planned by Our Children's Trust, a nonprofit organization that was taking state and federal governments to court on behalf of their youngest citizens over their disregard for greenhouse gas emissions.

Montana's state constitution enshrined the right of its citizens to a clean and healthful environment. Yet, in 2019, the state of Montana had extracted, processed, transported, and consumed enough fossil fuels to pump 166 million tons of carbon dioxide into the atmosphere. Thanks to its fossil fuel–based economy, Montana, the eighth least populous state in the country, was generating as much in greenhouse gas emissions as Pakistan and its 248 million inhabitants.

Doyle looked at the pictures of the CAT mini-excavator reposing on a patch of dirt on the shores of Twin Lakes that his friends in the Montana Wilderness Association had forwarded. Leuschen's building site was tucked in a remote spot; his cabin would be pretty well hidden from view. All in all, it could have been a lot worse, Doyle thought. "The guy's a billionaire. He's going to have a few toys up there." But it was clear that some response was called for. What if Leuschen—or some other private landowner in the Crazies—pushed the Forest Service for a permit to build a road to his new cabin? That would open the door to SUVs and dirt bikes and ATVs in the upper elevations of Awaxaawippíia.

Doyle and Crow Agency's historic preservation officer, Adrian Bird Jr., contributed statements to a press release expressing concern about private development in the Crazies, and their objection to new roads and expanded motorized access. The Montana Wilderness Association sent it out to their contacts in the media, and pictures of the building site with its mini-excavator appeared in the *Billings Gazette* and the *Bozeman Daily Chronicle*. Leuschen didn't respond to any of their requests for comment.

The Forest Service's revised land management plan for the Crazies incorporated many of the Crow Tribe's priorities. For the first time in the Crazies' history, nearly ten thousand acres of public land in the interior would be designated a wilderness area—the highest level of protection under federal law. An additional thirty thousand acres would be placed permanently off-limits to motorized access and mountain bikes. Sacred sites and traditional practices—making vision quests, gathering medicinal plants—would be protected.

Meanwhile, the land-swap deal the Yellowstone Club was brokering in the Crazies was inching forward. In the Forest Service's draft plan,

3,435 acres of national forest would be exchanged for 5,505 acres of private land. The public would relinquish its claim to several historic trails, and the Yellowstone Club would build a twenty-two-mile trail through new Forest Service land in Big Timber Canyon and Sweet Grass Canyon. A lot of that land had been off-limits to the public for generations.

Permanent legal access to Crazy Peak for Apsáalooke people was part of the deal negotiated by the club's private consultants in exchange for Crow support for the swap. The right to risk life and limb climbing to that island of rock and ice in the sky, that was something, Doyle said wryly. He would never give up his dream that Crazy Peak might someday be returned to the tribe—that they would regain the cathedral in the heart of Crow Country. Being granted permission to enter the sacred places that had been taken from them—that was not the act of reparation he envisioned. So, the plan wasn't perfect. But expanded access to the Crazies would still be a good thing—for everyone. "I want to take my kids on a hike there and picnic and just be able to enjoy it," he said.

But the outcry over Leuschen's cabin had emboldened his friends in the wilderness association. Maybe they could use it to pressure the billionaire, to get more out of the land-exchange deal. The billionaire should give Crazy Peak back to the Crow, they declared. If he was going to put his toys in the Crazies, it was the least he could do.

Connections were brokered, and a meeting was arranged. The wilderness people made their request; Leuschen turned them down flat. They'd never get Crazy Peak, he told them. Crazy Peak was his legacy.

"They really wanted to emphasize that to me," Doyle said. "'David Leuschen thinks that's his legacy, Shane. What do you think of that?'" He started laughing. "These billionaires are so caught up in legacy, legacy, legacy."

I met Rick Jarrett and Alfred Anderson in February 2020, a year after the injunction hearing. Harv gave me a ride to Rick's farmhouse. He used a hydraulic lift on the back of his truck to disburse giant round bales of hay to the pregnant cows as we passed through the pastures along Duck Creek. One cow's tail was sticking straight out, a sign she was about to calve.

It was gusting, but Harv's only concession to the windchill was a ripped hat with earflaps and a well-worn green sweatshirt over a frayed flannel shirt. His five border collies sprawled across the truck's two rows of seats, tongues lolling. Empty soda cans rattled across the floor of the truck with each bump on the dirt road. Cattle ear tags, pliers, and baling twine cluttered the dashboard. All the commodities markets were down that morning, Harv noted glumly. "So, that's 20 percent less for us," he said.

In the farmhouse, Rick sat in his suspenders at the kitchen table before a pile of mail, a broken electric hair clipper, and a can of WD-40. "Do you have—phone, pills, hearing aid, glasses," a note tacked by the door asked.

Harv pulled a pile of hamburgers and a bag of limp lettuce out of the refrigerator, threw the meat in a skillet, and opened a can of baked beans. He fished around in the freezer. "I can't vouch for the bun," he said. "It may have freezer burn."

As Harv made lunch, I asked Rick about the appeal Monica had filed with the state Supreme Court. He didn't have high hopes. Even if they were successful, it wouldn't bring back Crazy Mountain Wind.

"I don't think I'll make any fucking money off this lawsuit," Rick said. "I just didn't want to say that we gave up." He wanted to do what was right. If he made his rich neighbors miserable, so much the better. He explained that Crazy Mountain Wind had been about money. Not green energy or climate change, a subject that did not overly concern him. "That's it. That's the truth," he said. "If the wind farm goes or not isn't going to make a huge difference to anybody. Except me."

Harv served the burgers and then sat down to eat, layering two beef patties with cheese and mayonnaise. No bun. "I'm watching my weight," Harv said. "I'm watching it get bigger." Rick tsked and said his weight was fine.

He returned to the subject of his rich neighbors. He was convinced they'd go after his water rights next. Gordy took his water from Duck Creek, same as the Jarretts did. "Yeah. There's going to be a fight over water," Rick said. Water was a precious resource in the Crazies' high desert, and everyone wanted it. More men had been killed over that than anything else. "You can take another man's wife, but you don't fuck with his water," he said. Rick's water rights went back to the 1880s. He'd like to see Gordy try to take his water, because he was ready to shoot a hole in his butt. Rick knew his goddamn water rights.

"I don't think Russell Gordy would wish anything good on any-body in Sweet Grass County because he'd like to own the whole son of a bitch," he said. Unbidden, the broken electric clipper started buzzing, jittering across the table. Rick went to work on it with the can of WD-40.

The next day, I visited the Andersons. Two border collie puppies sat in a crate in the crowded main room. "They can't be licking on you if they're shut up," Alfred said. He wore a Western shirt with pearlized buttons; his elbow stuck out of a neat L-shaped tear in the left sleeve. Dorothy was boiling brats and broccoli in small saucepans on a hot plate. The home, which Alfred built himself, didn't have a full kitchen. Doro-thy, bright and effusive, said she couldn't tolerate solid food anymore. As Alfred and Kevin sat down to eat, she whizzed her brat up in a blender with some springwater and poured it in a glass.

Like Rick, the Andersons were under financial strain. They had borrowed money against the land, taking out a $515,000 mortgage in 2017. Wool prices were down worse than beef prices. Two years be-fore, Alfred had sold the wool from his Targhees and Rambouillets for $24,000. But the following year, the wool clip didn't sell. It sat in the wool house down by the rail yard for a full year. When it finally sold, they only got $13,000.

The wind turbines would have helped quite a bit financially, Alfred said. The cows and sheep could have still eaten grass under the turbines; it didn't make any difference to them. You could have still cut hay under them. Dorothy couldn't understand why people had been so opposed to the wind farm. The Crazies were beautiful, but you'd still have been able to see them with the wind farm. "You can block your mind and look at the mountains and forget the wind turbines—or I can," she said.

"I thought Pattern was going to win out, you know," Alfred said. They'd gone to all that expense, all the bird counting and bat tests and whatever else they'd done. They didn't quite have their financing, but he supposed they could get what little they were lacking, if they'd got it that far. The judge probably thought they should have had it all down on paper. Then everything Monica came up with, well, he kinda ruled agin her. "He ruled for them, the rich guys," Alfred said in a placid tone. "You'd think he was paid off. It looks like it, you know."

I felt like I was putting Alfred back on the witness stand when I asked the question Monica had put to him, over and over: Without Crazy Mountain Wind, were the Andersons in danger of losing their ground?

"Well, close, probably, I suppose," Alfred said. He asked Kevin what he thought.

"Oh, I don't think we're toast yet," said Kevin, who had sat down to lunch in his Carhartt overalls and flat wool cap. Kevin's income from his two jobs would help keep the ranch afloat. If it didn't, they'd sell the cows. The cows would pretty much pay everything off, and they could keep the ground. A guy could still farm it and sell the grain, Kevin said. He'd keep working for pay while working on the ranch, seeding and irrigating and haying. Then they'd start buying stuff back. But, for the time being, they'd just keep doing what they'd always done—stacking bales, feeding livestock. "Can't do nothing else," Alfred said.

I FaceTimed with Rick in April. Now that he couldn't work on the ranch, the question of how to transfer it to Jami and Harv had become a central preoccupation. Rick only owned 50 percent of the Crazy Mountain Cattle Company; his silent partner, Penny, owned the other half. Jami and Harv had to pay Rick enough for his ownership interest so he could retire. And his son, Jay, would have to be compensated for his share of the place—that worried him, too.

The past summer, Rick had taken me on a tour of his corrals and the calving barn he built himself. "I think I designed a really magnificent setup," he said, surveying his domain. His pride in the place was unwavering. But the ranch was encumbered with debt. Cattle prices were in the shitter. He wondered if there'd be a goddamn ranch left for Jami and Harv to buy in a year.

"Right now, I wouldn't sell it to them because the chances of success are so goddamn slim and I don't want to see them fail," Rick said. "I've been scratching my head a lot. It may break me. I don't see a real way out of this son of a bitch."

He felt like he was bordering on depression, he said. He had asked Jami to make him an appointment with a mental health doctor.

In August, Montana's Supreme Court reversed one part of Judge Oldenburg's decision, ruling that Rick Jarrett and Alfred Anderson had the right to file a counterclaim against their neighbors. Although the justices didn't weigh in on the validity of the ranchers' complaints, they cited David Chesnoff's overheard comments as fresh grounds for a lawsuit. Monica had made Lois's scrawled note the centerpiece of her appeal.

Their wealthy neighbors had moved on from the litigation—far beyond, in the case of Whitney MacMillan. America lost its 128th-richest citizen in March 2020, when he died in Vero Beach at the age of ninety. An obituary estimated his net worth at $5.1 billion.

Whitney's death had put Jim and Roxie Hogemark in a state of existential uncertainty. They worried that Betty might decide to sell Wild Eagle Mountain. She hadn't been out to the ranch much since Whitney's death, and she didn't check in regularly by phone the way he had. They heard from her every two or three months, at best.

"I says, we kind of wonder, 'Well, do we just keep going?' I guess as long as they're paying the bills, we'll just keep doing what we're doing until we hear different," Jim told me that summer.

He hoped he'd get another ten years to keep doing what he'd done on Wild Eagle all his life. But he and Roxie both knew what was coming. The ranch wasn't theirs; it never had been. "We just have to enjoy it while we are here," said Roxie, who had started taking lots of pictures so she'd have something to remember the place by. They weren't sure where they'd go—maybe a little house in town, though prices had skyrocketed since the COVID pandemic. In 2019, the median listing price for a house in Big Timber was $363,600. By 2020, it was $445,300. In 2021, it would hit $644,500. The Hogemarks hoped the MacMillan family would take care of them when the time came, the way Whitney and Betty had helped out Jim's folks.

The Engwises had not sold their ranch. After the judge's ruling against Crazy Mountain Wind, their real estate agent, James Esperti, posted a jubilant announcement on the brokerage's website listing for the ranch. "We just received exciting news . . . The threat of a neighboring windfarm has been mitigated! Local landowners worked together and were successful."

But by January 2020, the listing for the Engwis ranch had vanished. The Engwises had pulled it off the market. The magnificent observation point, with its spectacular viewscape, remained just that—a ridge with a view.

Y

The cow pastures of Hunter's Hot Springs were still tranquil in July 2020, when I met Russell and Glenda Gordy there. We walked through the high meadow grass with an eye out for snakes as Russell pointed out where the Natatorium and the Plunge had been, and the grand Dakota Hotel. The rusty old hydrants were still there—the only things to survive the fire. "There is irony in the world," said Glenda, who told me that people had tried to steal parts of them. Water gushed out of a pipe at 112 degrees, pouring into a narrow canal. The day before had been July 4, Independence Day. The Gordys had celebrated with a family picnic and fireworks. Colorful boxes of spent pyrotechnics were lined up by the side of the road. "We put on a heck of a display," Russell said.

The world had changed since the injunction hearing. The pandemic had shut down the tourism industry, along with so much else. Gordy said he was still thinking of creating some kind of spa at the hot springs someday, maybe.

"We might wind up building it just for ourselves," he said. "I've had my fill of the public."

After opening Gordy & Sons and getting into real estate development in Houston, Gordy said, people had found out who he was. "Nobody ever knew who I was before. And I liked it a whole lot better when they didn't," he said.

David Chesnoff continued to appear at arraignments and sentencing hearings alongside the wealthy and influential people who made up his clientele. In 2021, he'd be photographed in a black leather jacket at the opening of a glitzy cigar lounge overlooking the Las Vegas Strip—a new business venture with Giuseppe Bravo, son of his old client, convicted cocaine smuggler Joe Bravo. Chesnoff hadn't had much time to visit Montana, he told me.

Y

Monica set a date to meet the ranchers at Lions Club Park in Big Timber that August. The pandemic had made in-person meetings all but impossible, but Rick and Alfred were no good on the phone. They needed to hash out the next steps. It was time for Rick and Alfred to decide if they were ready to sue the Oligarchs.

It was a four-hour drive from Monica's home in Missoula to Big Timber. She settled behind the wheel of her minivan, wrapping a U-shaped travel pillow around her neck. The windshield was cracked, the back seats overflowing with kids' discarded clothes and snack wrappers. "I wanna drive your car, not mine!" Monica yelled at a blonde in a convertible, as she gassed up the minivan at a pump island.

She kicked off her sandals to drive barefoot, taking calls from her wind developer clients with her cell phone in one hand, the steering wheel in the other. "NorthWestern is not playing nice," she complained. "Oh, I don't know, Willy. I am so sick of people who lie." She asked him to pray for her. In between calls, she ate a cookie.

A blue-and-green sign flashed past on I-90: "MONICA TRANEL for Public Service Commissioner." A commissioner's seat on the PSC was up for grabs in 2020. After years of complaining about the climate deniers and right-wing idealogues on the commission, Monica had decided to do something about it.

The PSC had imploded that year. There was an uproar in February when it was revealed that the five Republican commissioners had quietly approved a $6.5 million increase for Montana ratepayers at NorthWestern Energy's request, without so much as a press release. Finger-pointing, leaked personal emails, and vicious infighting followed. One commissioner accused Commissioner Roger Koopman of threatening to bring a gun to a public hearing, leading to headlines like "Fear and Loathing at the Montana PSC" and "Terror in Helena! I'm Afraid Roger Koopman Will Bring a Gun to Work and Shoot Me."

"Get Rid of the PSC," the editorial board of the *Billings Gazette* implored. "How much longer are we willing to be embarrassed by this commission's unfitness for the task it has been given? . . . Blow it up. Get rid of it. Replace it with something that works."

Monica wanted to restore the rule of law and a respect for science to the PSC. She won the Democratic primary for District 4, a sprawling eight-county district that included Missoula. In November, she'd face off against a hard-right Republican state senator who was soliciting campaign donations by raffling off a "TRUMP 2020 special edition survival kit" that included a Winchester .44 magnum, a hunting knife, military rope, and "emergency tube shelter."

The PSC race consumed Monica. She put twenty thousand miles on the minivan that year, making campaign appearances across the district. But she couldn't let go of Rick and Alfred's case. The injustice of it nagged at her. She woke up at 3 a.m. thinking about the map she had used as a courtroom exhibit, with the vast oceans of privately owned, colorful squares engulfing Rick and Alfred's land. "Doesn't that map bother you?" she asked. "Isn't there something about it that just seems wrong?"

The highway ran parallel to the railroad tracks, and a freight train sped by. It was bound for a wind farm somewhere. Each car bore a single gleaming white turbine blade, as long and curvilinear as a whale.

Jami, Rick, Lois, and Alfred were sitting at a picnic table at Lions Club Park when she arrived, talking about how cold it had been that morning when they were out irrigating. The Montana Supreme Court ruling had made Rick feel better than he'd felt in a long time. "I'm taking the son of a bitch to court. I always thought we were right, but I didn't know that we were going to end up at the Supreme Court, for Chrissakes," he said. "I bet Gordy was mad as hell when he read that court decision."

Jami was pretty sure Gordy hadn't bothered to read it.

On the long drive to Big Timber, Monica had seemed weighed down by the psychic load of Crazy Mountain Wind. Litigation was hard, she said, emotionally hard. She wouldn't tell Rick and Alfred what to do; it was their case. But sitting with them in the sunshine invigorated her. "I'm not going to tell you I'm objective, because I think an injustice has been done," Monica said at the picnic table. This wasn't the Montana that she knew. She offered to take the case on contingency. It would be a long time before they recouped any damages—if they ever did. Five years at least, she cautioned.

"Well, I don't think they should be telling me how to use my land," Alfred said, hands shaking. It was his eighty-ninth birthday that day.

Rick was up for the fight. "I might goddamn enjoy it," he said.

Jami was torn. More litigation meant more anger and stress. It meant getting down and dirty to try and scrape money out of people she didn't like. "Maybe I'm just a little too prideful," she said privately. "But fuck these people. I don't want to ask them for another goddamn thing."

After the meeting broke up, I walked Alfred to his truck. His vision had gotten worse, but he still drove during the daytime. He could do that pretty much blind, he said. As for the lawsuit, if Rick wanted to go for it, Alfred would, too. They'd see it to the end, he guessed. Or close to, anyway.

"I won't be here to see the end of it," Alfred said with a smile.

It was a shame they were first meeting this way, after twenty years, Russell Gordy said.

It was July 22, 2021. Rick sat at a conference table in a Bozeman office building on Mendenhall Street, listening to Gordy talk about the view. That was his real interest, the viewscape. Gordy didn't want anything that would destroy it: not windmills or subdivisions or cell towers. Nobody wants to buy land with windmills on it, Gordy said. He was prepared to make an offer for Rick's wind rights, his and Alfred Anderson's. To pay them something, for taking that away. For the lost opportunity. Nobody called anybody names; there wasn't any yelling. In a legal services building on a street named for Rick's ancestors, the parties in *Rick Jarrett et al. vs. Wild Eagle Mountain Ranch, LLC, et al.* had met to try to negotiate a resolution to their conflict. The Jarretts and the Andersons were ready to settle.

Monica had poured her heart into the lawsuit. After the picnic bench summit in Big Timber, she filed a complaint that read like a novel, with villains and underdogs and hundreds of pages of exhibits and photographs. Rick Jarrett was a fifth-generation rancher, the descendant of homesteaders. Alfred Anderson was an eighty-nine-year-old rancher who couldn't afford to retire, still working the land his family had ranched since the early twentieth century.

There was no mistaking the bad guys. Rock Creek Ranch was "Oilman Russell Gordy"—thereafter shortened to "Oilman Gordy"—a

Texan who couldn't remember how many ranches he owned. Defendant Wild Eagle Mountain was "Cargill-MacMillan," a clan of billionaires with a reported net worth of $40 billion. Defendant David Chesnoff was "Las Vegas lawyer Chesnoff," who represented rich drug dealers. Defendant Jan Engwis was "a foreign limited partnership" with a $19.5 million ranch for sale.

The complaint accused these "corporate defendants" of waging a twenty-year campaign against Rick Jarrett and Alfred Anderson that had undermined their rights to pursue economic opportunities on their property. The wealthy landowners had abused the legal process, Monica argued, using litigation to create delays that they knew would kill the ranchers' wind farm.

But Rick and Alfred's lawsuit hit rough water from the beginning. During oral arguments that February, Judge Michael Hayworth chuckled the first time Monica said, "Oilman Gordy." Then he apologized. It wasn't funny, the judge said. He understood what Monica was trying to do—it was the David-and-Goliath thing. But that kind of rhetoric hurt her case, a case the judge seemed to think was weak to begin with. He doubted that the wealthy neighbors' lawsuit constituted an abuse of process, even if it ultimately resulted in the outcome they'd hoped for.

Monica was discouraged. It had been a tough winter. She lost her campaign for a seat on the Public Service Commission and spent weeks wondering where she had gone wrong. Was there a path to victory that she just hadn't seen? Her Christmas season was capped off with a painful wisdom-tooth extraction. As she recovered at home, Monica tried to get in the holiday spirit, digging out the nativity set and setting it up with the girls. "We lost Jesus," she said.

Judge Hayworth didn't like Monica's case. It was clear from the questions he asked at the February hearing, she thought. Jan and Karen Engwis sat directly behind Monica, in the first row of seats. She was convinced she could hear Jan harrumphing and sighing every time she spoke. She considered asking him to move, to give her social distance.

From the beginning, it had seemed overwhelming, going up against all that money. Monica was just one person, and sometimes she wondered if her brain was sharp enough. "I thought we had a good case, but nobody sees it the way I see it," she said. Maybe she had read it wrong from the beginning. Or maybe she was too close to it. Maybe it was a shitty case. It didn't matter. "I can't let it go," she said.

The judge dismissed Jarrett and Anderson's lawsuit. Monica filed a second amended complaint. Gordy, Chesnoff, MacMillan, and Engwis retaliated by threatening to sue for their legal costs. That spooked the ranchers, the possibility that they might get stuck with the Oligarchs' attorney bills. The Jarretts and the Andersons were weary. The fight had gone on for so long. Maybe they had been a big enough pain in the ass for the Oligarchs to pay them to go away.

Monica had another idea. One of her clients had some old wind turbines he wanted to get rid of. Why not plant them on Rick and Alfred's ranches? The turbines could defray the ranchers' electricity costs and give the Oligarchs a poke in the eye at the same time. "Let's put three turbines up on the pads Pattern built and see what happens," Monica said.

"They could be for decoration, I suppose," Alfred said, with the ghost of a smile.

The settlement conference was managed by an arbitration and mediation firm in Bozeman. The settlement master, a kind man with a grandfatherly air, showed the ranchers to the conference room and told them to help themselves to coffee and muffins from a table in the main lounge.

"I know the two sides don't like to see each other," he said, reassuring them that the "other side" would stay on the second floor. Elizabeth Greenwood and Inga Parsons, who had arrived together in a BMW sport utility vehicle, lingered over the pastry tray before heading upstairs.

Jami and Harv joined Rick at the long table. This was their fight now—the ranch was theirs. They had bought Rick's 50 percent share of the Crazy Mountain Cattle Company in January, making a large down payment and committing to monthly payments "forever and ever and ever," in Jami's words. After Rick's death, those payments would go to her brother, Jay, to compensate him for his interest in the ranch. Some days, Jami wondered what she and Harv had just signed themselves up for, wrapping this giant albatross around their necks.

Although Gordy usually wore T-shirts and shorts in Montana, he had opted for a business-casual look with a turquoise polo shirt and tan slacks. Chesnoff, who had arrived in his immaculate F-450 dually, wore a dress shirt, no tie. The ranchers were dressed for a different kind of weather, in long-sleeved flannel and jeans. Early mornings were always cold when you were out irrigating, and then you needed something to keep off the sun as it scorched its way up the sky. Alfred kept his tractor cap on as he settled into a high-backed swivel chair.

The attorneys negotiated for over an hour, going back and forth between the rooms where the two sides had established their beachheads. Jan Engwis had sent his lawyer, Stephen Woodruff; Nicholas Lofing was there for the MacMillans. At around 10:30, an alert lit up the attorneys' phones simultaneously. There was a pause as everyone checked their email. Judge Hayworth had dismissed Jarrett and Anderson's second amended complaint, with prejudice. The complaint was fatally defective, the judge said. The case was over.

Woodruff and Lofing left immediately. Gordy and Chesnoff, sensing an opportune moment for a permanent settlement on favorable terms, stayed. Monica, swallowing her sense of defeat, suggested that they go in and talk to the Jarretts and the Andersons directly. Only the mediator would be present; no lawyers.

They talked for about twenty minutes. "It was pleasant, wasn't any hollering or nothing like that," Alfred said. Gordy and Chesnoff were respectful. They were kind of wanting to take some responsibility, was how he'd describe it. They knew they owed him and Rick something, for taking away what they'd had coming with Crazy Mountain Wind.

Rick left the talking to Jami. When Gordy said nobody wanted to buy land with windmills on it, she wouldn't let it lie. "Respectfully, let's agree to disagree," she said. Who in that room was going to be around in thirty or thirty-five years? The younger generation had different ideas.

When Jami got back to her place on the Boulder, she changed into shorts and a tank top, stuck her cell phone in her bra, and pulled on hip-high waders. Then she went out to irrigate the forage winter wheat fields in the side-by-side with two dogs, a spray bottle of Roundup, and a tallboy of Arnold Palmer Spiked.

Jami didn't have wheel lines or center pivots at her place on the Boulder. The fields were flood-irrigated through a network of ditches. The flow of water had to be directed and redirected throughout the day to different sections of the grass crop; once you'd gotten water to one section, you'd block up that ditch with a weighted tarp so it could flow to the next. When it was hot and dry, you had to do this throughout the day. It had been very hot and dry that summer. Smoke from wildfires in Oregon and California had clouded the Crazies for days on end, swathing their peaks in acrid smog. Snowpack on the mountains was low. The Crazies weren't the pure white and blue of the mural on the Big T. They looked brown.

The ranchers and the Oligarchs hadn't come to an agreement on terms for the wind rights yet, Jami said. But the lawsuit was over. "That's done," Jami said. "This is the end game."

The final agreement, signed that December, would prohibit all forms of wind and solar development on the Jarrett and Anderson ranches for thirty-five years, "to preserve the scenic integrity." Not leaving anything to chance, Gordy and Chesnoff also banned their neighbors from building a nuclear power plant. The financial terms were confidential. "Well, it's better than nothing, you know," Alfred said. "It isn't what it should be, but it's better than nothing." Gordy was now free to build his boutique hotel at Hunter's Hot Springs without fear that windmills, met towers, or nuclear generators would spoil the view. But, years after the agreement was signed, the only patrons at the hot springs were his Black Angus cows.[*]

The morning after the settlement conference, I visited Chesnoff at Diana's Great Idea. He made herbal tea—"I don't drink coffee, I'm a tea guy"—and showed me around the lodge. The Yellowstone River sparkled through a wall of glass. The rustic stone fireplace—the biggest outside Yellowstone National Park, he told me—was decorated with elk antlers and a pouch of arrows, which hung from the uneven chinked stones. Little signs were propped on the hearth. "It Is What It Is," one read. "Life without Horses . . . I Don't Think So!"

Chesnoff pointed out the trophies lining the walls: the caribou bagged in Nova Scotia, the elk shot in New Mexico, the framed boxing champi-

---

[*] In August 2023, a sign would briefly appear on Convict Grade Road. "COMING SOON," it declared. "Hot Hunter Springs Magificent [sic] Mission Hotel Natural Hot Spring Spa. Rebuilding history . . . One Brick At A Time." "Let's hope they build better than they spell," someone wrote on the *Buzz*.

onship belt—a gift from his client and friend Mike Tyson. Tyson had yet
to visit Montana. "He wants to come," Chesnoff said.

We took a tour of the ranch in his dually, driving along the high
embankment overlooking the Yellowstone, past the large garage where
he kept his Harley and the handsome guesthouse with a "VIP Cabin"
sign. Chesnoff showed me the spot where he wanted to build an art stu-
dio for Diana, who loved to paint. He pointed out a bald eagle on a tree
branch—one of their three resident eagles, he said proudly.

Chesnoff asked if I had heard about the judge's ruling the day before. "The thing with the windmills, it's pretty much dead," he said.
Windmills really weren't good for the environment. "They kill birds—
they really kill birds," he said with a shudder. He had sympathy for the
ranchers. But it seemed like their attorney cared more about the wind
farm than they did. It wasn't good for a lawyer to become emotionally
involved in a case.

Chesnoff was due in Los Angeles later that day, where he was representing the infamous real estate scion Robert Durst, on trial for the 2000
murder of his friend Susan Berman. It was a waste of time and taxpayer
money, trying a dying old man, Chesnoff tsked. He apologized for having to cut our visit short.

I got in my car and headed toward Sanctuary River Lane. Chesnoff,
who had said goodbye at the lodge, suddenly reemerged from the yawn-
ing double doorway. He waved at me, then broke into a run across the
green lawn. Chesnoff is a big man; the sight of him barreling across the
grass was arresting. I stopped the car and rolled down the window. Chesnoff asked me not to repeat anything he had said about Monica Tranel.

"She'll come after me," he said, shaking his head.

19

Eighteen Inches of Rain

Keep Me Montana

If I could pick a place to die
I wouldn't think on it
I'd lay me under this big sky
Of sun and clouds and grit . . .
Her wind-scraped land is in my bones
Her rivers made me free
And all the times I walked alone
Her spirit sang to me
                    —Aud Steinfeldt

In Loving Memory
Richard Ralph "Rick" Jarrett
1950–2023

February 4, 2023
Big Timber Lutheran Church
Big Timber, Montana

They began arriving at the church an hour before the service, in tractor caps and cattleman hats, faces scoured by weather and wind. The oak pews filled, and still more people arrived, squeezing in where they could. Christ looked down from the painted altarpiece amid his herd of white-faced sheep, a lamb cradled in one arm, the Good Shepherd of the one-time wool capital of the world.

On behalf of Rick Jarrett's family, the Reverend David Gunderson thanked everyone for coming out to mourn the death and celebrate the life of a man who was a very large presence in their community. His decline had been so difficult to see. Rick was such a font of energy and joyfulness and playfulness. No one wanted to see someone they loved decline and fail, to lose themselves. So there was a kind of relief at his passing. But the grief was so deep. "It's such an ache," he said.

Rick's Parkinson's disease had progressed rapidly—more falls and failures of memory, a deepening depression. One night, he was driving to town on the county road and became disoriented, lost on a road he had traveled his entire life.

"I don't know how to describe what I'm going through, but it's pissing me off," he told me. He had started using a walker, which he hated. He fell in a snowdrift trying to brush snow off his car and couldn't get back on his feet. He fell out of his own damn recliner. "I think it has a lot to do with that cow beating the shit out of me. The kind of work I did and the way I did it was hard on my body. Damn horses, damn cows, damn vehicles, damn everything."

In January 2022, Jami and her brother helped Rick move out of the ranch and into Big Timber's assisted living facility, the place with the mural of the Crazy Mountains in the dining room. He took his recliner, some family photographs, and a favorite painting of a cowboy riding through the sagebrush. His old dogs, Bo and Spur, had to stay behind. Sophie, his favorite, had been hit and killed by a car a few months before. It was almost a relief, he said. He was glad he wouldn't have to leave her.

The next year was tough. Rick didn't give two shits about anything anymore, Jami said. His memory was shot. He forgot to take his pills, but refused to let the staff at the assisted living center administer them, got real owly. Then Jami took his car keys away, which made him fucking mad. He told Jami he was going to go up into the Crazy Mountains to die. "Let me know how far you get in your walker," she said.

My last conversation with Rick was in September, a few months before he died. He put up a good front. The assisted living place was adequate; he couldn't complain. The food kept you from starving to death. Mostly, we talked about the weather. It was hot—102 degrees, he said. Big Timber had been hit by a series of late-summer heat waves. In September, they usually irrigated the grass crops once a day; now they'd have to irrigate twice. Harv and Jami were running the ranch, raising cattle, and the cattle were doing good. "Same old shit we do every year," he said, though now they were doing it without him.

Some years were good years and some years were bad years, he said. Some years, you sold your calves in the spring; other years, the market was better in the fall. In a good year, you sold your calves and gave a bottle of whiskey to the scaleman at the stockyard and bought everyone a steak dinner at the Grand. In a bad year, you took that check straight to the bank because your account had a minus sign on it and you needed credit to buy feed. It had been many years since Rick drank whiskey at the Grand to celebrate the sale of his calves.

"I'm coming to another crossroads," he told me before saying goodbye. "I've given the ranch away."

Reverend Gunderson read from the book of Micah and the gospel of Luke. Mimi Cremer played the church's mahogany organ as the congregation sang "Morning Has Broken." Two of Rick's grandsons shared memories of summer days down by the creek, chewing on mint, and cattle drives to the grazing lease on the Taylor Fork. They remembered his jokes—jokes you couldn't tell thirty years ago, let alone today. They would try to remember Rick the way he was then, full of life and energy, and not the way he was in his last years. "A man that lived that hard didn't need to die so hard," Jami's son, Jess, said.

Rick's girlfriend, Geri, came and so did Stacey from Hollywood, his old bunkhouse friend. Lois used to tease Rick that she'd sit in the front row at his funeral between his other girlfriends, but she didn't get the chance. She had moved back to Portland a few months before. Lois was grateful she'd been able to visit with Rick and say goodbye before she left Big Timber. "Now he's free to ride again," she said.

Tony Carroccia, Page Dringman's brother, stepped up to the altar with his guitar and sang "Eighteen Inches of Rain." It's a hard-luck song about pickup trucks that won't go, bitter coffee, and harsh winds from the east. It was one of Rick's favorites. All the rancher wants is a good horse, a good woman, a good price for his calves—and eighteen inches of rain.

I could see why Rick had loved the song, even if one good woman had never been enough for him. Eighteen inches of rain was a winning lottery ticket for anyone who raised grass for a living. It's what you hoped for in the spring and summer when you seeded your hay—an overabundance of water. In a dry year, when you didn't get enough inches of rain, you couldn't grow enough hay to feed your cows. The Crazy Mountain Cattle Company was high desert; they got less than twelve inches most years.

Rick thought about rain all the time—rain and snow. When he looked at the Crazy Mountains, he didn't see the breathtaking postcard that his neighbors saw. He saw water. The snowpack on its southern slopes were his irrigation source, the lifeblood of the ranch. Snowmelt from the Crazies fed Duck Creek throughout the spring and summer, providing the water to irrigate the fields that grew the grass that fed the cows.

In his last winter on the ranch, Rick spent a lot of time staring at the Crazies, worrying about the snowpack. The Crazies didn't get a lot of snow that winter. There was about 30 percent less water stored in the mountains than in past years, he guessed. "White six inches deep and white six feet deep are two different things," he said. When there wasn't enough white on the Crazies in January, there wouldn't be enough water in Duck Creek come summer. No one had figured out a way to make it snow in July.

Things were changing, Rick told me. "You have to have a personal relationship with the Crazy Mountains to understand what's going on," he said. He saw the signs.

Reverend Gunderson gave a prayer of thanksgiving for Rick, for his resilience and his hopefulness, for his stewardship of God's creation and its creatures. "Let him be to you as a sheep of your own fold, a lamb of your own flock," he asked God. And then the funeral was over and everyone headed over to the Grand for a buffet reception with an open bar. The wind was blowing hard by then. A gust knocked me sideways as I walked down McLeod Street.

Chafing dishes with mini-hamburgers and chicken skewers had been set out on a long table in the banquet room off the bar, the same room where Pattern had held its meet-and-greet. Alfred filled a plate with Swedish meatballs in gravy and settled down to eat in a booth with his son, Kevin. Kevin had moved out of the camper in the front yard and was now living in his grandparents' old house—Kelly Engel's one-time dream home. The Andersons had bought it back from Pattern. Ward Marshall and Michael Thompson lobbied the higher-ups at Pattern to sell it to the Andersons, well below market price. The company lost money on it, but it was the right thing to do, Marshall said.

Alfred and I chatted about Monica, who had put another forty thousand miles on her minivan that year in a run for Congress. Her campaign video featured a clip from the 1996 Olympics—Monica pulling hard in the engine room of the women's eight. "The engine room isn't for show ponies," she said. "You keep your eyes in the boat and work as hard as you can." She won the Democratic primary by a wide margin and waged an aggressive campaign against Ryan Zinke, Trump's former interior secretary. Zinke had resigned his post amid a welter of ethics investigations, one of which involved a private land deal with a Halliburton executive. Monica made her rival's ties to the fossil fuels industry a centerpiece of her campaign, tweeting an open letter to ConocoPhillips about the $460,000 it had paid Zinke in consulting fees. Zinke vowed to "kick the hell out of her." They had one debate. When Zinke equated Monica's legal work for a climate action group with a call to defund the police, she grabbed the microphone out of his hand. She lost the race by three percentage points—a tighter margin than anyone had predicted.

Montana had doubled down on its commitment to fossil fuels since the 2020 election of Republican governor Greg Gianforte, a tech entrepreneur best known for body-slamming a reporter during his 2017 reelection run for Congress. Six months after settling into the governor's mansion in Helena, Gianforte pulled Montana out of the US Climate Alliance, a bipartisan coalition of governors committed to action on climate change. In 2023, a Republican supermajority in Montana's legislature would pass a measure barring state agencies from considering "greenhouse gas emissions and corresponding impacts to the climate in the state or beyond the state's borders."

Monica wanted to change that. So did Ruby and Lilian Doyle, Shane Doyle's daughters. In 2020, Ruby, Lilian, and fourteen other children, aged two to eighteen, filed a lawsuit against the Gianforte administration, the Montana Public Service Commission, and a clutch of other state agencies for violating their constitutional right to "a clean and healthful environment" with their "fossil fuel–based state energy system." The lawsuit was called *Held v. State of Montana*, and it was headed for trial in Montana's First Judicial District that spring—the first youth climate lawsuit ever to be heard in an American courtroom. The children would achieve a landmark victory that summer, when Judge Kathy Seeley found in their favor, ruling that every ton of greenhouse gas emissions the state allowed into the atmosphere exacerbated their injuries and risked "locking in irreversible climate injuries."*

Maybe these kids would show everyone else the way forward. As Monica said on the campaign trail, "The Stone Age didn't end because we ran out of stones." She would seek a rematch against Zinke in a run for Congress in 2024.

Monica couldn't make Rick's funeral. She was awaiting a jury verdict in a courtroom in Malta, some two hundred miles to the north. That was a disappointment for Alfred, who hadn't been able to call her since he wrecked his flip phone. I helped him enter Monica's number in his new iPhone. Dorothy had dementia pretty bad, he told me. Their daughter, Karen, was sitting with her so Alfred could attend Rick's funeral.

I remembered the summer day Alfred took me up into the hills of his ranch in his side-by-side. Temperatures would reach ninety-nine degrees that day, and the air was bitter with smoke. "Gee whiz, it's hot," Alfred said. We drove past pastures of sainfoin, a tall grazing grass with bright pink flowers that sheep like even better than alfalfa. A hawk wafted overhead on a hot-air current; a few pronghorns bounded past, the fluffy white bustles of their hindquarters flashing in the sun. The pads for the wind turbines had left large circular indentations on the land, platters of stubborn brown in the meadow grass. A line of three ascended in a neat row toward the Crazies. "I want my ashes scattered by that pivot there,"

---

* *Held v. Montana* made history as one of the strongest court decisions on anthropogenic climate change. But its broader implications were unclear. Montana is among only a handful of states with a constitutional provision about the environment, and the children's lawsuit targeted a specific regulation that prohibited the state from considering all greenhouse gas emissions in the permitting of energy projects. Judge Seeley's ruling directed state agencies to consider climate impacts in their decision-making—but not to withhold approvals. The state appealed the decision, and the matter was pending in the Montana Supreme Court at the time of writing.

Alfred said, pointing. For seventy years, he had walked that land and drove that land, raised grass on it and run livestock on it. "It seems like that's where my ashes should be scattered," he said.

It was right where Turbine A02 would have been.

The reception got noisier, more boisterous. Harv sat in a corner, nursing a Michelob Ultra in a fleece pullover, cleaner than I'd ever seen him. Grief made him quiet. He struggled to find a way to describe what Rick had been to him. More than a father-in-law, was what he finally came up with. Jami moved through the room, talking to everyone, giving hugs. She had cooked a big dinner the night before, for her family and Jay's family and Rick's two surviving brothers. Then everyone went to the bar at the American Legion. That evening ended in the Town Pump parking lot, where some of the younger Jarretts puked by the dumpster bins. Jami had a hangover.

She drank a Red Bull and vodka and surveyed the room, wondering how much the open bar was going to cost her. Rick would have loved it. It was the last thing she could do for him. "He was my hero," Jami said. Rick had calluses on his hands, but he loved cooking, discussing ideas, meeting new people, being challenged. "How many things can you say about a round baler?" he'd say, when the men peeled off from the womenfolk at gatherings to talk ranching.

The family had put together a posterboard display decorated with Rick's cattle brand—a stacked R Bar J. There were photographs of Rick as a teenager with his horse, Geronimo; Rick as a young husband and father; Rick splashing in a creek with his grandsons; Rick on the back of a horse, moving cows under an immense blue sky heaped with clouds. Rick's older brother Ron stood nearby in a black leather vest and string tie. He was easy to spot from the old pictures of the four Jarrett boys.

I offered my condolences. Ron Jarrett owned a small dude ranch in the mountains on a 160-acre parcel of land that the Jarretts once used as a way station when they drove sheep to their summer grazing leaseholds in the Absaroka forest. Ron told me that he had been opposed to his brother's wind farm. Then he heard about the millionaires and billionaires who were fighting it, and decided he was all for it. If Rick's windmills scared off the rich people and drove down the price of land, maybe he could afford to buy some of it. As it was, he didn't have enough ground to grow hay for his own horses.

Jordan, Jami's daughter, came over to say good night. A flinty beauty with a tiny gold nose ring and the Jarrett gift for creative cussing, Jordan hadn't trusted herself to speak at the funeral service. Her eyes were red as she hugged Jami. Jordan was finishing a doctorate in sheep production at Texas A&M. She was talking about moving back to the ranch, maybe building herself a house there. Jami thought it was too risky, building a house on land their family didn't necessarily own. "What if we go belly-up and have to sell?" she said. "The ranch can't support everybody."

I knew that Jami and Harv were working hard to make the Crazy Mountain Cattle Company more financially stable, cutting expenses where they could, trying different range management techniques. The terms of their monetary settlement with Gordy and Chesnoff were confidential. But it hadn't made them whole, Jami said, not even close.

A lawsuit that Monica had filed on the ranchers' behalf against Jan Engwis and Wild Eagle Mountain Ranch was languishing in court; in a few months, the judge overseeing the case would retire and a new one would have to be assigned. Jami wasn't expecting to see any money out of the lawsuit, but she had made her peace with that. Her family never wanted to take money from those people in the first place.

"What we had always wanted to do was use our land in a way that we chose," Jami said. "If the wind farm had happened, we could have done the things we needed to do to ensure that the next generation could be there. That's what we wanted. Nobody wanted to settle."

In the summer of 2021, I visited David Leuschen at Switchback Ranch in Roscoe, the thirty-five-thousand acre spread on the northern front of the Beartooth Mountains that was the homebase of his multiunit ranching operation. The scenery was spectacular. Robert Redford had wanted to shoot *A River Runs through It* and *The Horse Whisperer* there, Leuschen said. He turned Redford down, twice.

The Crazy Mountains were in the news again. Leuschen had agreed to place a permanent conservation easement on Crazy Peak as part of the proposed land-swap deal with the Forest Service. The easement would protect Crazy Peak and its environs from being developed in any way—no motorized access, no shipping-container cabins, no commercial heli-skiing outfits, despite the rumors that had been circulating, much to Leuschen's annoyance. He hadn't planned on building anything up there anyway, he told me.* The agreement would also enshrine permanent access to Crazy Peak for Crow tribal members—so long as they contacted the ranch in advance and could produce Crow tribal ID.

But did anyone ever say thank you? Leuschen was disgruntled. He hadn't received any formal expression of gratitude from the Crow tribe, beyond an email from Shane Doyle. Now Doyle was making new demands, asking for access to Leuschen's mountains to conduct his cultural resource survey in the Crazies. During a flyover in a fixed-wing plane, Doyle had apparently spotted signs of old villages, tipi rings and such. Well, Leuschen could see that one coming a mile away. Doyle would discover a tipi ring on his land and insist on new restrictions in the name of historic preservation. Once you started giving people what they asked for, they'd try to take everything.

The conversation turned to Crazy Mountain Wind. Leuschen didn't have a voice in the decision to pull the plug on the wind farm, he said; he had recused himself. After the project was halted by the courts, the guys at Pattern had done as much as they thought appropriate to salvage it. It wasn't a great loss: Crazy Mountain Wind was a small project and the world was a big place. Pattern could build an eighty-megawatt wind farm somewhere else.

I told Leuschen about Alfred Anderson and Rick Jarrett, and what the loss of Crazy Mountain Wind meant for them. He knew all about Gordy and MacMillan, but this was the first he had heard about the ranchers who had leased their land to Pattern for the wind farm. He considered their situation. For these ranchers, the wind farm represented a revenue source that they didn't get. It was too bad. But things

---

* In March 2024, conservation groups would object to the final draft of the Forest Service plan because it failed to prohibit residential and commercial development—specifically "resorts, lodges and other luxury destinations"—on the newly privatized land in the Crazies. The Forest Service announced that it would issue a decision in late fall 2024.

like that happened all the time. There were no bad guys in this story, no white hats and black hats.

"Frankly, this is where people write books and get it wrong," he said. "I mean, this is America. This is how things work. There is no villain in that."

The little hamburgers and Swedish meatballs had gone cold in their chafing dishes. The church ladies set out platters of cookies and cut fruit that they had prepared. I thought about what Leuschen had said. He was right, of course. These things happen all the time. Business deals fall through. Ranches change hands. Set against the grand sweep of time, the Jarretts and Andersons were newcomers to Montana. However much their families had lost—whatever they might yet lose—the Crow families who lived on the land before them had lost more.

Jami tried not to be sentimental about it. She and Harv had attended a ranching-for-profit seminar earlier that year. You shouldn't view your family's land as your legacy—that was one of the things they taught. Your legacy was the work ethic your parents had passed on to you. If the land wasn't sustaining your family, there was no dishonor in selling it. Jami knew that Rick would understand that way of thinking. "If I sold the ranch tomorrow, my dad would say, 'If that's what you needed to do, you needed to do it,'" she said.

But the ranch *was* her legacy. She couldn't make herself think any other way. The hard times that the generations before her endured, the sacrifices they had made to hold on to that ground, that was her birthright. "If my family sells this ranch, we're never owning land again. When we let this go, our landowning legacy—and our legacy in this place—is over. We're done, and probably none of our descendants will work the land again," she said. Jami refused to be the Jarrett who decided it was just too hard and took the money.

Crazy Mountain Wind would have been a lifeline for the Jarretts and the Andersons. Its loss was their loss. But what did its death mean for everyone else? It was a small project, just eighty megawatts. The world was a big place. What was one less wind farm?

I found my answer in a map—an analysis of various pathways to achieving a net-zero power grid by 2035, conducted by the National Renewable Energy Laboratory, a division of the US Department of Energy. The year 2035 was not chosen at random. If carbon emissions go unchecked, global temperatures will exceed 1.5 degrees Celsius of warming within the decade and barrel past two degrees soon after. On the other side of that climactic trip wire, catastrophe awaits: the melting of the Greenland Ice Sheet, the full coral bleaching of the Great Barrier Reef, forest collapse in the Amazon. Droughts and famines, species extinctions, and flooded cities. Over a billion climate refugees. War.

Although the energy analysts modeled multiple energy-source options and scenarios for achieving 100 percent clean electricity, every road to a net-zero grid led to the same place: a wind farm. Lots of wind farms. America's clean energy future will depend on an unprecedented increase in wind and solar power development. Wind energy provided less than 10 percent of America's electricity in 2022. To get to net-zero and still be able to turn on the lights by 2035, the study concluded, the nation's wind generation capacity will have to increase a thousandfold.

"The only way to do that is to have a massive scale-up, and the only way to do that is to do it all over the country," Paul Denholm, a lead author of the study, told me. "It really just comes down to math. You need to build a bunch of these things."

There is no silver bullet, just a lot of silver buckshot. Seen this way, every wind project, however small, becomes essential. Or, as Denholm put it, "How many can you walk away from?"

The party for Rick Jarrett went late into the night. The mourners crowded the bar until closing, whooping and laughing as the harried bartender struggled to keep up with the drink orders. The next morning, the woman at the front desk shook her head over how raucous that funeral had been. "People need to sleep," she said.

Before I left Big Timber, I drove along Convict Grade Road and

North Yellowstone Trail, retracing Judge Oldenburg's caravan through the land at the heart of *Diana's Great Idea v. Crazy Mountain Wind*. There was a new sign at the head of the private road to Chesnoff's lodge. Sanctuary River Lane had become Raptors Nest Drive. Maybe it was a tribute to the eagles that helped put an end to Crazy Mountain Wind.

The sky hung low and gray over the hills. Duck Creek carved a frozen white path through the cottonwoods and golden willows, their bare branches raking the wind. I passed the crumbling stone wall at Hunter's Hot Springs that was once the Dakota Hotel, and the ruined schoolhouse where Rick Jarrett rode his horse as a boy. Cows stood in pastures of bleached grass, banded with snow. They'd be calving soon. The Crazy Mountains towered above them, rising up from the plains in all their astonishing white and blue majesty. I wondered how many inches of white were on those mountains, and if it would be enough.

ACKNOWLEDGMENTS

A story like this comes along once in a lifetime. I am filled with gratitude for the people who trusted me with their share of it, and sadness that the man at its heart didn't live to see this book in print. Rick Jarrett, how lucky I was to know you.

I want to begin by thanking Jami Jarrett Moody. Rick never would have let me across his cattle guard if Jami hadn't said it was okay. Thanks to Jami, and to Harv Van Wagoner, for showing me how much hard work and heart it takes to be a rancher, every damn day.

Thanks to Alfred and Dorothy Anderson, and to Kevin Anderson, for the many hours at your kitchen table and under the shade tree, and for answering my endless questions with patience and kindness.

Thanks to Jim and Roxie Hogemark, for sharing your lives on Wild Eagle Mountain, and for letting me tag along as you moved the cows and calves down from the mountains.

Thanks to Russell and Glenda Gordy, for welcoming me to Double Arrow and Hunter's Hot Springs, and for answering every question with candor and courtesy. I'm grateful to have experienced the Crazies through your eyes.

Thanks to David Chesnoff, for being so generous with your time and your insights into a remarkable career, and for showing me your ranch on a rare day off.

Thanks to David Leuschen, for welcoming me to the Roscoe and Lazy K Bar units of Switchback Ranch, and for sharing your unique perspective on the Crazy Mountains.

I am profoundly grateful to Monica Tranel. Thank you for taking me behind the front lines of the legal battle over Crazy Mountain Wind, and so much more. My thanks to Greg Lind, Adrienne Tranel, Ben Tranel, and Virginia Tranel.

My deep thanks to Shane Doyle, for sharing your knowledge of Crow Country, and for a hike into Awaxaawippíia that transformed my understanding of what this book needed to be.

I'm grateful to Jaffe Wilde for our many conversations over the years, and to Chloe Wilde. Your stories brought Marty to life. Thanks to Annette Dea-Dart, and to Lockley Bremner and Pat Schildt, for sharing memories of Marty's time on the Blackfeet Nation.

I'm indebted to Charles Shawley. Thanks for sharing a fraction of your knowledge about wind power, the challenges of developing wind farms in Montana, and the complexities of the federal production tax credit. Any mistakes are mine.

Not everyone pays such close attention to the world around them as Lois Huffman. Lois, thanks for sharing your true superpower.

My thanks to Jean Chapel, curator at the Crazy Mountain Museum and a font of knowledge about Big Timber; Karen Reinhart, curator at the Yellowstone Gateway Museum; and Jerry Brekke, Park County historian emeritus. Thanks to Gary Barnhart, library technician with the Archives and Special Collections at Montana State University, and to Misti Titeca and all the librarians at Big Timber's Carnegie Public Library.

Thanks to Susan Badger Doyle for generously sharing documents about merchant trains on the Bozeman Trail. Thanks to Timothy Mc-Cleary at Little Big Horn College and Marsha Fulton with the Extreme History Project. Thank you, Rachel Sue Old Coyote and Sharon Rich Pohlman.

I'm grateful to the people of Big Timber. Thanks to Pastors Ron and Kathy Countryman, Brian Engle, and Lindsey Erin Kroskob. Thanks to Jess Moody and Jordan Moody. Thanks to Jennifer Breck, Brandon Droeger, Rob Fleming, Jerry Graves, Josiah Kalinauskas, Kent and Kathy Morgan, and Julie Hogemark Patterson. My thanks to the Chavez family.

Thanks to Sweet Grass County officials, past and present: Page Dringman, Pat Dringman, Bob Faw, Susan Metcalf, J. V. Moody, Susie Mosness, Vera Pederson, Melanie Roe, and Bill Wallace. Thanks to Julie Johnson and Monte Koch.

Thanks to Larry Lahren, Cathy Whitlock, and Eske Willerslev, whose work in archaeology, paleoclimatology, and evolutionary genetics have opened a window on the Crazy Mountains' past. Thanks to Sarah Anzick and the Anzick family, for sharing the place where it was found.

Thanks to Ross Crandall, Carol Endicott, and Adam Sepulveda, and all the aquatic ecologists and wildlife biologists who are charting the perilous future of the creatures that call the Crazies home.

I'm grateful to the wind industry veterans who shared their knowledge with me. Thanks to Ward Marshall, and to Greg Adams, Jeff Fox, and Michael Uda.

Thanks to the conservationists and public lands advocates: Emily Cleveland with Wild Montana, Pete Kolbenschlag with the Colorado Farm and Food Alliance, Alison Gallensky with Rocky Mountain Wild, Erica Lighthiser with the Park County Environmental Council, and Jessica Wiese, formerly with the Montana Land Reliance.

My thanks to Jeff Bollman at Montana's Department of Natural Resources and Conservation and Paul Denholm at the National Renewable Energy Laboratory. Travis Kavulla, thank you.

Thanks to Molly Bradberry, Park County clerk of district court, for helping me stay afloat on the river of legal filings over Crazy Mountain Wind, and to Phillip English, IT systems analyst at the Montana Public Service Commission.

Thanks to Dean Apostol, Alan Batkin, Eric Bernt, Susan Davis, Kelly Engel, Chris Dern, David Ferrara, Jonathan Foote, Tom Glass, Mavis Greer, Penelope Hatten, John Katsilometes, Isabel Lara, Fred Michini, Alicia Murphy, Marcia O'Neill, Tim Poster, Bill Roberts, Karen Searle, Jack Sheehan, John Surma, Mark Taylor, Thomas Usher, and Don Webb. Thanks to Jim Taylor, godfather of the modern ranch real estate industry, and to ranch brokers James Esperti, Greg Fay, Tom Morse, Tim Murphy, and David Viers.

I'm grateful for the support of my colleagues at the *Wall Street Journal*, past and present. Emily Gitter and Beth DeCarbo, thank you for sending me to Montana in the first place. Thanks to *WSJ* energy reporter Luis Garcia, and to Stephanie Capparell, Heather Halberstadt, Kat Malott, and the entire *WSJ* Mansion team.

My thanks to the poet Aud Steinfeldt, for your generous permission to reproduce verses from "Keep Me Montana." Thanks to Barbara Van Cleve for the photograph that graces the book's cover.

I am forever grateful to my agent, Sabrina Taitz, who believed in this book from the beginning, advocated for it tirelessly, and was at my side through every twist and turn. Thanks to my brilliant editor, Megan Hogan, for inspiring me with your vision of what this book could be, and for working so hard to help me achieve it. Thanks to the incomparable Julie Tate, for fact-checking every quote, date, and dollar sign (twice), and to Elisa Rivlin for your eagle-eyed legal review. Thank you, Jonathan Karp and the entire team at Simon & Schuster, for giving my book the best home a writer could hope for. Lloyd Davis and Amy Medeiros, thanks for your meticulous copyediting and tireless attention to detail. Thanks to Martha Kennedy for a beautiful cover, and to Carly Loman for making the inside of the book look just as good. Thanks to Brianna Scharfenberg and Elizabeth Venere for helping *The Crazies* find a wider audience.

Reporting and writing this book made me think a lot about family. Time and again, it made me appreciate how fortunate I am to have my own. I owe everything to my parents, Kenneth and Martha Gamerman. I finished this book during the last, hard year of my father's life. I could not have done it without the courage, heart, and grit that was his gift to me. Mom, thank you for your love and wisdom, which flow through everything I do. Thanks to my sisters, Nancy and Ellen, friends for life.

Max, Sarah, Jack, and Gloria, thanks to each one of you, for your patience and good cheer, and for your sustaining faith in me and in this project. In the toughest moments, you kept me going. I'm so lucky to have you in my corner.

And finally, my husband, Kevin Conley. My first reader, my last reader, and everything in between. Thank you for the countless ways you made this book—and all that is precious—possible. Two last words, just for you: still crazy.

NOTES

PREFACE

Amy Gamerman, "Oilman Russell Gordy has a $96 million collection—of ranches," *Wall Street Journal*, July 20, 2017.

PROLOGUE

Note: Descriptions of where people sat, how they dressed, etc., are drawn from interviews with multiple sources. The thoughts attributed to them are drawn from interviews, court filings, and sworn testimony, as recorded in the transcript of proceedings for Case No. DV 2018-161, *Diana's Great Idea, LLC, et al. v. Crazy Mountain Wind, LLC, et al.*, Sixth Judicial District Court, Park and Sweet Grass Counties.

7 **A former cop . . . Rick Jarrett's obsessive wind development efforts:** "Affidavit of Jan Engwis," *Diana's Great Idea v. Crazy Mountain Wind*.

1. RANCHING IT

Note: The histories of the Jarrett and Mendenhall families are interwoven with the history of Big Timber itself. The Crazy Mountain Museum in Big Timber features exhibits about both families.

9 **A year later, a railway surveyor platted:** Phyllis Smith, *Montana Sweet Grass Country: From Melville to the Boulder River Valley* (Big Timber, MT: Sweet Grass Museum Society, 2002).
21 ***Sunset* magazine ran a glowing feature:** Jeff Phillips, "Ranch Vacation: Reconnect with Your Inner Cowboy in Montana," *Sunset*, August 6, 2004.

2. THE TREASURE STATE

Note: The archives of the Crazy Mountain Museum and the Yellowstone Gateway Museum in Livingston contain a treasure trove of ephemera—old photographs and postcards, a battered cookbook—that opened a window into the past lives of Big Timber and Hunter's Hot Springs. When the coronavirus pandemic made visiting museums—or anywhere—impossible, I immersed myself in nineteenth-century newspapers, time-traveling to the Montana Territory through the portals of the Library of Congress's *Chronicling America* database and the Montana Historical Society's Montana Newspapers website—now sadly discontinued.

Susan Badger Doyle's two-volume history and compendium, *Journeys to the Land of Gold: Emigrant Diaries from the Bozeman Trail, 1863–1866* (Helena: Montana Historical Society Press, 2000), was an invaluable resource in reconstructing the Hunter family's travels through Crow Country, and Cyrus B. Mendenhall's passage with a merchant train in the final year of the Bozeman Trail.

23 **The first tourist to record his impressions:** Meriwether Lewis, William Clark, et al., *The Journals of the Lewis and Clark Expedition*, ed. Gary Moulton (Lincoln: University of Nebraska Press/University of Nebraska–Lincoln Libraries Electronic Text Center, 2005).

Clark's impressions of the Crazies and the land that would become Sweet Grass County are recorded in his journal entries for July 15–17, 1806.

24 **Fifty-eight years and one day after Clark's ride-by:** The Hunters seem to have traveled in the same party as Missouri banker John T. Smith: "John T. Smith Reminiscence, 1864," Doyle, *Journeys to the Land of Gold*, vol. 1.

25 **Large numbers of Southern secessionists:** Stanley R. Davison and Dale Tash, "Confederate Backwash in Montana Territory," *Montana: The Magazine of Western History*, Autumn 1967, 50–58.

The strong Confederate presence in Montana's mining camps spilled over into the territory's politics. The territorial legislature enacted a slew of racist laws against Black Montanans—enforcing school segregation, deeming Black people incompetent to testify in court proceedings—that, in the authors' words, "would not be equaled in the southern states for another decade."

25 **Dr. Hunter's war:** Sharon Rich Pohlman, a descendant of Andrew Jackson Hunter, has compiled a wealth of information about his Civil War service from the National Archives and the Civil War Descendants Society, among other sources, which she generously shared.

25 **"So we found ourselves in a short time":** Susan C. Hunter's "Reminiscence," handwritten on lined notepaper in 1912, recounts the Hunter family's experiences on the Bozeman Trail, their luckless sojourn in the Montana goldfields, and their early days at the hot springs. The "Reminiscence" is part of the Mary Hunter Doane Papers, 1860–1952, housed in the Merrill G. Burlingame Special Collections of the Montana State University Library.

26 **"Montana's growth, in one sense":** K. Ross Toole, *Montana: An Uncommon Land* (Norman: University of Oklahoma Press, 1959).

26 **Now, as he forded the Yellowstone:** Doyle, *Journeys to the Land of Gold,* vol. 1.

The Hunters and other emigrants who traveled the Bozeman Trail in the summer of 1864 followed Jim Bridger's route from Rock Creek to the Yellowstone River, fording the river at a spot about three miles east of Springdale—at the mouth of Duck Creek. This difficult ford became known as Bridger's Crossing.

27 **People on a wagon train . . . had the bright idea of washing their odiferous clothes:** This detail comes from a typewritten guide for the Park County Historical Society's Second Annual Historic Tour (August 3, 1986), Yellowstone Gateway Museum Archives.

28 **In the winter of 1867, some twenty Apsáalooke chiefs:** The French engineer and geologist Louis L. Simonin gave an eyewitness account of the summit at Fort Laramie in *The Rocky Mountain West in 1867*, translated and annotated by Wilson O. Clough (Lincoln: University of Nebraska Press, 1966).

28 **"The country across the river":** *Report of the Commission Appointed under Act of Congress Approved March 3, 1873, to Negotiate with the Crow Indians in Montana Territory* (Washington, DC: Government Printing Office, 1873).

29 **Bolts of calico, tin kettles, socks:** Frederick E. Hoxie, *Parading through History: The Making of the Crow Nation in America 1805–1933* (Cambridge, UK: Cambridge University Press, 1995).

   Marsha Fulton and Crystal Alegria's Extreme History Project created a website dedicated to the history of Fort Parker, the first Crow Agency: https://fortparkerhistory.org/the-history-of-fort-parker/.

30 **Dr. Hunter's health resort:** Michael A. Leeson, *History of Montana 1739–1885* (Chicago: Warner, Beers, 1885).

   Thomas H. LeForge described Dr. Hunter's compulsive tobacco-chewing and air of benign pomposity in his *Memoirs of a White Crow Indian (Thomas H. LeForge), as Told by Thomas B. Marquis* (Lincoln: University of Nebraska Press, 1974 [1928]).

31 **An Iowa farmer, Mendenhall followed the trail:** *Report of Trains Organized at Fort Laramie, June 1886*, National Archives, Record Group 393, Part 1, E3731, Box 1A, DP, LR, 1866.

   Note: Mendenhall figures in several early histories of Montana, including *Progressive Men of the State of Montana* (Chicago: A. W. Bowen, 1903[?]). A more personal glimpse of Mendenhall is provided by his daughter (and Rick Jarrett's great-grandmother) Inez Jarrett in her essay "Memories of Montana," published in the *Billings Gazette* on November 29, 1964.

31 **"This land has buffalo on it":** Hoxie, *Parading through History*.

31 **Shooting buffalo was a popular pioneer pastime:** Doyle, *Journeys to the Land of Gold*, vol. 1.

   John T. Smith, who traveled Bozeman's trail in the summer of 1864 with his two sons, reminisced about reaching the Big Horn River on Independence Day—a holiday "which the boys celebrated by killing over a hundred buffalo."

33 **He sponsored buffalo-hunting contests:** Buffalo Bill Cody's "Famous Hunting Parties of the Plains," published in *Cosmopolitan* magazine in June 1894, is part of the digital collections of the William F. Cody Archive.

35 **Mendenhall became one of the highest taxpayers:** "Heavy taxpayers," *Livingston Enterprise*, November 2, 1887.

35 **His bay Billy:** "How we celebrated," *Livingston Enterprise*, July 9, 1887.

35 **When paying guests were in short supply:** "From a letter received from Dr. A. J. Hunter," *Bozeman Weekly Chronicle*, November 19, 1884.

35 **Dr. Hunter's name appeared on a list:** "Delinquent tax list of Gallatin County, Montana," *Bozeman Weekly Chronicle*, February 11, 1885.

35 **The Northern Pacific platted a town:** Yellowstone Gateway Museum Archives, including photographs, postcards, and Northern Pacific Railway promotional material.

36 **Mendenhall hired a civil engineer:** Mendenhall plat, Park County public records.

37 **Mendenhall took measure of his losses:** Ray Jarrett, "The Hunter's Hot Springs Story," *Big Timber Pioneer*, Centennial Edition, June 29, 1983.

38 **John "Liver-Eating" Johnson:** "We have received from Fred Enzenbach, the photographer at Hunter's Hot Springs," *Big Timber Pioneer*, April 18, 1895.

38 **Walter Goodall, former secretary:** "A Montana reverie," *Livingston Enterprise*, August 20, 1887.

38 **Big Timber acquired all the accoutrements:** Sources include Smith, *Montana Sweet Grass Country*; Leslie Paulson Stryker and the Crazy Mountain Museum, *Images of America: Big Timber* (Charleston, SC: Arcadia Publishing, 2009); Sanborn Fire Insurance maps, Big Timber, August 1893 and September 1896; "John S. Solberg, last of the pioneer merchants, passes," *Big Timber Pioneer*, June 8, 1933; Brett French, "Big Timber's Chinatown: dig reveals a rich cultural past," *Billings Gazette*, June 12, 2008; Christopher William Merritt, "'The Coming Man from Canton': Chinese Experience in Montana (1862–1943)" (PhD diss., University of Montana, 2010), 5, https://scholarworks.umt.edu/etd/5/.

39 **An opium den did business:** Merritt, "'The Coming Man from Canton,'" 5.

39 **"Rich and poor, high and low":** "Funeral services held Sunday at local church for Thos. K. Lee," *Big Timber Pioneer*, March 31, 1938; "Pioneer files, Aug. 23, 1923: Judge T. K. Lee ate his first dinner," *Big Timber Pioneer*, August 21, 1941; Brett French, "Big Timber's Chinatown: Dig reveals a rich cultural past," *Billings Gazette*, June 12, 2008.

39 **In April 1903, the *Pioneer* reported:** "Additional Local," *Big Timber Pioneer*, April 16, 1903.

39 **Some men shot up a restaurant:** Judi Thompson, "Whatever became of Big Timber's Chinese?" *Big Timber Pioneer*, September 4, 1985.

39 **only three Chinese residents:** Merritt, "'The Coming Man from Canton,'" 5.

40 **Murray built the Dakota Hotel:** *Hunter's Hot Springs, in the Rockies of Montana*, Northern Pacific Railway brochure, 1910.

40 **A few decades later, it was gone:** Cindy Shearer, "Hunter's Hot Springs: The Forgotten Opulence of a Bygone Era," *Bozeman Magazine*, July 1, 2018; As-

sociated Press, "Blaze destroys Hunters Hot Springs," *Billings Gazette*, November 4, 1932.

40 **Various commercial enterprises:** "Hunter's Hot Springs closing greenhouse," *Livingston Enterprise,* October 21, 1992; "Growing tomatoes," *Big Timber Pioneer,* November 6, 1997.

3. IF YOU GIVE ANYBODY LUCK, SHIT WILL DO FOR BRAINS

41 **He declared himself shocked:** Scott McMillion, "Ranch buyer keeps a low profile," *Bozeman Daily Chronicle*, April 13, 2002.

43 **Russell grew up in a cramped single-story brick home:** Houston (Greater) Residence White Pages, Southwestern Bell, May 1956 (University of Texas, Austin Digital Collections). Harris County, Texas, public records.

43 **He grew to mind when his basketball team:** Cara Smith, "Meet Russell Gordy, one of Houston's most powerful developers you've never heard of," *Houston Business Journal*, June 1, 2017.

43 **Gordys had lived in the parish since the Reconstruction Era:** US Census records.

44 **Lumber merchants descended on Vernon:** Sources include "Visions of Vernon," *Beauregard (LA) Daily News*, August 17, 2020; Steve D. Smith, *A Good Home for a Poor Man: Fort Polk and Vernon Parish, 1800–1940* (Tallahassee, FL: Southeast Archeological Center/National Park Service, 1999).

The *Mississippi Rails* website offers a short history of the White-Grandin Lumber Company and its railroad: https://www.msrailroads.com/Leesv_Sla gle_Eastern.htm.

44 **Vernon Parish had been cut over . . . all the way to Lake Charles:** Vernon Parish Tourism Commission, "Logging in Vernon Parish," *Louisiana's Legend Country: Vernon Parish*, https://vernonparish.org/about-us/history/logging-in -vernon-parish/.

45 **At the time, a wildcat oilman named Joe Walter:** James P. Sterba, "Houston oil: A skyrocketing wildcatter comes of age," *New York Times*, November 6, 1977.

46 **In the mid-1980s, a friend of Gordy's brought him a deal on coalbed methane:** "Russell Gordy on business, land and elk," *Casper (WY) Journal,* June 11, 2012.

Sources on coalbed methane extraction and wastewater disposal include Gary Bryner, "Coalbed Methane Development in the Intermountain West: Primer," paper presented at Coalbed Methane Development in the Intermountain West, University of Colorado Law School, Boulder, CO, April 4–5, 2002; *Coalbed Methane Extraction: Detailed Study Report*, Environmental Protection Agency, December 2010.

49 **In between stints as George H. W. Bush's secretary of defense:** "Dick Cheney Resumes Role as Chairman of Halliburton Company," Halliburton press release, February 1, 2000.

50 **On his ninth day in office, Bush created the National Energy Policy Develop-**

ment Group: *Report of the National Energy Policy Development Group* (Washington, DC: US Government Printing Office, May 2001).

50 **The task force held some forty secret meetings:** The Cheney Energy Task Force records were released under court order to the National Resources Defense Council, which published them online: https://www.nrdc.org/resources/cheney-energy-task-force.

   See also *Energy Task Force: Process Used to Develop the National Energy Policy: Report to Congressional Requesters*, US General Accounting Office, August 2003.

51 **By 2004, wind power accounted:** *Renewable Energy: Wind Power's Contribution to Electric Power Generation and Impact on Farms and Rural Communities: Report to the Ranking Democratic Member, Committee on Agriculture, Nutrition, and Forestry, US Senate*, US Government Accountability Office, September 2004.

51 **Gordy was . . . buying up oil and gas exploration leases:** Rocky Mountain Wild, an environmental advocacy group, has created an interactive map that shows current and upcoming lease sales by the Bureau of Land Management. It can be accessed through their website: https://rmwild.maps.arcgis.com/apps/web appviewer/index.html?id=9d8b507edd81456a9f906813141114745.

53 **William—"Wild Bill" to his friends:** Kelly McMillan Manley, "Bill Koch's Wild West Adventure," *5280: Denver's Mile High Magazine*, February 2013.

53 **But when SGI and GEC's interests in the region began to collide:** Tim Mutrie, "Justice Dept. investigating power play on local gas pipelines," *Aspen (CO) Journalism*, October 14, 2012; Andrew Travers, "Settlement in gas lease case draws local criticism," *Aspen (CO) Daily News*, April 24, 2012.

55 **The Department of Justice launched a two-year investigation:** The complete docket of the DOJ's case against SGI and GEC, including public comments and the judge's final decision, is on the official website of the Antitrust Division of the US Department of Justice: https://www.justice.gov/atr/case/us-v-sg-inter ests-i-ltd-et-al.

57 **John Moreland cut his teeth:** A copy of John W. Moreland's 2007 self-published memoir, *As I Remember It*, can be found at the Carnegie Public Library, Big Timber, MT.

58 **"a view with some dirt under it":** "Bonhomme Ranch still for sale," *Bozeman Daily Chronicle*, December 28, 2001.

58 **He spent his days farming, fencing, and raising cattle:** "David Gibson [obituary]," *Big Timber Pioneer*, October 8, 2020.

59 **It was a mix of longtime ranching families and some moneyed newcomers:** Sweet Grass and Park County public records.

4. AWAXAAWIPPÍIA

Sources for this chapter include:
"Annual Report of F. D. Pease, agent Crow agency," *Report of the Commissioner*

of Indian Affairs to the Secretary of the Interior for the Year 1871 (Washington, DC: Government Printing Office, 1872).

Tim Bernardis, *Crow Social Studies: Baleeisbaalischiweé History, Teacher's Guide* (Crow Agency, MT: Bilingual Materials Development Center, 1986).

Frederick E. Hoxie, *Parading through History: The Making of the Crow Nation in America 1805–1933* (Cambridge, UK: Cambridge University Press, 1995).

Frank B. Linderman, *Pretty-Shield: Medicine Woman of the Crows* (Lincoln: Bison Books/University of Nebraska Press, 1974 [1932]).

———, *Plenty Coups, Chief of the Crows*, new ed., introduction by Barney Old Coyote Jr. and Phenocia Bauerle, afterword by Timothy P. McCleary (Lincoln: Bison Books/University of Nebraska Press, 2002 [1930]).

Joseph Medicine Crow, *From the Heart of the Crow Country: The Crow Indians' Own Stories* (New York: Orion Books, 1992).

Report of the Commissioner of Indian Affairs to the Department of the Interior for the Year 1873 (Washington, DC: Government Printing Office, 1874).

Father Pierre-Jean de Smet, *Life, Letters and Travels of Father Pierre-Jean de Smet, S.J., 1801–1873*, vol. 1, ed. Hiram Martin Chittenden and Alfred Talbot Richardson (New York: Francis P. Harper, 1904).

Two Leggings, *Two Leggings: The Making of a Crow Warrior*, based on a field manuscript prepared by Willem Wildschut for the Museum of the American Indian (Lincoln: University of Nebraska Press, 1982 [1967]).

Willem Wildschut and Ludwell "Bud" Lake, *Exploits of Plenty Coups, Chief of the Crows* (Meadville, PA: Fulton Books, 2022).

61 **Sediment cores drawn from the muddy depths:** James V. Benes, Virginia Iglesias, and Cathy Whitlock, "Postglacial Vegetation Dynamics at High Elevation from Fairy Lake in the Northern Greater Yellowstone Ecosystem," *Quaternary Research* 92, no. 2 (September 2019): 365–80.

61 **The first people arrived at the end of the last Ice Age:** Livingston archaeologist Larry Lahren has studied sites in and around the Crazy Mountains for decades. His book *Homeland: An Archaeologist's View of Yellowstone Country's Past* (Livingston, MT: Cayuse Press, 2006) offers a portrait of what Sweet Grass County would have looked like in the late Pleistocene, some thirteen thousand years ago.

62 **But the word that the Crow, or . . . offers a better portal:** The Apsáalooke Place Names Database, Little Big Horn College: http://lib.lbhc.edu/index.php?q=node/200.

63 **In 1873, Felix Brunot, an envoy:** Brunot's account of his meeting at Crow Agency is in *Report of the Commission Appointed under Act of Congress Approved March 3, 1873, to Negotiate with the Crow Indians in Montana Territory* (Washington, DC: Government Printing Office, 1873)

65 **"We stole the hunting grounds of the Crows":** Hoxie, *Parading through History*.

71 **Hargis and his friends had unearthed the oldest grave in the Americas:** Sources

for the discovery of the Anzick gravesite and the analysis of its contents include:

Lorena Becerra-Valdivia et al., "Reassessing the Chronology of the Archaeological Site of Anzick," *Proceedings of the National Academy of Sciences* 115, no. 27 (July 3, 2018): 7000–7003.

Lahren, *Homeland*.

Larry Lahren and Robson Bonnichsen, "Bone Foreshafts from a Clovis Burial in Southwestern Montana," *Science* 186, no. 4159 (October 11, 1974): 147–50.

Douglas W. Owsley and David R. Hunt, "Clovis and Early Archaic Crania from the Anzick Site (24PA506), Park County, Montana," *Plains Anthropologist* 46, no. 176 (May 2001): 115–24.

Philip J. Wilke, Jeffrey Flenniken, and Terry L. Ozbun, "Clovis Technology at the Anzick Site, Montana," *Journal of California and Great Basin Anthropology* 13, no. 2 (1991): 242–72.

Eske Willerslev et al., "The Genome of a Late Pleistocene Human from a Clovis Burial Site in Western Montana," *Nature* 506, no. 7487 (February 13, 2014): 225–29.

5. COYOTE WIND

78 **Dave, a fifty-four-year-old wind hippie:** "David Gregory Healow [obituary]," *Billings Gazette,* January 15, 2020.

81 **He won a Department of Energy grant:** Sources for Marty's wind energy projects on the Blackfeet Reservation include:

"Native Americans See Money in the Wind," *Windpower Monthly*, July 1, 1996.

Blackfeet Tribe—1995 Project, Office of Indian Energy Policy and Programs, US Department of Energy, May 1988.

"Blackfeet Wind Projects Provide Foundation for Future Development," *Nawig News: The Quarterly Newsletter of the Native American Wind Interest Group*, Summer 2004.

"The Future Is Green: Tribal Colleges Saving Water, Electricity—and Money," *Tribal College Journal* 17, no. 2 (Winter 2005).

Jeri Lawrence, "Blackfeet Nation Energy Organization Development: First Steps to Renewable Energy Grant Awarded by US Department of Energy," Blackfeet Renewable Energy Program, 2016.

84 **It was a busy week on the ranch:** Crazy Mountain Cattle Company guest log.

88 **In the summer of 1902 . . . visiting circus elephant:** Smith, *Montana Sweet Grass Country*.

88 **In 1978, Congress enacted the Public Utility Regulatory Policies Act:** For an overview of PURPA and Qualifying Facilities, see https://www.ferc.gov/qf.

89 **A NASA report on windmill technology:** Dennis G. Shepherd, *Historical De-*

velopment of the Windmill, Lewis Research Center, National Aeronautics and Space Administration, 1990.

90 **In 2005, Marty offered Rick a one-year wind lease agreement:** Sweet Grass County public records.

92 **Officials in the state's Department of Natural Resources and Conservation (DNRC):** Sonja Nowakowski, "Maximizing State Land Use for Energy Generation," in *2009–10 Energy Policy for Montana*, Energy and Telecommunications Interim Committee (Montana), September 2009.

92 **Their consultant flagged Section 36:** "Site Assessment for Coyote Wind, LLC," compiled by Martin H. Wilde, July 4, 2004, appendix C in *Draft Environmental Impact Statement for Coyote Wind Project*, Montana Department of Natural Resources and Conservation, August 2009.

93 **Internal emails by DNRC staffers:** A 2,208-page tranche of emails was released on March 31, 2011, during discovery for Case No. DV-2010-09, a lawsuit filed by Wild Eagle Mountain Ranch, Rock Creek Ranch, Engwis Investment Company, and R. F. Building Company (the latter two being Jan Engwis's holding companies), against the Montana Department of Natural Resources and Conservation in Montana's Sixth Judicial District Court.

96 **In January 2008, Bollman got a phone call:** Bollman references this call in an email included in State's Responses to Engwis/R. F. Building Company's First Combined Discovery Request to DNRC, Case No. DV-2010-09.

97 **Jan and Karen Engwis had moved . . . buying the first piece of a ranch:** Sweet Grass County public records.

97 **Along with three and a half miles:** "Featuring Engwis Ranch," *Farm & Ranch West* 38 (October 2, 2012).

97 **Their idyll was disrupted one morning:** Jan Engwis, direct testimony, transcript of proceedings, Case No. DV 2018-161, *Diana's Great Idea v. Crazy Mountain Wind*.

97 **That particular strip of land:** Sweet Grass County public records: See "Exhibit A" in Document 150925, Amended Special Warranty Deed (To Correct Legal Description).

97 **Two metal fence posts:** A photograph of the fence posts was attached to a thirty-one-page letter dated September 10, 2009, submitted by Jan Engwis's attorney, Stephen Woodruff, during the public comment period for Coyote Wind. It is included in Appendix A of the DNRC's *Final Environmental Impact Statement Amending and Adopting the Draft Environmental Impact Statement for Coyote Wind Project*, November 2009.

98 **As part of his due diligence, Marty had hired Dr. Al Harmata:** Dr. Harmata's "Complete Fish and Wildlife Service Impact Index" is included in Appendix C of the Montana DNRC's *Draft Environmental Impact Statement for Coyote Wind Project*.

99 **Prior to 2005, up to 117 golden eagles, 300 red-tailed hawks:** ICF International,

Final Report: Altamont Pass Wind Resource Area Bird Fatality Study, Monitoring Years 2005–2013, Alameda County Community Development Agency, April 2016.

100 **Every aspect of the state trust parcel was examined:** These findings are summarized in the Montana DNRC's *Draft Environmental Impact Statement for Coyote Wind Project*.

101 **Should the pipeline spring a leak:** There have been several pipeline spills and leaks in Montana in recent years:

Matthew Brown, "Pipeline that spilled into Yellowstone to be removed," *Great Falls (MT) Tribune*, April 7, 2015.

Cindy Uken, "Cleanup, investigation underway after Phillips 66 pipeline leaks gas on Crow land," *Billings Gazette*, July 4, 2013.

102 **Public hearings were held:** Transcript of public comments, "Springdale/Coyote Wind Farm Project Hearing, September 2, 2009," Appendix B of the Montana DNRC's *Final Environmental Impact Statement Amending and Adopting the Draft Environmental Impact Statement for Coyote Wind Project*.

106 **In 2016, Judge McKeon would make national headlines:** Sarah Begley, "Judge Defends 60-Day Sentence for Father who Repeatedly Raped His 12-Year-Old Daughter," *Time*, October 19, 2016.

6. ALFRED AND WHITNEY AND A $10,000 BULL

112 **He knew Jan Engwis . . . Hunter Hot Springs Canal Company:** Jan Engwis is named as the registered agent for the HHSCC on corporate filings and Montana Water Court decisions.

113 **Cargill Incorporated, the largest privately owned:** David Whitford with Doris Burke, "Cargill: Inside the Quiet Giant That Rules the Food Business," *Fortune*, October 27, 2011.

113 **He began working for the family company:** W. Duncan MacMillan's *MacMillan: The American Grain Family* (Afton, MN: Afton Historical Society Press, 1998), describes his cousin Whitney's rise to the summit of the family business.

115 **In 2006, Cargill and a few other Big Ag:** Christine MacDonald, "Green Going Gone: The Tragic Deforestation of the Chaco," *Rolling Stone*, July 28, 2014; David Yaffe-Bellany, "From environmental leader to 'worst company in the world," *New York Times*, July 29, 2019.

116 **"I didn't ask," Duncan said:** Kristin Tillotson, "A grain family's roots," *Minneapolis Star Tribune*, August 30, 1998.

118 **The ranch was so remote, its terrain so rugged:** "Dusting off the old ones," *Big Timber Pioneer*, December 9, 1992.

119 **Only a small fraction of this land would be used for tracks:** Derrick Jensen and George Draffan, *Railroads and Clearcuts: Legacy of Congress's 1864 Northern Pacific Land Grant* (Sandpoint, ID: Keokee Co. Publishing, 1995).

120 **Attached to the land were water rights:** The history of the Jarretts' water rights

on Duck Creek is set out in detail in "Decrees of Duck Creek and Tributaries, Case No. 236," in *Water Resources Survey, Sweet Grass County, Part 1: History of Land and Water Use on Irrigated Areas*, published by the State Engineer's Office in July 1950.

121 **Access to the Crazies shrank with each decade:** "Crazy Mountains History and Key Points," Environmental Quality Council, Montana State Legislature, March 22, 2018.

124 **Endicott proposed dosing:** Carol Endicott, "Duck Creek Wild Eagle Mountain Ranch: Initial Project Assessment," Montana Fish, Wildlife, and Parks, August 2007.

126 **"Wild Eagle has a direct and substantial interest":** Appendix A, *Final Environmental Impact Statement Amending and Adopting the Draft Environmental Impact Statement for Coyote Wind Project*, Montana DNRC.

126 **As it happened, Whitney MacMillan had just signed:** Memorandum of oil and gas lease, February 13, 2009, Doc. 145924, Sweet Grass County public records.

126 **Fracking fever had swept Sweet Grass County:** Linda Halstead-Acharya, "Tapping hopes and dreams," *Billings Gazette,* December 28, 2008.

A GIS map on the Montana Board of Oil and Gas Conservation website shows all active drilling leases—and dry holes—in Sweet Grass County: https://bogapps.dnrc.mt.gov/dataminer/MontanaMap.aspx. A list of fracking approvals by the board can be found at https://bogwebfiles.dnrc.mt.gov/Hydr aulicFracturing/ApprovedFracProposals.

128 **He collected over $25,000 in USDA crop subsidies:** The Environmental Working Group's Farm Subsidy Database tracks $478 billion in farm subsidies from commodity, crop insurance, disaster programs, and conservation payments paid between 1995 and 2021.

7. HIGH ON THE HORSE IN BIG TIMBER

Note: Audio recordings and minutes of Sweet Grass County Commission meetings held in December 2013 and throughout the winter and spring of 2014 are a primary resource for this chapter. All references to weather are drawn from historic data on the Weather Underground website.

134 **It was full of gorgeous vehicles . . . including a 1965 fire-engine-red coupe:** Mike McNessor, "Mid-year Convertible Is Tops at Kansas City, Selling for $188,000," Hemmings.com, March 24, 2011.

ProTeam Corvette owner Terry Michaelis posted a YouTube video about the Corvette—"one of the top three Corvettes I've ever owned"—in which he congratulates its new owner, "Jan," on November 4, 2011.

134 **A few years back, the Las Vegas attorney and his wife had petitioned:** "Private road will get a name," *Big Timber Pioneer,* February 26, 2009.

136 **But investment wizards at banks like J. P. Morgan:** Herman K. Trabish, "JP

Morgan's John Eber Bullish on Wind Markets," *Greentech Media*, April 9, 2013.

139 **After a court-ordered mediation, Engwis paid:** Judgment and decree in *Engwis Investment Co., Ltd., v. Crazy Mountain Cattle Company, et al.*, Case No. DV-09-13, Montana Sixth Judicial District Court, filed February 1, 2011.

139 **Jarrett had certainly acted maliciously:** Jan Engwis, direct examination, transcript of proceedings in Case No. DV 2018-161, *Diana's Great Idea v. Crazy Mountain Wind*.

139 **"But to a flatland boy":** Ibid.

139 **Engwis was born in 1946:** Public records.

139 **After graduating Midland High School:** *Chemic 1964* (Midland High School yearbook); *Delta 1966* (Delta Community College yearbook).

139 **Jan worked as a Michigan police officer:** Jan Engwis, direct examination, transcript of proceedings in Case No. DV 2018-161, *Diana's Great Idea, LLC, v. Crazy Mountain Wind*.

139 **POA president Engwis had strong views on crime:** "Police to stop using hollowpoint bullets," *Ann Arbor (MI) News*, March 18, 1975.

140 **By 1995, Engwis was the company's majority owner:** Associated Press, "Climbers' mission: Keep rocks off road," *Grand Junction (CO) Daily Sentinel*, June 12, 1995; Pat Dobbs, "Open Cut climbers keep rock at bay," *Rapid City (SD) Journal*, July 24, 1995.

142 **The more he spoke, the angrier Engwis became:** The language in this passage—"absurd," "abject idiocy," "on a whim," "without a cloud in the sky"—is drawn from an audio recording of Engwis's comments at the Sweet Grass County Commission meeting on December 6, 2013.

143 **Back in the 1970s, a group of ranchers had banded:** "Melville zoning district proposed," *Big Timber Pioneer,* September 20, 1978.

143 **Page's great-great-grandfather:** Page Dringman's grandfather, Spike Van Cleve, wrote about his family's history in the Crazies in his memoir, *40 Years' Gatherin's* (Kansas City, MO: Lowell Press, 1977).

145 **Chesnoff's exposure to rock music:** "Everyone's Man in Vegas," a profile of David Chesnoff by Michael Kaplan, appeared in the Winter 2014 edition of *Vegas* magazine right around the time of this county commission meeting.

147 **In 2005, he had taken out a mortgage on the Crazy:** Sweet Grass County public records.

148 **Marty, who wasn't particular . . . gotten a haircut:** "Commissioners hear abatement positions," *Big Timber Pioneer*, February 27, 2014.

148 **As the meeting got underway:** This account and all quotes are drawn from an audio recording of the Sweet Grass County public hearing on tax abatement for Crazy Mountain Wind, February 20, 2014.

149 **Susie Mosness, who was hunkered:** Photograph posted on the *Big Timber Buzz* Facebook page, February 20, 2014.

149 **Breck had leased his land:** New or Expanding Industry Classification Applica-

tion, Kelly Hills Wind Project, October 29, 2012, Sweet Grass County public records.

149 **But Jan Engwis . . . was dissatisfied:** Audio recording of the Sweet Grass County Commission meeting, March 5, 2014.

149 **"'I do not take this lightly,' Engwis said":** "Commission rescinds 2012 Crazy Mountain Wind support letter," *Big Timber Pioneer*, March 6, 2014.

149 **As far as Jan Engwis was concerned, the toothpaste:** Audio recording of the Sweet Grass County Commission meeting, March 5, 2014.

8. Diana's Great Idea

152 **Leonid the Magnificent . . . wrapped the birthday boy:** "Sightings," *Las Vegas Review-Journal*, May 16, 2005.

152 **"With as many prosecution enemies as Chesnoff has made":** "Chesnoff's odds," *Las Vegas Review-Journal*, May 13, 2005.

152 **If the FBI had been stationed . . . rap mogul Suge Knight:** "Sightings," *Las Vegas Review-Journal*, May 16, 2005.

153 **Hadn't he once gotten Suge a table for fifteen:** "Everyone's Man in Vegas," *Vegas* magazine, Winter 2014.

156 **As it happened, a pregnant Spears:** "Celebrating 5-0 and knots tied," *Las Vegas Review-Journal*, May 12, 2005.

157 **When he filed a story about the escaped parrot:** Laurie Gwen Shapiro, "The Little Mayors of the Lower East Side," *Lapham's Quarterly*, August 1, 2018.

157 **"Louis, as everybody knows":** "Lights and shades of life in a city court," *New York Times,* March 29, 1908.

157 **founded the New York League of Locality Mayors:** "The numerous neighborhood 'mayors' New York boasts of," *New York Tribune*, January 18, 1920; Shapiro, "The Little Mayors"; "Louis Zeltner, 77, East Side 'mayor' [obituary]," *New York Times*, May 13, 1953.

158 **As the chairman of Alfred's student assembly:** "Student Assembly," *Fiat Lux*, May 8, 1975.

159 **Gentile represented coke dealers:** John M. Broder, "In search of the best break, defense, vintage, bet and exit," *New York Times*, June 4, 2004.

159 **At lunchtime, you'd find him dining on squirrel stew:** Oscar Goodman, *Being Oscar: From Mob Lawyer to Mayor of Las Vegas* (New York: Weinstein Books, 2013).

160 **Soon, he was having lunch . . . and getting comped everywhere:** "Everyone's Man in Vegas," *Vegas* magazine, Winter 2014.

161 **He kept a plastic rat in his office:** *Mob Law: A Film Portrait of Oscar Goodman*, directed by Paul Wilmshurst (1998).

162 **During the trial of Jones:** "One of accused in drug ring has gambling past," Ken Pekoc, *Helena (MT) Independent-Record*, March 2, 1991.

163 **"No matter who you're dealing with, you go right to the top":** "Everyone's Man in Vegas," *Vegas* magazine, Winter 2014.

163 **Over the course of three election cycles starting in 2013:** David and Diana Chesnoff's political contributions are documented on the Nevada Secretary of State website.

166 **McKenna's lawsuit cited multiple conflicts of interest:** Case 2:14-cv-01773-JAD-CWH, *Michelle McKenna v. David Z. Chesnoff and Richard A. Schonfeld*, United States District Court for the District of Nevada, March 20, 2015.

166 **an ongoing representation of Pure's top executive:** Jeff German, "Former Pure nightclub owner faces sentencing in tax scheme," *Las Vegas Review-Journal,* June 25, 2012.

166 **Robert J. Cipriani . . . Vegas gadfly:** Devin O'Connor, "Resorts World Las Vegas gambler has felony charges dropped, but banned from casino," Casino .org, May 5, 2022.

166 **However dubious its merits:** Complaint for Damages and Injunctive Relief, *Robert J. Cipriani v. MGM Resorts International et al.*, Superior Court of the State of California for the county of Los Angeles, West District.

9. BOXING IN PRISON

Note: All work sessions and hearings of the Montana Public Service Commission are videotaped and/or recorded, then archived on its website under "Documents & Proceedings."

169 **one of Montana's smallest government agencies:** "What We Do for You," Montana PSC website: https://psc.mt.gov/About-Us/What-We-Do.

170 **NorthWestern Energy . . . the modern incarnation of the Montana Power Company:** "NorthWestern Energy: A 104-year timeline," *Montana Standard,* May 20, 2016.

170 **Today, NorthWestern Energy sells electricity:** "Electric Generation," North-Western Energy website, https://northwesternenergy.com/clean-energy/where -does-your-energy-come-from/electric-generation.

170 **States gave single utility companies monopolies:** "Power Market Structure," US Environmental Protection Agency website: https://www.epa.gov/green -power-markets/power-market-structure.

171 **There is an actual mathematical formula:** The formula: $R \equiv B \cdot r + E + d + T$. Mark A. Jamison provides a helpful breakdown of the revenue requirement formula in his paper "Rate of Return: Regulation" (Public Utility Research Center, University of Florida, 2007).

172 **A disillusioned former Montana Public Service Commissioner:** Travis Kavulla, "There Is No Free Market for Electricity: Can There Ever Be?" *American Affairs Journal* 1, no. 2 (Summer 2017).

173 **A *Harvard Law Review* study put it:** "Mandate versus Movement: State Public Service Commissions and Their Evolving Power over Our Energy Sources," *Harvard Law Review* 135, no. 6 (April 2022).

173 **The PSC has no say over firearms or abortion:** Koopman touted his endorsements by the National Rifle Association and the Montana Pro-Life Coalition on his Facebook page.

174 **Under the Montana Rule:** The Montana Rule, as described on the Montana Secretary of State website: https://rules.mt.gov/gateway/ruleno.asp?RN=38.5 .1902.

175 **Crazy Mountain Wind would be a good deal:** The Petition of Crazy Mountain Wind, LLC, for Certification of an Eligible Renewable Resource and Community Renewable Energy Project and Petition for Declaratory Ruling, Public Service Commission Docket No. D2014.1.7. All filings in Docket No. D2014.1.7 are archived on the PSC website under "Documents & Proceedings."

176 **Even NorthWestern's own representatives admitted:** Judge James Manley of Montana's 20th District Court cited this admission by NorthWestern Energy in his August 1, 2019, decision to overturn PSC-issued waivers for the utility.

177 **But in early February . . . attorneys for Jan Engwis, Whitney MacMillan:** All public comments in Docket No. D2014.1.7 are archived on the PSC website under "Documents & Proceedings."

177 **On February 25, the PSC commissioners met:** PSC work session on Docket No. D2014.1.7, February 25, 2014. The video recording is archived under "Archived Work Sessions."

178 **the Gordon Butte wind farm . . . owned by the powerful Galt family:** "Montana's top 5 landowners," *Billings Gazette*, February 10, 2013.

180 **The young would-be commissioner had studied:** Derrick Asiedu, "Travis Kavulla wants to be your energy man," *Harvard Crimson*, July 22, 2010.

183 **By 2018, there was widespread consensus:** Tom Lutey, "NorthWestern gets pass from PSC," *Billings Gazette*, October 3, 2018.

183 **George Stigler, a Nobel Prize–winning:** George J. Stigler, "The Theory of Economic Regulation," *Bell Journal of Economics and Management Science* 2, no. 1 (Spring 1971).

184 **like learning how to box in prison:** Karl Puckett, "Second wind farm going up near Fairfield," *Great Falls (MT) Tribune*, May 1, 2015.

184 **As if to confirm this . . . handed Marty a victory:** Federal Energy Regulatory Commission, Notice of Intent Not to Act and Declaratory Order in Docket No. EL13-73-000 et al., issued March 20, 2014.

185 **"My understanding is that there's quite a few forces":** Audio recording of the Sweet Grass County Commission meeting, April 1, 2014.

186 **The following week, Cindy Selensky had announced:** "Three races will have challengers," *Big Timber Pioneer,* March 13, 2014.

188 **"NorthWestern cannot bargain away":** Exhibit MHW-02, attached to Petition for an Order Setting the Terms and Conditions of a contract between NorthWestern Energy and Greenfield Wind, LLC, PSC Docket No. 2014.4.43.

188 **"This guy keeps pestering me":** Ibid.

10. THE ENGINE ROOM

191 **A clutch of pipe bombs:** Ken Stanford, "Venue security commander recalls safety training for '96 Olympic Games," *AccessWDUN* (WDUN radio website), July 27, 2016.

192 **"Women's crew route seems paved":** William N. Wallace, "Women's crew route seems paved in gold," *New York Times*, July 10, 1996.

192 **the ranch seemed the ideal setting:** Virginia Tranel, *Ten Circles upon the Pond: Reflections of a Prodigal Mother* (New York: Anchor Books, 2004 [2003]).

192 **The St. Labre school's dark history:** Sources for this passage include:
"More victims claiming sex abuse by Montana priests," *Indian Country Today*, July 30, 2012, updated September 13, 2018.
Seaborn Larson, "Montana reservations reportedly 'dumping grounds' for predatory priests," *Great Falls (MT) Tribune*, August 16, 2017.
Johnathan Hettinger, "Boarding school survivors share traumas at Road to Healing event in Bozeman," *Montana Free Press* (Helena, MT), November 6, 2023.
Paul Hamby, "Former St. Labre pastor named in Illinois sex abuse investigation," *Billings Gazette*, May 26, 2023.
Jenna Kunze, "Catholic group investigates its Indian boarding schools in Montana," *Native News Online*, July 11, 2023.

194 **Ned was an alcoholic:** Virginia Tranel writes about her husband's alcoholism and its impact on her family in *And the Light Strikes Home: Memoir of a Marriage* (Fairfield, IA: 1st World Publishing, 2020).

194 **Gonzaga's Jesuit Navy . . . "All this is about is pulling hard":** John Blanchette, "Whatever floats her boat," *Spokane Spokesman-Review*, July 23, 1996.

196 **The speed with which they inhaled:** Elizabeth Gleick, "8 Live Crew," *Time*, June 28, 1996.

196 **"As with other Olympic athletes":** William N. Wallace, "Women's crew route seems paved in gold," *New York Times*, July 10, 1996.

197 **Hours after the race, Linda Wertheimer:** "Olympic US women rowers place fourth," *All Things Considered*, National Public Radio, July 29, 1996.

198 **Monica tied her Team USA jacket:** Ann O'Hanlon and Brad Parks, "For Olympians, it's one big house party," *Washington Post*, August 8, 1996.

198 **When she wasn't dodging beavers:** Betsy Cohen, "Wake to an Olympic dream," *Missoulian* (Missoula, MT), September 10, 2000.

200 **That April, the PSC Commissioners left:** Notices of public meetings about the proposed hydroelectric dam purchase, Docket No. D2013.12.85, are archived on the PSC's website under "Documents & Proceedings."

200 **Monica gave them an earful:** Matthew Brown, Associated Press, "NorthWestern says changes would nix $900M dam deal," *Billings Gazette,* April 18, 2014.

200 **"Your rates are going up":** "PSC holds listening sessions on proposed NWE purchase of dams," *Bitterroot Star* (Stevensville, MT), May 13, 2014.

200 **The PSC held nine days of hearings at the state capitol:** Tranel's questioning of NorthWestern Energy CFO Brian Bird in Docket No. D2013.12.85 took place on July 10, 2014. All quoted material in this passage is drawn from that hearing. The audio recording is archived on the PSC website under "Archived Work Sessions."

202 **The PSC responded by scuppering the whole deal:** Hearing on Greenfield Wind, Docket No. D2014.4.43, held on December 16, 2014. The video recording is archived on the PSC website under "Archived Work Sessions."

202 **Two months later, Marty was back:** February 10, 2015, hearing on Greenfield Wind, Docket No. D2014.4.43. The video recording is archived on the PSC website under "Archived Work Sessions."

204 **Marty came to see Monica:** Marty's legal troubles with Fairfield Wind and Greenfield Wind are laid out in Affidavit of Martin Wilde, Case No. DV-2016-389, *WINData, LLC, vs Greenbacker Wind, LLC, et al.*, Lewis and Clark County District Court, filed May 9, 2016.

206 **So, Marty added more turbines:** Marty describes Crazy Mountain Wind's growth spurt in his Petition for an Order Setting Certain Terms and Conditions of a Contract between NorthWestern Energy and Crazy Mountain Wind, LLC, Docket No. D2016.7.56. It is archived on the PSC website under "Documents & Proceedings."

11. WHAT WOULD YOU DO?

209 **There had been sporadic calls and emails:** An email chain between Rick Jarrett's lawyer and lawyers for Jan Engwis, Russell Gordy, and Whitney MacMillan, discussing a possible settlement, was submitted as an exhibit in Case No. DV 2018-161, *Diana's Great Idea v. Crazy Mountain Wind.*

210 **In May, he signed a pair of mortgage agreements:** Sweet Grass County public records.

211 **"Our solicitation of an offer":** Email from Michael Begley, May 14, 2014.

211 **Through his attorney, Engwis declared:** Email from Stephen Woodruff to Michael Begley, July 23, 2015.

211 **MacMillan's attorneys were preoccupied:** A notice about a public hearing for the Alkali Creek RV Park appeared in the Classifieds section of the *Big Timber Pioneer* on July 23, 2015.

212 **By mid-November, the Darlene C. Fahrenbruch Living Trust had sold:** Sweet Grass County public records.

218 **Within a year, he had entered into a leasing agreement:** SEC filing, Coal Mining Lease between RGGS Land & Mineral, Ltd., and Sugar Camp Energy, LLC, July 29, 2005.

Information about Sugar Camp Energy's longwall mining operation can be found on Foresight Energy's website, https://www.foresight.com/operations/.

218 **Gordy's partner . . . Chris Cline:** John Lippert and Mario Parker, "Cline

Talking Clean as Coal Mines Supply Most Energy Since 1970," *Bloomberg Markets Magazine*, October 12, 2010; Lee Buchsbaum, "Foresight Energy invests in Illinois," *Coal Age*, December 7, 2010; Christopher Helman, "Chris Cline could be the last coal tycoon standing," *Forbes*, December 19, 2017.

219 **Sugar Camp was good for the Gordys, but not for the residents:** Kari Lydersen's three-part series on the Sugar Camp Mine for Energy News Network (March 2018) explores the profound environmental and social costs of the Sugar Camp Mine.

219 **Sugar Camp was charged with scores of environmental violations:** These violations are referenced in Securities and Exchange Commission filings for the 2014 IPO by Sugar Camp Energy's parent company, Foresight Energy.

220 **Don Webb, whose family had farmed:** Franklin County, Illinois, public records.

In RGGS Land & Minerals' lease agreement with Sugar Camp Energy, the Webb lease appears as Number 29 in Exhibit C, "Prior Agreements": "Farm lease between USX Corporation and Cyrus Webb dated January 1, 1987." The original lease was signed by J. T. Chenault and "N. J. Chenault, his wife" in 1910.

220 **In 2010, Gordy did another deal with Cline:** For context about RGGS Land & Minerals' holdings in Minnesota, see "Sidebar: Mining: Minnesota Minerals: Not just for Minnesotans," *Rural Minnesota Journal*, December 16, 2013.

221 **Gordy partnered up with Cline on a plan to turn:** Dan Kaufman's *The Fall of Wisconsin* (New York: W. W. Norton, 2018) details the secret campaign that Foresight Energy waged to advance the cause of its taconite mine in the Penokee Range. G-TAC lawyers worked behind the scenes with Republican legislators to draft a custom-tailored mining bill to accelerate the permitting process, limit public hearings, and ease environmental restrictions.

Additional sources:

Theodoric Meyer, "In Wisconsin, Dark Money Got a Mining Company What It Wanted," *ProPublica*, October 14, 2014.

Carol Pogash, "Wisconsin governor, Chippewas battle over open pit mine plan," *USA Today*, September 8, 2013.

Foresight would eventually declare bankruptcy:

Bruce Rushton, "Dark days for Foresight," *Illinois Times* (Springfield, IL), December 17, 2015.

12. CROW COUNTRY

Note: The Crazies' recent history and the conflicts over public access have been the subject of reporting by Brett French for the *Billings Gazette* and Amanda Eggert for the *Montana Free Press*. Their reporting helped inform my understanding of these complex issues.

226 **Medicine Horse nodded at Sarah Anzick:** Sources for the passage on the child's reburial include:

Nova, season 43, episode 16, "Great Human Odyssey," directed by Niobe Thompson, aired October 5, 2016, on PBS.

"The Anzick Children Laid to Rest," *Mammoth Trumpet* 30, no. 2 (April 2015).

Brett French, "Remains of ancient child ceremoniously reburied," *Billings Gazette*, June 28, 2014.

226 **He would compare himself to Marlow:** Maria Anderson, "Local Knowledge: Uncovering Ancestral Narratives," *Big Sky Journal*, Winter 2020.

227 **"We traveled by that dream":** Frank B. Linderman, *Plenty Coups: Chief of the Crows*, new ed., introduction by Barney Old Coyote Jr. and Phenocia Bauerle, afterword by Timothy P. McCleary (Lincoln: Bison Books/University of Nebraska Press, 2002 [1930]).

227 **Under Plenty Coups's leadership ... with the yellow eyebrows:** Plenty Coups's description of white officials as "yellow eyebrows" is from Wildschut's *Exploits of Plenty Coups*.

227 **"We had always fought the three tribes":** Linderman, *Plenty Coups: Chief of the Crows*.

227 **Crow warriors pointed their guns:** This passage is drawn from Pretty Shield's account of the Battle of the Little Bighorn, from Frank B. Linderman, *Pretty-Shield: Medicine Woman of the Crow* (Lincoln: Bison Books/University of Nebraska Press, 1974 [1932]).

228 **"The White Chief never paid us":** Linderman, *Plenty Coups: Chief of the Crows*.

228 **Pretty Eagle described their summit:** Pretty Eagle's description of his visit to the White House is one of several firsthand accounts by Crow leaders cited in Adrian Heidenreich's "The Crow Indian Delegation to Washington, D.C., in 1880," published in *Montana: The Magazine of Western History* 31, no. 2 (Spring 1981).

229 **Crow Agency was pushed eastward:** Frederick E. Hoxie, *Parading through History: The Making of the Crow Nation in America 1805–1933* (Cambridge, UK: Cambridge University Press, 1995).

229 **an honorary member of the Kiwanis Club:** Timothy P. McCleary's afterword to Linderman, *Plenty Coups: Chief of the Crows*.

229 **Today, Crow Agency is the largest:** "Crow Agency," Indian Affairs, US Department of the Interior.

229 **In 2015, Tribal Chairman Darrin Old Coyote:** Transcript of Senate Hearing 114-42, "Empowering Indian Country: Coal, Jobs, and Self-determination," Field Hearing Before the Committee on Indian Affairs, United States Senate, April 8, 2015.

229 **The tribe's economic mainstay:** Ibid.

229 **In 2013, Old Coyote complained that the houses:** Matt Hudson, "Crow: Waiting for Home," *Native News*, 2013.

230 **The Apsáalooke had lost ... Four Times' sixteen-year-old daughter:** Shane

Doyle explores the history of his ancestors in his PhD dissertation, *Decolonizing Collaborative Inquiry at the Absaroka Agency* (Montana State University, April 2012).

230 **the Earl of Dunraven, had been much impressed:** Windham Thomas Wyndham-Quinn, Earl of Dunraven, *The Great Divide: Travels in the Upper Yellowstone Valley in the Summer of 1874* (HardPress, 2017).

232 **"My tribe, through colonization":** *Awaxaawippíia: The Crow Nation's Sacred Ties,* directed by Eric Ian (2020; Helena, MT: Wild Montana and Shane Doyle).

233 **A Danish television crew captured him:** *DNA Detektiven,* season 1, episode 3, "The Legacy of the Anzick Child," directed by Linus Mark, aired May 17, 2015, on Danish television.

234 **The Smithsonian invited him to speak:** Smithsonian National Museum of the American Indian, "Native Peoples and Genetic Research 11: Dr. Shane Doyle," YouTube, June 23, 2014.

234 **It snowballed from there:** Doyle and the dancing lodgepoles appeared in *Standby Snow: Chronicles of a Heat Wave, Chapter One,* a performance piece staged by Mountain Time Arts in Bozeman in August 2019.

234 **Conservation groups invited him to join:** "Montana conservationists to Zinke: Protect Upper Missouri Breaks National Monument," *Missoula (MT) Current,* June 24, 2017.

235 **He made his first fast:** See Shane Doyle's essay "Crazy Mountain Cathedral," published on the website of the Montana Office of Public Instruction on June 1, 2020.

236 **in the Van Cleve family for generations:** Smith, *Montana Sweet Grass Country*; Spike Van Cleve, *40 Years' Gatherin's.*

236 **An 1877 photograph shows a man with large ears:** Herbert A. Coffeen, *Lieut. J. J. Crittenden, 20th Infantry, Fell Here in Custer Battle, June 25, 1876. From Photo Taken One Year Later,* postcard, Denver Public Library Digital Collections.

237 **Big Horn County . . . missing and murdered Indigenous people:** Letter from Senator Jon Tester to FBI Director Christopher Wray, November 20, 2019.

238 **"Decades ago, I was told":** "An Uncommon Energy," *All News,* Tuck School of Business, Dartmouth, October 30, 2013.

239 **In a full-circle Leuschen family moment:** Associated Press, "Riverstone completes buyout of Talen Energy, Colstrip owner," *Billings Gazette,* December 8, 2016.

239 **Leuschen hit a speed bump in 2009:** "Riverstone founder pays $20 million in pension case," Dealbook, *New York Times,* December 9, 2009.

239 **Leuschen invested $100,000 . . . in *Chooch*:** Bruce Handy, "The Worst Movie Ever Made?" *Vanity Fair,* August 4, 2010.

239 **initial public offering . . . raising $352 million:** "Wind energy company Pattern blows past IPO price in debut," Reuters, September 27, 2013.

240 **For a TEDx Talk:** TEDx Talks, "Why I Am a Carbon Optimist—David Leuschen—TEDxBigSky," YouTube, March 9, 2021.

240 **He bought houses:** Robin Finn, "Big Ticket: Sold for $42 million," *New York Times,* July 6, 2012.

240 **a privately published book about Switchback Ranch:** David Leuschen, *Good Cattle, Good Country: The Making of Switchback Ranch* (self-published, 2020).

245 **"Don't plan on a pristine campsite":** Fred Spicker and "B.," "Crazy Peak," Summitpost.org.

245 **The Lazy K Bar fired the first salvo:** "Crazy Mountains History and Key Points," Environmental Quality Council, US Forest Service, March 22, 2018.

245 **Alex Sienkiewicz, the Forest Service's district ranger:** Christopher Solomon, "The Fight for Public Land in Montana's Crazy Mountains," *Outside*, December 6, 2017, updated May 12, 2022.

247 **Reagan's veto of the Montana wilderness bill:** Philip Shabecoff, "Reagan vetoes bill to protect 1.4 million acres in Montana," *New York Times*, November 4, 1988.

248 **"Although our tribe lost our legal ownership":** The open letter signed by Shane Doyle, Adrian Bird Jr., and A. J. Not Afraid appeared in the *Billings Gazette* on May 21, 2019.

248 **"Generally, residents think there should be":** "Crow, environmentalists push for protections of Crazy Mountains," *Billings Gazette*, June 4, 2019.

249 **A reporter joined Doyle and Bird:** Brett French, "Crazy Mountains turbulence: Management sparks spirits, feuds," *Billings Gazette*, June 30, 2019.

13. EARTHQUAKE

252 **Monica Tranel, dressed in a brown pantsuit:** The source for all details and quoted remarks in this passage is the Public Service Commission hearing on November 9, 2016, In the Matter of the Petition of Crazy Mountain Wind for the Commission to Set Certain Terms and Conditions of Contract between NorthWestern Energy and Crazy Mountain Wind, LLC, Docket No. D2016.7.56. A video recording is archived on the PSC website under "Archived Work Sessions."

253 **Marty had paid a visit to the old Norwegian:** "Amended and restated wind energy lease and agreement" between Alfred and Dorothy Anderson and Crazy Mountain Wind, LLC (Pattern), Section A.

255 **The utility factored a $14.63 carbon adder:** Final Order, PSC Docket No. D2013.12.85, Order No. 7323k.

Note: Commissioner Roger Koopman references the carbon adder in his concurring opinion on the 2014 hydroelectric dam deal, Order No. 7323k, in which he writes that NWE's calculations for avoided carbon costs "resulted in placing as much as a 25–30 percent premium on the value of the hydro assets themselves."

256 **This aversion was rooted . . . Trump International Golf Links:** David A. Graham, "He'll Take the Low Road: Trump's Tortured History with Scotland," *The Atlantic*, December 18, 2015.

256 **"I am building what many are already considering":** Trump's testimony before the Scottish Parliament can be found on YouTube at https://www.youtube .com/watch?v=HX4J1a8gy6I.

257 **take down all his campaign yard signs:** PSC hearing regarding Docket No. D2016.7.56 on November 9, 2016. A video recording is archived on the PSC website under "Archived Work Sessions."

261 **The commissioners met shortly before Christmas:** PSC work session regarding Docket No. D2016.7.56 on December 12, 2016. A video recording is archived on the PSC website under "Archived Work Sessions."

262 **In a newspaper opinion piece:** Roger Koopman, "Federally imposed renewables come with cost attached," *Montana Standard* (Butte, MT), January 13, 2016.

262 **The PSC order, issued in early January:** Final order in Docket No. D2016.7.56, Order No. 7505b, January 5, 2017.

263 **Jan Engwis, on one of his periodic PSC website trawls:** Jan Engwis, direct testimony, transcript of proceedings, Case No. DV 2018-161, *Diana's Great Idea v. Crazy Mountain Wind*.

264 **In late March, a local television news program:** *Wake Up Montana*, KULR-TV, aired March 22, 2017.

265 **Crandall was tracking golden eagle nesting behavior:** Ross Crandall, Bryan Bedrosian, and Derek Craighead, "Habitat Selection and Factors Influencing Nest Survival of Golden Eagles in South-Central Montana," *Journal of Raptor Research* 49, no. 4 (December 2015): 413–28.

265 **Participating in the research study was a thrill for Jan:** The now-defunct EngwisRanch.com website referred to the Craighead Beringia South research project and featured photographs of Crandall and his fellow researchers, with this caption: "The active nesting site on the Engwis Ranch provided a thrilling experience again this summer."

265 **The Engwises' sense of connection . . . they *experienced* them:** Jan Engwis, cross-examination, transcript of proceedings, Case No. DV 2018-161, *Diana's Great Idea v. Crazy Mountain Wind*.

266 **lived in a home attached to an indoor riding arena:** Details about the Engwis Ranch property are drawn from multiple real estate listings, including photographs on the now-defunct Engwis ranch website; "Featuring Engwis Ranch" in *Farm & Ranch West*; and a Fay Ranches sales brochure.

266 **Karen's adult son, Mikey, who had cerebral palsy:** Affidavit of Jan Engwis, Case No. DV 2018-161, *Diana's Great Idea v. Crazy Mountain Wind*.

266 **But after less than a decade . . . Jan and Karen listed:** Email from Jeff Bollman, May 14, 2010, State's Responses to Engwis/R. F. Building Company's First Combined Discovery Request to DNRC, Case No. DV-2010-09.

268 **Monica filed an appeal . . . delay the carbon adder:** Petitioner Crazy Mountain Wind's Motion for Reconsideration, PSC Docket D2016.7.56, January 20, 2017. A video recording is archived on the PSC website under "Archived Work Sessions."

268 **This time, Marty had company:** PSC work session on February 28, 2017, regarding Docket No. D2016.7.56. A video recording is archived on the PSC website under "Archived Work Sessions."

269 **The BLM ruled that the federal leases:** Paul Tolmé, "The Fight over the Thompson Divide," *5280: Denver's Mile High Magazine*, March 2016.

269 **Vowing to fight the decision . . . Robbie Guinn:** Ryan Summerlin, "SG Interests files libel lawsuit against environmental activist," *Glenwood Springs (CO) Post Independent*, March 8, 2017.

269 **Kolbenschlag thought Guinn's remarks:** Guinn's comments appeared in John Stroud, "Divide lease decision likely to land in court," *Glenwood Springs (CO) Post Independent*, November 29, 2016.

270 **"Reasonable people reading this assertion":** *SG Interests I, Ltd., v. Kolbenschlag*, filed in Colorado's Delta County District Court on February 21, 2017.

270 **SG Interests pursued the case against Kolbenschlag:** The Colorado Court of Appeals' opinion in the case of *SG Interests I, Ltd., v. Kolbenschlag* can be found on the Justia online database: https://law.justia.com/cases/colorado/court-of-appeals/2019/18ca1316.html.

270 **"It's tough when people tell you":** Devon Pendleton, "America's billionaire playgrounds: rockets, ranches and rivers," Bloomberg, September 13, 2019.

271 **He spent about $100,000 in all:** Affidavit of Russell Gordy, Case No. DV 2018-161, *Diana's Great Idea v. Crazy Mountain Wind*.

272 **In early 2017, Gordy called Ward Marshall:** Ward Marshall, direct testimony, transcript of proceedings, Case No. DV 2018-161, *Diana's Great Idea v. Crazy Mountain Wind*.

272 **"It might have been in jest":** Ibid.

273 **Marty filed a sweeping lawsuit:** Karl Puckett, "Wind developer sues PSC, NorthWestern, over pricing," *Great Falls (MT) Tribune*, October 13, 2017.

273 **At a work session in June:** PSC work session, June 22, 2017—a video recording is archived on the PSC website under "Archived Work Sessions"; Tom Lutey, "Hot mic records troubling conversation about solar regulations," *Billings Gazette,* June 27, 2017.

274 **"The Montana Public Service Commission . . . have lost their regulatory minds":** Tom Lutey, "Montana's regulators are putting public at risk of high energy prices, NorthWestern says," *Billings Gazette*, August 2, 2017.

14. GOOD NEIGHBORS

Photographer Christine Bakke posted pictures of the Sweet Grass County Fair Pig Sale on the *Big Timber Buzz* on July 29, 2018.

282 **By the time the auction was over, Shawley had spent $3,391:** Pattern disclosed the purchase price of two hogs and a sheep at the Sweet Grass County Fair in Defendants Crazy Mountain Wind, LLC, Pattern Energy Group, Inc., and

Pattern Energy Group, LP's Answers to Plaintiffs' First Combined Discovery Requests in Case No. DV 2018-161.

284 **the 107-year-old elementary school was infested:** The Reed Point elementary school's bat and termite infestation was the subject of a story in the *Big Timber Pioneer* on August 16, 2018.

285 **That spring, George Hardie III:** Russell Gordy described the call from Hardie in his testimony at the injunction hearing. See the transcript of proceedings for Case No. DV 2018-161, *Diana's Great Idea v. Crazy Mountain Wind.*

285 **The Vault at Gordy & Sons:** I wrote about Russell Gordy's rod and gun shop for the November/December 2018 issue of *Departures.*

287 **Chesnoff began the conversation by saying:** David Chesnoff described the phone call in his testimony at the injunction hearing. Transcript of proceedings for Case No. DV 2018-161, *Diana's Great Idea v. Crazy Mountain Wind.*

288 **Just before the Pattern team arrived, Chesnoff and his partner:** "Charles Oakley cheated 3 times during Texas Hold'em . . . officials say," TMZ Sports, August 3, 2018; Tom Schad, "Charles Oakley pleads no contest, resolves case stemming from Vegas arrest, lawyers say," *USA Today*, August 7, 2018.

289 **"'Well, I guess the picture will speak a thousand words'":** David Chesnoff's testimony at the injunction hearing. Transcript of proceedings for Case No. DV 2018-161, *Diana's Great Idea v. Crazy Mountain Wind.*

290 **Every August, Chavez led:** "Crazy Mountain Stockgrowers Ranch Rodeo 2016," *Big Timber Pioneer*, August 25, 2016.

A picture of Orlando Chavez holding his prize bridle was posted on the *Big Timber Buzz* on August 22, 2016.

292 **"It kind of makes you think that it'll be okay to go ahead and get treatment":** "Orlando Chavez: 'One of those good guys,'" *Big Timber Pioneer*, November 17, 2016.

293 **the Chavezes put their brand on her shoulder:** Brand Book, Park County (Montana Department of Livestock, Brands Enforcement Division).

295 **"Human nature being what it is":** Holly Michels, "Facebook groups change the way information, gossip, spread in small-town Montana," *Billings Gazette*, December 29, 2015.

295 **When a helicopter was spotted:** *Big Timber Buzz* posts about the helicopter "harassing" eagles appeared on March 11 and 12, 2018.

296 **the 2013 study by Lawrence Berkeley National Laboratory:** Ben Hoen et al., *A Spatial Hedonic Analysis of the Effects of Wind Energy Facilities on Surrounding Property Values in the US*, Lawrence Berkeley National Laboratory, August 2013.

297 **"I don't have millionaires for neighbors":** Tom Valtin, "The Answer My Friend . . . ," Sierra Club, August 21, 2018.

297 **"My firm has been retained to consider":** Letter submitted into evidence in Case No. DV 2018-161, *Diana's Great Idea v. Crazy Mountain Wind.*

298 **A few days before Pattern's open house:** "Wind farm firm donates $100,000 to Reed Pt. Schools," *Big Timber Pioneer,* August 23, 2018.

299 **It wasn't enough to invite people for some food:** Elizabeth Greenwood recalled her comments to Wynn at a Sweet Grass County Commission meeting on August 28, 2018.

15. FIRE SEASON

303 **The Trippers were a tight-knit group:** "Timber Trippers," *Big Timber Pioneer,* September 17, 1974.

303 **Whitney and Betty were nice people, ordinary-type people:** Jim Hogemark's description of the MacMillans is drawn from his testimony at the injunction hearing. Transcript of proceedings for Case No. DV 2018-161, *Diana's Great Idea v. Crazy Mountain Wind.*

305 **The MacMillans only had so much time:** Ibid.

307 **As the hearing got underway, Chairman Faw:** Audio recording of the Sweet Grass County Commission hearing, August 28, 2018.

313 **It was from Jim Hogemark at Wild Eagle Mountain Ranch:** The thank-you announcements by Wild Eagle Mountain Ranch and the Crazy Mountain Cattle Company were published in the *Big Timber Pioneer* on September 13, 2018.

313 **After introducing herself as the attorney for Engwis:** Audio recording of the Sweet Grass County Commission hearing, September 13, 2018.

315 **Pattern was planning to make a donation to the high school:** Pattern disclosed that it gave $10,000 to Sweet Grass County High School for a cable cross machine for the weight room and new welders, in Defendants Crazy Mountain Wind, LLC, Pattern Energy Group, Inc., and Pattern Energy Group, LP's Answers to Plaintiffs First Combined Discovery Requests in Case No. DV 2018-161.

315 **JV's Democratic opponent didn't even show up:** "County, state candidates meet voters at forum," *Big Timber Pioneer*, September 27, 2018.

16. ANACONDA

322 **"It takes a ton of money away from the county":** "County, state candidates meet voters at forum," *Big Timber Pioneer*, September 27, 2018.

324 **In late September, Gordy made headlines with a $15 million gift:** Amber Elliott, "Houston oilmen set a Texas record, raise $83 million for new Texas Children's Hospital tower," *Houston Chronicle,* October 1, 2018.

325 **The article that ran in the *Pioneer*:** "Ranchers say they're looking to the future," *Big Timber Pioneer,* November 1, 2018.

325 **tax returns and decades of medical records:** Rick Jarrett's and Crazy Mountain Cattle Company's Responses to Plaintiffs' First Combined Discovery Requests and Alfred Anderson's Responses to Plaintiffs' First Combined Discovery Requests, Case No. DV 2018-161, *Diana's Great Idea v. Crazy Mountain Wind.*

326 **Gilbert faulted state environmental regulators:** Corrin Cates-Carney, "Proposed Paradise Valley mine needs more study," Montana Public Radio, May 25, 2018.

326 **the BLM cited Gordy's SG Interests:** Bruce Finley, "Texas oil company cited for improper drilling in Colorado that spewed waste," *Denver Post*, June 25, 2017.

326 **The rule is a relic from the War of the Copper Kings:** Sources for this passage include:

    C. B. Glasscock, *The War of the Copper Kings* (Helena, MT: Riverbend Publishing, 2002 [1935]).

    Michael P. Malone, *The Battle for Butte: Mining and Politics on the Northern Frontier, 1864–1906* (Seattle: University of Washington Press, 2006 [1981]).

    K. Ross Toole, *Montana: An Uncommon Land* (Norman: University of Oklahoma Press, 1959).

328 **"In this case, there are other landowners":** Wild Eagle Mountain Ranch, Brief in Support of Motion to Intervene, filed December 5, 2018.

332 **"Quick! Get your landscape photos":** Posted on the *Big Timber Buzz* on November 23, 2018.

334 **"We didn't do this for Pattern":** "County OKs wind project road use pact," *Big Timber Pioneer,* February 7, 2019.

17. Show Ponies

The transcript of the three-day injunction hearing in Case No. DV 2018-161, *Diana's Great Idea v. Crazy Mountain Wind*, is the primary source for this chapter.

337 **"a haunting foreshadow of the dramatic change":** Wild Eagle Mountain Ranch's brief in support of motion for site visit, February 13, 2019.

344 **Crandall had done a multiyear study:** Ross H. Crandall et al., "Survival Estimates and Cause of Mortality of Golden Eagles in South-Central Montana," *Journal of Raptor Research* 53, no. 1 (February 2019): 38–45.

    In 2022, Crandall's findings would be confirmed by the publication of a paper by Vincent A. Slabe et al., "Demographic Implications of Lead Poisoning for Eagles Across North America," in the journal *Science*. An eight-year study by scientists from the US Geological Survey, Conservation Science Global, Inc., and the US Fish and Wildlife Service found widespread chronic lead poisoning in bald and golden eagles across the North American continent, at levels that have harmed population growth rates for both species. The cause: lead ammunition fragments.

368 **Crandall was seeking funding:** "The Bridge," *Newsletter of Craighead Beringia South*, Quarterly Update, July 2020.

18. FINDINGS OF FACT

378 **The judge had rejected the central plank:** Case No. DV 2018-161, Hon. Jon A. Oldenburg, Findings of Fact, Conclusions of Law, Order on Preliminary Injunction, March 22, 2019.

383 **The newest asset in Riverstone's portfolio:** Pam Rosacia, "Three Rivers IV receives up to $500M commitment from Riverstone," *S&P Global Market Intelligence*, February 7, 2019.

384 **After Pattern asked to be dismissed . . . Monica filed a counterclaim:** Case No. DV-20-142, *Rick Jarrett, Crazy Mountain Cattle Company, and Alfred Anderson v. Wild Eagle Mountain Ranch, LLC, Rock Creek Ranch I, Ltd., Yellowstone River Ranch, d/b/a Diana's Great Idea, LLC, Engwis Investment Company, Ltd., and R. F. Building Company, LP*, filed in Montana Sixth Judicial District Court, Park County.

386 **A similar exchange had been in the works for years:** "Forest Service moves forward with two Crazy Mountain land swaps, drops one," Montana Public Radio, December 15, 2020.

388 **Thanks to its fossil fuel–based . . . Pakistan and its 248 million inhabitants:** Findings of Fact, Conclusions of Law, and Order, Case No. CDV-2020-307, *Rikki Held et al. v. State of Montana et al.*, filed in Montana First Judicial District Court, Lewis and Clark County, August 14, 2023.

388 **Doyle and Crow Agency's historic preservation officer:** Brett French, "Cabin in the Crazy Mountains worries Crow tribal members," *Billings Gazette*, October 1, 2019.

388 **The Forest Service's revised land management plan for the Crazies:** *Custer Gallatin Land Management Plan—Sharing the Decision*, US Forest Service, US Department of Agriculture, Winter 2022.

388 **the land-swap deal the Yellowstone Club was brokering:** For more on the Forest Service's East Crazy Inspiration Divide Land Exchange, see the US Forest Service website (https://www.fs.usda.gov/project/?project=63115) and the Crazy Mountain Access Project website (https://www.crazymountainproject .com/east-side-land-swap).

392 **In August, Montana's Supreme Court reversed:** Opinion in Case No. DA 19-0594, filed August 11, 2020.

393 **America lost its 128th-richest citizen:** "Whitney MacMillan [obituary]," *Minneapolis Star Tribune*, March 12, 2020.

393 **In 2019, the median listing price:** The data for single-family home list prices was compiled by analysts at Move, Inc.

395 **The PSC had imploded that year:** Phil Drake, "Fear and Loathing at the PSC: Battle among some members escalates," *Great Falls (MT) Tribune*, February 29, 2020; "Get Rid of the PSC," *Billings Gazette*, May 13, 2020.

397 **Monica had poured her heart into the lawsuit:** Amended Complaint and De-

mand for Jury Trial on Behalf of Jarrett and Anderson, Case No. 20-142, filed December 7, 2020.

399 **Gordy, Chesnoff, MacMillan, and Engwis retaliated:** Defendants' Motion for Rule 11 Sanctions, filed May 21, 2021.

19. EIGHTEEN INCHES OF RAIN

413 **I found my answer in a map:** Paul Denholm et al., *Examining Supply-Side Options to Achieve 100% Clean Electricity by 2035*, National Renewable Energy Laboratory, 2022.

ABOUT THE AUTHOR

Amy Gamerman has written about real estate and culture for the *Wall Street Journal* for more than two decades. *The Crazies* is her first book.